NATO, the European Union and the Atlantic Community

NATO, the European Union, and the Atlantic Community

The Transatlantic Bargain Reconsidered

STANLEY R. SLOAN

ROWMAN & LITTLEFIELD PUBLISHERS, INC.
Lanham • Boulder • New York • Oxford

ROWMAN & LITTLEFIELD PUBLISHERS, INC.

Published in the United States of America
by Rowman & Littlefield Publishers, Inc.
A wholly owned subsidiary of The Rowman & Littlefield Publishing Group, Inc.
4501 Forbes Boulevard, Suite 200, Lanham, Maryland 20706
www.rowmanlittlefield.com

PO Box 317
Oxford
OX2 9RU, UK

British Library Cataloguing in Publication Information Available

Library of Congress Cataloging-in-Publication Data

Sloan, Stanley R.
    NATO, the European Union, and the Atlantic community : the
transatlantic bargain reconsidered / Stanley R. Sloan.
        p. cm.
    Includes bibliographical references and index.
    ISBN 0-7425-1759-4 (cloth : alk. paper) – ISBN 0-7425-1760-8 (pbk. : alk.
paper)
1. North Atlantic Treaty Organization. 2. European Union. 3. Europe–Defenses.
4. North America–Defenses. I. Title.

  UA646. 3.S5836 2002
355'.031091821–dc21
2002009852

Printed in the United States of America

♾™ The paper used in this publication meets the minimum requirements of American
National Standard for Information Sciences—Permanence of Paper for Printed Library
Materials, ANSI/NISO Z39.48-1992.

Contents

Foreword

For more than fifty years, the North Atlantic Treaty Organization (NATO) has been a powerful force for peace and security. NATO has been essential to maintaining the transatlantic link, the mechanism that was so vital to deterrence during the Cold War and that today helps keep the West united on security issues. NATO's consultative mechanisms have been a positive source of stability on the Continent and were central to the solution of bilateral problems among its members. NATO forces, policies, and procedures proved to be an essential and irreplaceable foundation for the US-led coalition's success in Operation Desert Storm, reversing the consequences of Saddam Hussein's aggression against Kuwait. NATO has been the linchpin for the process of peace enforcement, peacekeeping, and stabilization in the Balkans. Its programs of outreach and enlargement are key ingredients for European stability today and tomorrow.

With all this said, however, the transatlantic alliance faces a contemporary crisis. The terrorist attacks against the United States on September 11, 2001, and their aftermath have raised serious questions about the future role of the alliance. The NATO allies invoked Article 5 of the North Atlantic Treaty, considering the attack on the United States an attack on the entire alliance. But when the United States developed a military strategy to respond to the attacks and to initiate a "war on terrorism," it initially found very little that NATO or even individual NATO allies, save for the British, could contribute to the military aspects of the campaign.

It is my belief that a healthy transatlantic relationship remains vital to the interests of the United States and the nations of Europe. The United States is currently the only true "global power" and is capable of taking on demanding military missions with little assistance from other powers. But it still needs allies. It cannot afford, financially or politically, to be the world's policeman. The American people will not stand for it. Other countries must share the responsibility for maintaining international stability. Moreover, the war on terrorism requires international collaboration that goes well beyond unilateral use of force. This war will be won by good intelligence, appropriate strategy and diplomacy, and effective international policy and financial collaboration and with progress toward resolution of the global problems that fill the coffers of terrorist organizations and create pools of recruits ready to sacrifice their lives for the cause. The cooperation of European and other allies is essential to such a campaign. Military force will be an element, but a successful overall strategy will use the credible threat to deploy force to dissuade countries from hosting terrorist operations combined with discrete military operations against specific terrorist targets.

The members of the European Union are trying to give the process of European unification a military dimension to accompany the Union's well-developed economic integration and its fledgling common foreign and security policy. Some day that effort may make "Europe" a key military as well as political and economic player on the world stage. Even when that day comes, Europe will still benefit from a close transatlantic relationship. Until then, Europe will remain dependent to one degree or another on the United States for the US contribution to European and international peace and security.

Since the end of World War II, successive generations of civilian and military leaders, opinion makers, business leaders, academics, and interested citizens on both sides of the Atlantic have ensured that the transatlantic alliance would be adapted to changing international circumstances. The process of adaptation has guaranteed the continued vitality of the relationship. Today, the current "new world disorder" calls for leaders who understand the centrality of the transatlantic bond as well as the need for change.

As always, planning the future will benefit from an understanding of history. This is where Stan Sloan's book comes in. Just as governments on both sides of the Atlantic begin to grapple with a new period of transition in international relations, the author has produced an analysis of the transatlantic relationship that captures the essence of the past, revealing many of the factors that will continue to influence the future. It is essential that future leaders, many of whom are now in colleges and universities in Europe, the United States, and Canada, understand the path that the nations of the Atlantic Community have traveled and the challenges that lie ahead. In particular, I hope that his analysis will become required reading in military schools and training programs across the United States.

This book challenges all of us to "reconsider" the transatlantic bargain. Its conclusion that NATO remains an essential but insufficient foundation for future transatlantic relations is right on the money. Whether the time is ripe for the shaping of a "new Atlantic Community" remains to be seen. But we must meet the challenge of ensuring that our children and grandchildren will live in a world where an Atlantic Community of values and interests serves as a stabilizing core and a source of democratic inspiration for nations around the world.

Gen. John Shalikashvili (US Army ret.),
former Chairman of the US Joint Chiefs
of Staff and NATO Supreme Allied
Commander, Europe (SACEUR)

Acknowledgments

This book is built on a foundation originally established when the Congressional Research Service (CRS) allowed me to accept the generous invitation of the National Defense University (NDU) to spend a sabbatical year at NDU during 1983–84. During that time, I wrote the book titled *NATO's Future: Toward a New Transatlantic Bargain*. Now long out of print and much of it out of date, that book serves as the precursor to the present one. In the earlier book, I concluded my analysis of NATO's history with a proposal intended to stimulate progress toward a new transatlantic bargain in which Europe would play a more substantial and unified role. Since the publication of that book in 1985, not only have the members of the European Union begun the process of building a more coherent Europe in defense and security affairs, but the world has changed in major ways.

This book represents the culmination of more than thirty years of research and analysis of transatlantic relations. It is the product of a lifelong policy analyst, not an academic, although I hope the book will be of value to scholars as well as students of transatlantic relations. To some extent, it draws on firsthand experience. But the work also stands on the shoulders of many colleagues in the field who have written perceptively about the alliance—its past, present, and future.

In particular, I want to acknowledge some of my friends and colleagues who encouraged my work over the years by generously offering friendship, support, guidance, and constructive criticism. Former mentors at the Central Intelligence Agency, particularly Joe Zaring and the late Keith Clark, helped a young analyst develop his research and analysis skills. I am indebted to Fred Kiley and Jan Hietala—my publisher and editor at the NDU Press, respectively—for ensuring that my first book on NATO's future met high standards. There are others, many friends and former colleagues at CRS, who helped me along the way. They include Warren Lenhart, Karen Donfried, John Collins, Joe Whelan, Mark Lowenthal, and Charlotte Preece. A steady stream of US and European interns passing through

CRS provided solid assistance as well as new and helpful perspectives on old issues. Over the years, Larry Chalmer gave me the opportunity to try out ideas before his knowledgeable students in the NATO Staff Officer Orientation class at NDU and, on a personal level, has been the source of many helpful ideas of his own. NATO's leading historian, Larry Kaplan, not only provided wise guidance but also encouraged me to write what became this book. Steve Szabo, Simon Lunn, Maurizio Cremasco, and Robert Grant have been both good friends and supportive professional colleagues over many years.

This book benefited greatly from the work of Louis Golino, who drafted the chronology that appears in appendix 2 and who also provided research assistance and reviewed each chapter carefully for both content and style. Very helpful comments at various stages of the project also came from professional colleagues Marten van Heuven, Sean Kay, and Heiko Borchert. I appreciate the work of Susan McEachern, Matt Hammon, Lori Pierelli, Bruce Owens, and the entire team at Rowman & Littlefield who ensured that the book came out clean and in a timely fashion. Responsibility for any mistakes or roads not taken in this book is, of course, mine.

Generous support for the project was received from the German Marshall Fund of the United States, an independent US foundation created to deepen understanding, promote collaboration, and stimulate exchanges of practical experience between Americans and Europeans.

Finally, my biggest debt of gratitude is to the love of my life, Monika, whose tolerance for an author often lost in his next paragraph was exceeded only by her expert editorial comments on the text as it evolved. My love of writing and interest in foreign affairs came from a family environment in which creativity was honored and valued, and I have Mom, Dad, Ba and Grandpa, and Flon and Ed to thank for their love and encouragement over the years. Unfortunately, only Aunt Flon remains to read this appreciation, but I am sure the others know of it.

This book is dedicated to the memory of our son, Scott Rawson Sloan, whose love for life, creativity, and positive spirit remain an inspiration to us both. I hope that this work will contribute to understanding, cooperation, and peace in the world whose stewardship we entrust to his generation and those that follow.

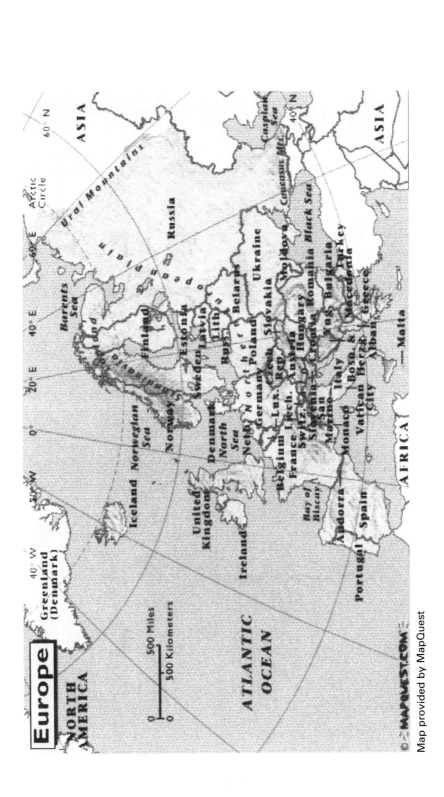

Map provided by MapQuest

List of Acronyms

ABM	Anti-Ballistic Missile Treaty
AFSOUTH	Allied Forces Southern Europe [NATO]
AWACS	Airborne Warning and Control System
BENELUX	Belgium, the Netherlands, and Luxembourg
CAP	Common Agricultural Policy [EU]
CDE	Conference on Security and Confidence Building Measures and Disarmament in Europe
CEE	Central and East European countries
CESDP	Common European Security and Defense Policy [EU]
CFE	Conventional Forces in Europe Treaty
CFSP	Common Foreign and Security Policy [EU]
CIS	Commonwealth of Independent States
CJTF	Combined Joint Task Force [NATO]
COMECON	Council for Mutual Economic Assistance
COPS(I)	(Interim) Political and Security Committee [EU] (French acronym)
CSCE	Conference on Security and Cooperation in Europe
DCI	Defense Capabilities Initiative [NATO]
DPC	Defense Planning Committee [NATO]
DSACEUR	Deputy Supreme Allied Commander in Europe [NATO]
EAPC	Euro-Atlantic Partnership Council [NATO]
EC	European Community(-ies)
ECSC	European Coal and Steel Community
EDC	European Defense Community
EEC	European Economic Community
EFTA	European Free Trade Area
EMS	European Monetary System [EU]

EMU	European Monetary Unit [EU]
EPC	European Political Cooperation [EU]
EUROCORPS	European Rapid Reaction Force [includes troops from Belgium, France, Germany, Luxembourg, and Spain]
EPC	European Political Cooperation [EU]
ESDI	European Security and Defense Identity [WEU/EU]
EU	European Union
EUMC	European Union Military Committee [EU]
EUMS	European Union Military Staff [EU]
EURATOM	European Atomic Energy Community
Euro	European Union currency unit
Eurogroup	Informal grouping of NATO European defense ministers dissolved in 1993
FSU	Former Soviet Union
FYROM	Former Yugoslav Republic of Macedonia
GATT	General Agreement on Tariffs and Trade
IEPG	Independent European Programme Group
IFOR	Implementation Force (for Bosnia) [NATO]
IGC	Intergovernmental Conference [EU]
INF	Intermediate-Range Nuclear Forces
KFOR	Kosovo Force [NATO]
LANDCENT	Allied Land Forces Central Europe [NATO]
LTDP	Long Term Defense Plan [NATO]
MBFR	Mutual and Balanced Force Reductions
MC	Military Committee [NATO]
MLF	Multilateral Force [NATO]
NAC	North Atlantic Council [NATO]
NACC	North Atlantic Cooperation Council [NATO]
NATO	North Atlantic Treaty Organization
NPA	NATO Parliamentary Assembly (formerly NAA, North Atlantic Assembly)
NPG	Nuclear Planning Group [NATO]
NPT	[Nuclear] Non-Proliferation Treaty
NSC	US National Security Council
OECD	Organization for Economic Cooperation and Development
OSCE	Organization for Security and Cooperation in Europe
PARP	[Partnership for Peace] Planning and Review Process [NATO]
PFP	Partnership for Peace
PJC	NATO–Russia Permanent Joint Council [NATO]

PSC	Political and Security Committee [EU]
RMA	Revolution in military affairs
SACEUR	Supreme Allied Commander, Europe [NATO]
SACLANT	Supreme Allied Commander, Atlantic [NATO]
SDI	Strategic Defense Initiative
SFOR	Bosnia Stabilization Force [NATO]
SHAPE	Supreme Headquarters Allied Powers, Europe [NATO]
SNF	Short-Range Nuclear Forces
STANAVFORMED	Standing Naval Force Mediterranean [NATO]
START	Strategic Arms Reduction Talks
TEU	Treaty on European Union, "The Maastricht Treaty" [EU]
UK	United Kingdom
UN	United Nations
UNPROFOR	United Nations Protection Force (in Bosnia)
US	United States of America
USSR	Union of Soviet Socialist Republics
WEAG	Western European Armaments Group
WEU	Western European Union
WMD	Weapons of mass destruction

1

The Bargain as a Framework for Analysis

The glue that has held the allies more or less together is a large, complex and dynamic bargain—partly an understanding among the Europeans, but mostly a deal between them and the United States of America.

—Harlan Cleveland, *NATO: The Transatlantic Bargain*[1]

Crafted in the late 1960s, Harlan Cleveland's description of NATO as a "transatlantic bargain" remains, in the early years of the twenty-first century, a helpful prism through which to analyze the North Atlantic alliance. Cleveland, a former US permanent representative to NATO, knew the alliance was far more than the sort of deal struck between business partners. Although the transatlantic bargain is based firmly on unsentimental calculations of national self-interest on both sides of the Atlantic, it also depends on some amorphous but vital shared ideas about man, government, and society. It is a "bargain," to be sure, but a bargain with roots in the hearts as well as in the minds of the partners.

WHAT WAS THE ORIGINAL BARGAIN?

The original transatlantic bargain, described in chapter 2 of this book, was a bargain between the United States and its original European partners with the militarily modest but politically important participation of Canada.[2] The deal, based on interpretations of the diplomacy of the time, was that the United States would contribute to the defense of Europe and to Europe's economic recovery from the war if the Europeans would organize themselves to help defend against the Soviet threat and use the economic aid efficiently.

The European allies were quite successful in developing the second half of the bargain. In 1948, the Organization for European Economic Cooperation was created to coordinate utilization of Marshall Plan assistance from the United States and to promote European economic cooperation. The Europeans constructed a European Coal and Steel Community (1951) and then, through the 1957 Rome Treaties, the European Economic Community and the European Atomic Energy Community, the precursors of today's European Union.

The allies were not nearly so successful in the security area. As discussed in chapter 2, France had proposed the creation of a European Defense Community to organize Europe's military contribution to the bargain. When that initiative failed in 1954, the arrangements adopted in place of the European Defense Community, considered in chapter 3, left the transatlantic bargain highly dependent on US nuclear weapons and a substantial US force presence in Europe to give credibility to NATO's defense against the Soviet threat.

Throughout the Cold War, the alliance lived with the 1954 "revised" bargain and a persistent burden-sharing debate between the United States and its European allies as well as between successive US administrations and the US Congress.

Congress, given the crucial constitutional roles of the Senate in the process of ratifying treaties and the House of Representatives in legislating funding for government programs, participated actively in shaping and overseeing the transatlantic bargain. The involvement of Congress, judiciously sought by President Harry Truman's administration in the late 1940s, ensured a solid foundation for US participation in the transatlantic bargain. But it also guaranteed that senators and representatives would, for the life of the deal, closely inspect its terms and conditions. From the beginning, this inspection process has focused particularly on whether the costs of the deal were being fairly shared. For most of the history, they have found the sharing process lacking; this continues to be the case today, even under much-changed conditions.

In addition to the important congressional "clause" in the transatlantic bargain, there were many subordinate bargains that were more important to individual allies than to the United States. For example, France wanted the deal to ensure that it would not have to face a resurgence of German power on its own. The United Kingdom wanted US participation in European defense to provide an effective deterrent to Soviet expansionism so that some British military assets would be available maintain its position as a global power. Canada wanted the bargain to be about more than military power, of which it had little, and more about political values, which it held high. When the Federal Republic of Germany joined in the bargain, it accepted constraints on its military capabilities in return for sovereignty over its internal affairs.

Every addition to the membership of the alliance brought new subordinate bargains as European states sought specific benefits from the alliance. Contemporary candidates for membership see belonging to NATO and the European Union as the two key tokens of acceptance in the Western community of nations and as protection against external domination by Russia or any other power.

Among all the changes and adjustments in the bargain over the years (discussed in chapters 4 to 8), the step-by-step development of European integration may be of the greatest importance. The allies were unsuccessful in fulfilling the original transatlantic bargain because Europe was not politically prepared for the degree of unity that would have been required to produce a coherent contribution to Western defense.

The future of the transatlantic bargain depends heavily on whether the European integration process is able to produce such coherence within the framework of continued cooperation with the United States and Canada. The attempt by the members of the European Union to develop a Common European Security and Defense Policy and its implications for the bargain are considered in chapter 9.

WHAT HAS NATO BECOME?

For now, NATO remains at the heart of the transatlantic bargain. Chapter 10 analyzes current challenges to the alliance, and chapter 11 concludes that a new Atlantic Community Treaty should be prepared as the basis for a broader and deeper transatlantic bargain. However, NATO provides the starting point for any such venture, so it is important to consider where NATO's evolution has brought the alliance at the beginning of the twenty-first century.

Today, more than a decade after the Berlin Wall fell, many diverse views about what NATO is—or should become—remain. The discussion of NATO's essence recalls the Indian fable about the king who asked a group of blind men to feel various parts of an elephant and describe the elephant on the basis of the part they had touched.[3] Naturally, each blind man produced a different description of the elephant. This analysis starts from the premise that an objective assessment of NATO's purpose and mission can be based on several sources: on the provisions of the 1949 North Atlantic Treaty, on the declared goals and intentions of its members, and on the fact that an organization is in many respects defined by its activities.

NATO has always been more than simply a defensive alliance. The North Atlantic Treaty provides a broad and flexible mandate through which to defend and promote allied interests and security. Moreover, preserving the attributes of a collective defense system, including an integrated command structure, a vital defense planning process, and thoroughgoing political and military consultations strengthens NATO's ability to play new roles and assume new missions that respond to the post–Cold War challenges to the values and interests of the members.

NATO Is a Community of Values

The North Atlantic Treaty was designed to counter Soviet expansion and military power. But the Treaty itself was based on common values, identified no enemy, protected the sovereign decision-making rights of all members, and was written in sufficiently flexible language to facilitate adjustments to accommodate changing international circumstances. British Foreign Secretary Ernest Bevin, one of NATO's "founding fathers," urged the creation of a "Western Union" in a speech to the British Parliament on January 22, 1948. He asserted that "our sacrifices during the war, our hatred of injustice and oppression, our party democracy, our striving for economic rights and our conception and love of liberty are common among us all." During the negotiation of the Treaty, the government of Canada argued the need to reflect "the ideological unity of the North Atlantic powers." US Secretary of State Dean Acheson subsequently maintained that "the central idea of the treaty is not a static one" and that "the North Atlantic Treaty is far more than a defensive arrangement. It is an affirmation of the moral and spiritual values which we hold in common." During the 1949 Senate hearings on the Treaty, Acheson and other Truman administration witnesses argued that what they were proposing was very different from previous military alliance systems.[4]

What made NATO different from previous military alliances was that the Treaty's preamble clearly articulated allied support for "democracy, individual liberty, and the rule of law." It is true that, during the Cold War, the values of democracy, rule of law, and individual freedom occasionally took second place when authoritarian regimes in NATO were tolerated in the interest of maintaining a militarily strong alliance. But NATO's survival beyond the end of the Cold War suggests that its value foundation and the inherent logic of Euro-Atlantic cooperation remain important ingredients in the glue that holds the alliance together. It is these same factors that make NATO membership so attractive to the new European democracies.

NATO Is Based on a Broad and Flexible Mandate

The North Atlantic Treaty's relatively simple language does not spell out in great detail how its objectives should be implemented. There is no specified military strategy and no requirement for any particular organization or even military arrangements beyond the creation of a North Atlantic Council and a defense committee. This suggests substantial latitude for adaptation and adjustment to changing circumstances. The only limits on such changes are imposed by national interests, values, inertia, and other human and institutional factors, not by the Treaty.

NATO's flexibility was demonstrated, for example, by the military buildup and elaboration of an integrated command structure in the early 1950s that had not been anticipated when the Treaty was signed and that was judged necessary only after North Korea invaded South Korea. The alliance was adjusted again following the failure of the European Defense Community in 1954. In the mid-1960s, NATO was forced to adapt to France's departure from the Integrated Command Structure. In 1967, the allies revamped NATO's strategy with the doctrine of "flexible response" to a possible Warsaw Pact attack. That same year, they approved the "Harmel Report," which gave the alliance the mission of promoting détente as well as sustaining deterrence and defense. And, in the 1990s, the allies reoriented NATO's goals and activities to take into account the peaceful revolutions that brought democracy to Eastern and central Europe and gave Russia, Ukraine, and other former Soviet republics the opportunity for independence and democratic reform.

NATO Is a Collective Defense System

At its founding, the most prominent aspect of the Treaty was its requirement for individual and collective actions for defense against armed attack. Article 3 of the Treaty provides that the allies "separately and jointly, by means of continuous and effective self-help and mutual aid, will maintain and develop their individual and collective capacity to resist armed attack." In Article 5, the Treaty's collective defense provision, the parties agreed that "an armed attack against one or more of them in Europe or North America shall be considered an attack against them all." They specifically agreed that each party to the Treaty would "assist the Party or Parties so attacked by taking forthwith, individually and in concert with other Parties, such action as it deems necessary, including the use of armed force, to restore and maintain the security of the North Atlantic area."

During the Cold War, NATO's strategy and the way in which the United States, Canada, and the United Kingdom deployed their forces on the Continent gave Article 5 more substance in practice than suggested by the words in the Treaty. Beginning in the early 1950s, the United States deployed its military forces and nuclear weapons forward in Europe, mainly in Germany, in a fashion ensuring that a Soviet attack on the West would, in its early stages, engage US forces, thereby constituting an attack on the United States as well as on the host nation. In the mid-1950s, the United States threatened massive nuclear retaliation against the Soviet Union should it attack a NATO country. After massive retaliation's credibility was undermined by Soviet acquisition of long-range nuclear weapons, NATO adopted its "flexible response" strategy. Flexible response suggested that battlefield nuclear weapons might be used early in any European conflict. Such weapons were deployed well forward in West Germany to ensure that they were seen as part of NATO's first line of defense.

Today, the collective defense commitment still endows the North Atlantic Treaty with special meaning. It is a potential deterrent against would-be enemies of the allies and a source of reassurance should future threats develop. With no imminent Soviet-style threat currently facing the allies, they have been adapting NATO strategy and force deployments to fundamentally new circumstances. Most activities of the alliance have turned toward purposes of defense cooperation that lie beyond collective defense, even though the institutions and processes developed to implement collective defense, including the Integrated Command Structure, remain critically important to NATO's future. Article 5 still provides a continuing rationale for maintaining the Integrated Command Structure and the day-to-day political and military consultation and planning that make NATO a unique facilitator of defense cooperation among the member states. They are now seeking to translate their commitment to cooperate against threats posed by terrorist operations and weapons of mass destruction into NATO strategy, force planning, capabilities, and operations.

NATO Is a Cooperative Defense Organization

NATO has been and always will be a political as well as a military alliance. In recent years, it has been increasingly common for observers to say that NATO would have to adapt to new circumstances by becoming "more political." In 2002, following the US failure to use NATO military structures to help conduct military operations in Afghanistan and the decision to intensify cooperation with Russia, many said that NATO was clearly in the process of becoming, for all intents and purposes, a political organization. But NATO's activities in the past and today make clear that its unique role is as an instrument of both political and military cooperation among member and partner states. The process involves consultations in the North Atlantic Council and its many subordinate bodies, practical coordination developed in the work of the Military Committee, and day-to-day collaboration in the Integrated Command Structure. In the 1990s, consultation and cooperation with partners, including Russia and Ukraine, became a critical part of NATO's role. The goals of such cooperation today, however, are more diverse and complex than during the Cold War.

NATO Creates Policy Options for Crisis Management

At the end of the Cold War, the allies questioned whether they still needed an elaborate system of political and military cooperation at a time when the Soviet threat had all but vanished. Their answer, in the November 1991 "new strategic concept," was that political consultation and defense cooperation, so essential in the Cold War, could be broadened to include other purposes. NATO cooperation was widely accepted as having facilitated an effective US-led coalition response to Iraq's invasion of Kuwait, and the experience had a significant influence on the directions taken in the 1991 strategic concept. Since that time, most of NATO's military activities have been focused on "non–Article 5" requirements, most significantly in the Balkans. The mandate for such activities is found primarily in Article 4 of the North Atlantic Treaty, which authorizes cooperation to deal with circumstances that threaten the security of one or more NATO members.

NATO remains an organization of sovereign nation-states in which no member can be compelled to participate in a military operation that it does not support. Therefore, no guarantee exists that the allies will respond to any given political or military challenge. But NATO can be used to build political consensus and create military options to implement political goals. The allies would have fewer credible military options if their military leaders and forces were not working together on a day-to-day basis, developing interoperability of those forces, planning for contingency operations, and exercising their military capabilities. This day-to-day routine develops political and military habits of cooperation that underpin the ability to work together under pressure and, more important, under fire.

The interests of the allies will clearly require the application of military force around and beyond Europe in the twenty-first century. The political-military cooperation that is unique to NATO gives them the option of facing such circumstances as an effective coalition rather than as individual nation-states.

NATO Defense Cooperation Is a Burden-Sharing Tool

NATO can also be seen as a way to ensure that allies carry a fair share of the burdens of maintaining international peace. This is a role that can be seen as a glass half full or half empty. During the Cold War, some Americans saw NATO as a creator of burdens for the United States rather than as an instrument for sharing them. Some may still hold this view, particularly in light of the growing gap between US and European military capabilities. On the one hand, the US military presence in Europe, down to fewer than 100,000 troops on shore, is now increasingly oriented toward force projection and peace operations rather than toward defense of European territory. The NATO framework provides the United States with leverage to push for additional European defense efforts, presuming that the Europeans want the United States to remain involved in European security, which they apparently do. On the other hand, it could be argued that the habit of European security dependence on the United States is perpetuated by NATO, and that new means of cooperation, for example, by giving the European Union a homegrown role in defense, are needed to increase European self-reliance and reduce US burdens.

NATO Defense Cooperation Is an Instrument to Promote Political Change

NATO defense cooperation is now being used more prominently for political goals beyond its members' borders as well. Perhaps for this reason, some see NATO as becoming "more political." The Partnership for Peace (PFP) was initiated to develop cooperation with non-NATO states. Through the PFP, Europe's new democracies have been learning how to develop systems of democratically controlled armed forces as well as habits of cooperation with NATO nations and neighboring partners. The partnership approach has helped the Czech Republic, Hungary, and Poland meet the requirements for NATO membership and remains the principal path through which other nations can prepare to enter the alliance. Countries that were formerly neutral during the Cold War are using the PFP to participate in NATO's efforts to promote stability in and around Europe.

The allies are also using political/military cooperation with Russia as a means to change Russian perceptions of the alliance and, it is hoped, to change the political relationship between Moscow and NATO by gradually integrating Russia into a cooperative Euro-Atlantic security system. In a sense, the 1997 Founding

Act with Russia, creating a NATO–Russia Permanent Joint Council, updated NATO's attempt to promote improved relations with Russia, a goal that was prominently advanced in the 1967 Harmel Report. The strengthening of that tie in 2002 continues the process. If NATO succeeds, the defense cooperation relationship with Russia, which began with military cooperation in Bosnia, could leapfrog over the arms control accords that were designed during the Cold War to regulate relationships between parties that otherwise were in conflict with one another. Moving from a Russia–NATO relationship governed by arms control to one characterized by the transparent, predictable, and confidence-building nature of defense cooperation would mark a sea change in the European security system.

NATO Is an Open Organization

The drafters of the North Atlantic Treaty made it clear in Article 10 that accession to the Treaty would remain open to "any other European state in a position to further the principles of this Treaty and to contribute to the security of the North Atlantic area." This "open door" policy led to the membership of Greece and Turkey in 1952, Germany in 1955, and Spain in 1982. After the countries of central and Eastern Europe freed themselves from communism and began establishing democratic systems of government, NATO's rejection of their desire for membership in the alliance would have repudiated everything the North Atlantic Treaty stands for. Acceptance by the allies of the Czech Republic, Hungary, and Poland in 1999 and of other qualified nations in the coming years highlights the fact that NATO is organized around transcendent values and goals that do not require an enemy to validate their continuing relevance.

NATO Is a Source of Stability

It is clear that NATO serves a variety of purposes for individual member states beyond these broadly stated goals. Many such secondary agendas help explain why current members of NATO want the alliance to continue and why so many countries want to join. For example, although former members of the Warsaw Pact do not fear attack from today's Russia, they do see NATO as a guarantee against falling once again into the Russian sphere of influence as well as an insurance policy against any future resurgence of a Russian threat. Most European governments hope that the process of European unification will lead to more intensive security and defense cooperation among European states. But they continue to see the transatlantic link as essential to security in and around Europe.

Further, many Europeans believe that the US role in Europe, particularly as translated through NATO, provides an important ingredient of stability that facilitates cooperation among European states. For example, even though Germany is not seen as a threat by its neighbors, both Germany and its neighbors feel more comfortable with Germany's role in Europe thoroughly integrated within the framework of both the European Union and the transatlantic alliance. From the

US point of view, NATO cooperation is a way to ensure that the burdens of maintaining international stability are fairly shared with like-minded states.

NATO Is at the Center of a Cooperative European Security System

Finally, it is necessary to address the somewhat academic but politically important question of whether NATO is a collective security organization. The term "collective security" is widely and loosely used in today's discussion of NATO's future role. According to its classic definition, collective security is a system of interstate relations designed to maintain a balance of power and interests among the members that ensure peaceful relationships within that system. The League of Nations, established after World War I without US participation, is usually regarded as such a system.

From the outset, NATO was designed as a system of cooperation among member states to deal with challenges and problems originating outside that system, not within it. Granted, NATO has to some extent tried to promote peaceful settlement of problems within the system in support of its mission of defending against external threats. It is credited with having helped heal World War II wounds inflicted by Nazi Germany on its neighbors. NATO has served to mitigate conflicts between Greece and Turkey. Indeed, the requirements of collective defense promoted a degree of cooperation between these two NATO members that might not have been realized in NATO's absence. Today, several NATO activities support the goal of collective security. Russia–NATO cooperation, the PFP, and the Euro-Atlantic Partnership Council, for example, have helped maintain peaceful and cooperative relations among all states in Europe. Such efforts enhance collective security and make it less likely that any NATO country will be attacked by any other European nation. But when the allies began preparing for enlargement, they made clear to potential applicants that they must resolve differences with their neighbors in order to be seriously considered for NATO membership. The NATO countries insist that new members leave their old baggage of bilateral and ethnic differences with their neighbors by the wayside when they join NATO. So far, in the cases of Poland, the Czech Republic, and Hungary, not all issues related to ethnic nationals residing in neighboring states have been "resolved." However, the NATO commitment helps keep such differences within bounds and promotes peaceful resolution.

From a legal perspective, NATO does not have principal responsibility for collective security in Europe—the North Atlantic Treaty does not suggest such a role. In fact, the Conference on (now Organization for) Security and Cooperation in Europe (OSCE) was designed to promote peaceful relations among states "from the Atlantic to the Urals." The 1975 Helsinki Final Act of the OSCE established a series of agreed principles, or "rules of the road," to govern relations among states in Europe. The OSCE member states (all European states plus the United States and Canada) have adopted further agreements and principles, have given the organization some diplomatic tools for conflict prevention, and convene regular meetings under OSCE auspices to try to address problems before they develop more serious proportions.

THE FUTURE OF THE TRANSATLANTIC BARGAIN

In the fable of the blind men and the elephant, the king finally observes, "Well is it known that some Samanas and Brahmanas cling to such views, sink down into them, and attain not to Nirvana." An "ideal" NATO is probably beyond the reach of member governments today. And participants in the debate on the future of the transatlantic bargain may well continue to "fight among themselves with their fists," as in the fable, declaring that "such is an elephant, such is not an elephant." The future of the bargain most likely must be built on a foundation that accommodates all these perceptions to one degree or another.

In sum, the North Atlantic Treaty still accurately represents the values and goals articulated by the United States and its allies despite persistent differences among them concerning how best to promote those values and defend their interests. The collective defense commitment in the North Atlantic Treaty is an obligation assumed by all current and future members, even though Article 5 leaves much room for nations to decide collectively and individually what to do under any given crisis scenario. This was clearly demonstrated when NATO invoked Article 5 following the September 11, 2001, terrorist attacks on the United States. Continuing defense cooperation in NATO keeps alive the potential to mount collective responses to aggression against alliance members. Defense cooperation also creates policy options, though no obligation, for responses to crises beyond NATO's borders and serves as a tool for changing political relationships between NATO countries and other nations, most importantly Russia. NATO is not a collective security organization; it is designed primarily not to keep peace *among* its members but rather to protect and advance the interests of the members in dealing with the world around them. But some of NATO's activities contribute to the goal of collective security, helping maintain peaceful and cooperative relations among all states in Europe.

These attributes of NATO bear witness to the continuing relevance of the North Atlantic Treaty and the importance of continued US–European security cooperation. However, more than a decade has passed since the dramatic changes at the end of the Cold War. In that decade, the transatlantic allies have sought to understand and relate effectively to a fundamentally new international system. Now the time may be approaching for the United States, Canada, and the European allies to decide whether their thoroughly intertwined interests and still-potent shared political values require a broader framework for cooperation than that provided by NATO, the US–EU dialogue, and other bilateral and multilateral Euro-Atlantic institutions. The concept of an "Atlantic Community" is not a new one. It has been brought forward many times during the history of the alliance, and on each occasion it has been judged an idea whose time has not yet come. But as the United States and its allies focus on the newly framed threats of terrorism and weapons of mass destruction, it may now be the hour in which a serious reconsideration is warranted to ensure that this historic transatlantic bond survives into the uncertain future.

NOTES

1. Harlan Cleveland, *NATO: The Transatlantic Bargain* (New York: Harper & Row, 1970).

2. Canadian priorities and diplomacy resulted in the Treaty's Article 2: "The Parties will contribute toward the further development of peaceful and friendly international relations by strengthening their free institutions, by bringing about a better understanding of the principles upon which these institutions are founded, and by promoting conditions of stability and well-being. They will seek to eliminate conflict in their international economic policies and will encourage economic collaboration between any or all of them." For discussion of the Canadian role in shaping the treaty, see Sean Kay, *NATO and the Future of European Security* (Lanham, Md.: Rowman & Littlefield, 1998), 21–31.

3. According to *The Udana*, or the *Solemn Utterances of the Buddha*, the story goes something like this:

> And the King went to where the blind men were, and drawing near said to them: "Do you now know what an elephant is like?"
> And those blind men who had felt the head of the elephant said: "An elephant, Sir, is like a large round jar."
> Those who had felt its ears said: "it is like a winnowing basket."
> Those who had felt its tusks said: "it is like a plough-share."
> Those who had felt its trunk said: "it is like a plough."
> Those who had felt its body said: "it is like a granary."
> Those who had felt its feet said: "it is like a pillar."
> Those who had felt its back said: "it is like a mortar."
> Those who had felt its tail said: "it is like a pestle."
> Those who had felt the tuft of its tail said: "it is like a broom."
> And they fought amongst themselves with their fists, declaring, "such is an elephant, such is not an elephant, an elephant is not like that, it is like this."

4. US Senate Committee on Foreign Relations, *North Atlantic Treaty, Hearings before the Committee on Foreign Relations*, 81st Cong., 1st sess., April 27–29 and May 2–3, 1949.

2

Genesis of the Bargain

The transatlantic bargain finds its origins in a series of political decisions and diplomatic events in the mid- to late 1940s. As the end of World War II neared, US President Franklin D. Roosevelt was particularly sensitive to fact that President Woodrow Wilson's failure at the end of World War I to engage the United States in the League of Nations had been a contributing factor to the rise of Adolf Hitler in Germany and the events leading to World War II. Roosevelt wanted to ensure that the United States played a leading role in constructing a new international system under the auspices of a United Nations organization. Unlike Wilson, Roosevelt carefully engaged leading members of Congress in the process, including the influential and prewar isolationist Senator Arthur H. Vandenberg, to increase the chances that the United States would commit to the venture.[1]

Meanwhile, wartime ally Great Britain, led by Prime Minister Winston Churchill, was naturally focused on how postwar Europe could be organized to protect British interests and particularly on how to keep German power contained and prevent further Soviet advances into Western Europe. Roosevelt died in 1945, just before the end of the war in Europe and the signature of the UN Charter in San Francisco. In Great Britain, the Labour Party, led by Clement R. Attlee, defeated Churchill's Conservatives, putting the postwar conclusion and reconstruction in the hands of successors in both countries.

The United States, under President Harry Truman, moved into a debate on how best to deal with the Soviet Union as it increasingly appeared that the wartime cooperation between Roosevelt and Soviet leader Joseph Stalin was turning toward a more competitive and even hostile relationship. British Foreign Secretary Ernest Bevin set out to convince the United States to lend its power and influence to a postwar system in Europe that would prevent further Soviet political and military advances. Out of office, Winston Churchill, speaking in Fulton, Missouri, warned of the expansionist tendencies of the Soviet Union, saying, "From

Stettin in the Baltic to Trieste in the Adriatic an iron curtain has descended across the Continent."

Responding to the growing perception of a Soviet threat, in March 1947, President Truman promulgated what became known as the Truman Doctrine, urging the United States "to support free peoples who are resisting attempted subjugation by armed minorities or by outside pressure." A few days later, Great Britain and France, demonstrating that they worried not just about the Soviet threat but also about the possibility of a resurgent German challenge, signed the Treaty of Dunkirk, agreeing to give mutual support to each other in the event of renewed German aggression. The process of shaping the transatlantic bargain had begun in earnest.[2]

In a June 5, 1947, speech by Secretary of State George C. Marshall, the Truman administration proposed what became known as the Marshall Plan to provide funds for economic reconstruction to war-ravaged nations in western and southern Europe. The plan was warmly welcomed by Great Britain and other European countries not only because it would provide much-needed assistance but also because it was a sign of US commitment to Europe's future. Then, speaking before the British House of Commons on January 22, 1948, Foreign Secretary Bevin proposed creation of a Western Union comprised of the United Kingdom, France, and the Benelux countries. As one author has observed, this step "launched the making of the Atlantic Alliance."[3]

Over the course of the next two years, three formative steps shaped the transatlantic bargain: the Brussels Treaty (1948), which resulted from the Bevin initiative; the Vandenberg Resolution (1948); and the North Atlantic Treaty, also known as the Washington Treaty (1949; the text of the treaty is given in appendix 1). These events outlined the objectives of the bargain, identified the partners in the deal, and suggested some of the reciprocal obligations to be borne by the participants.

In the Brussels Treaty of Economic, Social and Cultural Collaboration and Collective Self-Defence of March 17, 1948, the governments of France, the United Kingdom, Belgium, the Netherlands, and Luxembourg provided the initial framework for postwar West European cooperation. More important, these five countries signaled to the United States their intent to structure postwar intra-European relations to encourage internal stability and defense against external threats. The treaty stated the basic European commitment to the bargain. To make sure that the signal would be heard loudly and clearly where it needed to be heard the most—in the halls of the US Congress—President Truman, coincident with the Brussels Treaty signing, told a special joint session of Congress that he was "sure the determination of the free countries of Europe to protect themselves will be matched by an equal determination on our part to help them protect themselves." And so the first part of the bargain was in place, and the stage was set for the next act of alliance construction.

The second part of the bargain was America's response to the European signal. The basic structure of the bargain was being hammered out behind the scenes primarily by officials of American and European governments. But these officials recognized that the bargain's political viability ultimately depended on its acceptance by Congress. They were keenly aware, as had been Franklin Roosevelt, that Woodrow Wilson's plan for US engagement and leadership in the League of Nations had failed because it lacked the essential support of Congress. Midcentury statesmen were determined not to ignore history only to pay the price of repeating it. On the US side, Congress had to be a partner in the deal.

Vital congressional acceptance of the bargain was given political life in the so-called Vandenberg Resolution, personalized, as are many important congressional actions, to acknowledge the role of the principal congressional architect, Senator Arthur Vandenberg, the sponsor and chairman of the Senate Committee on Foreign Relations. The Truman administration went to great lengths to encourage Vandenberg's postwar conversion from isolationism to a more "internationalist" inclination. Christopher S. Raj, in *American Military in Europe,* relates, "The Administration had skillfully placated Vandenberg by including him in US delegations, and the State Department cultivated him assiduously by consulting him often on European affairs."[4]

Following signature of the Brussels Treaty, the State Department asked Vandenberg to prepare a resolution that would express congressional support for the administration's desire to affiliate the United States with the European self-help project. Vandenberg complied and crafted a resolution that, in part, suggested that the United States should support "the progressive development of regional and other collective self-defense in accordance with the purposes, principles, and provisions of the [United Nations] charter." The resolution was approved by the Senate on June 11, 1948, with overwhelming bipartisan support, providing political sustenance, in principle, for the emerging bargain.

The Soviet Union infused the project with added urgency by imposing a blockade of Berlin late in June 1948. After six more months of debate and negotiation among the founding partners in the bargain, the deal was consummated. By the spring of 1949, ten European governments, the United States, and Canada were prepared to sign the North Atlantic Treaty.

The document, finally signed on April 4, 1949, reflected a compromise between the European desire for explicit US commitments to provide military assistance to prospective NATO allies and the American desire, strongly expressed in Congress, for more general, less specific assistance provisions. In this fundamental aspect of the bargain, the Europeans had to settle for a general commitment that was more consistent with the mood in Congress.

Between Congress and the Europeans, the Truman administration practiced a form of diplomatic footwork that subsequently became a standard part of the repertoire of every American administration from Truman to George W. Bush. In the 1949 context, the Truman administration was challenged "to convince Western Europe that the American commitment through the North Atlantic Treaty was a strong one, and . . . to assure Congress that the treaty did not involve the United States in an 'entangling' military alliance."[5] Since that time, subsequent administrations have been required, under a great variety of circumstances, to continue to reassure the Europeans of the validity of the American defense commitments to Western Europe while justifying to Congress the expensive price tag attached to the "entangling alliance" that NATO became.

Consequently, when the Senate approved ratification of the treaty in 1949, it did so despite some strong concerns about the potential long-term costs of a US commitment to defense of Europe—misgivings that then-opponents of the Treaty today might well believe to have been justified.[6] On the other hand, most of those senators who voted for ratification based on the strategic arguments for the alliance would probably today see their action as having been legitimized by history, particularly in light of NATO's contributions to deterrence during the Cold War and the alliance's role promoting stability and cooperation in post–Cold War Europe. Some of the issues raised in the halls of Congress in recent decades over NATO enlargement, burden sharing, Bosnia, and Kosovo echo those heard in the ratification debate of 1949.

At the end of the day, as Lawrence Kaplan has observed, "an awareness of America's new weight in the world combined with the weakness of Europe and the power of Soviet Communism to win over the Senate and the nation."[7] Importantly, the Senate's close involvement in the treaty's development and its approval implied that the bargain was not a simple partnership. It was a deal struck among governments, to be sure, but with the clear implication that two branches of the American government were parties to the deal and that management of the bargain would be a shared responsibility as long as the alliance endured.

UNRESOLVED ISSUES

With signature and subsequent ratification of the North Atlantic Treaty in 1949, NATO's founding fathers had shaped the basic deal: the United States had pledged its continued involvement in European security arrangements in return for a European commitment to organize itself for both external defense and internal stability.

But two central and intimately related issues were left unresolved by these formative steps. The first was how the US commitment would be implemented. The Treaty neither suggested the institutional framework for US involvement nor specified whether the US military contribution would consist primarily of strategic bombing and naval capabilities or whether it would also include substantial

US ground forces in Europe—issues whose contemporary counterparts are still raised in debates about the US military role in NATO.

The second issue was how western Germany would fit into this Euro-Atlantic framework of defense obligations. The treaty did not clarify Germany's status vis-à-vis its West European neighbors, leaving open the question of whether western Germany would be permitted to rearm and, if so, under what circumstances.

In 1949, there was no consensus among the allies or between the Truman administration and Congress concerning how best to deal with these two issues. The national security priorities of the United States, Britain, and France were sharply in contrast. These three leading powers agreed that the Euro-Atlantic partnership, in its broadest form, was designed for the dual purpose of balancing Soviet power and providing an acceptable way to integrate western Germany into the Western community of nations. But it was by no means self-evident how this would be accomplished.

The basic conflict was between French and American priorities—another underlying factor that still affects Euro-Atlantic relations today. The French government, not without good cause, was obsessed with preventing Germany from acquiring any substantial independent military capabilities and placing political constraints on Germany in both the European and the Atlantic framework.

In 1949, the French government, doubting the US willingness to remain involved in any European power balance, was not confident it could provide, on its own, the economic or military counterweight to a Germany already demonstrating its potential for industrial recovery and resurgence. As Timothy P. Ireland has observed, "As it became apparent to the allies that (1) the defense of Europe would have to begin with the Federal Republic and that (2) West Germany's industrial strength was necessary for a successful rearmament program, traditional French apprehensions vis-à-vis Germany became more and more manifest."[8]

The United States was not unsympathetic to France's preoccupation but was fixed on its own priority: balancing the power of the Soviet Union in central Europe. From the American perspective, German industrial capabilities and manpower were assets that could not be overlooked, particularly given Germany's geographic position in the center of Europe. Furthermore, Secretary of State Dean Acheson, sensitive to the fact that the North Atlantic Treaty might not win Senate approval if it appeared to commit the United States to a large military buildup in Europe, had assured the Senate Committee on Foreign Relations that the United States would not, as a consequence of treaty ratification, be required to send large numbers of troops to Europe.[9] Thus, Congress, one of the important partners in the bargain, had signed on to the deal with the tacit understanding that the US contribution to the alliance would consist largely of strategic bombing (the nuclear guarantee) and sea control.

To complicate the problem further, the British absolutely opposed any suggestion that they maintain a substantial presence on the Continent to help balance potential German power. The reluctance of the British to play a large military role in the central European balancing act reflected London's own priorities. Even though the United Kingdom remained strongly committed to a transatlantic alliance, the British Labour government of the time viewed a major political and military commitment on the Continent as less important to British interests than its Commonwealth ties and global responsibilities. Britain's eyes were still turned away from the Continent, across the Atlantic toward the "special relationship" with the United States and around the world to its vast colonial holdings.

In retrospect, this British orientation was as unfortunate for the postwar alliance as the French paranoia concerning Germany was troublesome for the United States. More than two decades would pass before Britain even tentatively acknowledged that its future world role and internal well-being were intimately dependent on the United Kingdom's relationship with its neighbors across the English Channel. But in the meantime, the British attitude denied the postwar allies the potential for a more coherent and effective European pillar for the Atlantic partnership. It is therefore ironic, and perhaps historically appropriate, that in 1999 another Labour government under Prime Minister Tony Blair helped jump-start the process aimed at creating a defense capability for the European Union.

The contrasting French and American preoccupations, combined with the British orientation away from continental involvement, produced two distinctly different sets of preferences for the way Euro-Atlantic relations should be structured to serve the "agreed" purposes of the alliance. The American preference was to help balance Soviet power in central Europe by rearming western Germany. To ensure that Germany's rearmament took place within a stabilized framework, the United States envisioned West Germany's membership in NATO as well as its cooperation in a multilateral European framework growing out of the Brussels Treaty. From the American perspective, German, French, and other continental nations should provide the bulk of ground force manpower in central Europe, with less substantial, primarily symbolic, contributions by the United States, Great Britain, and Canada. West German membership in NATO would legitimize German participation in the military effort, and the European cooperative arrangements would provide France a means of monitoring and controlling German power.

The French preference was, first and foremost, to avoid German rearmament. France also opposed German entry into NATO, viewing such entry as validation of a rearmament program, eventually permitting Germany to escape from any control provisions established in a European framework. Second, the French hoped to convince the United States to commit substantial forces to forward defense of Western Europe in Germany. Third, Paris wanted to weave a web of political and economic relationships within Western Europe that would reinforce German self-interest in cooperation and deter any possible future hegemonistic or aggressive behavior.

In fact, the French National Assembly authorized ratification of the North Atlantic Treaty with the understanding that the pact would not lead to Germany's rearmament. Foreign Minister Robert Schuman reassured French parliamentarians prior to the Assembly's vote for the treaty, saying, "Germany has no army and should not have one. It has no arms and will not have any. . . . It is therefore unthinkable, for France and her allies, that Germany could be allowed to adhere to the Atlantic pact as a nation capable of defending itself or of aiding in the defense of other nations."[10]

The conflict between French and American priorities could not have been sharper. While the United States had refocused its policies toward confronting the threat posed by the Soviet Union, French vision remained fixed on the "German problem," which it hoped to solve once and for all by denying Germany the armed forces with which it could once again threaten France.

THE KOREAN CATALYST

On June 25, 1950, North Korean troops attacked the Republic of South Korea. This aggression, almost halfway around the world from Western Europe, proved to be the catalyst for shaping postwar Euro-Atlantic relations and resolving the Franco-American impasse on German rearmament. The Korean War, seen as demonstrating the global threat of communist aggression, provided the political momentum required to overcome congressional resistance to a substantial deployment of US ground forces in Europe. Such an American commitment undoubtedly was essential in helping to ease French concerns about the potential of a resurgent German neighbor.

For more than a year, the State Department and the Pentagon had argued the issue of German rearmament. The Pentagon, and particularly the Joint Chiefs of Staff, contended that German armed forces would be required if the West hoped to balance Soviet power in central Europe. But the Department of State resisted any formal discussion of German rearmament with the allies, believing that the political costs of such an initiative would be greater than the military benefits. Secretary of State Acheson "feared that any plans to associate Germany with the Atlantic alliance would undermine the whole structure of western defense by running the risk of alienating France."[11]

The Pentagon was not anxious to take on what appeared to be a massive and potentially open-ended commitment in Europe without parallel development of West European defense forces. Given the British reluctance to play a major role on the Continent and the fact that France, with forces tied down in Indochina, would not provide sufficient ground forces to balance the Soviet Union in central Europe, German rearmament seemed an inescapable prerequisite for any major US commitment to continental defense. This position was considerably strengthened by the reasonable expectation that Congress too would not approve a buildup of US forces in Europe without a parallel European effort.

And so, stimulated by the Korean War, a most significant elaboration of the original bargain began to take shape. The United States would deploy substantial ground forces to Western Europe and place them within an integrated NATO command structure. This structure would serve the practical role of coordinating Western defense efforts in Europe as well as providing the crucial Atlantic framework for bringing German military forces into the Western defense against the Soviet Union.

President Truman announced his decision to send a substantial number of American troops to Europe on September 9, 1950, after difficult negotiations during the previous summer had forged a common Defense and State Department position on the question. The decision marked a momentous change in US policy toward Europe, declaring that the United States would commit combat troops to peacetime defense forces in Western Europe. Truman's declaration linked this commitment to the efforts expected from the European allies, without specifically raising the issue of German rearmament, even though reconstituting the German military had become a principal goal of US policy:

> On the basis of recommendation of the Joint Chiefs of Staff, concurred in by the Secretaries of State and Defense, I have today approved substantial increases in the strength of the United States forces to be stationed in Western Europe in the interest of the defense of that area. The extent of these increases and the timing thereof will be worked out in close coordination with our North Atlantic Treaty partners. *A basic element in the implementation of the decision is the degree to which our friends match our action in this regard.* Firm programs for the development of their forces will be expected to keep full step with the dispatch of additional United States forces to Europe. *Our plans are based on the sincere expectation that our efforts will be met with similar action on their part.*[12] (emphasis added)

The Truman administration recognized that it would first have to get the French government to move away from its strong opposition to German rearmament in order to make the deployment of US troops to Europe acceptable to Congress. American pressure on the French government throughout the summer of 1950 intensified in September. Truman's statement of September 9 added a sense of even greater urgency, and the French understood that they would have to respond to the US action. The United States, after all, had now expressed its willingness to deploy combat troops in Europe, just as Paris had desired.

But the French acceptance of the need to act did not mean that Paris was yet prepared to contemplate German rearmament within the NATO framework. The French still hoped to win acceptance for some European organization within which future governments in Paris would be able to control German military efforts.

The French responded to their apparent dilemma by proposing the creation of a European Defense Community. The so-called Pleven Plan, named for French Premier René Pleven, envisioned the eventual creation of a European army within which token German units would be included. The army would not be formed until a European decision-making framework had been established, with a European defense minister and a European parliament to approve funds for the operation. The French National Assembly approved the plan on October 24, 1950.

The Pleven Plan did not respond fully to the American requirement for German rearmament, and American officials were skeptical concerning the motives of the French (to put off German rearmament indefinitely?). They also questioned whether it would be wise to allow the French to exercise the greatest influence of any European nation over the future role of Germany.[13] Nonetheless, the Pleven Plan moved the French one step closer to the American position and helped prepare the way for compromise at the NATO meetings of foreign and defense ministers scheduled for December.

THE COMPROMISE AND CONGRESS

As the allies prepared for the regular end-of-year meetings of NATO foreign ministers, both Secretary of State Acheson and French Foreign Minister Schuman signaled their interest in reaching a compromise on the German rearmament issue. Encouraged by signs of flexibility from Paris, US Deputy Representative to the North Atlantic Council Charles Spofford crafted a compromise proposal that suggested that the United States endorse the long-term concept of an integrated European defense force in return for French acceptance of short-term measures to start bringing German manpower into use "under strong provisional controls" until a more permanent system of European cooperation could be developed.[14] Under the Spofford Compromise, the United States would appoint a Supreme Allied Commander and begin deploying US forces to Europe without waiting for German troops to materialize.

A number of factors convinced Acheson that moving too rapidly on the rearmament issue could be destabilizing in Germany as well as in France. The opposition Social Democrats in Germany were not at all enthusiastic about the prospect of integration into a Euro-Atlantic framework, believing that it would destroy chances for eventual German reunification. In response to domestic criticism, Chancellor Konrad Adenauer felt compelled to press for equal treatment for Germany in return for Germany's willingness to join in the economic and military enterprises that were being designed mainly in Paris, London, and Washington. Adenauer had his own agenda: independent statehood for Germany. But Acheson apparently was convinced that the French government might lose a vote of confidence in the National Assembly should it be forced to move too far too fast on the rearmament issue.

Acheson communicated to Schuman his willingness to compromise in a letter sent to Paris on November 29; the American secretary of state tried to reassure Schuman of the US intent to appoint a supreme commander and, by implication, to begin deployment of American troops to Europe. Acheson argued that the United States had already demonstrated "the depth and permanence of its interests in Europe, its support for closer European association, its willingness to cooperate with Europe." He told Schuman that cooperation between France and the United States in NATO was "an essential corollary to an orderly progression from German cooperation in defense, to European integration, and thus final solution of the problem of relations with Germany."[15]

On December 17, 1950, the North Atlantic Council—NATO's decision-making body—approved the package Spofford had designed and the French and American governments had ultimately accepted. The council approved the French plan for creating a European Defense Force on the condition that the plan not delay the availability of German manpower for Western defenses, and it authorized the establishment of a supreme headquarters with the expectation that a US officer would be appointed supreme commander. At the meeting, Secretary of State Acheson announced that President Truman had appointed General Dwight D. Eisenhower as supreme commander and that the number of US forces in Europe would be increased in the near future.

According to Timothy Ireland's study of this period, the compromise satisfied the principal objectives of the French government and the US administration: "The United States had gained French adherence to at least the idea of German rearmament. The French gained an immediate American military commitment to the defense of Europe while delaying the rearming of Germany."[16] The deal, however, had not yet been approved by another party to the original bargain: the US Congress. While the path for approval of the original North Atlantic Treaty had been carefully prepared in the Senate, Congress had not been formally involved in the steps leading to the Franco-American compromise. As the subsequent "Great Debate" in Congress would demonstrate, Congress had no intention of relinquishing its role in managing the transatlantic bargain.

Congress was in recess following the midterm elections when the NATO meetings concluded, but when the legislators returned to session in January 1951, the new American commitment moved rapidly to the top of the congressional agenda. Troop deployment was most severely questioned by conservatives among the Republican majority in the Senate. They were supported by some influential conservative spokesmen outside Congress, most notably former President Herbert Hoover. On December 19, 1950, Hoover, reacting to the appointment of General Eisenhower as Supreme Allied Commander, Europe (SACEUR), had commented the next day that "the prime obligation of defense of Western continental Europe rests upon the nations of Europe. The test is whether they have the spiritual force, the will and acceptance of unity among them by their own volition. America cannot create their spiritual forces; we cannot buy them with money."[17]

The conservative Republicans focused on two principal issues: whether it was appropriate for the United States to deploy substantial ground forces to Europe as part of an integrated Atlantic defense structure and whether the president could, without congressional authorization, deploy American troops overseas—the "war powers" question that later returned to prominence with the Vietnam War and has remained a sticking point between subsequent US administrations and Congress. The war powers issue was pointedly raised by Senator Robert Taft, who argued, "The President has no power to send American troops to fight in Europe in a war between the members of the Atlantic Pact and Soviet Russia. Without authority he involved us in the Korean war. Without authority, he apparently is now adopting a similar policy in Europe."[18] The administration and its supporters in Congress argued that the president did not need specific congressional approval to make such a deployment. The argument, however, was not convincing for those senators who questioned not only the constitutional validity of the action but also the defense and foreign policy rationale underlying the troop deployment and participation in an integrated command structure in NATO.

Following Truman's January 8 State of the Union Address, in which he strongly defended American involvement in the defense of Western Europe, the debate was joined in Congress. Senator Kenneth Wherry, the Republican floor leader, introduced Senate Resolution 8, which asked the Senate to resolve "that it is the sense of the Senate, that no ground forces of the United States should be assigned to duty in the European area for the purposes of the North Atlantic Treaty pending the formulation of a policy thereto by the Congress."[19] The Wherry resolution was referred to the Foreign Relations and Armed Services Committees, which then held joint hearings on the troop deployment issue. During these hearings, the Truman administration sought to avoid a direct conflict with Congress on the central war powers issue raised by Wherry's resolution. Administration strategy apparently was to defend the president's constitutional right to deploy US forces while at the same time not attacking directly the congressional prerogatives in this area. The administration carefully avoided any acceptance of the idea that it needed congressional approval to do what it had already told the allies it would do.

After extensive hearings, in which a wide range of constitutional, strategic, and economic aspects of the issue were aired, the committees submitted a joint report to the full Senate. Senator Tom Connally, chairman of the Senate Committee on Foreign Relations, then introduced Senate Resolution 99 on behalf of the committees. With Senate Resolution 99, the committees attempted to deal with concerns that had been raised by Senator Taft and others while, at the same time, supporting the appointment of General Eisenhower as SACEUR and the deployment of four US Army divisions to Europe.

Senate Resolution 99 was approved by the Senate on April 4, 1951, by a vote of 69 to 21. Senator Taft, who had so severely questioned the commitment, voted with the majority, apparently believing that his concerns were reflected in the bill.

And so the Truman administration's decision was vindicated in the Senate vote, but not without qualification. The resolution endorsed General Eisenhower's appointment and approved the four-division Army deployment. The Senate also declared, however, that the Joint Chiefs of Staff should certify that the European allies were making a realistic effort on behalf of European defense, that the European allies should make the major contribution to allied ground forces, and that provisions should be made to utilize the military resources of Italy, West Germany, and Spain.

Perhaps most important, although the form of the congressional action—a "sense of the Senate" resolution—did not insist on congressional authority over the president's decision, neither did the Senate give up its claim to exercise such control in the future. Incorporated in the final version of the resolution was an amendment offered by Senator John McClellan that expressed the Senate's desire that "no ground troops in addition to such four divisions should be sent to Western Europe in implementation of Article 3 of the North Atlantic Treaty without further Congressional approval."

The Senate once again had made clear that it wanted to be regarded as an active partner in the transatlantic bargain. It remained reluctant to contemplate an extensive, open-ended US commitment to the defense of Europe, and it expected Europe to carry the bulk of responsibilities, particularly in ground forces, for the Continent's defense. The Senate sought the rearmament of Germany as central to the success of the NATO effort, and it pointedly reminded the administration that it retained the right to involve itself more decisively in US policy toward the alliance should its wishes be overlooked.

WRAPPING UP THE PACKAGE IN LISBON

With the requisite congressional mandate in hand, the Truman administration could move toward firming up the deal with the allies. Throughout the remainder of 1951, administration officials worked with allied counterparts on plans for NATO's future organization and force posture, developed the outline for a European Defense Community, and planned for the relationship between NATO and the defense community. The significant progress made in these discussions was confirmed at a meeting of NATO foreign, defense, and finance ministers in Lisbon, Portugal, in February 1952.

The Lisbon meeting is perhaps remembered best for the fact that it set force goals that remained elusive for the alliance until they no longer needed them at the end of the Cold War. A report adopted by the ministers set NATO force goals of fifty allied divisions, 4,000 aircraft, and substantial additional targets for future years. The allies never reached these so-called Lisbon Goals. The failure of the European members of NATO to build up their conventional military forces to balance those of the Warsaw Pact created the burden-sharing issue that, in one way or another, dominated congressional consideration of the US role in NATO throughout the Cold War.

The NATO ministers also reorganized the civilian management of NATO, making the North Atlantic Council a permanent body, with member governments represented by senior officials and supporting delegations at NATO headquarters in Paris. This organizational change established NATO as a permanent forum for diplomatic exchanges and foreign policy consultations among the allies.

And the allies took note of NATO's further expansion into the Mediterranean region, welcoming the accession of Greece and Turkey to the alliance. Both countries, in advance of the Lisbon meeting, had signed and ratified the North Atlantic Treaty. (The addition of these two countries was a critical move to block expansion of communist influence in southeastern Europe. But it also brought subsequent problems to the alliance. Greece and Turkey's bilateral disputes over the control of Cyprus and the territorial waters between them frequently disrupted internal alliance cohesion and, from time to time, verged on war between the two allies.)

In diplomatic exchanges prior to the Lisbon session, some of the most intensive negotiations among the allies had dealt with the question of West Germany's future role in the Western alliance. The Franco-American compromise formally endorsed in Lisbon had taken shape over the two previous years. A year prior to the Lisbon gathering, France had hosted the first session of the Conference for the Organization of a European Defense Community. The early meetings of the conference were attended by representatives of West Germany, Belgium, Italy, Luxembourg, and the host government, France. The Netherlands had joined the project in October 1951. In Lisbon, these countries presented a report on their progress to the NATO ministers.

The conference report on the European Defense Community described in detail the considerable technical progress that had been made toward establishing a defense community. The participants were, in fact, able to report that they had begun preparation of a draft treaty and associated protocols. In the conclusion of the report, they reaffirmed the purpose of their work:

> To create a European Defense Community which can fulfill the imperative requirements of military effectiveness; to give the Western World a guarantee against the rebirth of conflicts which have divided it in the past; and to give an impetus to the achievement of a closer association between the Member countries on a federal or confederate basis.[20]

When the Lisbon session adjourned on February 25, the ministers announced that they had concluded that the principles underlying the treaty to establish a European Defense Community conformed to the interests of the parties to the North

Atlantic Treaty. They also said they had agreed on the principles that would govern the relationship between the proposed community and NATO. And so, when the thirty-five foreign, defense, and finance ministers and their delegations completed the intensive round of meetings in Lisbon, they had seen the bargain through another significant stage of development. NATO now had an integrated military command structure with a Supreme Allied Commander. The NATO countries had agreed to make substantial ground, air, and naval commitments to the integrated command. Greece and Turkey had been welcomed into the alliance. Progress had been recorded toward the establishment of a European Defense Community, designed to reassure France against future German power and to provide a constructive framework for the creation of a united Europe.

The stage was set for Secretary of State Acheson to travel to Bonn to negotiate and sign, on May 26, 1952, the Convention on General Relations among the Federal Republic of Germany, France, the United Kingdom, and the United States. Acheson then flew to Paris to participate in the May 27 signing of the treaty establishing a European Defense Community and the various associated agreements specifying the intended relationship between that community and NATO. Not too long after these historical ceremonies, however, the package started to come undone.

NOTES

1. Chapters 2 to 5 are based on the analysis in Stanley R. Sloan, *NATO's Future: Toward a New Transatlantic Bargain* (Washington, D.C.: National Defense University Press, 1985).

2. Professor Lawrence S. Kaplan, known to most of his colleagues as NATO's premier historian, has produced a number of books that chronicle in detail NATO's evolution from its origins through the Cold War. They include *The United States and NATO: The Formative Years* (Lexington: University Press of Kentucky, 1984) and *NATO and the United States: The Enduring Alliance* (New York: Twayne, 1988).

3. Don Cook, *Forging the Alliance* (New York: Arbor House, 1989), 114.

4. Christopher S. Raj, *American Military in Europe* (New Delhi: ABC Publishing House, 1983), 8.

5. Timothy P. Ireland, *Creating the Entangling Alliance: The Origins of the North Atlantic Treaty Organization* (Westport, Conn.: Greenwood, 1981), 119.

6. For a discussion of the concerns raised by senators and administration efforts to deal with those concerns, see Phil Williams, *The Senate and U.S. Troops in Europe* (London: Macmillan, 1985), 12–27.

7. Lawrence S. Kaplan, "The United States and NATO: The Relevance of History," in *NATO after Fifty Years,* ed. S. Victor Papacosma, Sean Kay, and Mark R. Rubin (Wilmington, Del.: Scholarly Resources, 2001), 246.

8. Ireland, *Creating the Entangling Alliance,* 177.

9. US Senate Committee on Foreign Relations, *Executive Sessions of the Senate Foreign Relations Committee,* vol. 4, 82d Cong., 2d sess., 1952. Historical Series, 1976.

10. *Journal Officiale,* July 25, 1949, p. 5277, as cited in Michael M. Harrison, *The Reluctant Ally: France and Atlantic Security* (Baltimore: The Johns Hopkins University Press, 1981), 14.

11. Ireland, *Creating the Entangling Alliance,* 186. This discussion of events in 1950–51 benefited substantially from Ireland's account, which is based largely on the US State Department's Foreign Relations of the United States series covering this period (hereafter cited as FRUS).

12. *New York Times,* September 10, 1950, as cited in Raj, *American Military in Europe,* 22.

13. Such reactions are found in detail in diplomatic exchanges recorded in FRUS, 1950, vol. 3, *Western Europe.*

14. FRUS, 1950, vol. 3, *Western Europe,* 480.

15. FRUS, 1950, vol. 3, *Western Europe,* 498.

16. Ireland, *Creating the Entangling Alliance,* 207.

17. *New York Times,* December 21, 1950, as cited in Raj, *American Military in Europe,* 26–27.

18. *New York Times,* January 6, 1951, as cited in Raj, *American Military in Europe,* 27.

19. US Senate Committee on Foreign Relations, *Executive Sessions of the Senate Foreign Relations Committee,* vol. 3, pt. 1, 82d Cong., 1st sess., 1951, Historical Series, 1976, 559.

20. FRUS, 1952–1954, vol. 5, *Western European Security,* 246.

3

The Transatlantic Bargain Revised

The ink was barely dry on the European Defense Community (EDC) treaty when the Lisbon package started to come apart. The force goals so bravely adopted in Lisbon soon appeared unreasonably optimistic. Neither the British nor the French government could fit substantial troop increases into budgets already stretched thin by non-European military commitments—the French bogged down in Indochina, and the British struggling to keep a global role intact. Rumors spread around Europe that the United States was reducing its aid to the NATO countries. Press sources speculated that the entire NATO structure was on the verge of collapse (a prediction heard many times since).

THE LONG ROAD FROM LISBON TO PARIS

The State Department, alarmed by the emerging trends in US as well as European public opinion, drafted a message to send to the embassies in London and Paris. The cable expressed Washington's concern with all-too-common suggestions in the press that "(1) [the] NATO force plan has already been revised unilaterally; (2) Sov[iet] tension has diminished; [and] (3) [the] entire NATO defense program is facing collapse."[1]

The secret cable noted that it apparently was becoming popular in Europe to blame cutbacks in American assistance for French and British inability to meet force goals. The cable suggested that should such misleading information continue to be so prominent in the European press, the US government would be forced to point out some facts—"US defense expenditures [are] four times [the] total [of] all other NATO countries combined; [the] US with smaller population has more men under arms than all other NATO countries combined; [the] percentage of GNP spent by [the] US is above all others and twice [the] NATO average; US per capita defense expenditures are six time[s the] NATO average." Noting the potential impact on US domestic opinion, the cable argued that placing the blame on the United States for European shortfalls would "infuriate Amer[icans] and cause them [to] recall with indignation vast US contributions to Eur[opean] recovery and defense." The message continued with the warning that such duplicity reinforces the arguments of NATO critics who assert that Europe is a "'bottomless pit' and will 'do nothing for itself.'"[2]

After making the State Department's concerns so clear, the cable instructed the embassies in London and Paris to encourage the British and French governments to "find opportunities" to clarify the situation to the public, especially making these tersely worded points:

a. There has been no revision NATO targets adopted at Lisbon; cannot be revised unilaterally. What we face is possible shortfall in meeting targets.
b. US is fulfilling aid commitments and has not reduced them.
c. There is no evidence easing of Soviet threat, and NATO defenses remain inadequate.
d. Prospective shortfall, while increasing and prolonging security risks, should not be interpreted as NATO "breakdown." Defense buildup will continue forward as rapidly as possible.[3]

The NATO ministers met in December 1952, following the elections in the United States in which NATO's first Supreme Allied Commander, Europe, General Dwight David Eisenhower, had won his campaign for the White House. Perhaps with little anticipation of how crucial events in Indochina could be for the NATO alliance, the ministers issued a communiqué proclaiming that the campaign being waged in Indochina by the forces of the French Union deserved the support of the NATO governments.[4]

When the new secretary of state, John Foster Dulles, returned from his first NATO ministerial meetings in April 1953, he reported that the allies had accepted, though with some qualms, the new administration's inclination to concentrate on the quality rather than the quantity of assistance to the NATO allies. The Eisenhower administration was working toward a "new look" at American defense policy— an approach that, fifty years later, the George W. Bush administration brought to the table during its first year in office.

The administration, while seriously concerned about the Soviet challenge, was equally intent on rationalizing US commitments abroad as part of an overall program of economic austerity. The Truman administration had not been able to decide to what extent US strategy should depend on nuclear weapons, but the Eisenhower administration was inclined virtually from the outset to use nuclear weapons deployments to meet national security objectives while pursuing fiscal solvency. Dulles had attempted to reassure the allies that rationalization in no way suggested a US tendency toward isolationism.

At the same time, the new administration clearly hoped that closer cooperation among the NATO European allies would eventually relieve the United States of some of its European defense burdens—a theme of US policy that has persisted until today. In his 1953 New Year's message to Chancellor Konrad Adenauer, Eisenhower made a special point of saying that the development of an EDC "would contribute much to promote peace and the security of the free world."[5] At a meeting at the Pentagon a few weeks later, Eisenhower argued strongly for support of the EDC, saying, "The real problem is that of getting German participation. Anything which does not accomplish that doesn't mean very much." The general-turned-president went on to recall, "In hearings before the Congress, I have always had to face the question as to when we were going to get German help in defending Europe. It would be difficult to justify Congressional appropriations for Europe if there were no such prospect."[6]

It is therefore no surprise that Dulles was concerned, as had been the previous administration, by the slow progress toward implementation of the EDC plan. On his return from Europe, he reported to a meeting of the National Security Council that his "one great worry in retrospect . . . was the delay and failure to ratify the EDC treaties and to secure the desired German contribution."[7] Dulles felt that the political steam had gone out of the drive toward an EDC. The post-Stalin leadership in the Soviet Union, through its first "peace campaign," had already managed to dispel some of the sense of urgency that had earlier helped motivate work toward an EDC.

As 1953 passed without any of the six EDC signatories having ratified the treaty, the dilemmas inherent in European security arrangements became increasingly apparent to US officials. At a meeting of the National Security Council on December 10, 1953, preparatory to a scheduled NATO ministerial meeting in Paris, Secretary of Defense Charles Wilson expressed his "distress" that the United States seemed "hopelessly caught between the fear of the Europeans as to the use of atomic weapons, and our own desire to bring our forces home."[8]

Responding to Wilson's concerns, President Eisenhower explained, "Our one great objective at the moment was to secure the ratification of EDC." Eisenhower said that the United States could not afford "to take any steps toward redeployment, or even to talk about redeployment [of troops in Europe to the United States], until these objectives have been reached." To buttress his point, the president added, "The French have an almost hysterical fear that we and the British will one day pull out of Western Europe and leave them to face a superior German armed force."[9]

When Secretary of State Dulles left for the Paris meetings, he apparently hoped to provoke some new movement toward realization of the EDC, which had become key to the US goal of German integration in Western defenses and eventual withdrawal of some US forces from Europe. At a press conference held during the NATO meetings on December 14, Dulles administered shock treatment in an attempt to resuscitate the defense community project when he said,

> We also understand that action [creating a united Europe to prevent future Franco-German antagonism] will be taken within the framework of the North Atlantic

Treaty, which will bring into association with the European Defense Community (E.D.C.) this strength which lies around the periphery of E.D.C.

It is that policy, in regard to Europe, to which the United States is committed. In essence that is the European policy which we are trying to cooperate with, and we earnestly hope that policy will be brought to a successful conclusion.

If, contrary to our hopes and beliefs, it should not happen that way, it would force from the United States *an agonizing reappraisal* of its foreign policy.[10] (emphasis added)

The implication that the United States would reconsider its commitment to European defense should the EDC not be approved appeared reasonable from Washington's perspective. The US Defense Department, impatient with the slow progress toward ratification of the EDC, had already considered some contingency plans for incorporating German forces in Western defenses in the absence of an EDC. But in Paris, the Dulles statement probably looked like a strong-arm tactic, raising the hackles of the consistently nationalistic and sensitive French.

The US minister in France at the time, Theodore Achilles, observed in a memorandum to Dulles that "it is too soon to tell whether your press conference has arrested [an] unfavorable trend [in France against the EDC], but it has certainly provided food for thought and again posed clearly the issue and the urgency."[11] But Achilles also recorded the prophetic reaction of one French Foreign Ministry official who reportedly said that

the press conference had finished EDC, that it must have been deliberate, that the problem now was to save the Atlantic Alliance, that some new way would have to be found to tie Germany to the West, perhaps through NATO, and finally that France would now have to do some painful rethinking of its own policies.[12]

In the first half of 1954, US policy struggled to shore up the transatlantic bargain with constant reassurances to France and its prospective EDC partners that the United States remained supportive of the EDC concept and committed to European defense. The United States was unable to dispel a lingering concern in France that once the EDC was in place, the United States would take its leave of Europe, exposing France to German power. There was, of course, some cause for this concern. The Eisenhower administration did see the EDC as a potential source of relief, though not an escape, from the burdens of European defense. Many in Congress, however, hoped that the EDC would in fact provide the escape route many Europeans feared the United States would take all too quickly once the EDC was set up.

Congress had demonstrated clearly its desire to see the EDC ratified. The Mutual Security Act of 1953, governing military assistance to the NATO allies, required that the administration withhold a portion of the aid intended for EDC nations that had not ratified the treaty. In the spring of 1954, a modified form of the provision was incorporated in the Mutual Security Act of 1954, effectively preventing future deliveries of military equipment to the two countries that had not yet ratified the EDC: Italy and France. The Eisenhower administration had originally opposed the prohibition but supported the version incorporated in the 1954 legislation, apparently believing that it might add pressure to the campaign for EDC ratification.

At the same time, however, the administration's nuclear weapons policies may have undermined the credibility of its case for French ratification of the EDC. The administration's intent to increase substantially US and consequently NATO reliance on nuclear weapons, tactical as well as strategic, suggested that the United States had given up hope of mounting a credible nonnuclear defense against the Soviet Union in central Europe, even if West German forces were incorporated in Western defenses via the EDC. Under such circumstances, why should France be willing to risk sacrificing substantial national sovereignty for the sake of participation in a European army that US nuclear weapons policy was making increasingly less relevant?

Despite the potentially counterproductive interaction between the new-look strategy, which emerged full blown in 1954, and the EDC goal, the United States moved assertively on both fronts. At the NATO ministerial meetings in April 1954 (by then the Netherlands, Belgium, Luxembourg, and the Federal Republic of Germany had ratified the EDC treaty), Secretary of State Dulles cautioned the gathered ministers:

> Without the availability for use of atomic weapons, the security of all NATO forces in Europe would be in grave jeopardy in the event of a surprise Soviet attack. The United States considers that the ability to use atomic weapons is essential for the defense of the NATO area in the face of the present threat.

Then Dulles summarized his argument with a judgment undoubtedly not accepted by all his colleagues around the table: "In short, such weapons must now be treated as in fact having become 'conventional.'"[13]

THE DEFEAT OF THE EDC

As Secretary of State Dulles was preaching the gospel of nuclear dependence, the EDC story was moving toward a dramatic conclusion. The French government formed by Pierre Mendes-France in June 1954, the latest in a succession of politically vulnerable Fourth Republic regimes, was preparing a ratification vote on the EDC treaty in the French National Assembly. Mendes-France suspected that the treaty as it stood would probably not be approved by the Assembly or that it would be approved by such a slim margin that it might undermine the entire program of his government. Apparently hoping to generate a more substantial majority for the treaty, Mendes-France asked the other EDC signatories to approve a package of modifications in the treaty. The foreign ministers of the six nations met in Brussels from August 19 to 22 to consider the French proposals. The Belgian foreign minister, Paul-Henri Spaak, submitted a set of compromise proposals that was accepted by all the other countries except France. The conference adjourned without agreeing on modifications to the EDC plan, and Mendes-France prepared with little enthusiasm to move toward a vote in the National Assembly.

It is still not clear whether Mendes-France, had he obtained the changes he requested, could have won ratification of the accord. In any case, with an unenthusiastic governmental advocacy of the EDC case, the treaty failed on an August 19, 1954, procedural vote by a margin of 264 deputies for and 319 against.

According to a postmortem on the ratification vote, completed by the American embassy in Paris early in September 1954, changes in French perceptions of the threat influenced the outcome. Although the French remained concerned about the potential German threat, they had become more relaxed about the Russian threat and somewhat more wary of American intentions. The embassy's analysis suggested that

> in 1954, the fear of Russia was less than in 1953, when it was less than in 1952 and much less than in 1951 and 1950. Correspondingly, there existed, perhaps not only in France, a greater fear of some future action or reaction on the part of the US which might lead to world war; and in the specific case of EDC a greater fear that the US might in some way back the irredentist aspirations of Germany in a manner detrimental to French security interests.[14]

French perceptions of the threat had changed, but a number of other factors also influenced the mood in Paris. The French had been freed from their Indochinese dilemma by the July 1954 Geneva accords, but only in the wake of military defeat. This defeat, combined with the prospect of a long struggle against an independence movement in France's North African Algerian colony, presumably made more than a few French deputies wary of taking on additional military commitments. Furthermore, the structure of the Fourth Republic consistently produced weak governments, and as the embassy postmortem pointed out, "No French government ever dared to challenge the opponents of EDC and carry the battle to them. Indeed, they could not have done so without breaking up the governing coalition."[15]

History has yielded no single explanation for France's defeat of a French idea that had been adopted in principle by the entire Western alliance. Some analysts have speculated that a deal had been cut between Mendes-France and Soviet Foreign Minister V. M. Molotov. According to this theory, in return for Soviet cooperation in the Geneva negotiations in July 1954 bringing an end to the war in Indochina, Mendes-France chose not to compromise at Brussels, thereby guaranteeing defeat of the treaty in the National Assembly. Moscow was strongly opposed to the EDC, and its active peace campaign of 1953–1954 bore witness to the depth of Soviet concern. But there is still no firm evidence of any deal between Moscow and Paris to receive a graceful exit from Indochina in return for defeat of the EDC.

The Soviet campaign certainly contributed to the delay and indecision that characterized the French approach to EDC ratification between 1952 and 1954, and French Communist Party deputies, closely following the Moscow line, were unalterably opposed to the treaty. The Soviet campaign's main influence, however, probably was on the large number of French Socialist deputies, many of whom could have gone either way on the treaty.

In the final analysis, France's fear of a resurgent Germany remains the most prominent factor in the rejection of the EDC. Had France been in an optimistic frame of mind, perhaps the nation would have been able to suppress its sense of insecurity toward the Germans and take on the challenge. But the economic outlook was gloomy, France had lost the war in Indochina, and the French governmental system was weak and ineffective. As a result, "the whole debate took place in an atmosphere of a tremendous national inferiority feeling." And noting this mind-set, the embassy commented further, "One of the most important, though usually unspoken arguments against EDC had long been the belief that in any community including France and Germany the latter would inevitably gain the upper hand because the Germans are more capable soldiers, organizers, businessmen and politicians."[16]

Almost fifty years later, the same sorts of concerns about Germany still haunt many French politicians and influence French attitudes toward European integration and transatlantic relations—*plus ça change, plus c'est la même chose!* (the more things change, the more they remain the same).

The decision against the EDC was a tragic chapter in the history of Western postwar alliance construction. Ironically, it was France, the original author of the EDC plan, which had become uncertain about its work and had finally torn up the script. The embassy concluded, "This deep pessimism, it must be recognized, is perhaps justified," awkwardly adding the phrase "at least in part" to the end of the sentence, seemingly trying to take some of the edge off this dark assessment of the French national psyche. The phrase perhaps also reflected some acknowledgment that the policies of the Eisenhower administration had helped undermine the EDC project by intensifying French fears of being seduced into the defense community with Germany and then abandoned by the United States.

PICKING UP THE PIECES

France's rejection of the EDC removed what had been intended as a vital link between the postwar Western alliance arrangements and the goal of a sovereign and rearmed West Germany. While the action destroyed the intended framework for Germany's integration into the Western community as a sovereign and equal participant, it by no means meant that such a link would be impossible.

The United States had quietly been considering possible alternatives to the EDC for more than a year and had discussed such options with the British early in 1954. All along, the United States had viewed the EDC principally as a means to an end: the rearming of western Germany as part of the Western alliance against the Soviet Union. Secretary of State Dulles affirmed this priority in a statement issued just two days after the vote in the National Assembly. Expressing regret that France had turned "away from her own historic proposal," Dulles stated that the United States would now be required to "reappraise its foreign policies, particularly those in relation to Europe," as he had promised eight months earlier. At the heart of this reappraisal would be the place of the Federal Republic of Germany in the Western alliance:

> The Western nations now owe it to the Federal Republic of Germany to do quickly all that lies in their power to restore sovereignty to that Republic and to enable it to contribute to international peace and security. The existing Treaty to restore sovereignty is by its terms contingent upon the coming into force of EDC. It would be unconscionable if the failure to realize EDC through no fault of Germany's should now be used as an excuse for penalizing Germany. The Federal German Republic should take its place as a free and equal member of the society of nations. That was the purport of the resolution which the United States Senate adopted unanimously last July, and the United States will act accordingly.[17]

Officials in the United States did in fact move very quickly, as Dulles wished, to develop alternative arrangements. Interagency discussions, although revealing somewhat different (and natural) priorities among the State and Defense Department officials involved, nonetheless produced agreement on the general objectives. By mid-September, Dulles had met with Chancellor Adenauer in Bonn and British Foreign Secretary Anthony Eden in London, and a strategy had been agreed on. The goal was a four-power meeting among the United States, Great Britain, the Federal Republic of Germany, and France to obtain French agreement on three points:

(1) Further progress toward European unity by expansion of the Brussels Pact so as to admit Germany and Italy.

(2) Admission of Germany to NATO.

(3) The working out of "accompanying arrangements" by the Federal Republic and the occupying Powers, who should at the same time declare their intentions with regards to restoration of sovereignty.[18]

This agenda, based on a British initiative, stimulated a flurry of diplomatic activity in September that culminated in the Nine-Power and Four-Power Conferences at London from September 28 to October 3. The Four-Power Conference meetings involved foreign ministers from the United States, the United Kingdom,

France, and West Germany, and the Nine-Power Conference added foreign ministers from Belgium, Canada, Italy, Luxembourg, and the Netherlands. Those present decided to end the occupation of Germany, allow West Germany to join NATO, and strengthen and expand the Brussels Treaty with the membership of West Germany and Italy.

The foreign ministers of the same countries reconvened in Paris on October 20 and were joined by those of the remaining NATO countries: Denmark, Norway, Iceland, Greece, and Turkey. The formal decisions were confirmed on October 23 at three different levels. First, the foreign ministers of the United States, the United Kingdom, France, and the Federal Republic of Germany signed the Protocol on the Termination of the Occupation Regime in the Federal Republic of Germany, the Convention on the Presence of Foreign Forces in the Federal Republic of Germany, the and the Tripartite Agreement on the Exercise of Retained Rights in Germany.

Next, the foreign ministers of the United Kingdom, France, Belgium, the Netherlands, and Luxembourg signed the Declaration Inviting Italy and the Federal Republic of Germany to Accede to the Brussels Treaty and its four protocols. (Italy was an original signatory of the North Atlantic Treaty but not of the Brussels Treaty.) Finally, the fourteen NATO foreign ministers signed the Protocol to the North Atlantic Treaty on the Accession of the Federal Republic of Germany.

With these agreements, the three occupying powers had recognized the Federal Republic of Germany as a sovereign state and ended their occupation. In return, the Federal Republic agreed to authorize the stationing on its territory of foreign forces at least equal to the strength existing at the date the agreements came into force. West Germany and Italy joined the Brussels Treaty, and the "Western Union" became the Western European Union (WEU). West German military capabilities would be monitored within the WEU framework, but Germany would become a member of NATO. The United States and the United Kingdom agreed to station forces on the European continent for as long as necessary.

The French National Assembly voted in favor of the London/Paris agreements on December 30, 1954, and the bargain was put back together again—but not according to the original plan. West Germany became a NATO member on May 5, 1955, and nine days later the Soviet Union concluded the Warsaw Pact with the governments of Albania, Bulgaria, Czechoslovakia, East Germany, Hungary, Poland, and Romania, with whom Moscow had earlier negotiated bilateral defense pacts.

Meanwhile, the US campaign for allied approval of the new-look strategy had also moved to a conclusion. The NATO ministers, meeting in mid-December 1954, adopted a report prepared by the NATO military committee designated "MC 48," modestly titled "The Most Effective Pattern of NATO Military Strength for the Next Few Years." In a memorandum to President Eisenhower in November 1954, the presidential staff secretary, Colonel Andrew J. Goodpaster, summarized the proposed change in NATO strategy by writing, "An effective atomic capability is indispensable to a maximum deterrent and essential to defense in Western Europe." Goodpaster continued,

> [The first] element of proposed action is to secure NATO-wide approval of the concept of the capability to use A-weapons as a major element of military operations in event of hostilities. For this purpose, the US should be prepared, if required subject to constitutional limitations, to give assurances that A-weapons would be available in the hands of US forces for such operations.[19]

On his return from the NATO sessions, Secretary of State Dulles reported to the National Security Council that a number of allies were concerned that the new policy might take vital crisis decisions out of the hands of civilian leaders of allied countries. Dulles had met with British Foreign Secretary Anthony Eden and Canadian Secretary for External Affairs Lester Pearson prior to the NATO meetings, and the three worked out a formula whereby the new strategy would be adopted under the condition that "there was to be no delegation by the NATO governments of their right as the civilian leaders to give the signal for bringing the atomic defense into action."[20] With this reassurance and the belief that any crisis would allow time for allied consultation prior to the use of nuclear weapons, NATO Secretary-General Lord Ismay formally put the proposal before the ministerial session of the North Atlantic Council. Dulles reported that the resolution occasioned "virtually no discussion or debate, and was unanimously approved by the Council."[21]

And so, apparently with little controversy, the alliance quietly mortgaged its future strategy to nuclear weapons. The mortgage came with relatively small payments in the early years, a consideration that, at the time, seemed more important than any foreseeable future costs. By the end of 1954, therefore, the alliance had assumed its basic shape, with the way cleared for the admission of the Federal Republic of Germany. Alliance strategy had evolved toward heavy dependence on nuclear weapons and a continuing US ground force presence in Europe.

But this formative period for the Western alliance had left two fundamental desires unfulfilled. First, the plan to coordinate European contributions to the alliance through an EDC had failed to materialize. This failure meant that Germany would not remain a military midget within a French-controlled EDC; it also frustrated American hopes that such a community would eventually make it possible for the United States to withdraw most of its ground forces from Europe.

Second, even at this early stage of alliance development, it became clear that the United States and its allies would not match the quantitative force levels fielded by the Soviet Union and its allies. Despite a continued substantial American troop presence and the rearming of West Germany, the Lisbon force goals had become little more than paper promises, even though the alliance was not as yet willing to backtrack formally on the commitments made at the Lisbon ministerial meetings.

As a result of these two changes in the goals agreed on at Lisbon, the military strategy of the alliance came to rest heavily on the threat of the United States to use nuclear weapons against the Soviet Union should Soviet forces attack Western Europe. At the same time, the credibility of that threat depended on a continuing and substantial American military presence in Europe. These two changes in the original bargain bequeathed a legacy that troubled the alliance throughout the Cold War. The fact that NATO's military credibility was so dependent on the US force presence in Europe ensured that burden sharing would remain an issue between the United States and Europe as well as between successive US administrations and Congress.

NOTES

1. US State Department, Foreign Relations of the United States (hereafter cited as FRUS), 1953–1954, vol. 5, *Western European Security,* 313.

2. FRUS, *Western European Security,* 314.

3. FRUS, *Western European Security,* 314.

4. *NATO Facts and Figures* (Brussels: NATO Information Service, 1981), 32.

5. *New York Times,* January 7, 1953, A1.

6. FRUS, *Western European Security,* 711–12.

7. FRUS, *Western European Security,* 398.

8. FRUS, *Western European Security,* 451.

9. FRUS, *Western European Security,* 451.

10. FRUS, *Western European Security,* 468.

11. FRUS, *Western European Security,* 868.

12. FRUS, *Western European Security,* 469.

13. FRUS, *Western European Security,* 511–12.

14. FRUS, *Western European Security,* 1112.

15. FRUS, *Western European Security,* 1112.

16. FRUS, *Western European Security,* 1113.

17. FRUS, *Western European Security,* 1121.

18. FRUS, *Western European Security,* 1221.

19. FRUS, *Western European Security,* 534–35.

20. FRUS, *Western European Security,* 561.

21. FRUS, *Western European Security,* 561.

4

The Bargain through the Cold War, 1954–1989

It is difficult to look at the roots of the original transatlantic bargain without being impressed by the persistence of some factors. After more than fifty years, US policy toward the alliance is debated by Congress in virtually the same terms that it was in the early 1950s, with a focus on better burden sharing and more European self-reliance. Presidential administrations have not always been comfortable with the bargain but have consistently defended it in the face of congressional skepticism. The United States and France continue to pursue different visions for the future of transatlantic relations, and traditional French concern about US "hegemony" is now stimulated by US missile defense plans and massive military spending. France still worries about Germany, but it is now a reunited Germany's "soft" power that worries Paris the most.

Despite these and other continuities, the bargain has constantly evolved, even while the Cold War helped sustain NATO's basic strategy and structure. More dramatic change was to come after the Cold War ended, but even in the thirty-five years between 1954 and 1989, a number of things changed. The allies, acting unilaterally in some cases and in concert in others, made conscious changes in and amendments to the bargain. Some of these changes were inspired by developments over which the allies had little control (such as the Soviet Union's drive toward nuclear parity with the United States, calling into question NATO's nuclear strategy), while political and economic trends rooted primarily within the alliance spawned other changes.

Identifying certain events or developments as representing significant changes in the bargain while leaving some others aside is in itself a subjective exercise. With that in mind, the following alterations in the bargain before the end of the Cold War are suggested as having produced changes that were important in their time and relevant to the Atlantic Community's future:

1. France's development of an independent security policy, culminating in withdrawal from NATO's integrated military command structure;

2. NATO's adoption of the "Harmel formula," giving the alliance a dual defense and détente role in East–West relations;
3. NATO's approval of the military strategy of "flexible response" and the efforts to keep the strategy viable with deployment of intermediate-range nuclear forces in Europe;
4. British acceptance of an active role in continental Europe's future through membership in the European Community (now European Union);
5. the political maturation of the Federal Republic of Germany;
6. the development of European Political Cooperation as a forum for shaping common European positions on foreign policy issues and as a foundation for a European "pillar" in the alliance.

All these developments represented fundamental changes in the nature of the transatlantic bargain. There were other shifts, to be sure, such as the wavering commitments of some allies (e.g., Greece) and the admission of Spain to NATO. There were attempted shifts that failed, such as Secretary of State Henry Kissinger's "Year of Europe" initiative in 1974, designed to convince the European allies that the transatlantic bargain should take into account "out of area" challenges to Western interests and redress the balance between economic costs and benefits of the transatlantic bargain for the United States.[1] Enthusiasm about and policies toward the alliance fluctuated over time in most alliance countries. But the factors discussed in this chapter are the ones that most fundamentally influenced the core of the transatlantic bargain.

THE FRENCH REBELLION

When President Charles de Gaulle withdrew France from NATO's integrated military command structure in 1966, he unilaterally altered the transatlantic bargain with a flair befitting this most French of modern French leaders. The general's move, however, was not so much a break from Fourth Republic policies as it was the culmination of attitudes and frustrations that had roots in a uniquely French mixture of historical doubts about the reliability of the United States and concerns about US domination. France had never been comfortable with the way the bargain turned out. De Gaulle's strong will and unique leadership ability, combined with the powers that he had insisted be built into the constitution of the Fifth Republic, simply provided the means for translating French displeasure into political action.

From the beginning, France had substantially different objectives for and interests in the Atlantic alliance than did the United States. The earliest French proposals for tripartite French, British, and US management of the alliance emanated from Fourth Republic governments, even though this approach may best be remembered as a "Gaullist" line. The directorate concept was an expression of the French image of itself as the leading continental European power as well as of the

French desire to be acknowledged clearly as having rights and powers superior to those available to the Federal Republic of Germany. The structure of the alliance favored by the United States, granting in theory equal rights to all members, provided a framework for the American superpower to exercise a primus inter pares role within the alliance, subordinating France to a position, in this sense, no more privileged than that of West Germany.

Fourth Republic governments had already decided that France, in order to obtain the status it thought essential to French security and national independence, would be required to take unilateral measures. One route available to France but denied to Germany was to become a nuclear power. When the Fourth Republic gave way to de Gaulle and the Fifth in 1958, development of a French nuclear weapons capability was well under way. It remained only for de Gaulle to articulate a political philosophy and develop a military strategy to give the *force de frappe* a major role in projecting French independence.

Perhaps from a French perspective, this stunning unilateral change in the transatlantic bargain was not totally unprovoked. France had hoped, indeed expected, from the early days of the alliance that its role as a global power would be acknowledged as an asset to the Western alliance and that the rhetorical support that the NATO countries accorded the French role in Indochina in the December 1952 ministerial communiqué would be followed by more substantive assistance. From the French perspective, however, the United States not only failed to provide that assistance but also eventually turned against French interests in the Third World. The disenchantment in this regard perhaps began with the French defeat in Indochina, when the United States was faulted by Paris for not providing crucial military assistance to besieged French forces at Dien Bien Phu. The "lesson" of Indochina for Paris was bitterly repeated with American failure to support France's struggle in Algeria and, in 1956, with active American opposition to France and Great Britain in the Suez crisis. France, for its part, may well have perceived the United States as having made the first unilateral change in the original bargain. Michael Harrison, in his book *The Reluctant Ally,* reaches this conclusion: "NATO's value to France never recovered from the allied failure to support her cause in Africa, from the American reaction to Suez, and from the conviction that the United States had morally and materially turned against France and violated the Alliance tie."[2]

Whether or not one is sympathetic to the French case, it remains clear that the experiences of the Fourth Republic governments had set the stage for de Gaulle's rebellion against the Western "order." This is not to say that de Gaulle was simply following through on Fourth Republic initiatives. De Gaulle's wartime experiences had galvanized his doubts that the United States could be counted on to defend French interests. This skepticism eventually was reinforced by postwar-era nuclear politics, which led him to believe that France (or any other country for that matter) could not expect the United States to risk nuclear destruction of an American city to defend that of any ally. Only if France had an autonomous nuclear deterrent could it truly be independent. And de Gaulle believed strongly that a nation, once robbed of its independence, would soon lose its spirit and eventually die. These beliefs made de Gaulle suspicious of American plans for nuclear sharing with Europe, as manifested by the US/United Kingdom Nassau Agreement of December 1962, which made modernization of British nuclear capabilities dependent on American assistance, and by the abortive multilateral nuclear force plan of the early 1960s. His concerns about French independence were heightened by what appeared to be a growing tendency toward US–Soviet condominium in the wake of the Cuban Missile Crisis and by the signature of the Test Ban Treaty in July 1963, which de Gaulle saw as symbolizing a US–Soviet collaboration to monopolize the nuclear arena and eventually squeeze France into a nonnuclear status.

Just prior to de Gaulle's ascent to the presidency of France in 1958, the Rome Treaties had taken effect, establishing the European Economic Community, precursor of the European Community (EC) and now the European Union. De Gaulle, believing as strongly as he did in the nation-state as the heart of the international system, hoped to lead his European partners away from the supranational inspiration of the Rome Treaties and toward a *Europe des patries*, a European unity based on sovereignty of the nation-states and led, of course, by France. An important part of the French plan was the so-called Fouchet initiative for political cooperation among the European Community members, conceived to build the foundation for an independent European coalition positioned between the American and Soviet superpowers.

When the uncompromising Gaullist approach to European unity proved unacceptable to the other five Community members, de Gaulle became convinced that only unilateral French action, within Europe as well as toward the United States and in East–West relations, could effectively promote French interests. In 1963, de Gaulle vetoed the British application to join the European Economic Community, seeing the United Kingdom as still too Atlanticist to be a committed "European" partner. De Gaulle also provoked an internal crisis within the Community in order to block a scheduled transition to qualified majority voting on certain Community policy decisions. The move had been intended to subordinate national interests in specified policy area to broader "community" interests as well as to make Community decision making more effective.

Then, in 1966, de Gaulle finally announced France's decision to leave NATO's integrated military command and asked NATO to remove its headquarters, forces, and facilities from French territory by April 1, 1967. De Gaulle made it clear that France would continue as a participant in the political aspects of NATO and would remain true to its treaty obligations. But from that point forward, France would declare itself independent of American leadership as symbolized and, to a certain extent, operationalized by NATO's integrated commands.

What could have been a devastating event for NATO actually was turned into a positive stimulus for the alliance. The fourteen other allies carefully avoided emotional responses to the French action and concentrated on the practical challenges that the withdrawal posed. Harlan Cleveland, US ambassador to NATO at the time, recalls, "President Johnson, whose private references to General de Gaulle stretched his considerable talent for colorful language, imposed an icy correctness on those who had reason to discuss French policy in public."[3] The allies quickly relocated NATO headquarters to Brussels, Belgium, and went on with the business of the alliance almost as if nothing had happened.

In fact, the French move appeared to have had so inconsequential an impact on the alliance that some observers questioned whether it had any importance at all other than producing domestic political points for de Gaulle. One such observer, a NATO diplomat, described the action as "a cheap anti-American gesture, which changed almost nothing militarily, certainly did no harm to French security, yet enabled the General to crow that he had 'withdrawn from NATO'—for home consumption."[4]

In retrospect, however, de Gaulle's withdrawal from the alliance did have some long-term consequences, some of them quite detrimental to the transatlantic bargain despite the admirable fashion in which the fourteen other allies adjusted to the French action.

Militarily, the French move weakened NATO's lines of supply and communications. Even if the allies could in theory have counted on France to join in the battle should Warsaw Pact forces have attacked Western Europe, the infrastructure for supporting NATO's front lines and for bringing in new supplies and reinforcements would be closer to the front and more vulnerable to enemy interdiction. Some of the negative effects were mitigated by continued French participation in certain NATO infrastructure projects and by the fairly extensive but low-key military cooperation that developed between France and the other allies in subsequent years. But the benefits to allied defense plans that full access to French territory would have offered were lost.

The political costs to the alliance, however, may have been far more important than the military consequences. The French withdrawal substantially altered the political balance within the alliance. With France conferring on itself an "independent" status, the alliance became even more dependent on American leadership than it was before. This strengthening of American preeminence in the alliance ironically came at a time when Western Europe was moving toward a more powerful position in the Atlantic relationship as a result of its economic strength, the increasingly important role of West German forces in the alliance, and the growing strategic importance of French and British nuclear forces.

It was also ironic that one consequence of the French move was to enhance the importance of the German role within the alliance. The withdrawal virtually guaranteed that the Federal Republic, even without nuclear weapons of its own, would become the second most influential ally in NATO and the leading European member. Even though France remained a participant in all aspects of the alliance *not* directly associated with the integrated military command structure, its voice in alliance councils became less influential as a consequence of its decision to limit its formal military participation in the alliance.

The French withdrawal also raised serious political and structural obstacles to the chances for European defense cooperation within the alliance. In the years following the withdrawal, the allies actively tried to develop ways to expand cooperation with the French. The West Germans sought to exploit the avenue of bilateral Franco-German military cooperation, which de Gaulle saw as preferable to such cooperation within the NATO framework. The West Germans walked a fine line in such cooperation, attempting to expand the relationship in every way possible without jeopardizing in any fashion Germany's NATO obligations and its relations with the United States. But the political conditions imposed by France's qualified participation in NATO severely limited the options available for closer defense cooperation among the European allies.

It is difficult, in retrospect, to see any unequivocal gains for France as a consequence of the withdrawal. French security may not have been damaged, but it also was not appreciably enhanced by the move. Perhaps it could be said that an "independent" French position resulted in more political energy and financial resources being devoted to defense than if France had remained in the integrated military structure, but this is hard to prove. Furthermore, France did not become a more valued interlocutor with the Soviet Union because the United States and the Federal Republic of Germany held the cards of greatest interest to Moscow. An independent position might have seemed of some tactical value to the Soviet Union from time to time, but in the end Moscow sought to deal principally with the two Western countries that could most benefit or harm Soviet interests.

The alliance may, in fact, have benefited in one regard from the French withdrawal. The establishment of a truly independent alternative Western nuclear decision-making center produced additional complications for Soviet strategy. Whatever uncertainty French nuclear forces and strategies created for Moscow may have enhanced Western deterrence. This was in fact recognized in Washington and officially by NATO. As Pascale Boniface has written,

> Once the French *force de frappe* became a reality . . . the United States was obliged to accept it. Washington eventually made a virtue out of necessity—by acknowledging in the Ottawa Declaration of 1974 that France's nuclear capability was in fact useful for the defense of the West and for greater European security.[5]

On balance, however, the French rebellion was to the detriment of the long-term viability of the Western alliance. Most important, the withdrawal made it more difficult for the alliance to translate increased European strength into a more substantial European role in the alliance. This alteration in the bargain, therefore, is one of the most important factors that had to be accommodated when the allies turned to the business of building a European pillar for the alliance after the end of the Cold War.

NATO'S ROLE IN DEFENSE AND DÉTENTE

The French rebellion had shaken the foundations of the alliance. But another fundamental challenge lay at hand. The North Atlantic Treaty was approaching its twentieth anniversary, auspicious primarily because the Treaty's escape clause gave members the opportunity to leave the alliance after twenty years. As the alliance closed in on the 1969 opportunity for desertion, the greatest challenge to its political viability was not the French challenge. Rather, it was the question of whether this alliance, constructed in the chilly atmosphere of the Cold War, could survive in the warming climate of East–West détente.

In Germany, Social Democrat Willy Brandt had come into government as foreign minister in a "grand coalition" with the Christian Democrats, assuming the position of foreign minister on December 6, 1966. He believed that the Federal Republic's policy of nonrecognition of East Germany and of existing European borders stood in the way of improving human conditions in Europe and particularly in the German Democratic Republic. Brandt's concept of "Ostpolitik" represented a major shift from Germany's orientation under Chancellor Konrad Adenauer, and he brought this new philosophy to his first NATO foreign ministerial meeting in Paris later that month.[6]

Brandt's Belgian counterpart, Foreign Minister Pierre Harmel, felt strongly that the alliance would have to respond to critics who charged that NATO had become irrelevant under the changed international conditions. On the basis of Harmel's initiative, at least partly inspired by Brandt's philosophy that NATO defense and East–West détente could be compatible, the December 1966 meeting of NATO foreign ministers commissioned a yearlong study of "The Future Tasks of the Alliance." According to Harlan Cleveland, even the title of the study took on special meaning in the context of the mid-1960s. Cleveland, who represented the United States in the North Atlantic Council in the period before, during, and after the study, recalled that "if the 'Future of the alliance' had been studied, that would have implied doubt about continuation of the Alliance beyond 1969. 'Future tasks' assumed that NATO would survive its twentieth birthday, and called only its functions and priorities into question."[7]

The critique of NATO that inspired the Harmel exercise suggested that NATO's emphasis on the military aspects of security tended to undermine prospects for political solutions to East–West problems. The alliance had, of course, focused primarily on ways to maintain and improve Western defenses. It had not, however, been totally blind to the political aspects of security. Already by the mid-1950s, the allies had recognized that a narrowly focused Western military approach to the Soviet threat would not be sufficient to serve the broad range of allied political and economic as well as security objectives. The communiqué issued by the NATO foreign ministerial meeting in Paris in December 1955 marked the first formal alliance initiative broadening its perspectives on security, taking the Soviet Union to task for Moscow's refusal to consider intrusive systems of arms control verification, such as President Eisenhower's "Open Skies" proposal.

In 1956, the allies began developing the rationale and mandate for arms control consultations in the alliance. The spring ministerial of that year appointed a "Committee of Three on Nonmilitary Cooperation" to study ways in which NATO nonmilitary cooperation could be expanded. The "three wise men"—Foreign Minister Gaetano Martino of Italy, Halvard Lange of Norway, and Lester Pearson of Canada—reaffirmed the necessity for collective defense efforts but strongly emphasized the need for better political consultation among the members. In particular, their report, approved by the North Atlantic Council in December 1956, observed that consultation "means more than letting the NATO Council know about national decisions that have already been taken; or trying to enlist support for those decisions. It means the discussion of problems collectively, in the early stages of policy formation, and before national positions become fixed."[8]

"The habit of consultation," strongly advocated by the three wise men, became an important part of alliance rhetoric, almost approaching theological heights. Even before the report—and ever since—NATO problems, to one extent or another, have been blamed on the failure of one or more allies to consult adequately. Virtually no report or commentary on the alliance can reach its conclusion without recommending "improved consultations."

The Harmel Report appropriately commended the virtues of improved consultation. The report's most important contribution, however, was its conclusion that "military security and the policy of détente are not contradictory but complementary." The report, the product of a prestigious committee led by Harmel, asserted that the alliance had two main functions. The first function, and the one with which the alliance had become most closely identified, was "to maintain adequate military strength and political solidarity to deter aggression and other forms of pressure and to defend the territory of member countries if aggression should occur." The second, newly assigned function of the alliance was "to pursue the search for progress towards a more stable relationship [with the East] in which the underlying political issues can be solved." Approved by all the allies, including de Gaulle's France, the report offered this summary perspective:

> Collective defense is a stabilizing factor in world politics. It is a necessary condition for effective policies directed towards a greater relaxation of tensions. The way to peace and stability in Europe rests in particular on the use of the Alliance constructively in the interest of détente. The participation of the USSR and the USA will be necessary to achieve a settlement of the political problems in Europe.[9]

The allies adopted the Harmel Report at their ministerial meeting in December 1967 and, in this bold stroke, fundamentally altered the objectives, image, and "future tasks" of the alliance. The report's "defense and détente" combination provided an intellectual and political framework for NATO policies that accommodated the growing split in the alliance between left and right. By bridging two different views of how best to ameliorate East–West tensions, it broadened the potential base of political support for NATO in European countries and in the United States. Subsequently, instead of polarizing Western politicians, policy elites, and publics, the alliance could serve as a fulcrum for balancing divergent perspectives on the requirements for the West's security policy in Europe. Not inconsequentially, this critical addition to NATO's role provided the foundation for NATO to become a viable political instrument following the end of the Cold War, when its military relevance appeared open for debate following disappearance of the Soviet threat.

Acceptance of the Harmel Report also provided a way to deal with another problem that had been brewing between the United States and the European allies. The United States had become actively involved in bilateral arms control discussions with the Soviet Union, and these discussions occasionally left the allies wondering whether their interests would be protected by their American ally. At the same time, American officials had become increasingly concerned that the European allies would become "infected" by the Soviet peace campaign, with individual allies drifting off to cut their own deals with Moscow. The Harmel Report implied that NATO consultations could serve to coordinate Western approaches to the East. This coordination function would help alleviate European concerns about US–Soviet bilateralism while providing a brake on any European tendencies toward excessive détente fever.

In a very practical sense, the Harmel exercise created a whole new set of responsibilities for NATO. A few weeks after the Harmel Report had been approved, the allies agreed to strengthen the political institutions of the alliance by establishing a "Senior Political Committee." This step could be regarded as institutional sleight of hand because the new box on the organizational chart simply referred to meetings of the NATO Political Committee, with the allies represented by the deputy permanent representatives (instead of the lower-ranking political counselors). Nonetheless, to the extent that bureaucratic structures can be manipulated to send political signals, the alliance in this way marked the increased importance of the political side of alliance activities. A further institutional signal was issued later in 1968, when a new section in the NATO international staff was created to deal with disarmament and arms control issues.

The allies wasted no time translating the Harmel mandate into alliance policy. When the North Atlantic Council met in Reykjavik, Iceland, in June 1968, the allies issued a "Declaration on Mutual and Balanced Force Reductions." The so-called Reykjavik signal announced allied agreement that "it was desirable that a process leading to mutual force reductions should be initiated." They agreed "to make all necessary preparations for discussions on this subject with the Soviet Union and other countries of Eastern Europe," and they urged the Warsaw Pact countries "to join in this search for progress toward peace."[10]

The Reykjavik signal echoed NATO's June 1967 expression of interest in mutual force reductions. However, the Reykjavik declaration was notable in that it not only expressed interest but also voiced NATO's intention to prepare for discussions that the East was invited to join. The Reykjavik signal, therefore, marked NATO's formal entry into the world of arms control initiatives, making operational the recommendations adopted in the Harmel Report six months before.

The Harmel exercise revitalized the foundations of the alliance. It reiterated NATO's commitment to maintain a strong defense, but it broadened substantially the goals of the alliance. This amendment to the original transatlantic bargain provided a political framework more relevant to the challenges posed by the East–West environment of the 1960s. It also responded to the evolving relationships between the United States and its West European allies. The Harmel formula gave the alliance a new lease on life and a renewed sense of purpose.

Perhaps the most lasting contribution of the Harmel exercise was the change in NATO's mission that would become so relevant at the end of the Cold War. For many years, NATO's search for the fruits of détente appeared unproductive and to some perhaps even counterproductive. Negotiations on Mutual and Balanced Force Reductions (MBFR)[11] opened in 1973 but droned on for more than a decade before being converted into negotiations on Conventional Forces in Europe in the mid-1980s; the latter negotiations finally produced a deal, largely because the fading Cold War finally made it possible. That deal not only provided the framework for dramatic cuts in military forces and equipment across Europe but also established an intensive, cooperative monitoring system that would eventually help ease the transition from Cold War confrontation to a more cooperative security system in Europe.[12]

In addition, in 1975, NATO's initiatives helped turn Moscow's propagandistic proposals for a "Conference on European Security" into the Conference on Security and Cooperation in Europe (CSCE), a meaningful East–West forum on a broad spectrum of issues.[13] The East–West dialogue in the CSCE may well have contributed to undermining the control of communist regimes in the East and to the unraveling of the East–West conflict.[14]

Despite the opening of MBFR talks and the beginning of the CSCE process, many Americans saw little in the way of demonstrable benefits for NATO's pursuit of détente. When President Gerald Ford (in 1974 Ford succeeded President Richard Nixon, who had stepped down after the Watergate scandal) suggested that the term "détente" should be removed from the West's political vocabulary, many Europeans winced but hoped that the comment would not be prophetic. Ford's declaration, inspired by some deeper trends in American thinking, in fact did project accurately the future course of American policy.

The administration of President Jimmy Carter (1977–80) was unsure in its early years what it would do about the growing disenchantment, particularly among American conservatives, with the era of détente. The administration revealed a split personality in its approach to the Soviets. On the one hand, it wanted—and negotiated—a strategic arms control accord with Moscow. On the other hand, the administration's fixation on human rights issues produced a strong critique of the Soviet Union's treatment of its own citizens, criticism that cohabited very uncomfortably with the administration's attempts to sell a US–Soviet arms control deal to the US Congress.

While the Strategic Arms Limitation Talks (SALT II) treaty was languishing someplace between life and death in the US Senate, the Soviet Union provided the stimulus for resolution of the dilemma in Carter administration policy. In the closing days of 1979, Moscow sent troops into neighboring Afghanistan, collapsing whatever was left of US–Soviet détente. A US Atlantic Council report in 1983 noted, "The death of détente was sounded when the Soviets invaded Afghanistan in 1979. President Carter imposed sanctions, withdrew the SALT II agreement from Senate ratification, and recommended substantial increases in US defense spending which were further enlarged under the Reagan Administration."[15]

Washington's unilateral declaration of the death of détente, however, was never fully accepted in Europe. The Soviet invasion of Afghanistan was seen as distasteful evidence of Soviet insecurity and interventionism but not as a direct threat to Europe and certainly not as a sufficient rationale for jeopardizing the fruits of détente in Europe. As Josef Joffe put it, "For the United States, détente did not 'work,' for the Europeans it did—hence their almost obsessive attempts to snatch as many pieces as possible from the jaws of the rattled giants."[16]

Even before the invasion of Afghanistan, Henry Kissinger had argued that the Harmel formula was inappropriate for the circumstances of the late 1970s. Addressing a conference on the future of NATO in Brussels in September 1979, Kissinger dismissed NATO's détente role as an intrusion on the real business of the alliance. European (and some American) participants in the conference shook their heads in amazement that Kissinger could so lightly dismiss a political aspect of NATO that had been so important to the credibility of the alliance for more than a decade. Kissinger's approach, however, was a clear warning that the critique from the political right in the United States was increasingly affecting American perspectives on the alliance.[17]

In the late 1970s and into the 1980s, the United States and the European allies struggled with the great variety of issues raised by their differing perspectives on the importance of détente and whether détente was "divisible," applicable to Europe but not the Third World. The debate intensified with the advent of the Reagan administration in 1981, which was determined to implement a tough new American policy toward the Soviet Union, backed by a substantial defense buildup.

The allies managed to work out compromises on many of the specific issues raised by the differing American and European perspectives. But European governments never accepted the American contention that détente was dead or that the alliance should jettison its mandate for pursuing improved relations and arms control agreements with the Soviet Union.

Ironically, the hard-line Reagan administration, which had troubled the Europeans so much, managed to initiate the end-game negotiations on both intermediate range nuclear missile cuts and conventional force reduction negotiations in Europe. In subsequent years, supporters of President Reagan claimed that his tough policies toward the Soviet Union had helped bring about its collapse. Critics of the American president suggested that Soviet leader Mikhail Gorbachev should be given most of the credit for opening both the Soviet Union and the Warsaw Pact for change. Looking back, it would appear that both factors played a role and that, to some extent, the outcomes that unraveled the Warsaw Pact and dissolved the Soviet Union were unexpected consequences of Soviet and American policies. In any case, the relevance and importance of the Harmel doctrine appear in historical perspective to have been borne out by the end of the Cold War and the need for NATO to adapt its role further to accommodate the dramatically new international realities.

NATO'S NUCLEAR STRATEGY

From Massive Retaliation to Flexible Response

NATO's reliance on the threat of a massive nuclear attack on the Soviet Union had been suspect virtually from the day MC 48 was approved in December 1954. NATO's first nuclear strategy was not quite as simple as implied by the image of "massive retaliation" most frequently used to describe the essence of MC 48. The strategy spelled out in this document did not exclude the possibility that nuclear weapons might be used only within the confines of the battlefield. Despite US deployment in the 1950s of a variety of nonstrategic nuclear weapons in Western Europe, however, alliance strategy remained at least implicitly reliant on the suggestion that the Soviet Union would risk a massive nuclear strike on its territory should its forces attack Western Europe.

This nuclear strategy, driven principally by the austerity program of the Eisenhower administration and the failure of the allies to meet the Lisbon convention force goals, did not sufficiently anticipate the implications of Soviet nuclear force deployments. The Soviet Union had successfully tested an atomic device in 1949 and a hydrogen bomb in 1953, but when MC 48 was approved, the Soviet Union had only limited means for delivering its few weapons on Western targets and virtually no credible means for threatening American territory. The United States, meanwhile, had surrounded Soviet territory with a bomber force capable of devastating strikes on the Soviet Union. This situation was, for obvious reasons, intolerable for the Soviets, and even as the NATO ministers were approving MC 48, Moscow was developing its own long-range bomber force and planning to deploy medium- and intermediate-range ballistic missiles targeted on Western Europe. The launch of the *Sputnik* satellite in 1957 symbolized the dramatic progress the Soviet Union had made in a very few years toward developing its own strategic nuclear weapons force capable of holding both European and American cities hostage to a nuclear threat, calling into question the US policy of massive retaliation.

The NATO allies struggled from the mid-1950s with attempts to adjust NATO's strategy and force posture to the evolving strategic environment. In 1959, the Eisenhower administration deployed US medium-range ballistic missiles to Europe: sixty Thor missiles to England and ninety Jupiter missiles divided evenly between Italy and Turkey. The missile deployments were intended to help offset the Soviet deployment of SS-4 and SS-5 missiles that had begun in the late 1950s and to bolster the confidence of European governments in the ability of the United States to implement its nuclear guarantee.

The alliance was at the same time grappling with some internal political dynamics that had begun to undermine its nuclear weapons strategy. European fretting about civilian control of nuclear weapons, so much in evidence when the United States had first attempted to sell the new-look strategy to the alliance in 1954, developed into a more specific European desire to have a say in Western nuclear decision making. By the late 1950s, the British had an independent nuclear capability, and the French were on the way toward nuclear power status. The United States was by no means anxious to encourage the proliferation of nuclear weapons states and would have preferred that neither France nor Great Britain develop nuclear forces.

Between 1959 and 1963, a number of schemes emerged for some form of nuclear sharing among the NATO allies. These schemes were motivated to varying degrees by Soviet nuclear weapons advances and by the tension within the alliance about the American monopoly in nuclear decision making. Of these proposals, only the Multilateral Force (MLF) made any headway. The MLF would have been a force of twenty-five surface ships, each carrying eight Polaris nuclear missiles, manned and funded by multinational crews and assigned to the NATO Supreme Allied Commander. The United States would have retained ultimate veto power over the use of the MLF weapons.

The MLF proposal, ingenious as it might have been, never had much chance of political acceptance. President de Gaulle interpreted the scheme simply as a means for the United States to retain control over Western nuclear policies while appearing to share it. He saw his suspicions confirmed when the British, seeking to modernize their nuclear forces, chose to purchase Polaris missiles from the United States. According to de Gaulle, British Prime Minister Harold Macmillan "mortgaged" Britain's future nuclear capability to the United States in the Nassau Agreement with President John F. Kennedy in December 1962, when he agreed to buy

Polaris submarine-launched ballistic missiles from the United States. After further NATO discussions of various MLF variants that continued into the administration of Lyndon B. Johnson, MLF joined the ranks of historic curiosities.

The MLF failure left unresolved the issues it had been designed to address, in particular, the political requirement for broader allied participation in nuclear decision making. Even if France and Great Britain were determined to maintain their own nuclear forces, US officials remained convinced that West Germany would have to be given a more acceptable role in nuclear decision making given Bonn's increasingly central role in the alliance.

By the early 1960s, the United States had positioned in Western Europe a wide array of nuclear weapons, ranging from intermediate-range systems to short-range weapons intended for use on the battlefield. However, it kept either full control over the weapons or joint control by retaining one of two keys necessary to release them. This massive infusion of US nuclear weapons in NATO defenses, combined with the desire of some West European allies for a more influential role in NATO nuclear planning, led to the creation of the Nuclear Planning Group (NPG) in 1966. The NPG was designed to allow alliance members to influence planning for the potential use of nuclear weapons and to give them a role in nuclear decision making in a crisis. The United States also agreed to assign sixty-four Polaris submarine-launched ballistic missiles directly to NATO along with the British Polaris force, both of which would be responsive to requirements of the SACEUR.[18]

The abortive MLF project and the subsequent creation of the NPG were responses largely to developments within the alliance. During the same period, the alliance was also moving toward a substantial shift in its nuclear strategy. Although massive retaliation had died years before, it had never been formally buried; the United States started pushing for a proper interment in the early 1960s.

From an American perspective, the steady growth of Soviet nuclear capabilities clearly necessitated a more flexible set of guidelines for the use of nuclear weapons. It was no longer credible simply to threaten attacks on the Soviet heartland with nuclear weapons in response to a Warsaw Pact offensive in Western Europe—the American heartland had become vulnerable to a response in kind. The need for change had been signaled by Secretary of Defense Robert McNamara in 1962. Such a momentous change in nuclear strategy, however, met with skepticism in Western Europe, largely from fear that the credibility of the nuclear guarantee would be destroyed by a strategy that foresaw the possibility of limited or controlled nuclear exchanges. The concepts that lay behind MC 48 had been of American origin, but they had been embraced by the European allies, and in the 1960s the threat of a massive nuclear strike still seemed a needed deterrent to Soviet aggression in Europe.

In 1967, following France's departure from NATO's integrated military command structure and after several wrenching years of discussion and debate among the allies, NATO adopted the doctrine of flexible response. According to the new strategy, NATO would be prepared to meet any level of aggression with equivalent force, conventional or nuclear, and would increase the level of force, if necessary, to end the conflict. The doctrine attempted to accommodate the American desire for more flexible nuclear options and West European concerns about the nuclear umbrella. Under the doctrine, Chicago might not be put at risk in the early stages of a conflict, but the possibility of escalation supposedly "coupled" the fate of Chicago to that of Paris, Hamburg, or London.

The new strategy, substantially altering the original transatlantic bargain, compromised conflicting US and European perspectives on the requirements of deterrence. As Simon Lunn wrote, "While theoretically sound, it [flexible response] left considerable latitude for differences concerning the levels of forces necessary at each stage to insure credible deterrence. This ambiguity permitted the accommodation of conflicting American and European interests, but it did not represent their reconciliation."[19]

The new nuclear doctrine did not reconcile American and European differences on nuclear strategy, but it did provide a formula that was sufficiently ambiguous to achieve political credibility on both sides of the Atlantic—at least for a while. The strategy, combined with the advent of allied consultations on NATO's nuclear policy in the NPG, formally accorded nuclear weapons, from the smallest-yield battlefield systems to the strategic forces of the United States, their own unique places in NATO military strategy. Not only would nuclear weapons serve as a deterrent against a Warsaw Pact attack, but, under flexible response, the entire range of nuclear weapons had a potential role to play in wartime scenarios. Furthermore, the United States had acknowledged the legitimate interests of the allies in shaping NATO nuclear doctrine and sharing the responsibilities of decision making in a crisis. The United States provided no iron-clad guarantee about how extensive consultations might be in a crisis, but at least the NPG provided the ways and means for such consultations.

The decision also recalled the long-standing but unfulfilled NATO objective of mounting a credible nonnuclear defense against the Warsaw Pact. A more substantial conventional capability would fit comfortably within the flexible response framework. In this regard, the new strategy was at least superficially consistent with the original bargain, in which substantial European nonnuclear forces were to be a key support for NATO strategy. Under the circumstances of conventional insufficiency, however, the new doctrine implied greater reliance on the possible use of short-range nuclear weapons as well as the possibility that a nuclear exchange might be limited to the battlefield or to the European continent.

Flexible response, in this sense, was a double-edged sword. Reliance on a wide range of battlefield nuclear weapons implied an even more permanent US commitment to its force presence in Europe because virtually all of NATO's nuclear weapons were under exclusive US control or subject to US veto. NATO's defense options as well as its deterrent strategy had become more dependent on the US troop presence. The October 1954 American commitment to maintain troops in

Europe for "as long as is necessary" therefore became longer and more necessary under the flexible response strategy.

At the same time, whether or not the US intent was to provide a greater buffer between its homeland and a possible war in Europe, the new doctrine clearly left open the possibility that the United States would place a higher value on avoiding nuclear strikes on the United States than it would on protecting West European territory. Although the first edge of the sword therefore committed the United States even more firmly to participate in the defense of Europe, the second edge of the sword cut away some of the credibility of that commitment.

In fact, the Soviet Union's drive, first to obtain the means to threaten the United States directly and then to achieve nuclear parity, changed one of the most important conditioning factors for the original transatlantic bargain. The American homeland became dangerously exposed for the first time since the young upstart of a nation had chased the European powers from the Western Hemisphere. Technological advances had given the Soviet Union the potential to threaten all of the United States with its nuclear weapons. But the Atlantic Ocean still separated the United States from its European allies, and it therefore remained possible, at least in theory, for the United States to limit its involvement in a war in Europe in order to save the American homeland, and, given the emerging Soviet nuclear capabilities, it had much more reason to do so.

Flexible Response Undermined

With the advent of flexible response and the development of limited nuclear options, the certainty implied by massive retaliation was replaced by the elusive goal of "escalation control." That NATO "advantage" was countered in the 1970s by Soviet nuclear force improvements, including deployment of the SS-20, a mobile, accurate missile system capable of carrying three independently targeted warheads on each missile.

For many West Europeans, the nuclear deterrent had remained credible throughout the perturbations in the nuclear balance and adjustments in Western nuclear policy. There was no certain guarantee that the American president would push the button for Europe, but no iron-clad commitment could be expected. The Soviet Union had not risked an attack on Western Europe and did not seem likely to do so. A qualified guarantee, therefore, appeared sufficient for deterrence. For many nuclear strategists, however, there was no such confidence.

In the 1970s, West German Chancellor Helmut Schmidt became the single most influential European commentator on alliance strategy and force posture. By the mid-1970s, Schmidt had become convinced that Soviet conventional force advantages over NATO, combined with its superiority in theater nuclear forces, put Europe at risk. Schmidt was concerned that the codification of a US–Soviet balance of strategic weapons in the SALT process could make these weapons of "last resort," weaken extended deterrence, and leave Europe exposed to Soviet power.

He highlighted such concerns in a major address to the London International Institute for Strategic Studies in October 1977. Although Schmidt's comments did not refer to theater nuclear forces, they "focused public attention on the concept that a gap was appearing in NATO's deterrent capability."[20]

In the fall of 1979, Henry Kissinger, having served earlier as national security adviser and then secretary of state under Presidents Nixon and Ford, strongly criticized European and American governments for permitting the fate of their nations to rest on such a foundation of hope rather than on adequate deterrence forces. Kissinger "confessed" to a Brussels meeting of Western defense experts and officials that he had "sat around the NATO council table in Brussels and elsewhere and uttered the magic words [promising extended deterrence for Western Europe] which had a profoundly reassuring effect and which permitted [allied] ministers to return home with a rationale for not increasing defense expenditures." Then Kissinger stunned much of his European American audience with his conclusion:

> If my analysis is correct, these words cannot be true. And we must face the fact that it is absurd to base the strategy of the West on the credibility of the threat of mutual suicide. Therefore, I would say—which I might not say in office—the European allies should not keep asking us to multiply strategic assurances that we cannot possibly mean, or, if we do mean, we should not want to execute, because if we execute we risk the destruction of civilization.[21]

Kissinger urged that NATO modernize its European-based nuclear forces (an action that the alliance was already preparing to take three months later) and encouraged the allies to strengthen conventional defense, an objective sought with varying degrees of enthusiasm since the alliance was founded. In other words, Kissinger argued primarily for more "credible" nuclear options combined with a stronger conventional defense to deal with NATO's nuclear dilemma. His analysis suggested that extended deterrence had been invalidated by the advent of Soviet strategic nuclear parity and that the expansion of Soviet theater nuclear forces, particularly deployment of the SS-20 missiles capable of striking targets throughout Western Europe, had checkmated NATO's adoption of the flexible response strategy and deployment of thousands of short-range nuclear weapons in Europe. Kissinger's argument, framed by a politically conservative analysis and a pessimistic perspective on trends in the East–West military balance, represented the conventional wisdom that justified NATO's December 1979 decision to deploy new long-range theater nuclear forces.

Kissinger's message, while compelling, gave short shrift to some additional requirements of Western policy. First, NATO's political viability had come to depend on a fine balance between allied defense efforts and Western attempts to reach mutually acceptable accommodations with the East. Second, any unilateral NATO efforts to improve its nuclear force posture would likely produce a countervailing response from the Soviet Union. As a consequence of the first requirement, NATO's plan for dealing with the perceived deterioration in the nuclear deterrent would have to make sense to European and American publics. In order to gain public confidence, the allies would have to make a serious arms control proposal to the East. Furthermore, the only way to reduce the threat posed by Soviet SS-20 missiles and to forestall a countervailing Soviet response would be to negotiate limits on such systems with the Soviet Union.

And so, in December 1979, led by the US administration of President Carter, the NATO allies decided to modernize its theater nuclear forces while seeking to negotiate limits on such forces with the Soviet Union.[22] The decision came despite growing public opposition to new missile deployments in several West European countries.

The debate between East and West and within the Western community that preceded the initial deployments tended to obscure rather than illuminate the rationale of the original decision. The debate between East and West became a contest for the "hearts and minds" of the Europeans. Within the West, the issue became part of a larger struggle between competing concepts of how best to deal with the Soviet Union. The 1979 decision therefore became a surrogate for the discussion of much broader aspects of East–West relations. The initial deployments, marking as they did a "victory" for one side of the debate, perhaps opened the way for a more reflective look at the fate of the 1979 decision and its implications for the future of NATO.

The 1979 "dual-track" decision was, after all, perfectly consistent with the stated objectives and strategies of the alliance. The decision attempted to deal with conflicting American and European perspectives on deterrence by providing more flexible nuclear systems—in response to the American requirement for credible nuclear options—which, nonetheless in their ability to strike Soviet territory, could be seen as strengthening the link between the European theater and the strategic nuclear standoff—in response to the European requirement for extended deterrence.

According to the decision's rationale, deterrence for Europe would be strengthened because the Soviet Union, in contemplating any attack on Western Europe, would be forced to calculate that the West might respond by striking Soviet territory with the new systems. And, in using the systems, the West would know that the Soviet Union might respond by striking American, not just European, targets. Therefore, both sides would be aware that hostilities initiated in Europe might escalate rapidly to a strategic exchange.

This logic was no foolproof guarantee of extended deterrence. The American president could, in theory, decide not to use the new systems in case of a Soviet attack and could even choose to "lose" them rather than invite strategic retaliation. That decision, however, would have to be made much earlier in the conflict than might previously have been the case. The new deployments, therefore, compressed the time in which the Soviet Union could advance through Western Europe without risking a nuclear strike on Soviet territory. So the new missiles were not principally intended as a means for targeting the Soviet SS-20 missiles. Given the linkage rationale for deploying the new weapons, there was no magic number of missiles that had to be deployed. The deployment would have to be sufficiently large to guarantee (in combination with other factors, such as mobility) survival of enough weapons to remain a serious option in a crisis. Beyond this pragmatic rationale, the final number of 572 missiles was also influenced by the desire to deploy systems in a number of allied countries to "share" the risks and responsibilities of the decision.

The arms control "track" of the dual-track decision also had a very specific purpose. It brought the decision in line with the Harmel formula, which the allies had developed in 1967 to give NATO a role in promoting détente with the East as well as sustaining defense and deterrence. It undoubtedly was clear to the allies that they might need to demonstrate their interest in arms control in order to defend the deployment decision before their publics. The arms control initiative, however, could do something that the deployment would not accomplish on its own. Only if there were an arms control agreement with the Soviet Union to limit intermediate-range nuclear systems could the West restrict the extent of the SS-20 threat to Western Europe.

Why, when the decision on intermediate-range nuclear forces seemed so well designed to serve the strategy of extended deterrence, did it ultimately provoke in Europe fear of nuclear war rather than produce increased confidence that war would be deterred? The answer lies in the fact that the viability of extended deterrence rested on three pillars: the weapons themselves, a credible strategy relating the weapons to the purpose of the alliance, and political confidence that the weapons and the strategy would make it less rather than more likely that war would occur. Historically, the United States has tended to place greater emphasis on the weapons and the strategy for their use than on the political context for their deployment. Europeans, on the other hand, have tended to place greater emphasis on the political context, believing that wars usually are "about something," the product of political disagreements rather than spontaneous unexplainable events. Critiquing the 1979 decision, one European analyst suggested,

> The historical record since the Second World War demonstrates that the faith of Europeans in Washington's ability to use its power in a measured and prompt way to defend Western interests, whether inside or outside the NATO area, is a far more important determinant of their confidence in the reliability of the US nuclear umbrella and of their acceptance of nuclear defence than is the nuclear balance between the Superpowers.[23]

Even under the best of circumstances, it would not have been easy to negotiate an arms control agreement limiting intermediate-range nuclear systems. As it happened, the negotiations began under a dark cloud because of the general deterioration in US–Soviet relations that had begun in the years immediately prior to the NATO decision and that quickened in its wake.

The Soviet invasion of Afghanistan, only two weeks after the NATO 1979 decision, provided a rallying point for the critique of Soviet global intervention that had been building in the United States for a number of years. The critique had already been a major factor in the failure of the Senate to ratify the SALT II treaty. The invasion brought consideration of the treaty to a full stop.

Ronald Reagan, after trouncing Jimmy Carter in the 1980 elections, set American foreign policy on a new course. President Carter had already begun a defense buildup that the Reagan administration promptly accelerated. Just as important, the Reagan administration came to office infused with great skepticism about arms control based on a perception of unrelenting Soviet antagonism toward US interests. The administration put arms control on a back burner and concentrated on developing its defense program.

The Reagan administration's approach to the 1979 decision was based on its dominant philosophy that the Soviet Union—the "evil empire"—would not act seriously in arms control negotiations until Moscow saw that an expensive arms race was the alternative to arms control agreements. It took six months for the administration even to announce that it intended to open arms control negotiations on intermediate-range nuclear weapons. That decision came only after urgent pleading from the allies and a contentious decision-making process within the administration in which officials argued whether arms control negotiations would undermine deployment plans or, on the other hand, make it easier to deploy the missiles.

Almost another six months passed before the administration set its goal for the negotiations. The famous "zero-option" proposal, announced by President Reagan on November 18, 1981, called for the total elimination of all Soviet intermediate-range nuclear weapons in return for cancellation of NATO deployment plans. The plan was received with skepticism by many experts. Some suspected that the far-reaching nature of the approach was designed to produce a Soviet rejection, allowing deployment to proceed.

The initial Soviet response was negative, as was to be expected. Tough negotiations stretched out over several years, seemingly destined to become an arms control failure. Meanwhile, however, other factors were working on the Soviet Union. At home, the Soviet system was proving increasingly incapable of providing basic necessities. As a consequence, Soviet President Gorbachev judged that the Soviet Union could not afford to engage in an open-ended arms competition with the United States. He decided to cut a deal.

On December 8, 1987, the United States and the Soviet Union signed the Intermediate-Range Nuclear Forces (INF) Treaty designed to eliminate two categories of their intermediate-range nuclear missiles: long-range INF, with a range between 600 and 3,400 miles, and short-range INF, with a range between 300 and 600 miles. The treaty did not cover short-range (under 300 miles) nuclear force missiles. In this shorter-range category, NATO countries still had the aging LANCE missile system with approximately 700 warheads. The United States deployed some thirty-six LANCE missile launchers in Western Europe. Belgium, the Netherlands, West Germany, Italy, and the United Kingdom deployed around sixty LANCE launchers with nuclear warheads available under dual-key arrangements with the United States. These missiles could not reach Soviet targets from their launch sites in Europe and therefore were not of great concern to Moscow and did not accomplish the same strategic objectives intended in deployment of the INF missiles.

Although European as well as American public opinion strongly supported the INF Treaty, some observers judged that elimination of the missiles would undermine the credibility of flexible response and argued that the alliance would have to compensate for the loss of the INF missiles to keep its strategy intact. Others argued, however, that the United States still committed a small but strategically significant portion of its relatively invulnerable sea-launched ballistic missile force for use by NATO's Supreme Allied Commander, and that this force, plus nuclear weapons carried on FB-111 and B-52 bombers based in the United States, preserved a strategic strike potential for NATO. They also argued that a substantial US troop presence in Europe served as a "trip wire" and thus ensured linkage to US strategic nuclear forces.

In addition, British and French strategic capabilities, capable of hitting targets in the Soviet Union, which were not included either in the INF negotiations or in US–Soviet strategic arms talks, were being modernized and expanded.

In any case, implementation of the INF Treaty became part of the process of winding down the Cold War, a circumstance anticipated by no one when the treaty was signed in 1987. The intensive inspection regime associated with provisions for dismantling the missiles created a vehicle for testing the possibilities for US–Russian cooperation in the post–Cold War era.

With the end of the Cold War and the dissolution of the Soviet Union, NATO's struggles with nuclear doctrine and extended deterrence promised to enter a dramatically new phase. The aspect of the transatlantic relationship that, in many ways, had been the most difficult for the allies to sustain in capabilities and public support was suddenly overtaken by welcome events.

BRITAIN JOINS EUROPE

The original transatlantic bargain had been seriously flawed by the British refusal to become more closely involved in postwar continental European affairs. The United Kingdom had been centrally involved in shaping the Western alliance and had promised to maintain forces on the Continent, at least as long as the troop presence in Europe did not conflict with British global commitments. But the British commitment to Europe was highly qualified and purposefully distant. The United Kingdom had wanted no role in a European Defense Community and could not see itself as any part of a European unity movement. The United Kingdom's European role in the 1950s was, in effect, an extension of its special relationship with the United States and a distraction from British global political and military involvements. Furthermore, British foreign trade with the Common-wealth was more substantial than that with continental Europe.

The United States valued the special relationship and appreciated the impor-tant role that the United Kingdom had played in the formative years of the al-liance. Only in retrospect, perhaps, is it possible to see so clearly how Great Britain's distance from the Continent handicapped efforts to organize a more co-herent European pillar for the alliance. Had the United Kingdom been willing to join in the European Defense Community or to make a stronger commitment to European defense, perhaps French concerns about balancing Germany on its own would have been allayed. Of course, such speculation serves very little purpose other than to suggest how much the alliance needs British involvement on the Eu-ropean side of the bargain. It would have been unreasonable to expect this global power to acknowledge in the early years of its decline that its future would have to be more intimately linked to that of its neighbors across the English Channel. Luigi Barzini captured the British attitude with this colorful portrait:

> Most of the men who at the beginning rejected the European idea had had respon-sible roles in World War II. They kept on considering their country what it had been indisputably only a few years before, one of the three great powers. . . . Such men nat-urally found it unthinkable to join a condominium of defeated, weak, frightened, and impecunious second-rank nations. . . . Were they not still better than any Con-tinental in every—well, practically every—field that really counted? Didn't the ordi-nary inferior humans still begin at Calais? To be sure, some individual Continentals could be brilliant and sometimes admirable, but most of them were bizarre, slippery, and often incomprehensible. They ate inedible things such as octopuses, frogs, and snails. "Only foreigners waltz backward," Englishmen said contemptuously in the past, when the waltz was still fashionable.[24]

A new generation of British politicians in the 1960s decided the United King-dom should join the European Economic Community, but the commitment to Europe remained highly qualified. When the British finally joined the Commu-nity in 1973, they did so, according to Barzini's interpretation, "reluctantly and somewhat squeamishly, though politely concealing their feelings, like decayed aristocrats obliged by adverse circumstances to eat in a soup kitchen for the needy."[25]

Britain's first tentative approach to Europe, of course, ran into General de Gaulle's veto in 1963. De Gaulle accurately perceived Great Britain's commitment to Europe as still prejudiced by its Commonwealth ties and, most important, by its special relationship with the United States. Seeing Great Britain as an "Atlanti-cist" Trojan horse, de Gaulle explained his action by saying that with Britain in the Community, European cohesion would not last for long, and "in the end there would appear a colossal Atlantic Community under American dependence and leadership which would completely swallow up the European Community."[26]

By the time Britain made its second attempt to join the Community, much had changed. De Gaulle had been replaced by a Gaullist but more pragmatic leader, President Georges Pompidou, whose prestige was not at issue over British membership in the European Community. More important, the United Kingdom's circumstances had substantially altered. British defense policy had become more Eurocentric with the withdrawal of its forces east of Suez. British trade with the Commonwealth had declined in the 1960s as a share of total British foreign trade, while commerce with continental Europe had steadily increased. The special relationship with the United States had become less and less of an equal partnership as symbolized by the British withdrawal from a far-flung global presence.

The English, as a people, still had not fully accepted their place as a "European" country. Even now, some still talk of "going to Europe" when they cross the Channel. But by the early 1970s, it was already more than clear to objective observers that Britain's strategic interests could be served only as a European power, "waltzing backwards," following Barzini's image, as a member of the European Community even while resisting the temptation to eat snails.

The British turn toward Europe represented a fundamental change in the transatlantic bargain. British membership in the European Community could not change the fact that the bargain might have been a far different deal had the United Kingdom joined Europe twenty years earlier. It nonetheless enhanced the potential for Europe to become a true second pillar for the alliance, and this became a crucial factor as the Europeans—not only including the United Kingdom but also with British leadership—began moving to create a new transatlantic bargain at the end of the twentieth century.

WEST GERMANY'S ASCENDANCE

When the original transatlantic bargain was struck, it was principally a deal between the United States and France. The British actively participated as facilitators, negotiators, and mediators. The Germans were actively involved but more like lobbyists, trying to protect German interests from just outside the formal negotiating process rather than as full-fledged participants. After all, the bargain was partly about Germany's future, about how German power could be contained as well as utilized within the Western alliance.

Luigi Barzini observed, in mock-Germanic style, "The future of Europe appears largely to depend today once again, for good or evil, whether we like it or not, as it did for many centuries, on the future of Germany."[27] Germany was a central issue when the alliance was formed. Throughout the Cold War, Germany remained at the heart of Europe's future, and the Federal Republic gained in strength, stature, and influence within and outside the alliance.

By the late 1980s, Germany had become a key player in the Western alliance. Only because it was not a nuclear weapons state did Germany rank second in power to any other European country. German armed forces provided the backbone of NATO active-duty forces in central Europe as well as a large reserve component. The German economy, even as it struggled in the recession of the early 1980s, had become more vibrant than that of either France or Great Britain. The fact that the German question remained at the core of intra-Western as well as of East–West relations granted the Federal Republic substantial political influence in both Western and Eastern capitals. In the late 1960s and early 1970s, Foreign Minister and then Chancellor Willy Brandt's Ostpolitik exercised a major influence on Western alliance policy by seeking to overcome East–West divisions with contacts and cooperation rather than confrontation.

West Germany, however, remained constrained in unique ways—the residue of World War II and the postwar division of Europe. The Western powers continued to exercise certain rights with regard to Germany, and some of the constraints that were wrapped up in the 1954 London and Paris accords remained in effect. Most of the limitations on nonnuclear West German military operations and arms production had been removed or liberalized, but there still were legal constraints on the production or possession of chemical or nuclear weapons. And the Soviet Union still held effective veto power over the future of relations between the two Germanies, with Berlin's hostage status as the leading symbol of Moscow's line of influence to Bonn.

The Germans accepted the constraints placed on them by the Western postwar security framework as a price of the war and a ticket to independent statehood and renewed respectability. Over time, those constraints were woven into the fabric of West German political life. One close observer of German–American relations, Gebhard Schweigler, has observed that the outside constraints on Germany became progressively irrelevant as West German policies and political behavior were shaped according to the preferences of Bonn's Western allies. Once West Germany had "internalized" those constraints, Schweigler maintained, many policy differences with the United States grew out of the fact that West Germany was not willing to change from directions originally taken at the insistence or urging of its Western allies.[28]

Despite these external and internalized limitations, West Germany became America's most important NATO ally. The fact that West Germany's development as an independent power included its emergence as a potent military ally, at least within the confines of Western Europe, represented a major geostrategic gain for the United States.

The progress of West German national growth can be observed in many aspects of US–German relations. One of the best examples, perhaps, is the evolution in the financial aspects of the relationship. In the early 1950s, the United States was still providing substantial financial assistance to support West German rearmament. As the US balance of payments weakened in the late 1950s and the German economy accelerated, the United States looked for ways to retrieve some of the costs of its military presence in Europe. In 1961, the United States and West Germany agreed to an offset program whereby West Germany would purchase military equipment in the United States to compensate for US military expenditures in West Germany. These agreements were renewed and expanded in the Johnson and Nixon administrations to include German purchases of US Treasury bonds and, in the 1970s, the repair of barracks used by US forces in Germany.

By the early 1970s, however, the Germans had grown uncomfortable with the idea of paying the United States to maintain troops in Germany. Bonn did not like the idea of paying for American "mercenaries" and preferred to concentrate its resources on improving German military capabilities. The United States accepted German arguments for a more "normal" relationship between the two allies, and the offset agreement was allowed to expire in 1975. As the German "White Paper 1983" on defense recalled, "The changes that had meanwhile taken place in the international monetary structure and the extensive contribution made by the Federal Republic of Germany to common defense no longer justified these additional burdens on the Federal budget."[29]

By the mid-1980s, some Germans were arguing that US economic policy was effectively making Germany (and other countries as well) pay for the US defense buildup. The logic of the argument ran something like this: Continuing deficits in the United States kept US interest rates high, attracting investment capital to the United States and artificially elevating the value of the dollar on international exchange markets; the investment capital attracted to the United States was therefore not available to help prime a German economic recovery while the elevated value of the dollar kept energy prices high in Germany (because oil is traded in dollars), also restricting German economic recovery. Although the argument certainly does not tell the whole story of Germany's economic problems, it does illustrate how substantially the defense economics of US–German relations had changed since the early 1950s.

The German assertion that the United States was making Germany pay for the American defense buildup suggested that Germany's maturation had brought with it some changes that have been difficult for the United States to accept. Over the years, a number of the factors that guaranteed the United States substantial influence over West German policies had eroded. The United States no longer served as the model of society and government it once did for many Germans. West Germans might not have been fully satisfied with their own political and social institutions, but they no longer felt burdened with a sense of systemic inferiority toward the United States. As a consequence, the West Germans no longer believed it was necessary to look to Washington to define West German security interests. The Federal Republic, with greater confidence than ever since World War II, began basing its foreign and defense policies more and more on homegrown assessments of German interests.

The process of German maturation could have been viewed as one result of the then-perceived deterioration in the US position of international leadership. Alternatively, it could be seen as a logical consequence of the Federal Republic's development into a more normal participant in the international system in the Western alliance.

The emergence of West Germany as a more independent participant in international relations produced a fundamental change in the transatlantic bargain. In many ways, Germany filled the vacuum that France created when it abandoned NATO's integrated commands in search of a defense policy more independent of the United States.

Virtually no one expected that Germany's situation would change even more radically with the end of the Cold War. West Germany's evolution during the Cold War helped prepare German leaders and citizens to face the consequences of what they had long hoped for but dared not expect: a peaceful and sudden reunification of the two Germanies.

FOREIGN AND DEFENSE POLICY IN THE PROCESS OF EUROPEAN UNIFICATION

A central feature of the original transatlantic bargain had been the pledge of the European allies to work toward greater unity among their separate nations. The United States, in fact, had made Marshall Plan assistance contingent on the development of coordinated European approaches to the use of that aid. While the Europeans were unable to translate their unification efforts into a European Defense Community, they did expand economic cooperation through a community approach.

The cooperative West European efforts encouraged by the Marshall Plan were transformed into the European Coal and Steel Community in the early 1950s. The scope of West European cooperation was dramatically expanded when, on March 25, 1957, the governments of France, West Germany, Italy, Belgium, the Netherlands, and Luxembourg signed the Rome Treaties. These six original Community members agreed in Rome to establish the European Economic Community and the European Atomic Energy Community as sister organizations to the Coal and Steel Community. The treaties sought progressively to eliminate obstacles to trade among the six countries while building up common policies among them. A common agricultural policy was the original centerpiece, designed in particular to benefit French farmers. Over the years, these three communities, with their decision-making processes and civil servants, were combined under one institutional roof. By the mid-1980s, the European acronymic stew was most accurately referred to as the "European Community," capturing in one simple phrase most of the activities and institutions that formed the core of a uniting Europe.

Even though de Gaulle's rebellion had frustrated plans for expansion of the membership and powers of the Community, Europe's healthy economic growth in the 1960s provided the economic margins for steady integration in the near term and lofty dreams of full economic union in the not-too-distant future. But the oil price–induced recessions of the 1970s, carrying into the early 1980s, combined with strong nationalistic approaches among the members, slowed the integrative process to an almost imperceptible crawl and dashed hopes for early progress toward full economic and monetary union.

Nevertheless, the "six" became "nine" in 1973 when the United Kingdom, Ireland, and Denmark became EC members and "ten" when Greece joined in 1981. The Community became "twelve" with the accession of Spain and Portugal in 1986. This expansion of the Community, however, brought with it additional economic problems, and the integration process stalled in the mid-1980s, waiting for renewed economic growth to provide the financial margins to underwrite further integration.

While the process of European unification was struggling through the bad economic weather, the European Community members moved forward on the political front. The foundations of the Community remained firmly planted in the economic integration process established in the Rome Treaties. Advocates of European unity nonetheless always recognized that the economic heart of the Community would eventually need to be guided by a political soul.

For many years, the search for greater political unity was caught up in debates over the purposes and methods of cooperation—between advocates of a supranational Europe and partisans of a Europe of nation-states, between the Gaullists and the "Communitarians," and between the "Europeanists" and the "Atlanticists." Finally, in December 1969, the leaders of the original six EC members, meeting in The Hague, bypassed these traditional conflicts and instructed their foreign ministers "to study the best way of achieving progress in the matter of political unification, within the context of enlargement" of the Community.

When the foreign ministers reported back to the heads of state and government on October 27, 1970, they recommended that the EC members initiate a process of European Political Cooperation. The report was accepted, recording agreement of the six countries to ensure through regular exchanges of information and consultations a better mutual understanding on important international problems and to strengthen their solidarity by promoting the harmonization of their views and the coordination of their positions and, where it appears possible and desirable, common actions.

Over the years, the members of the European Community expanded the scope and content of their consultations to the point where, by the end of the Cold War, European Political Cooperation had become a regular and accepted part of the process of foreign policy formulation in the twelve EC countries. One result of this decade of foreign policy coordination was a proliferation of foreign policy issues on which there was a European consensus or a record of previous joint actions. Political cooperation produced a number of results (many of which could also be called "successes"): coordinated positions in a variety of international forums, including the CSCE and the United Nations; various declarations on the Middle East; agreement on a package of sanctions in response to the declaration of martial law in Poland; and a coordinated reaction to Argentina's occupation of the Falkland Islands.

This expansion of topics and problems covered by the political consultations inevitably led the European Community in the direction of "security policy." The EC members consciously stopped short of what could be considered "military policy," an area that until the late 1990s remained reserved almost exclusively for NATO consultations. But even though the EC members were careful to steer clear of actions that would conflict with NATO's prerogatives, EC consultations by the mid-1980s regularly included issues that were on NATO's consultative agenda as well.

In 1987, the European allies took some significant steps toward European defense cooperation. France and Germany agreed to form a "European brigade," and in September of that year, the two countries conducted a major joint military exercise in Germany with combined French and German forces operating under French command.[30] Perhaps most notably, the Western European Union (WEU) countries in October 1987 issued a "Platform on European Security Interests" that constituted the most explicit and far-reaching European statement to date on common approaches to European security issues. The document emphasized the continuing importance for Western security interests of both nuclear weapons and American involvement in European defense. The West Europeans also used WEU consultative and decision-making procedures to coordinate their enhanced naval contributions to the Western presence in the Persian Gulf in 1987.[31]

The political consultations in the European Community and the revival of activity in the Western European Union remained exercises of coordination among the member states rather than a process of political integration. They nonetheless established the foundation for much more dramatic developments during the 1990s, after the end of the Cold War and the dissolution of the Soviet Union had created an entirely new set of international, transatlantic, and European circumstances.

LESSONS FROM COLD WAR HISTORY

Judged by the outcome of the Cold War, the North Atlantic Alliance had served the allies well despite the failure of the European allies to deploy the nonnuclear forces they had promised at Lisbon in 1952. The hallmark of the alliance was its adaptability. The transatlantic bargain was revised and reshaped almost constantly from 1949 to 1989. Some of the internal battles were bitter and left scars. But, on balance, there was much more success than failure and much of which NATO's founding fathers would be proud. The next period of history would bring with it even more dramatic changes. The way in which the NATO allies would deal with those changes was influenced by their experiences and interactions during the Cold War. The next chapter turns to some observations about the transatlantic bargain drawn from the Cold War years.

NOTES

1. Kissinger's so-called Year of Europe in US foreign policy heightened European suspicions of US intentions and laid bare a number of conflicting interests, particularly regarding how to deal with Western vulnerability to a disruption of Middle East oil supplies. The exercise yielded a "Declaration on Atlantic Relations," approved by the NATO foreign ministers in Ottawa in June 1974. The document reflected no fundamental change in the transatlantic bargain, but the difficulties encountered in producing the declaration perhaps provided a foretaste of things to come.

2. Michael M. Harrison, *The Reluctant Ally: France and Atlantic Security* (Baltimore: The Johns Hopkins University Press, 1981), 48.

3. Harlan Cleveland, *NATO: The Transatlantic Bargain* (New York: Harper & Row, 1970), 106.

4. Unnamed diplomat as cited in Cleveland, *NATO*, 104.

5. Pascale Boniface, "The Specter of Unilateralism," *Washington Quarterly* 24, no. 3 (summer 2001): 161.

6. Anthony Glees, *Reinventing Germany: German Political Development since 1945* (Oxford: Berg, 1996), 154–56.

7. Cleveland, *NATO*, 144.

8. Report of the Committee of Three, *NATO Online Library*, www.nato.int/docu/basictxt/b561213a.htm [accessed August 4, 2002].

9. *NATO Online Library*, www.nato.int/docu/basictxt/b671213a.htm [accessed August 4, 2002].

10. *NATO Online Library*, www.nato.int/docu/comm/49-95/c680624b.htm [accessed August 4, 2002].

11. MBFR was the Western term for their initiative, emphasizing the word "balanced" to imply the need for larger Warsaw Pact than NATO reductions to overcome Pact numerical advantages. Moscow, of course, objected to this term, and the agreed title of the negotiations was Mutual Reduction of Forces and Armaments in Central Europe (MURFAAMCE!).

12. At a summit meeting of the Conference on Security and Cooperation in Europe in Paris on November 19, 1990, the twenty-two member states of NATO and the Warsaw Treaty Organization signed a major Treaty on Conventional Armed Forces in Europe and published a joint declaration on nonaggression. The treaty included major reductions of military manpower and equipment in Europe as well as a wide array of cooperative inspection and compliance measures.

13. On August 1, 1975, the heads of state and government of thirty-three European states, Canada, and the United States signed the Helsinki Final Act establishing the CSCE.

14. John Fry, *The Helsinki Process: Negotiating Security and Cooperation in Europe* (Washington, D.C.: National Defense University Press, 1993), 165–73.

15. Atlantic Council of the United States, "Arms Control, East–West Relations and the Atlantic Alliance: Closing the Gaps," Washington, D.C., March 1983, 62.

16. Josef Joffe, "European-American Relations: The Enduring Crisis," *Foreign Affairs* 59 (spring 1981): 840.

17. The September 1979 gathering in Brussels received its greatest notoriety for Kissinger's warning to the European allies that they could no longer count on the American nuclear guarantee against the Soviets. Kissinger's observations were substantially edited and revised before publication, taking some of the rhetorical edge off the more dramatic statements made in the conference session (based on author's notes taken at the session). Kissinger's (revised) speech and other major statements to this conference can be found in Kenneth A. Myers, ed., *NATO—The Next Thirty Years: The Changing Political, Economic, and Military Setting* (Boulder, Colo.: Westview, 1980).

18. The Nassau agreement had included a British pledge that its Polaris force would be assigned to the alliance and withdrawn only when "supreme national interests are at stake."

19. US House of Representatives, *The Modernization of NATO's Long-Range Theater Nuclear Forces* (report prepared for the Committee on Foreign Affairs by the Congressional Research Service, Library of Congress, by Simon Lunn, Washington, D.C., 1981), 11.

20. US House of Representatives, *The Modernization of NATO's Long-Range Theater Nuclear Forces,* 16.

21. Joseph Fitchett, "Kissinger Cites Gaps in US Nuclear Role," *International Herald Tribune,* September 3, 1979, 2.

22. NATO members agreed to modernize the Europe-based US nuclear arsenal by deploying a total of 572 new ground-launched systems capable of reaching Soviet territory from West European sites. The deployment would consist of 108 Pershing II ballistic missiles and 464 ground-launched cruise missiles, all with single nuclear warheads. The missiles would be deployed in five European countries: P-IIs and cruise missiles in West Germany and cruise missiles only in the United Kingdom, Italy, the Netherlands, and Belgium. The allies also agreed to attempt to negotiate with the Soviet Union East–West limitations on theater nuclear forces in the context of SALT. For a detailed discussion of the decision, see US House of Representatives, *The Modernization of NATO's Long-Range Theater Nuclear Forces.*

23. Simon May, "On the Problems and Prerequisites of Public Support for the Defence of Western Europe" (paper presented at the annual conference of the Centre for European Policy Studies, Brussels, November 23–26, 1983), 2.

24. Luigi Barzini, *The Europeans* (New York: Simon & Schuster, 1983), 58, 59.

25. Barzini, *The Europeans,* 60–61.

26. Press conference, Ambassade de France, *Major Addresses, 1958–1964,* January 14, 1963, 214.

27. Barzini, *The Europeans,* 70.

28. Gebhard Schweigler, *West German Foreign Policy: The Domestic Setting,* Washington Papers no. 106 (New York: Praeger, 1984), 6–24.

29. Federal Republic of Germany, Federal Minister of Defence, *White Paper 1983, The Security of the Federal Republic of Germany* (Bonn, 1983), 126.

30. "Manoeuvres," *Atlantic News,* no. 1951 (September 25, 1987), 3.

31. "Allies End Week of Hesitation by Sending Ships to Gulf Region," *NATO Report* 2, no. 45 (September 21, 1987): 8.

5

The United States and Europe at the End of the Cold War: Some Fundamental Factors

When, in sudden historical succession, the Berlin Wall was breached, communist regimes were swept from office throughout Eastern Europe, the Warsaw Pact was dissolved, and the Soviet Union broke apart, the NATO allies could not believe their good fortune. These events raised concerns in Washington and in West European capitals about potential instability growing out of so much change in such a short time. But a forty-year struggle had been resolved in their favor without a shot fired in anger. The Cold War had never turned hot, deterrence had worked, and the values on which the transatlantic alliance was founded had triumphed.

The time for celebration, however, was short. The allies almost immediately found themselves dealing with the consequences of their victory and asking questions as fundamental as "Do we still need NATO if there is no more Soviet threat?"

The following chapters discuss how the allies responded to this challenge. This chapter, however, reflects on some of the fundamental factors in transatlantic relations as seen in the Cold War experience. It is, in a sense, an assessment of the assets and liabilities that the transatlantic bargain brought to the table at the end of the Cold War. Such an assessment may seem particularly timely with the advent in the United States of a Republican administration that, in some respects, seems still be attracted to perspectives and policies that were prevalent in the United States during the last decade of the Cold War.

NATO: MORE THAN A MILITARY ALLIANCE

Had the transatlantic bargain been inspired by no more than the desire to balance Soviet power in central Europe and to control Germany, it might have survived through the Cold War and beyond, but it certainly would not have prospered. The founding of NATO reflected hopes as well as fears, and those were recorded in the North Atlantic Treaty. The treaty's preamble declared that the parties to the treaty were "determined to safeguard the freedom, common heritage and civilizations of their peoples, founded on the principles of democracy, individual liberty and the rule of law." With an economy of language that characterized most of the Treaty, the allies described the alliance as more than a traditional arrangement among nations to preserve a favorable balance of power. The treaty recorded fundamental beliefs and interests shared by the allies that might have drawn them together even in the absence of a common threat to their security.

The allies also agreed that their belief in democracy and individual liberty should be translated into some common goals in their relations with other nations. They pledged to "contribute toward the further development of peaceful and friendly international relations by strengthening their free institutions, by bringing about a better understanding of the principles upon which these institutions are founded, and by promoting conditions of stability and well-being."

After recognizing their common political heritage and ideals, the allies noted the importance of economic factors in their relationship. Fully aware that economic factors had played a major role in provoking both wars of the twentieth century, the allies pledged in Article 2 of the Treaty that they would "seek to eliminate conflict in their international economic policies" and would "encourage economic collaboration between any or all of them."

These political and economic statements of purpose have been inscribed so frequently in books about the alliance that their repetition is now regarded as an obligatory part of the NATO analyst's ritual. These phrases usually are read over quickly in order to get to the meat of the matter. Do these motherhood and apple pie declarations perhaps deserve more attention? From a cynical perspective, it would be quite easy to dismiss such exhortations as little more than treaty niceties, paid only lip service in practice. After all, the Treaty, one among believers in "the principles of democracy, individual liberty and the rule of law," was originally signed by a Portuguese regime that fell far short of democratic standards. In subsequent years, military regimes in Greece and Turkey were allowed to continue full participation in the alliance because of their geostrategic significance despite protests heard from some northern European quarters. Furthermore, the international economic policies of the allies were anything but free of conflict.

A measured dose of skepticism may indeed be warranted. The alliance has not always lived up to its own standards. The Treaty drafters understood that the alliance would work most effectively if the policies of the member states demonstrated sensitivity to their shared political beliefs and intertwined economic destinies. What made the Treaty special was the allies' belief that they were defending a way of life and a means of governing that were most likely to benefit the well-being of their citizens as well as enhance the stability of the international system.

From the signing of the Treaty in 1949 until the end of the Cold War, troubles in the alliance were provoked primarily by nuclear and East–West issues, but the degree to which they threatened the solidarity of the alliance was undoubtedly influenced by the quality of relations within the West.

The alliance, like any partnership, depended on the willingness of the partners to understand and respect what is motivating each other. Each had to walk a mile in the other's shoes in order to make the arrangement work. Eventually, through compromises, the partners developed sufficient common ground to provide the basis for joint action. The beginning resided, however, in understanding.

WE ARE HERE, AND THEY ARE THERE

Perhaps the most basic differences between European and American approaches to East–West relations during the Cold War could be traced to the fact that the Atlantic Ocean and many miles separate the United States from Europe, and that Western Europe occupies the same land mass as did the Soviet Union and its Warsaw Pact allies. It is less than 1,000 air miles from Moscow to Berlin, about the same distance as between Washington and New Orleans. It is approximately the same distance from Moscow to Paris or London as it is from New York to Denver. But Washington is almost 5,000 miles from Moscow.

Many Americans wondered during the Cold War why Europeans, much closer to the Soviet Union, appeared far less concerned about the "Soviet threat." The short answer, "We are here, and they are there," identified the puzzle but did not resolve it. Proximity to Soviet military power should have led to greater concern, according to the logic of the American question. But it clearly did not, suggesting that even in an age of instantaneous communications and space travel, the Atlantic Ocean divided us more than it united us.

Western Europe's proximity to Soviet power, in fact, made Europeans particularly concerned about the consequences of war and, therefore, particularly determined to avoid them. For Americans, the European "theater" could be separated, at least intellectually, from their homeland; for Europeans, the homeland was the potential battlefield, whether or not nuclear weapons were used by either side. As a result, Americans and Europeans placed different emphases on deterrence versus war-fighting capabilities, on conventional versus nuclear weapons, and on arms control versus defense improvements.

These geographically based differences asserted themselves strongly in the early 1980s. Once of the principal themes of the antinuclear movement in Europe was that the United States was moving toward a nuclear war-fighting posture in Europe, and the installation of new long-range theater nuclear weapons was evidence of that tendency. This charge was set against the enunciation by the Carter administration of a more flexible nuclear employment strategy (PD-59) in 1980 and the decision of the Reagan administration to construct (but not deploy) enhanced-radiation warheads—the "neutron bomb"—that would have killed people but left inanimate objects standing. The final proof for many Europeans of American willingness to contemplate "limited" nuclear war in Europe came on October 16, 1981, when President Reagan remarked that he "could see where you could have the exchange of tactical weapons against troops in the field without it bringing either one of the major powers to pushing the button."

When geography is married with history and related to the implications of war, the "European" perspectives as opposed to the "American" view takes on special meaning. As one observer noted in the early 1980s, "Nobody in Europe, West or East, imagines that war means only fighting overseas. For all Europeans, the question of war is the question of survival, not just of superiority."[1]

But geography is a complex factor. How would you explain that Canadians, in the same relative geographic position as the United States, display some very "European" traits when it comes to defense efforts and arms control? With regard to defense spending, the Canadians have never been among NATO's big spenders by any measure. In the Canadian case, the reason (or excuse) for not doing more may be the geographic proximity to the United States. In other words, Canada relies on the fact that the United States must regard Canada's defense as vital to its own security.

This is simply to say that the end of the Cold War did not change the geography of the Atlantic alliance, and it did not erase some of the instincts and strategic predispositions that developed on either side of the Atlantic during the Cold War. The same can be said of the profound influence of history on transatlantic attitudes.

THE DIFFERENT LESSONS OF HISTORY

It is an objective fact that the United States and Europe have passed through their own unique historical experiences and naturally have drawn somewhat different lessons from those experiences. Europe was the site of two devastating wars in the twentieth century and was the principal host to the Cold War as well. Most continental European countries, at one time or another in the past century, have been defeated and occupied by foreign forces. From a European perspective, the desire to avoid war remains an immediate and meaningful imperative.

Fritz Stern, an American historian, describes the effects of these differing experiences with war:

> The Europeans cherish a different historic memory from ours. To Europeans the increase in overkill capacity is an irrational art, an absurdity: they know that we have enough to kill and be killed a hundred times over again. Their historic experience in this century—unlike America's until Vietnam—has not been the triumphant use of power but the experience of brute and futile power, blindly spent and blindly worshiped. Even an unhistorical generation in Europe remembers World War I as the epitome of the mindless worship of force; they remember the guardians of morality sanctifying violence. For the Europeans, this century has been the experience of the absurd, first as an intuition of artists, then as drama produced by history. Having lost their preeminence in repeated wars, the Europeans today seek alternatives to force.[2]

Americans also want to avoid war. But no major hostilities have been fought on American soil since the Civil War, 140 years ago. The United States emerged from both world wars "victorious," suffering neither occupation nor the ravages of war on its territory, save Pearl Harbor. The most popular American historical perspective on World Wars I and II is that the United States was forced to join the hostilities because Europe had not dealt effectively with threats to the peace. One consequence, particularly growing out of the World War II experience, is that Americans tend to view appeasement of an antagonistic power as the greatest danger for their interests.

Many Americans would say that European nations, in seeking alternatives to the use of force throughout the Cold War, opted out of responsibility to their citizens as well as to their alliance. The European starting point appeared to be the possible rather than the desirable. History, on the other hand, left Americans with an expectation of virtually unlimited possibilities—a theme that has helped elect more than one American president.

The United States emerged from World War II wearing a "white hat." America had come to the rescue of democracy and freedom and had provided the additional force needed to defeat fascism. After the war, Americans saw themselves as the main barrier to the spread of communism. America's involvement in Vietnam called into question its moral posture and raised issues about the role that the United States should play in the world—issues that still are unresolved and perhaps are even more pointed at the opening of the twenty-first century than they were in the 1980s. But Americans still see themselves mostly as reluctant warriors who, when called into action, fight to win.

An even longer-term factor reinforces the American tendency to seek the desirable rather than to work within limits. This country matured with one frontier after another to cross and with a record of sustained accomplishment and growth. Throughout most of its history, the United States had seemingly unlimited resources to call on to support its national objectives. Some analysts and politicians have argued that the United States must begin to shape its world role in ways more compatible with finite resources. But the American psychology still inclines Americans to reach beyond their grasp and to regard limits as new frontiers to be crossed rather than as boundaries to be observed. Thus, in the Cold War competition with the Soviet Union, the United States was inclined to push beyond limits that the European allies found more judicious to accept.

Europeans are more willing to accept limits in part as a consequence of painfully bumping into each other for hundreds of years. Innumerable attempts to change national boundaries—to alter political realities by the use of force—have produced unimaginable death and destruction. The Germans, in particular, have been forced to accept limits on their sovereignty as well as on their freedom of international maneuver. Economic and geostrategic factors, not legal limits, have constrained France and the United Kingdom. Most other European countries are so small and relatively weak that their ability to influence international events is effective only in the context of their participation in larger groups, such as the European Union, NATO, and the United Nations. Limits, therefore, tend to be accepted facts of life for most Europeans rather than the frustrations they are for most Americans.

American scorn for the ways of the "old world" is well engrained in US national history, and American national attitudes result in part from rejection of those ways. As Louis J. Halle wrote,

> We have to recall that the American nation had its beginnings in the seventeenth century, as a nation of refugees from the tyrannies, the persecutions and the power-politics of the Old World. . . .
>
> In our American mythology, the refugees and their children had established in their God-given land a new and entirely different kind of society in which all men were free and equal, in which all men were brothers, in which the wicked devices of the Old World . . . were happily unknown. . . .
>
> Not only had God given us a virgin continent, replete with all goods, on which to establish our society, he had given us the great oceans to protect it. Part of our American mythology, then, was that we were beyond the reach of the wicked.[3]

Europeans, including Russians, were of course never beyond the "reach of the wicked." And in another marriage of geography and history, West Europeans generally view Russian behavior as conditioned by the numerous times that marauding armies have marched across Russia's naturally exposed frontiers. Americans tended to see the Soviet Union as an expansionist power attempting to spread communism across the world. Today, as Americans watch an enfeebled Russia struggle to survive by calling on some instincts drawn from the Soviet period, these differing American and European perspectives on how to deal with Russia still come into play.

Debates between Americans and Europeans over East–West relations during the Cold War often turned toward what Stanley Hoffman called the "game of historical analogies." As with most historical analogies, those used in this debate could be turned to favor either side of the argument. Both Europeans and Americans hearkened back to the beginning of World War I to prove the validity of their approach to the Soviet Union. Americans likened Soviet Russia to imperial Germany, while Europeans compared the competing Cold War alliances with those of 1914. Hoffman described the scenario:

> To the Europeans, Washington's view of 1914 suggests that war is the only way to curb Moscow, just as it was the only way to cut down German expansionism. To the Americans, the Europeans' view of 1914 means that—as in the Thirties—they are in effect willing to appease Moscow's expansionism. . . . To the Americans, if the Europeans failed to react strongly to as clearcut an aggression as the recent one [the Soviet invasion of Afghanistan in 1979], what are the chances of their standing up in cases that may well be more ambiguous. . . . To the Europeans, if Americans overreact in this instance, aren't they going to push the Soviets onto a collision course that could still be averted by a wider policy?[4]

One measure commonly applied to analysis of differing US and European attitudes toward East–West relations was the (false) dichotomy between being "red or dead." During the Cold War, Europeans appeared more willing to opt for the "red" option than did Americans. It seems clear that differing historical experiences help explain the contrast between American and European perspectives on this issue. Most European countries have, at one time or another, been occupied by foreign powers or subjugated by domestic authoritarian regimes. Their more recent political freedom and relative economic well-being tell many Europeans that a condition of occupation or subjugation is not necessarily permanent and that resistance and recovery are possible. Death is quite permanent. Americans have experienced neither authoritarian subjugation nor foreign occupation and find the prospect essentially intolerable.

Importantly, US and European historical experiences have produced differences in transatlantic attitudes toward vulnerability. The United States never came to terms with its vulnerability in the nuclear age and continued to long for a return to its historic invulnerability to direct external threats. This psychological orientation lay behind the Reagan administration's search for a ballistic missile defense shield, dubbed the "Star Wars Program" by its critics. This focus of US policy moved into the background in the early years of the post–Cold War period but never left American minds. The American unwillingness to tolerate vulnerability may be just as potent a motivation for US national security policy as was the Soviet Union's deep security paranoia for its military programs and policies.

On the other hand, Europeans have tended to accept vulnerability as a fact of life. From an American perspective, the European allies are much too willing to tolerate vulnerability. Europeans, meanwhile, find the American search for invulnerability verging on the incomprehensible. This is not, however, a question of right or wrong but rather one of differing historical experiences and contemporary capabilities. Nevertheless, different American and European attitudes toward vulnerability create sharply differing standards for judging the requirements of a viable security policy for an ever-changing global environment.

Finally, one exception must be noted to this discussion of historical sources of divergent transatlantic perceptions. The exception is England. The United Kingdom's experience in the two world wars of the past century created a perspective distinct from, but perhaps in fact a blend of, the American and the continental points of view. Britain suffered substantial military casualties in both wars and took heavy bombardment of its homeland in World War II. But the United Kingdom, like the United States, emerged from both wars victorious, never having been occupied.

A MIXED IDEOLOGICAL HERITAGE

Americans and Europeans are united in their desire to protect individual rights, defend their democratic political systems, and sustain equitable and strong social and economic systems. Common ideological objectives are, in fact, explicitly expressed in the North Atlantic Treaty. But despite a wide area of shared ideological commitments, there are some fundamental differences between the European and American ideological experiences and cultures—differences that were highlighted during the Cold War and that remained in the background of transatlantic relations in the post–Cold War world.

The Marxist critique of capitalism has deep historical and political roots in Europe. A number of European countries had large Communist parties during the Cold War (most of which have been transformed or marginalized in the post–Cold War period). Many Europeans regard Marxist ideals as a source of inspiration even if they reject the systems that were spawned by the Russian Revolution. All European countries have important Socialist or Social Democratic parties, all of which support intervention of the government in the social and economic realm to allocate more equitably the costs and benefits of life within the country. In the continental European NATO countries, such programs are so thoroughly a part of the fabric of society that even conservative parties in government embrace a much more extensive social safety net than that acceptable to American conservatives.

The Marxist critique of capitalism has virtually no roots in the United States. The Democratic Party could by no stretch of the imagination be described as having a socialist program by European standards. The very term "socialism" still attracts a visceral negative reaction in the United States (except perhaps in Vermont, which in 2000 elected self-styled socialist Bernie Sanders to his sixth term in the US House of Representatives). Even though the United States has over the years developed extensive social programs, they were adopted and developed within a pragmatic rather than an ideological framework.

During the Cold War, these differing ideological perspectives contributed to divergent outlooks on East–West relations. Americans viewed the Soviet Union's communist system as more threatening than did many Europeans and saw it as the main threat to American democracy. The end of the Cold War and the dissolution of the main enemy, the Soviet Union, was seen by many Americans as a huge "victory" for the United States and its system of government.

The perspective from Europe was somewhat different. The ideology that motivated the Soviet system was unacceptable to the vast majority of West Europeans. The end of the Cold War was seen as a victory of sorts, but not one to be celebrated at the expense of the former Soviet Union and by no means as a rejection of the more generous social services safety net deployed by European nations.

On balance, Americans at the end of the Cold War still saw most Europeans as having been too "soft" on communism, and most Europeans viewed the United States as having been too hard line. The contrast in images is sharpest when the United States is being governed by a conservative Republican presidency, as it was during the Reagan–Bush years and as it is once again under President George W.

Bush. Socially conservative US governments usually find themselves with few soul mates among the European allies.

ROLES AND CAPABILITIES

It is a simple fact that, at the end of the Cold War, the United States was a global power with global military capabilities while the European nations were, with the exception of France and to a lesser extent Great Britain, regional powers with military capabilities limited to Europe. It was not always so, and the reversal of world roles has much to do with disagreements between the United States and Europe concerning how best to deal with the Soviet challenge in the Third World in the closing years of the Cold War.

Slowly but surely, following World War II, European nations retreated from extensive Third World military involvement. The international consensus favoring the process of decolonization was the prime political factor behind Europe's withdrawal; the economic impetus was provided by Europe's need to reconstruct its devastated industrial capacity and its desire to concentrate resources on economic recovery and the process of regional economic integration. France retained a military intervention capability in Africa and an impressive naval presence in the Mediterranean and the Indian Ocean. But for the most part, Europe's ability to influence global events with military forces became limited. The United States attempted to fill vacuums left by the European withdrawal to ensure Western interests by limiting territorial or political gains for the Soviet Union and protecting access to Third World markets and sources of vital natural resources.

The decline in Europe's ability to influence events in the Third World was accompanied by an evolution in European strategies toward Third World problems. European policies became increasingly dependent on political and economic instruments to influence events in the Third World. The American experience in Vietnam confirmed for many Europeans their skepticism regarding the utility of military force beyond Europe's borders. And the fact that the former colonial powers retained or reestablished close ties with their former colonies, based in many cases primarily on the strength of political, economic, cultural, and linguistic links, reinforced the faith of our allies in these policy tools.

As the end of the Cold War approached, the United States and the European allies carried forward fundamentally different attitudes toward the use of force in international relations. European leaders believed, for the most part, that diplomacy, development aid, and trade policies should be the weapons of first resort in dealing with Third World instability. Many Europeans feared what they saw as an American tendency to concentrate too narrowly on military responses to security challenges, believing that other approaches might be more productive and less costly in terms of Western interests. They were at least equally, if not more, interested in developing economic ties and political bonds that would both ensure cooperative relations

with less developed states and discourage adventurism by the Soviet Union or potential rogue states. The 1980 British White Paper on defense, the product of a Conservative government, put the European perspective quite clearly:

> The best answer is to try to remove the sources of regional instability which create
> opportunities for outside intervention. In some circumstances, military measures
> will not be appropriate at all; in others, they may form only one component of the
> total response. Diplomacy, development aid and trade policies will usually have a
> greater contribution to make.[5]

Furthermore, Europe had gained far more in tangible benefits than the United
States from the period of détente with the Soviet Union in the form of reduced
tensions, increased trade opportunities, and improved human contacts. This
made Europeans more inclined to see détente as "divisible," that is, to want to protect the gains of détente in Europe even if the Soviet Union misbehaved in the
Third World. The United States, carrying the majority of Western global military
burdens, had a much greater interest in treating détente as "indivisible," with Soviet actions outside Europe seen as providing cause for Western responses within
the European framework.

The Cold War experience left several interesting questions open. Does military
weakness generate faith in economic and political instruments of national purpose? To what extent did US global military capabilities permit the West European
allies to concentrate on nonmilitary approaches? Does military strength generate
an inclination to use force to further national objectives? These questions remain
just as valid and important for the transatlantic relationship at the beginning of
the twenty-first century as they did at the end of the Cold War, particularly as the
United States and its European allies search for the most effective ways to deal
with the threats posed by terrorism and weapons of mass destruction.

During the 1990s, while most European allies dramatically reduced spending on
defense and particularly on investment in new technologies and systems, the US focus on the "revolution in military affairs" (RMA) created a growing gap between US
and European military capabilities. The US RMA began revolutionizing the modern
battlefield with new intelligence, communications, target identification and acquisition technologies, and "smart weapons" capabilities. After President George W. Bush
declared a "war on terrorism" in September 2001, it became clear that the transatlantic divergence in capabilities was enhancing the different perspectives about
threats and how to deal with them that are deeply rooted in the Cold War transatlantic military relationships (this issue is considered in more detail in chapter 10).

BURDEN SHARING AS A PERPETUAL ISSUE
Elected officials in sovereign, democratic allied states usually seek to get the best
security for their populations at the most reasonable price. This means that al-

liances among sovereign states will always face questions concerning an equitable balance of costs and benefits among the members. This reality caused constant friction between the United States and its allies throughout the Cold War.

The burden-sharing issue was built into the transatlantic bargain, rising up in many ways from the foundation provided by contrasting US and European geographic realities, historical experiences, and military capabilities. The original concept of the alliance was that the United States and Europe would be more or less equal partners and would therefore share equitably the costs of alliance programs. When the original transatlantic bargain was reshaped in 1954 following the failure of the European Defense Community, the seeds for a burden-sharing problem had been planted. As described in chapter 3, the revision of the original bargain meant that the alliance would become heavily dependent both on US nuclear weapons and on the presence of US military forces in Europe to make those weapons credible in deterrence as well as to fortify nonnuclear defense in Europe.

The US burden-sharing complaint took many forms and was translated into a great variety of policy approaches between 1954 and the end of the Cold War. In the early 1950s, the allies made arrangements for common funding of NATO infrastructure costs, such as running NATO civilian and military headquarters and building and maintaining fuel pipelines, communication systems, and so on. Each ally was allocated a share of the infrastructure costs, according to an "ability to pay" formula. As European nations recovered from World War II and experienced economic growth, the US share of infrastructure expenses was progressively reduced. However, such expenses were not the main cost of alliance efforts. The large expenses were the monies spent by nations to maintain their military forces. In this category, the United States always outpaced its European allies.

The administration of President John F. Kennedy in the early 1960s sought a greater European contribution to Western defense. Its policy optimistically advocated an Atlantic partnership with shared responsibilities between the United States and an eventually united Europe. The Kennedy presidency also witnessed the beginning of the financial arrangements between the United States and West Germany designed to "offset" the costs of stationing US forces in that country. These agreements were renewed and expanded in the administrations of Lyndon B. Johnson and Richard M. Nixon to include German purchases of US Treasury bonds and, in the 1970s, the repair of barracks used by US forces in Germany.

The US experience in Vietnam, French withdrawal from NATO's integrated military structure in 1966, and US economic problems all diminished support in the US Congress for US overseas troop commitments in general and led the Johnson administration to press the Europeans to increase their defense efforts. This period saw a strong congressional movement, led by Senator Mike Mansfield, to cut US forces in Europe. Senator Mansfield introduced the first of the Mansfield Resolutions on August 31, 1966. The resolution judged that "the condition of our European allies, both economically and militarily, has appreciably improved since large contingents of forces were deployed"; the commitment by all members of the North Atlantic Treaty is based on the full cooperation of all treaty partners in contributing materials and men on a fair and equitable basis, but "such contributions have not been forthcoming from all other members. . . . Relations between the two parts of Europe are now characterized by an increasing two-way flow of trade, people and their peaceful exchange," and "the present policy of maintaining large contingents of United States forces and their dependents on the European Continent also contributes further to the fiscal and monetary problems of the United States." The Senate was asked to resolve that "a substantial reduction of United States forces permanently stationed in Europe can be made without adversely affecting either our resolve or ability to meet our commitment under the North Atlantic Treaty."[6]

Senator Mansfield reintroduced the resolution in 1967, 1969, and 1970, when the resolution obtained the signatures of fifty cosponsors. However, US presidents, Republican and Democrat alike, consistently opposed such efforts, and these resolutions and similar efforts through 1974 failed to win final passage.

The Nixon administration, after unsuccessfully attempting to get the Europeans to increase "offset" payments, took a new tack. The Europeans objected to the prospect of American troops becoming little more than mercenaries in Europe and argued that the US troop presence was, after all, in America's as well as Europe's interests. Nixon shifted to a focus on getting allies to improve their own military capabilities rather than paying the United States to sustain its. The so-called Nixon Doctrine, applied globally, suggested that the United States would continue it efforts to support allies militarily if they made reasonable efforts to help themselves.

Despite the Nixon Doctrine, which was at least implicitly applied by all US administrations through the end of the Cold War, Congress continued to focus on offset requirements, passing legislation such as the 1974 Jackson–Nunn Amendment requiring that the European allies offset the balance-of-payments deficit incurred by the United States as a result of the 1974 costs of stationing US forces in Europe. However, a combination of events in the mid-1970s decreased congressional pressure for unilateral US troop reductions in Europe. The East–West talks on mutual force reductions that opened in Vienna, Austria, in 1973 aimed at producing negotiated troop cuts, and US administrations argued that US unilateral withdrawals would undercut the NATO negotiating position. Congress turned toward efforts to encourage the Europeans to make better use of their defense spending, and President Jimmy Carter, in 1977, proposed a new "long-term defense program" for NATO in the spirit of the Nixon Doctrine, setting the goal of increasing defense expenditures in real terms 3 percent above inflation for the life of the program.

In 1980, Congress, frustrated by allied failures to meet the 3 percent goal, required preparation of annual "allied commitments reports" to keep track of allied contributions to security requirements. Throughout the 1980s, Congress developed a number of approaches linking the continued US troops presence in Europe to improved allied defense efforts. However, the burden-sharing issue was never "resolved." In fact, the growing US concern with Soviet activities in the Third World put even more focus on the fact that the Europeans did little militarily to help the United States deal with this perceived threat to Western interests.

In sum, throughout the Cold War, the United States felt strongly that the Europeans needed to "do more." US arguments included the following:

1. By all quantitative measures, the United States spent more on defense than its allies (well documented in the annual reports on allied defense spending produced by NATO at the end of each year and published in the NATO Handbook).
2. American global military commitments contributed to Western security; growing US military commitments in the Persian Gulf region in particular benefited European as well as US security.
3. The economic strength and political maturity of the allies required them to play a larger role on behalf of their own security interests.
4. American military efforts had allowed the Europeans to modernize their industrial plants, producing competitive advantages for European over American firms.
5. American spending on its strategic nuclear capabilities contributed directly to Europe's security.

Although some Europeans agreed that their countries should increase their relative share of the Western defense burden, the prevalent feeling was that many American criticisms of their defense efforts were unwarranted. Their responses to the US critique included a variety of arguments, including the following:

1. The United States overreacted to the threat. Particularly toward the end of the Cold War, the Soviet Union was growing weaker, and Soviet President Mikhail Gorbachev was looking for ways out of the Cold War confrontation.
2. American attitudes toward the Soviet Union swing unpredictably from great pessimism to great optimism. This produces an irregular pattern of US defense spending, with dramatic peaks and valleys, while the Europeans maintain more steady modest growth in defense efforts.
3. Through NATO, the United States protects itself and its global interests more effectively than it could if its defense perimeters were withdrawn to North America and adjacent waters.
4. Some allied contributions to Western security cannot be measured in terms of defense expenditures alone. Most European countries provide much more development assistance to less developed countries than does the United States, and such efforts help promote stability. Some provide important real estate for NATO bases.
5. British and French strategic nuclear capabilities enhance deterrence.

6. During the Cold War, the allies purchased far more military equipment from the United States than the United States purchased from European arms manufacturers. American industrial profits, employment, and balance of payments all benefited from this fairly one-sided trade.

When the Cold War ended, the foundation for the burden-sharing debate was cut away. The Soviet Union's military capabilities did not vanish overnight, but its capacity to attack Western Europe vanished almost immediately with the democratic revolution in central and Eastern Europe that demolished the Soviet bloc and the Warsaw Pact. Soviet nuclear forces remained a concern, but more because it was unclear whether they would remain under reliable control at a time when the Soviet Union and its empire were disintegrating.

Perhaps ironically, the biggest burden-sharing issue at the end of the Cold War was how the allies should work together to deal with security problems beyond NATO's borders and beyond collective defense. That would become one of the biggest challenges for the allies in the 1990s. However, the end of the Cold War in itself was not sufficient to produce dramatic shifts in the burden-sharing equation and did not change the fact that leaders in all NATO nations would continue to look to buy an acceptable level of security at the best price. At least in the first decade after the end of the Cold War, the United States and all its allies would look for a peace "dividend" by reducing defense expenditures, taking the opportunity to shift resources to other priorities. The burden-sharing issue would remain a permanent feature of the transatlantic bargain for as long as it should last.

The end of the Cold War totally changed the context for the tensions and debate among the allies about the best policies to pursue in the face of Soviet power and ideology. However, the underlying sources of differing perspectives that were so prominent during the Cold War did not disappear with the end of that period of history. They simply went underground for a time, waiting to reappear in other ways at other times and perhaps to be changed and modified by future circumstances.

NOTES

1. Flora Lewis, "How Europe Thinks of War," *New York Times,* June 8, 1981, A15.

2. Fritz Stern, "A Shift of Mood in Europe," *New York Times,* September 2, 1981, A27.

3. Louis J. Halle, *The Cold War as History* (New York: Harper & Row, 1967), 12–13.

4. Stanley Hoffman, "The Crisis in the West," *New York Review of Books,* July 17, 1980, 44.

5. Government of the United Kingdom, *White Paper on Defence* (London: Ministry of Defence, 1980).

6. For analysis of the resolution, see Phil Williams, *The Senate and U.S. Troops in Europe* (London: Macmillan, 1985), 139–67.

NATO's Post–Cold War Military Missions in Theory and Practice

NATO'S NEW ROLES

NATO had been the West's indispensable institution during the Cold War. But as the Cold War era came to an end, many wondered whether NATO would or should be swept away by the breathtaking winds of change.[1] The NATO members had already been working hard to improve security relations in Europe, largely through negotiating arms control and confidence-building measures with the Soviet Union and its Warsaw Pact allies. Now the authoritarian regimes that had held the Warsaw Pact together were leaving, and the Warsaw Pact itself was not far behind. The West Germans and the postcommunist East German authorities began negotiating reunification under the watchful eyes of the Soviet Union, the United States, France, and the United Kingdom. A new Europe was on the horizon.

In this heady atmosphere, many thoughtful analysts and officials questioned what NATO's place might be in a world in which the Warsaw Pact had crumbled, the Soviet Union was withdrawing its forces from central Europe, and new leaders of former Warsaw Pact nations were already speculating about joining NATO (in February 1990, Hungarian Foreign Minister Guyla Horn said that he could "imagine that, in a few years, Hungary could become a member of NATO"[2]).

Early in 1990, very few observers were willing to talk about NATO opening its membership to former Warsaw Pact states. In fact, a variety of quite different concepts for the future organization of European security competed for official and public approval. Some experts speculated that it might be best to keep the Warsaw Pact in business to help organize future security in Europe. Others argued that NATO had outlived its usefulness because there was no longer any threat. Such advocates believed that the Conference on Security and Cooperation in Europe, to which all European states, the United States, and Canada belonged, could take over responsibility for maintaining peace and security on the Continent. Some Europeans, including French President François Mitterrand and British Prime Minister

Margaret Thatcher, tried to find alternatives to German reunification while the United States facilitated accomplishment of West Germany's long-term goal.[3]

With the world changing all around them, the leaders of NATO countries decided that they should address the question of whether NATO was needed. Instinctively, all the governments of all member states, as well as NATO Secretary-General Manfred Woerner,[4] believed that NATO should be preserved—even if they were not fully agreed as to why. Some officials argued that NATO was more than a military alliance and was based, in fact, on a community of values that rose above any specific military threat. Others maintained that the Soviet Union remained an alien society that could produce new threats to its neighbors in the future. They saw NATO as an "insurance policy" against a future fire in the European house. Others pointed to new risks and uncertainties that could best be dealt with through NATO's approach, in which like-minded countries work together to handle security problems.

Meeting in London in July 1990, less than nine months after the Berlin Wall had come down, the heads of NATO governments issued the "London Declaration on a Transformed North Atlantic Alliance," announcing a "major transformation" of NATO.[5] They offered to join the Soviet Union and other Warsaw Pact states in declaring that they were no longer enemy states and offered both friendship and cooperation to the former adversaries. Importantly, the leaders also agreed that NATO should revise its military system and its nuclear and nonnuclear strategy. They set in motion a major overhaul of alliance strategy, aimed at producing a "new strategic concept" for the alliance in the course of 1991. With this decision, the NATO members began the process of defining NATO's place in the post–Cold War world.

NATO's evolution throughout the 1990s responded to the changing international environment that the allies encountered after the end of the Cold War. The process of change did not come quickly enough to prevent the conflict in the former Yugoslavia from becoming a bloody civil war. A multinational institution with no supranational powers and an established bureaucracy moves slowly in reaction to change. But the NATO allies worked their way through the inertia of past success and political resistance to new approaches in order to adapt their alliance to the new security environment.[6] And, ultimately, the changes written down in the early 1990s provided the foundation for NATO's critical role enforcing peace in the former Yugoslavia later in the decade.

The next four chapters discuss the process of challenge and change that faced the Atlantic Community nations in the 1990s and the way it affected the transatlantic bargain. This chapter focuses on the evolution of NATO's military tasks and strategy and the influence of NATO's role in the Balkans on that evolution. Chapter 7 examines NATO nuclear strategy and forces since the end of the Cold War. Chapter 8 looks at the process of reaching out to other European countries by creating the Partnership for Peace program, offering membership to qualified candidates, and trying to build a new cooperative relationship with Russia and Ukraine.

Chapter 9 explores the development in the 1990s of a new transatlantic bargain, first through the creation of a "European Security and Defense Identity" and then through the establishment of an autonomous "Common European Security and Defense Policy" among the members of the European Union.

ADAPTATION OF NATO'S MILITARY MISSIONS

NATO has survived for more than fifty years in large part because the allies have constantly adapted a fundamentally sound, principled relationship to changing international circumstances. This continuing process of adaptation began with the military buildup and elaboration of an integrated command structure in the early 1950s after North Korea invaded South Korea—measures not anticipated when the North Atlantic Treaty was signed. The alliance was adjusted again following the failure of the European Defense Community in 1954. In the mid-1960s, NATO was forced to adapt to France's departure from the integrated command structure. In 1967, the allies revamped NATO's strategy with the doctrine of "flexible response" to a possible Warsaw Pact attack, broadening NATO's military options. In the same year, they approved the Harmel Report, which gave the alliance the mission of promoting détente as well as sustaining deterrence and defense. The process continued in the 1970s and 1980s as NATO allies adapted their alliance to the emerging period of détente in relations with the Soviet Union and sought arms control accords with Moscow to reduce the dangers of an East–West confrontation.

NATO's 1991 Strategic Concept

Since 1949, NATO always had a strategic concept to guide its policies and force structures. All previous concepts, however, had been classified and were available only in summary form for public consumption. The London Declaration of July 1990 authorized preparation of a new strategic concept. The allies decided that new times required new approaches. In November 1991 in Rome, NATO leaders approved the new concept and released it for all to see.[7]

In Rome, the allies established three areas of particular emphasis for future NATO policies. First, they said that, as part of a "broader" approach to security, they would actively seek cooperation and dialogue among all European states and particularly with the former Warsaw Pact adversaries. Second, they declared that NATO's nuclear and nonnuclear military forces would be reduced and that remaining forces would be restructured to take into account the need for militaries that could handle crisis management tasks (such as the one that soon emerged in Bosnia) as well as collective defense. Third, the allies agreed that the European members of NATO would assume greater responsibility for their own security.

In the 1991 concept, the allies acknowledged the radical changes that had recently occurred in the world and in Europe in particular. When the concept was released, the Soviet Union still existed and still deployed powerful nuclear and nonnuclear military forces. But virtually everything else had changed. Democratic governments were getting organized across central and Eastern Europe, the terms on which Germany would be reunified had been negotiated, the Treaty on Conventional Armed Forces in Europe had been signed, the Warsaw Pact had been disbanded, an antidemocratic coup against Soviet leader Mikhail Gorbachev had been defeated, and governments in Poland, Hungary, and Czechoslovakia had expressed their wish to be included in NATO activities.

The 1991 concept said that NATO's policies and force posture should be adapted to the remarkable changes. But the allies also reaffirmed some elements of continuity. NATO's core function, they declared, was to defend its members against attack, and NATO's integrated command structure and coalition approach to defense remained essential to the interests of the members. The transatlantic link between Europe and the United States and Canada continued to be vital to NATO's future relevance. Defense of democracy, human rights, and the rule of law still constituted the heart and soul of the alliance. Allied leaders noted that, even with all the positive changes, the world remained a dangerous place and that NATO cooperation would be essential to help them deal with the remaining risks and uncertainties. They agreed that the North Atlantic Treaty, in addition to providing for collective defense, included a mandate to work together to deal with threats to the security interests of the members, not just an attack on one of them.

This concept provided a new foundation for NATO initiatives throughout the 1990s and for substantial changes in NATO's military priorities. The allies dramatically reduced and streamlined military forces and NATO's command structure. In 1993, the allies agreed that peacetime strength of their forces could be reduced approximately 25 percent below 1990 levels. In subsequent years, additional cuts were taken. NATO's command structure was reduced from sixty-five headquarters down to twenty in the new system.

The force structure implications of the post–Cold War security environment were recognized early in the 1990s, even if most NATO governments were not prepared to act on the implications. The new challenges to allied security arose almost entirely well beyond the borders of NATO countries. Most allies, however, had forces designed largely to defend their own territory or that of a neighbor. They had little capacity to project and sustain forces in operations beyond their borders. The 1991 strategic concept assumed that allies would be reducing military spending and forces in view of the reduced threat. The concept also envisioned, however, that allies would restructure remaining military forces to give them greater force projection capabilities. The Balkan conflicts of the 1990s brought home the importance of these words in the 1991 concept.

The allies addressed directly the reality that the end of the Cold War did not resolve all sources of conflict and tension in the world, even though it certainly improved the prospects for a more peaceful future. Unfortunately, there remained countries and subnational groups, including terrorists, who did not accept the post–Cold War distribution of territory, resources, political influence, or generally accepted norms of international behavior. In some cases, these countries and groups saw the threat or use of force as a way to change the status quo—Saddam Hussein's attack on Kuwait in 1990 was a good example, as have been the terrorist acts instigated by the radical Islamic militant Osama bin Laden. Some of these activities rely on conventional weapons and terrorist tactics. But there was reason to be particularly concerned about access of such countries and groups to nuclear, chemical, and biological weapons of mass destruction (WMD) and modern means to deliver such weapons.

At the time, only the United States and a few other allied governments were prepared to move ahead with new military programs designed to respond to the terrorist/WMD problem. Thus, the allies focused initially on the politics of the issue, examining the underlying causes of dissatisfaction with the status quo that gave rise to WMD threats and terrorist activities. They also sought to identify the political, economic, and security tools available to the international community to eliminate the sources of proliferation or to prevent it in some way, including the active support for existing arms control regimes. The NATO allies pledged to support political and diplomatic efforts aimed at preventing proliferation without duplicating the work of other organizations. However, the allies never made a serious commitment to coordinate their approaches to terrorist threats or their possible responses to terrorist attacks. This failure was due in part to underlying disagreements about the sources of and appropriate responses to terrorist threats. In addition, the terrorist activities of greatest concern to date had been the responsibility of internal, not external, groups (e.g., bombings of British targets to protest the United Kingdom's involvement in Northern Ireland and attacks by Basque separatists in Spain) and were regarded by the target states as domestic affairs.

At the same time, weapons of mass destruction and terrorism raised specific security problems for NATO. A terrorist's missile carrying a weapon of mass destruction fired at any NATO country would become a collective defense issue for all the allies. And political efforts to prevent proliferation or deter the use of weapons of mass destruction might not always be successful on their own. The NATO members therefore decided that NATO's military posture must make it clear to any potential aggressor that the alliance cannot be coerced by the threat or use of weapons of mass destruction and could respond effectively to threats to its security as they develop.

NATO's 1991 strategy called for maintaining military capabilities that would be sufficient to signal how seriously NATO took the proliferation threat. Under post–Cold War conditions, the allies decided that they could best communicate their intentions by maintaining a mix of nuclear and nonnuclear response weapons, passive and active defenses, and effective intelligence and surveillance means. NATO forces, they determined, should be capable of anticipating (through high-quality intelligence information and analysis), deterring (through maintenance of credible forces), defending (by protecting against a variety of delivery systems and the effects of biological and chemical agents on troops), and, if necessary, defeating (using whatever force may be required) any threat from weapons of mass destruction that might emerge from any source in the future.

NATO's approach to the new challenges of weapons of mass destruction and terrorism was a contemporary application of the commitment the allies made in the North Atlantic Treaty to cooperate in preserving the peace and dealing with threats to the security of the alliance. Such threats were likely to remain politically complex, they might arise from several different possible directions, and they could be difficult to predict and assess. NATO, however, could help coordinate allied diplomatic efforts to prevent such challenges from arising and, if necessary, develop appropriate responses to more imminent and dangerous military threats that do emerge. Unfortunately, the alliance did little in real terms to respond to the terrorist challenge prior to the September 11, 2001, attacks on the United States.

The allies did, however, make an active commitment to military cooperation with their former adversaries. Even before the 1991 new strategic concept was issued, the allies began engaging their military forces in cooperative programs with former Warsaw Pact and other European nations. In support of the dialogues with Russia and Ukraine, NATO military forces tried to reach out to the militaries that had formed the core of the Soviet Union's defense establishment. Thus, while the NATO force structure was being reduced, new roles and missions were being added to the plate of allied military forces. This expansion of functions and responsibilities preceded the burdens that were subsequently imposed by the peace operations in Bosnia and Kosovo.

Perhaps the most fundamental reform of the NATO integrated command structure began at the January 1994 NATO summit meeting in Brussels when the allies approved the US-proposed idea of establishing Combined Joint Task Force (CJTF) headquarters as part of NATO's integrated command structure.[8]

The intent of the CJTF initiative was to provide flexible command arrangements within which allied forces could be organized on a task-specific basis to take on a wide variety of missions beyond the borders of alliance countries. Specifically, the concept sought the following:

1. Giving NATO's force and command structure sufficient flexibility to respond to alliance security requirements and new missions other than responses to an attack on a NATO country.
2. Facilitating the dual use of NATO forces and command structures for alliance and/or operations run by the Western European Union, the defense organization whose membership included only European countries and that had been chosen as the framework for constructing a "European pillar" in NATO; the purpose would be to encourage European nations to undertake missions with forces that are "separable but not separate" from NATO in the context of an emerging European Security and Defense Identity.

3. Permitting non-NATO partners to join NATO countries in operations, exercises, and training as envisioned in the Partnership for Peace program of cooperation open to all non-NATO European states.[9]

All these new directions had direct implications for the NATO command structure, and, in April 1994, the Chiefs of the Defense Staffs of NATO countries initiated the "Long-Term Study" intended to form the basis for a new command structure. For starters, it was decided to reduce major NATO commands from three to two—Allied Command Europe and Allied Command Atlantic—with the elimination of the Allied Command Channel. But more difficult issues lay immediately ahead.

NATO'S BOSNIA EXPERIENCE: FROM THEORY TO PRACTICE

While the NATO nations were trying to calculate how the alliance would relate to and operate in the new international environment of the post–Cold War world, that world was already posing new and difficult challenges. With very little concern for allied preferences and priorities, the real world reminded the United States and its European allies that "life is what's happening while you are busy doing other things."

By 1991, life in the Balkans had already become increasingly conflicted. Yugoslavia was a multiethnic communist state that remained relatively independent of the Soviet Union during the Cold War. Following the death of the communist dictator Josip Broz Tito in 1980, the country had been tenuously held together with a power-sharing approach that more or less continued to balance the interests of the country's main ethnic groups (Serbian, Croatian, Muslim, and Albanian). But attempts to modernize Yugoslavia's economic and political system were failing just as the world celebrated the end of the Cold War. The failure became a new Balkan tragedy when the process of disintegration turned violent. The Slovene Republic, a part of the former Yugoslavia that was blessed with a relatively homogeneous population and no substantial minority concentrations, managed to break away with limited fighting. But the Republic of Croatia's breakaway was strongly resisted by the Serbian-controlled military, producing approximately 20,000 dead and more than 350,000 displaced persons.[10]

The conflict quickly spread to Bosnia-Herzegovina, where Serbian, Croatian, and Muslim populations were interspersed around the republic and where the conflict became a brutal and bloody internecine battle among the ethnic populations. When the Bosnian War began in March 1992, the NATO countries had just issued their new strategic concept, which, in principle, suggested that they should prepare to deal with such circumstances. But they were nowhere near being ready to do so. In fact, NATO leaders in Rome had made clear their desire to keep NATO at arm's length from the conflict, proclaiming their concern but suggesting that the parties to the Balkan conflicts "cooperate fully with the European Community in its efforts under the mandate given it by the CSCE [Conference on Security and Cooperation in Europe], both in the implementation of cease-fire and monitoring agreements and in the negotiating process within the Conference on Yugoslavia."[11]

A key reason for NATO's reticence was the reluctance of the United States to get involved. President George Bush was facing a reelection contest in which it was clear that the Democratic opposition would charge him with spending too much time on foreign policy at the expense of domestic issues. Bush may have been additionally motivated by Soviet President Gorbachev's warning in the spring of 1991 that the West should not intervene in Yugoslavia, obviously not wanting a precedent for Western intervention to be set that subsequently could be applied to a crumbling Soviet Union.[12]

If the Bush administration needed additional cover for a reticent US approach, a way out had been provided earlier by the European allies. On June 28, 1991, Jacques Poos, the foreign minister of Luxembourg, speaking for the members of the European Community, bravely claimed that the problems in the Balkans presented an opportunity for the Europeans to take charge of their own security affairs, pronouncing that it was "the hour of Europe." According to Poos, "If one problem can be solved by the Europeans, it's the Yugoslav problem. This is a European country and it's not up to the Americans and not up to anybody else."[13] Under these circumstances, the Bush administration was satisfied to leave it at this. NATO's role was restricted to helping enforce the UN embargo against weapons deliveries to any of the warring parties in Yugoslavia. The operation was conducted in parallel with a seaborne monitoring operation organized through the Western European Union.[14]

With the United States unwilling to get involved, NATO's role clearly would remain limited. However, the brutality of the conflict and the suffering of noncombatants, broadcast up close and personal for the world to see, could not be ignored.

The international community responded to the immediate consequences of the conflict by mounting a humanitarian relief operation backed up by a UN protection force (UNPROFOR), manned largely by lightly armed French, British, and other European troops whose mission was effectively limited to ensuring the safety of the relief efforts. Despite the care that President Bush took not to get involved in the Balkan conflicts, the criticism that he had spent too much time and energy on foreign policy and not enough on the US economy apparently hit home with the American people. In November 1992, George Bush lost the presidency to Democrat Bill Clinton, who came to office in 1993.

During the US presidential election campaign, Clinton had criticized Bush's Bosnia hands-off policy but, after taking office, followed much the same approach. In April 1993, the UN Security Council agreed to impose an embargo of all land, sea, and air traffic attempting to enter Serbia and Montenegro. The Clinton administration and the European allies agreed that NATO would help enforce the enhanced embargo, but the new administration remained reluctant to get too deeply involved, fearing that the presidency could in its early months be drawn into what Secretary of State Warren Christopher called "the problem from hell."[15]

Transatlantic relations over Bosnia policy were also troubled by the fact that the United States saw and understood the conflict largely as one involving an aggressor—the Bosnian Serbs, supported by Serbia—against the much weaker Bosnian Muslims. The Europeans, for the most part, believed the conflict should be seen as a civil war in which all parties were to blame. These two different interpretations of the conflict produced divergent policy preferences. The approach to the conflict favored by many members of the US Congress was to lift the embargo against military assistance to Bosnia in order to equip and train Bosnian forces to produce a balance of power in Bosnia that would provide the necessary incentives for peace. This approach was based on the model of Serbia as the aggressor and the assumption that the United States should provide only air power and no ground forces to help resolve the conflict. The European allies strongly objected to any such "lift-and-strike" approach, particularly since the forces they had deployed in UNPRO-FOR depended on being seen as "neutral" in the conflict and were there only to help mitigate the humanitarian tragedy. The fact was that the Europeans were willing to put troops in harm's way and the United States, at that point, was not led to the growing perception in the 1990s that the United States would involve itself in overseas conflicts only if risks to American forces could be minimized.

Despite US desires not to touch the Bosnian tar baby, when it became increasingly clear that international relief efforts and UNPROFOR were dealing with some of the consequences but none of the causes of the conflict, the United States, and therefore NATO, were slowly drawn toward deeper involvement. The Clinton administration still hoped to avoid placing US troops on the ground in Bosnia unless they were sent to help enforce a negotiated peace accord. Clinton sent Secretary of State Christopher on a mission to Europe to try to convince the allies to accept the lift-and-strike approach. Christopher made what has been described as a halfhearted pitch to the allies, reportedly conveying the message that he had come in a "listening mode."[16] The Europeans perceived accurately the lack of the administration's commitment to the initiative.

However, by the summer of 1993, Bosnian Serb forces were winning military victory after victory. They had encircled virtually all the "safe areas" that UN-PROFOR had established to help protect civilian populations, including the major center of Sarajevo. In response, the NATO members agreed to draw up plans for air strikes by NATO forces against those threatening the viability of UNPRO-FOR's mission, mainly the Bosnian Serbs. The option was created with a "dual-key" arrangement in which both NATO and the United Nations would have to agree on striking any particular target.

The UN–NATO collaboration was necessitated by the fact that international involvement in the Balkans was largely under the mandate provided by UN Security

Council resolutions.[17] Most countries wanted it that way, but the arrangement made for difficult relations between the United States, which provided most of the military capabilities necessary for the NATO air strikes, and the European allies, led by the British and French, whose troops were on the ground and exposed to retaliation by Bosnian Serb forces.

The Bosnian Serbs fully recognized the advantages to their cause of the split between the United States and its allies. They responded to NATO air strikes by backing off when necessary, taking UNPROFOR soldiers hostage when advantageous, and playing for time to complete their military victory.

During 1995, it became increasingly clear that the UNPROFOR approach, even backed up by NATO air strikes, could not be sustained much longer. The European allies suggested that UNPROFOR would have to be withdrawn, and this would require that the United States fulfill its pledge to protect allied forces as they were being pulled out. But such a withdrawal also would mean a victory for those seen by the United States as the aggressors, and such an outcome would have been a serious setback for US foreign policy. Trying to escape from its policy dilemma, the Clinton administration was impelled forward by the Bosnian Serb attack on the UN safe area of Srebrenica early in July 1995. The United Nations rejected the request from Dutch UNPROFOR troops for air strikes to deter the Serb attack. When it came, the Bosnian Serbs conducted a brutal campaign of blatant war crimes in the wake of their military victory. Serbian forces executed some 8,000 Bosnian boys and men and tortured and sexually abused thousands of women and children. The shocking story emerging in the aftermath of Srebrenica began to galvanize an international view that something more had to be done. The commander of the Bosnian Serb forces bragged that Srebrenica was simply the beginning of the end of the conflict. As one observer has written, "This challenge confronted the United Nations, NATO and especially the leading member states with a fundamental choice. They could act to oppose what was unfolding before them by force of arms or they could declare defeat."[18]

At a meeting in London following the Srebrenica disaster, the United States and its key European allies agreed that Serbian preparations for an attack on the safe area of Gorazde would be met with a strong air campaign, hitting Bosnian Serb targets throughout Bosnia. The United States also produced a plan for negotiations that the allies readily accepted as a way out of the crisis. Operation Deliberate Force began on August 30 after it was determined that a deadly artillery attack on a marketplace in Sarajevo had been conducted by Bosnian Serb forces. The bombing campaign, combined with a successful Croatian offensive against Serbian forces that had begun in early August, brought the Serbs and the other combatants to the bargaining table.

The United States, represented by the bright, ambitious, and controversial Richard Holbrooke and a very capable interagency team of officials, provided much of the energy behind the talks.[19] Following complex and difficult negotiations, a peace accord was completed in Dayton, Ohio, and then signed in Paris on December 14, 1995. The United Nations gave NATO a mandate to help implement the accord, and on December 16, the allies decided to launch what was at the time the largest military operation ever undertaken by NATO. NATO sent to Bosnia an Implementation Force (IFOR) of more than 60,000 troops from NATO, partner, and other nations to maintain the peace, keep the warring factions separated, oversee the transfer of territory between the parties as specified in the peace accord, and supervise the storage of heavy weapons of the parties in approved sites. IFOR had been given one year to accomplish its tasks—a time frame recognized by most observers as inadequate for the purpose of establishing peace but perhaps necessary to appease domestic politics in the United States. At the end of that year, in December 1996, it was decided that peace would not yet be self-sustaining without continued external encouragement. NATO, with a UN mandate, replaced IFOR with a Stabilization Force (SFOR), which was still in Bosnia in 2002.

Over the years, NATO helped establish relative peace in Bosnia-Herzegovina, but questions remained about whether the goal of producing a self-sustaining peace in the multiethnic state cobbled together at Dayton would be achieved. According to most observers, international civilian assistance had not achieved a level of effectiveness to stimulate progress toward a more stable society. In addition to a less-than-effective international response to Bosnia-Herzegovina's civilian needs, the three ethnic communities—Bosnian, Croatian, and Serbian—had made insufficient efforts to start a serious process of reconciliation that would be needed for a multiethnic state to function in the long run.

In 2002, although NATO had reduced the size of SFOR in recognition of the less imminent chance of open conflict, it was still not clear whether the Dayton approach to peace in Bosnia-Herzegovina would succeed or fail. Nevertheless, the Bosnia experience demonstrated that the 1991 new strategic concept had been on target when it suggested that NATO needed to prepare for non–Article 5 military contingencies. Even though Article 5—the pledge to respond to an attack on another ally—remained the most profound commitment made by each NATO ally, a major attack on a NATO country had become the least likely near-term challenge to the security of the NATO members.

The conflicts in the Balkans did not directly threaten the security of most NATO allies, particularly the United States. This assessment produced the reticence of the United States and its allies to respond effectively when the Balkan wars broke out. However, the lofty goals of making Europe whole, free, and at peace were challenged directly, as were the moral standards embraced by the United States and its allies. The danger that the conflict would spread to the borders of NATO allies and perhaps lead to political and even military conflicts between NATO allies did pose a threat to allied security. And if NATO was not going to be used to deal with this crisis in Europe, would it simply become an insurance policy, ceasing to be an important vehicle for the future management of Euro-Atlantic relations?

NATO's role in helping promote and then enforce a peace in Bosnia-Herzegovina answered, at least temporarily, some of these questions. NATO's continued value as an instrument for transatlantic consultation and as a vehicle for political and military action became more obvious. The original European preference to handle the crisis through the United Nations and the US preference to avoid putting troops on the ground caused a costly delay in bringing an end to the brutal conflict. The fact that NATO's "habits of cooperation" facilitated putting together collaborative responses to contemporary security challenges was demonstrated, as was the utility of NATO's integrated command structure.

Some questions, however, were not answered. Could the allies in the future respond to an emerging crisis more quickly and therefore minimize the civilian casualties and dislocations that characterized the Balkan conflicts? How could rapid responses be produced by an organization in which one ally, the United States, had a wide range of military options available to it—and therefore might be more inclined to use them—while the rest of the allies had more limited military options and therefore might be more inclined to rely more heavily on diplomacy before resorting to the use of force? Would responses to future crises be hampered by the fact that the United States had grown suspicious and mistrustful of the United Nations while the European allies still believed in the necessity of obtaining a UN mandate for military operations? Would the fact that France, one of two European allies with meaningful intervention forces, still did not participate fully in NATO's integrated military structure hamper the construction of future NATO coalition operations? Would the United States be a reluctant participant—and therefore an ineffective leader—in future NATO peace operations, particularly given the attitude of many US conservatives that US military forces should be held in reserve for the "big" contingencies and not wasted on the more menial labor of "doing the windows" in peace operations?

BACK TO THE NATO ADAPTATION PROCESS

These and other questions remained very much open in 1996 when, with the Bosnia experience in hand and the difficult process of implementing the Dayton peace accord under way, the allies prepared to take the next steps needed to adapt the alliance to the new security environment. In many respects, the allies found it almost as difficult and time consuming to agree on the principles to guide new arrangements as they did arriving at a common approach to the conflict in Bosnia.[20]

The allies still faced the challenge of implementing agreements that they had made in principle in 1994 designed to give NATO a more flexible structure that would facilitate responses to new security problems. In June 1996, following months of difficult negotiations which on many occasions found the United

States and France at loggerheads, the allies neared a breakthrough concerning how to organize responses to future non–Article 5 security challenges. The French had interpreted the Clinton administration's initiatives at the January 1994 Brussels summit as a sign that the United States was prepared for "Europeanization" of the alliance. The administration, on the other hand, was thinking more in terms of an evolutionary development toward more European responsibility.[21]

At a critical meeting in Berlin, NATO foreign ministers agreed on significant new steps that, when implemented, would constitute a major transformation of NATO's missions and methods of operation. In Berlin, the allies agreed to move ahead with implementation of the CJTF concept that had been agreed on in principle at Brussels in 1994. In addition, they agreed that a European Security and Defense Identity would be created within the alliance by making NATO "assets and capabilities" available for future military operations commanded by the Western European Union (WEU), the defense organization whose membership included only European countries based on the 1948 Brussels Treaty. Such decisions would be made by consensus on a case-by-case basis. To facilitate such operations, European officers in the NATO structure would, when appropriate, shift from their NATO responsibilities to WEU command positions.[22]

The allies determined that adaptation of the alliance should be guided by three fundamental objectives: to ensure the alliance's military effectiveness and ability to perform its traditional mission of collective defense while undertaking new military roles, to preserve the transatlantic link by strengthening NATO as a forum for political consultation and military cooperation, and to support development of a European Security and Defense Identity by creating the possibility for NATO-supported task forces to perform missions under the direction of the WEU nations.

NATO forces in Europe have always been commanded by an American officer who occupies the position of Supreme Allied Commander, Europe (SACEUR), and the allies unanimously agreed that the United States should retain this top command. But the allies decided that the Deputy Supreme Allied Commander, Europe (D-SACEUR), a senior European officer, and other European officers in the NATO command structure would in the future wear WEU command hats as well as their NATO command hats.[23] This multiple-hatting procedure would, without duplicating resources and personnel, permit the WEU countries to use the NATO command structure to organize and conduct a military operation largely under European auspices.[24]

The Berlin Accord was designed to help transform NATO's role for the post–Cold War world, respond to calls from Congress for more effective sharing of international security burdens, and accommodate a more cohesive European role in the alliance. The government of France facilitated the outcome by deciding to move toward much closer military cooperation with its NATO allies to help deal with new challenges to security in Europe. The United States and other allies made major contributions to the outcome by agreeing to fundamental changes in the way that NATO had traditionally organized and run its military forces.

Agreement did not come easily. SACEUR General George Joulwan and the US Joint Chiefs of Staff had objected to the plan for strengthening the Deputy SACEUR's role and for making NATO (US) military assets available for some European-led military operations. The resistance was overcome only hours before the Berlin meeting was set to convene. President Clinton overruled Joulwan and the Joint Chiefs, giving the green light for the reform to proceed.[25]

The Berlin Accord suggested the importance the allies attached to the need for a flexible and dynamic alliance. It demonstrated the commitment of the United States, Canada, and the European allies to ensure that NATO could respond to contemporary security needs. It revealed transatlantic consensus on the need to accommodate development of greater European defense cohesion and military capabilities.

It was hoped that the agreement, giving the Europeans the potential for a more prominent role in NATO's military affairs, would also lead France to return to NATO's integrated military command. French President Jacques Chirac had implied that such a move might be possible. In the wake of the Berlin Accord, however, a series of events prevented the deal from being consummated. First, in the summer of 1996, Chirac sent a letter to President Clinton suggesting that the reform of NATO should include transfer of the position of Supreme Allied Commander Allied Forces South from the United States to a European country. The French saw such a potential shift in commands as a necessary token of the US willingness to let Europe take more responsibility in the alliance. Given the importance of the Mediterranean region to US interests and the fact that Clinton had just overruled the Joint Chiefs in order to agree to the Berlin Accord, Clinton was not going to "give away" such an important position. Following the small crisis that this request and its rejection caused in US–French relations, the door to a French return apparently was firmly closed early in 1997, when Chirac called early legislative elections (which his party lost, ceding control to the left) and did not want to be accused of abandoning an important Gaullist policy of independence from NATO's integrated command.

Meanwhile, implementation of the Berlin Accord moved ahead slowly, particularly with divergent US and French interpretations of what the agreement actually meant. Even though NATO had already constructed a combined joint task force (IFOR) to conduct the peace enforcement operation in Bosnia and a second one (SFOR) to help keep that peace, the alliance could not declare the CJTF concept operational until the allies had worked through all the details and conducted the requisite tests and exercises. This highly deliberate process gave rise to the circulation of a number of anecdotes. Most quoted is the one about a NATO discussion of the CJTF concept in which, after the US representative had described the great virtues of the concept, the French representative supposedly replied, "It looks as though it will work in practice, but will it work in theory?"

THE KOSOVO CAMPAIGN

Even as NATO conducted a relatively successful peace enforcement operation in Bosnia, the story of conflict in the Balkans was far from over, and the allies were to get yet another chance to test the CJTF theory in practice. As noted earlier, the disintegration of the former Yugoslavia unleashed several power struggles among ethnic and religious groups whose animosities toward one another had been suppressed for decades. Kosovo, a region in southern Serbia (more formally known . as the Federal Republic of Yugoslavia), was populated mainly by ethnic Albanians. In 1989, Serbian leader Slobodan Milosevic removed the region's former autonomy. Kosovo became an explosion waiting to happen.

During 1998, open conflict between Serbian military and police forces and ethnic Albanian forces in Kosovo resulted in more than 1,500 ethnic Albanian deaths and displaced 400,000 from their homes. The NATO allies became gravely concerned about the escalating conflict, its humanitarian consequences, and Milosevic's disregard for diplomatic efforts aimed at peaceful resolution. In October 1998, NATO decided to begin a phased air campaign against Yugoslavia if the Milosevic regime did not withdraw part of its forces from Kosovo, cooperate in bringing an end to the violence there, and facilitate the return of refugees to their homes. A UN resolution had called for these and other measures. At the last moment, Milosevic agreed to comply with the resolution, and the air strikes were called off. In addition, it was agreed that the Organization for Security and Cooperation in Europe (OSCE) would establish a verification mission in Kosovo to observe compliance with UN resolutions.

NATO assumed two special responsibilities in support of the OSCE mission. First, it established an aerial surveillance mission, Operation Eagle Eye, to observe compliance with the agreement. Several partner nations agreed to participate in the operation. Second, NATO established a special military task force, led by France, to be deployed in the former Yugoslav republic of Macedonia. Under the overall direction of NATO's SACEUR, this force was designed to rescue members of the OSCE Kosovo verification mission if renewed conflict should put them at risk.

The deteriorating situation in Kosovo in late 1998 led the international Contact Group (the United States, Britain, France, Germany, Italy, and Russia)[26] to produce a draft peace plan on January 29, 1999, that they then proposed to the Serbian authorities and representatives of the Kosovo Serbian population. On January 30, the North Atlantic Council agreed to authorize NATO Secretary-General Javier Solana to initiate NATO air attacks against Serbian targets if Milosevic did not accept the terms of the plan. The Kosovo Albanian authorities accepted the plan on March 18, but the Serbians rejected it. NATO initiated air strikes against Serbian targets in both Serbia and Kosovo on March 24. In response, Serbian forces began driving Kosovo ethnic Albanians from their homes, killing some 10,000 ethnic Albanians and torturing and raping many others.

The NATO air campaign, conducted largely by US forces with high-tech capabilities, lasted for seventy-eight days, targeting Yugoslav military forces and important civilian and military infrastructure.[27] The campaign was conducted without a mandate from the UN Security Council, where it could have been vetoed by the Russian and Chinese permanent members. The European allies would have much preferred having such a mandate but accepted the US argument that it was more important in this case to send a forceful message to Milosevic and stop the ethnic cleansing than to stick to international niceties. The allies pledged in the North Atlantic Treaty to "refrain in their international relations from the threat or use of force in any manner inconsistent with the purposes of the United Nations." In this case, the allies judged that use of force against Serbia was consistent with the purposes of the United Nations, even if they could not get a UN mandate.

Serbian President Milosevic agreed to a peace plan based on NATO conditions on June 3. It required the removal of all Yugoslav forces from Kosovo and provided for the deployment of a NATO-led peacekeeping force (KFOR) to keep the peace while Kosovo was put under international administration until autonomous, elected institutions and officials could be established. Kosovo's final status was left unsettled.

The Kosovo operation ultimately succeeded in driving out Serbian forces and allowing the Albanian population to return, in many cases to homes, neighborhoods, and entire towns that had been destroyed by the Serbs. But the victory was not without a price. Even during the operation, critics complained that NATO's military campaign had provoked the final and most brutal phase of Serbia's ethnic cleansing operation. As the air campaign dragged on with no sign of a Milosevic concession, differences arose among allies and in domestic political debates about an air campaign that was conducted under rules intended to minimize the risks to allied forces and that denied strategically important targets to NATO forces. Some argued strongly that ground forces would have to go in to drive Yugoslav forces out. The debate produced partially accurate images of a United States that thought all wars could be fought without risk to friendly forces versus Europeans who better appreciated the facts on the ground. Perhaps the most dramatic impact, however, was on the perception of a growing gap in deployed technology between the United States and its allies and, from the European side, a realization that Europe could influence the conduct of future military operations only if it could bring more capable forces to the table.

Thus, the end of the war over Kosovo and the beginning of peacekeeping and reconstruction was a victory for NATO albeit a qualified one. The successful outcome of the air campaign meant that the allies avoided the potential casualties, intra-allied divisions, and domestic unrest that a ground force campaign could have produced. However, the interaction between political objectives and military strategy will likely be debated well into the future.

The ultimate success of NATO's strategy surprised the vast majority of military experts and pundits. Most of them had blamed President Clinton, his advisers, and Supreme Allied Commander General Wesley Clark for concocting an air-only campaign designed to avoid NATO casualties but, in their judgment, unlikely to bring Milosevic to heel. In retirement, General Clark answered his critics in a book that argued that constraints imposed on his operations by Washington and interference from other NATO allies, particularly France, in targeting decisions had delayed a successful end to the campaign.[28] Meanwhile, a US General Accounting Office report released in July 2001 added to the critique. The report found that the need to maintain alliance cohesion during the conflict led to important departures from standard US military doctrine and resulted in a limited mission with unclear objectives. Many American military officers and civilian officials who participated in this campaign felt that these departures resulted in a longer conflict, more extensive damage to Yugoslavia, and significant risks to alliance forces.[29]

Such critics were half right and half wrong. They were right that the air campaign allowed Milosevic to continue his ethnic cleansing policies. They were right that Milosevic would have been more convinced of Western resolve if ground forces had been on the table from the beginning. In fact, the buildup of Western forces around Kosovo prior to the end of the conflict did begin to bring ground forces into the military equation, particularly as seen from Belgrade. Moreover, the military revival of the Kosovo Liberation Army, the main Kosovo Albanian fighting force, played a crucial role in forcing Serbian units out of concealment, making them more vulnerable to Western air strikes. NATO did, in the end, have a ground force component to its strategy, even if it developed tacitly rather than explicitly.

Given Milosevic's calculating but stubborn behavior, such critics did not believe that a tacit ground force threat would be sufficient. In addition, the general anti-Clinton perspective of many such experts and, in Europe, the prevailing belief that the United States was no longer willing to take casualties in conflicts not directly linked to "vital" US interests tended to block an objective evaluation of the other important factors at work.[30]

Clinton may have been reluctant to envision US casualties, but he also faced other serious constraints. Only one NATO ally, the United Kingdom, avidly supported the threat of a ground campaign. Some allies were actively opposed, and Clinton supported the air campaign as the only approach that could keep the alliance united and at the same time avoid substantial US casualties. The second important constraint was the absence of good invasion routes, created by a combination of difficult terrain, limited infrastructure in neighboring countries, and the reluctance of some states in the region to be used as launching points for a ground campaign.

At the beginning of the air campaign, and even toward its end, there was no NATO consensus on behalf of even threatening a ground force invasion of Kosovo. The most important missing links were Germany and Greece. If the United States had tried to impose such a strategy on the alliance, divisions among NATO members, never too far beneath the surface, would have burst into the open. The German government might have fallen, and the Greek government, by denying NATO access to its port and road facilities, could have severely hampered a ground campaign. Even though it was popular in Europe to see NATO as following US policy in lockstep, the fact is that neither the Clinton administration nor its predecessors led the alliance successfully by dictating NATO policy.

The big plus for NATO, in addition to achieving its main declared objectives, was that, not without some difficulty, NATO unity was preserved throughout the conflict. In addition, the fact that the air campaign was conducted with such efficiency left a strong impression concerning the readiness and condition of NATO air forces. The loss of only two aircraft and no NATO military casualties in action was both objectively and statistically convincing of US and NATO military effectiveness.

There may never be another contingency that replicates the Kosovo experience. This likelihood, however, suggested the importance of flexible contingency planning, the training and equipping of NATO forces to deal with a wide range of geographic and climatic conditions, and the availability of excellent tactical and strategic intelligence resources. These directions, however, would require political commitment and resources to implement.

The reality that political factors inhibited NATO's ability to show a stronger hand to Milosevic from the beginning threatened to leave a lasting mark on alliance decision making. The NATO allies, in the future, might again face a choice between two options: keeping allied unity but compromising its military strategy or abandoning NATO unity, operating with an ad hoc coalition but deploying a more robust military strategy.

NATO theology, followed to a capital "T" by President Clinton, holds that it is almost always better to maintain a unified alliance than to abandon attempts to produce alliance consensus. However, the Kosovo experience suggested that it would not be a surprise if, in some future noncollective defense military contingency, ad hoc approaches were to appear more attractive to NATO's main military players (the United States, the United Kingdom, and France). The United States obviously chose this course when planning its campaign against Taliban and al-Qaeda forces in Afghanistan, partly as a result of the "lessons learned" from the allied management of the Kosovo conflict.

Some European and even American critics of the Kosovo air campaign portrayed it as another example of the United States imposing its hegemonic solutions on a hapless Europe. Such critics echoed themes that came with a vengeance from Chinese and Russian commentaries on the war. The facts of the matter, when fully assessed, suggest the opposite. The role of the United States in this affair was to provide the critical military components for a strategy that was handicapped by political realities in Europe as well as in the United States.

The heavy European reliance on US military capabilities, once again, added urgency to the initiatives of British Prime Minister Tony Blair and other key leaders in the European Union to develop military capabilities more in keeping with Europe's economic and financial resources. There was good cause for Europeans to be concerned about their military capabilities because a healthy US–European security relationship requires that both burdens and responsibilities be shared equitably. It was no accident that the first peacekeeping forces entering Kosovo were, and remained, mainly European, not American. General Clark and NATO's political leadership were sensitive to the need to balance the perception of the US-dominated air operation with the equally accurate perception of a peacekeeping operation that would rely heavily on European troops. The implications of these aspects for a developing Common European Security and Defense Policy are discussed in chapter 9.

The question left over from the Kosovo campaign, with its full mix of positive and negative features, is whether the alliance would in the future use the experience to improve its military preparedness and command arrangements for such conflicts. The fact that the United States and Europe apparently learned different lessons may make it difficult to translate the experience into constructive changes for the alliance. The United States learned that it did not like to run military operations largely with US forces but with substantial allied political interference; the Europeans learned that they would prefer to have more influence on the course of a conflict whose outcome directly affected their interests.

THE WASHINGTON SUMMIT AND NATO'S
EVOLVING MISSION PROFILE

In April 1999, the NATO allies met at the summit in Washington with the intent of celebrating NATO's fiftieth anniversary and approving guidance to carry the alliance into the twenty-first century. However, before the allies could issue the revised strategic concept on which they had been working for some two years, they were forced by developments in the Balkans to move from debates on principles to decisions in practice. Despite claims by some US officials that the 1999 strategic concept would guide NATO for a decade or longer,[31] the summit produced what was largely an incremental step down the road toward twenty-first-century security requirements.

The summit was held under a Kosovo cloud that the summit leaders were unable to dispel. At the time of the summit, it was unclear whether the Kosovo air campaign would ultimately have the desired result. The Clinton administration decided that the main goal of the summit should be to demonstrate allied unity. Most other allied leaders apparently agreed. British Prime Minister Tony Blair clearly had hoped to move allied leaders toward a commitment to bring ground forces to bear in Kosovo. But the desire for at least a facade of unity won out. Compromise formulations were fashioned that papered over allied differences about the relationship of NATO to the United Nations and the limits on application of NATO's crisis management operations.

The Washington summit was the first for NATO's three new members—the Czech Republic, Hungary, and Poland (for a discussion of NATO's enlargement process, see chapter 8). All additional aspiring candidates for NATO membership were given some cause for hope. The allies created a Membership Action Program (MAP) that promised cooperation beyond possibilities in the Partnership for Peace and, perhaps more important, feedback from NATO concerning their progress toward membership. MAP participants were promised that NATO would formally review the enlargement process again no later than 2002.[32]

The allies repeated support for the development of a more coherent European role in the alliance. But the goal of giving new impetus to the European Security and Defense Identity largely fell by the wayside, left for the European allies to develop further in subsequent European Union gatherings.

One of the problems addressed by allied defense ministers prior to the summit had been the challenge of preserving the ability of NATO militaries to fight as coalition forces in the future. The greatest concern was the growing technology gap between US armed forces and those of most European nations. European allies had been feasting on the post–Cold War "peace dividend," using reductions in military spending to help meet the requirements for European monetary union. Meanwhile, the United States had continued developing new technologies for its military forces. The consequence, a large capabilities gap between the United States and its allies, was evident in the air campaign against Serbia.

At the summit, the allies agreed on a "Defense Capabilities Initiative"[33] designed to try to preserve the ability of allied forces to operate effectively with one another in future decades. The initiative put new political focus on the issue, which surely was needed. But the real problem was money. NATO agreement on what capabilities were needed at a time when threat perceptions were so low throughout Europe would not necessarily open up European treasuries to provide the required funding. In 2001, a NATO Parliamentary Assembly report observed that "the continuing decline in most European defence budgets may jeopardise the success of DCI, and with it the ability of the Alliance to carry out the roles and missions that it set out for itself in the 1999 Strategic Concept."[34]

NATO's 1999 Strategic Concept

One of the most anticipated products of the summit was the preparation of an updated strategic concept. The negotiations leading up to approval of the 1999 concept faced some key differences about NATO's future role and mandate. Perhaps the most important one was the question of how far NATO's mandate should extend beyond collective defense. The United States, with support from the United Kingdom, lobbied for increased alliance focus on new risks posed by the proliferation of nuclear, chemical, and biological weapons of mass destruction and by terrorism.

The North Atlantic Treaty authorizes the allies to cooperate on "threats" to allied interests, and these emerging risks certainly qualified. The Treaty imposes no formal constraints on the ability of the allies to decide to use their cooperative framework to deal with challenges that do not qualify as Article 5 (collective defense) missions. The United States preferred that the 1999 strategic concept impose no formal geographic limits on the relevance of NATO cooperation. Most European allies, however, did not want NATO to be seen as a "global alliance" and preferred that decisions on NATO's future operations be made on a case-by-case basis.

In the early months of 1998, as the allies began work on the strategic concept that was to be issued in April 1999, a major issue developed between the United States and several European allies concerning the relationship between NATO non–Article 5 operations and the United Nations. In preparing the new concept, the United States wanted to keep open the possibility that NATO would from time to time be required to act in the absence of a mandate from the United Nations. France and some other European governments did not disagree with the logic of the US assessment but strongly opposed turning possible exceptions into a new rule. From the French perspective, the rule should be to seek a UN mandate and then decide what to do should such a mandate appear blocked by Russia or China.

This debate, conducted in the corridors at NATO, turned into a real and imminent policy issue over Kosovo. By the autumn of 1998, Russia and China had made it clear that they would not support a UN Security Council resolution authorizing the use of force against Serbia for its activities in Kosovo. Despite this opposition, all NATO allies accepted that Slobodan Milosevic's policies of repression against the ethnic Albanian majority in Kosovo posed a threat not only to internationally accepted values but also to peace in the Balkans and therefore to stability in Europe.

By late 1998, France and most other allies had accepted that Kosovo could constitute the kind of exception that they still objected making into a new rule. When in March 1999 the allies saw no choice but to conduct air strikes against Serbia after the breakdown of the Rambouillet negotiations, they went ahead without the blessing of the Security Council.

Nevertheless, French and American differences over how to treat the mandate issue in the new strategic concept persisted, requiring carefully crafted compromises in the document issued by allied leaders in Washington. The strategic concept agreed to in Washington[35] acknowledged that the UN Security Council "has the primary responsibility for the maintenance of international peace and security and, as such, plays a crucial role in contributing to security and stability in the Euro-Atlantic area." The concept also noted that the OSCE "plays an essential role in promoting peace and stability, enhancing cooperative security and advancing democracy and human rights in Europe." The concept pledged that NATO "will seek, in cooperation with other organizations, to prevent conflict, or, should a crisis arise, to contribute to its effective management, consistent with international law, including through the possibility of conducting non-Article 5 crisis response operations." This language essentially met the French requirement for UN Security Council primacy regarding international security but left the door open for the allies, on a case-by-case basis, to act again in the future without a UN mandate if necessary.

The European preference for an international mandate is motivated partly by the need to demonstrate to public opinion that force is being used for the right purposes. Moreover, Europeans have a general preference for basing their foreign and security policies on international law. This is particularly important in Germany for solid historical reasons that have been embedded in both Germany's constitution and its political consciousness. Both the United Kingdom and France prefer to act on the basis of a Security Council mandate, given their positions as permanent (and veto-holding) members of the Council. France feels this need rather more strongly than the United Kingdom, which believes that it derives influence over US actions through its close ties to Washington. Other European countries, unable to take the law into their own hands, believe that their interests are best served by an international system that runs on a set of predictable rules and regulations to the maximum extent possible. In addition, most Europeans would far prefer to have the Russians on board in support of any military operation in Europe. From their perspective, Russia remains an important European influence even if it is currently weak in virtually all respects (except in its possession of superpower inventories of both strategic and theater nuclear weapons—another good reason for wanting to bring them along).

All the European allies accepted that the new threats identified by the United States were serious and merited their attention. They agreed with the United States when it appeared that NATO might have to use force against Serbia without a specific UN mandate to do so. But most were reluctant to make cooperation in any given peace enforcement or counterproliferation operation more or less automatic. They saw their willingness to act against Serbia without a UN mandate as an exception. In the end, such decisions were left to be made on a case-by-case basis, with Kosovo seen neither as a new rule nor as the last time NATO might act without a UN mandate. Nonetheless, the allies agreed to establish a new NATO center to monitor these threats and help plan NATO responses.

The allies agreed that NATO should always act in a way "consistent with international law" and made it clear that "the United Nations Security Council has the primary responsibility for the maintenance of international peace and security and, as such, plays a crucial role in contributing to security and stability in the Euro-Atlantic area." These words, however, did not settle the question of whether a UN mandate should always be required. By the same token, the concept placed no formal geographic limitations on NATO's activities, nor did it identify a specific area of operations for those activities.

This somewhat "fuzzy" outcome in the new concept on such issues accurately reflected the fact that NATO is an alliance of sovereign nation-states that prefer to reserve decisions on future NATO operations that do not involve an attack on a member. In the future, some might argue, most such operations could be organized on an ad hoc basis, if necessary.

The Washington summit did not, as some US officials had hoped, lay out the course for NATO's next decade. It made a start down that road but left many crucial questions unanswered. This was not necessarily a failure of allied governments but rather a reflection of the extent to which the Kosovo experience could affect NATO's future development and the more traditional fact that no one meeting in NATO's history has ever resolved all outstanding issues.

Another issue not resolved by the 1999 concept was the question of how to distinguish between Article 5 and non–Article 5 missions, neither of which have ever been differentiated by the scope of the operations. Rather, the distinction is determined by the reason for the operation.

Article 5 is frequently seen as an "automatic" commitment, requiring all allies to come to the defense of one or more under attack. The language in the Treaty, however, is more qualified. Allies are committed to regard an attack on one as an attack on all, but then each may "take such action as it deems necessary, including the use of armed force." The virtual automaticity of the guarantee actually was a product not of the language in the Treaty but in the way the allies deployed military forces on the front lines in Europe. Multinational layer-cake deployments assured that an attack on frontline ally Germany would at the very outset engage the military forces of the United States and other allies, ensuring that they would have very little choice but to respond with military force sufficient to end hostilities on terms favorable to the allies.

There is no such automaticity either in the Treaty or in practice regarding non–Article 5 operations. The response of the alliance in such cases must be determined by individual, independent national judgments, all of which must be at least permissive of the proposed action, if not actively supportive. The strength of the Treaty's non–Article 5 provisions is that Article 5 does not provide a mandate to act in the case of threats to interests of the allies, only to deal with circumstances created by an attack on one of them. Article 4, on the other hand, specifically takes into account the possible need to consult concerning threats and to consider joint actions to deal with those threats.

That said, from a military planning perspective, the operations in Bosnia and Kosovo were of impressive size and scope. They were politically complex and militarily demanding. But they differed from traditional Article 5 planning in a number of ways. Most important, NATO planners had a fairly clear idea of what forces would be available in the case of a Warsaw Pact attack on NATO. In both the Bosnia and the Kosovo operations, there was no way to know far in advance what forces member states would send to the operation. This meant that NATO planners were forced to develop a variety of theoretical options to present to their political leaders and then hope that forces would be made available to implement the option selected by NATO national officials. In addition, while a hard core of NATO forces was deployed forward during the Cold War to form the first echelons of a defense against a Warsaw Pact attack, NATO's response to non–Article 5 contingencies must be based on forces that are capable of being moved, establishing themselves in the theater of conflict, and then conducting military operations. The logistics for such deployed operations are much more complicated than those required to support frontline forces engaging in border defense.

NATO'S FUTURE MILITARY ROLE

By the beginning of the twenty-first century, NATO's military forces were expected to be able to perform at least five diverse missions, compared to one major mission during the Cold War. These missions include the following:

1. *Maintaining collective defense preparedness* for possible future major challenges and more limited collective defense contingencies that might develop in the nearer term;
2. *responding to crises* such as the ones in the Balkans to promote stability and protect members' interests;
3. using defense and political cooperation to *support ad hoc coalition formation* when a full-fledged alliance response is blocked by political circumstances;
4. using military-to-military cooperation with applicant countries to *support the enlargement process;*
5. using military-to-military cooperation to *build mutual confidence and transparency* with nonmember states (particularly Russia and non-NATO countries in the Mediterranean region).

These five missions are more complex militarily and much more diverse politically than the old Cold War collective defense mission, even though the potential costs of failure during the Cold War were much higher than they are today. NATO's military leaders and forces must accomplish these missions with significantly reduced resources than those available during the Cold War. These missions require forces that are much more flexible and agile. Forces must be adaptable to many different circumstances. No longer can forces from European states plan to operate only in their native climate and on familiar terrain. To be relevant, they have to be designed, equipped, and trained to work effectively in a much broader variety of topographic and climatic conditions.

In addition, military leaders, down to the unit level, have to be much more politically aware and sophisticated, particularly when dealing with the unstable environments found in crisis response operations and the politically sensitive setting for cooperation with Russia and other nonapplicant states.

It is not beyond the capacity of NATO's militaries to deal with this broad mission profile. The question is whether political leaders in NATO countries will provide the resources to prepare forces for such diverse operations and then supply the political will required to make the most effective use of those forces.

Balancing New Mission Priorities

The most fundamental policy issue faced by NATO at the end of the Cold War was how NATO should strike a balance between its traditional Article 5 collective defense mission and the new crisis management mission symbolized by NATO's operations in Bosnia, Kosovo, and Macedonia.

At the end of the Cold War, the NATO countries began asking whether NATO could be sustained entirely under the umbrella of its collective defense mission. The answer in the early 1990s was mixed. In the 1991 strategic concept, the allies concluded that NATO could and should be utilized to deal with new threats to security, but they also agreed that collective defense should remain the heart and soul of the NATO commitment.

When the Soviet Union was dissolved and as Russian military capabilities deteriorated progressively throughout the 1990s, it became clear that collective defense might be at the heart of the NATO commitment but would not necessarily dominate the alliance's day-to-day activities. Rather, conflict management and preparations for a variety of peace operations would likely become the bread and butter of NATO military cooperation.

During the mid- to late 1990s, NATO's day-to-day activities became almost entirely dominated by new roles and missions. This began with a shift in planning and exercising following the mandate of the 1991 strategic concept and then took a real and demanding form with the military missions in Bosnia (IFOR and SFOR), in Kosovo (the air war against Serbia and KFOR's peace implementation role), and in Macedonia beginning in 2001.

The Kosovo operation, coming on top of the ongoing peace operation in Bosnia-Herzegovina, suggested that both NATO and the European Union would find themselves preoccupied with Balkan security and stability for many years to come. The indeterminate status of Kosovo (technically still part of Serbia but under a form of international occupation and protection) leaves many questions open. The situation is complicated by the fact that at least some Albanians not only seek revenge against Serbs in Kosovo but also pursue a broader ethnic Albanian agenda.

The potential for continuing Balkan instability was underlined in 2001, when conflict between ethnic Albanians and government forces in neighboring Macedonia threatened to develop into another full-blown civil war in another part of the former Yugoslavia. The situation in Macedonia developed as a spillover crisis from the one in Kosovo. Both NATO and the European Union intervened diplomatically to attempt to promote a peaceful settlement. NATO agreed to send in some 3,500 European troops under Operation Essential Harvest to collect weapons and ammunition from the rebel ethnic Albanian National Liberation Army.

Thus, the Balkans became the main focus of NATO military activity and burdens. At least for the time being, NATO's collective defense mission was put in the alliance's back pocket, still a core commitment among the allies but not the main focus of NATO's activities.

Nevertheless, many NATO government and military officials and members of Congress continued to believe strongly that collective defense should remain NATO's "core mission." The logic for retaining collective defense as NATO's primary purpose goes beyond simply clinging to the old and familiar (although this tendency plays a part as well). There are some strong substantial reasons for keeping collective defense at the heart of the alliance.

First, something can be said for the role of the collective defense commitment as an insurance policy against a new Russian threat emerging in the future. Even though the allies hope that the hand of cooperation NATO has extended to Moscow will eventually be grasped by the Russians, it appears that many in the Russian elite still consider NATO, the United States, and the West as inevitable antagonists toward Russia. They are inclined to resist the development of extensive NATO–Russia cooperation. These Russians include a significant number who still think like Soviet rather than Russian leaders. They aspire to restoration of the Soviet Union's superpower role under a revitalized Russia.

Under current circumstances, it cannot be excluded that, regardless of the goodwill of NATO countries, future Russian leaders will choose some form of confrontational relationship with NATO rather than cooperation. Keeping NATO's collective defense commitment alive reassures those allies that would be most exposed to a more aggressive Russia and also could serve as a disincentive for a Russian choice of confrontation over cooperation.

Second, Russia is increasingly the least likely future threat to NATO allies. Turmoil to the south and east of Europe, in North Africa, and in the Middle East—fed by various forms of extremism antagonistic toward the NATO countries and their values, combined with modern weapons of mass destruction and their delivery systems—could produce direct threats to the security of NATO countries. This point was brought home all too sharply with the September 11, 2001, terrorist attacks on the United States and the military campaign against the terrorist organizations in Afghanistan that followed. The NATO collective defense commitment provides reassurance and potential deterrence and also a rationale for allied cooperation in trying to mitigate or eliminate such threats through diplomacy and other means.

Third, and perhaps most important from a practical perspective, NATO's collective defense commitment helps sustain a core of war-fighting military capabilities around which conflict management capabilities can be built and without which conflict management policies would appear much less credible. It also provides a continuing rationale for the integrated command structure, without which critical day-to-day cooperation among allied militaries would dissipate, eventually undermining the ability of NATO countries to operate in coalition formations. Former head of the NATO Military Committee, General Klaus Naumann, argued strongly during the late 1990s that NATO's collective defense mission and military capabilities were essential to NATO's future. If all NATO countries developed forces capable of no more than peacekeeping operations, the alliance would become largely irrelevant to contingencies such as those already seen in Bosnia and Kosovo. The high-intensity air campaign against Serbia over the Kosovo crisis demonstrated how important collective defense instruments, such as high-tech air capabilities, can be to non–Article 5 operations.

One way of looking at the relationship between collective defense and NATO's new tasks is to see them as "inner" and "outer" core missions.[36] Collective defense and the military forces and command structure associated with it provide a solid core for NATO's mission profile. Such capabilities both hedge against an uncertain future and provide a solid foundation for NATO's new missions.

In the future, the allies will have to ensure that there is a seamless continuum between all political and military aspects of NATO's inner- and outer-core missions and capabilities. In this regard, NATO military authorities will be called on to develop training, exercising, deployment, and rotation concepts that enable regular forces to maintain combat capabilities while being employed in non–Article 5 operations. In addition, NATO nations will have to focus increased political attention and defense resources on emerging outer-core, non–Article 5 missions, including promoting stability in Europe, dealing with the proliferation of weapons of mass destruction, responding to the terrorist challenge, and providing options to deal with threats to security that can arise beyond NATO borders. From this perspective, NATO's outer-core missions will have to be designed and executed with the goal of diminishing the chance that NATO's inner-core mission of collective defense will need to be invoked.

Finally, NATO's collective defense commitment carries with it a degree of serious intent and political will that would not be demonstrated by a less demanding form of cooperation. Article 5, in effect, constitutes a statement by all the allies that they consider their security to be indivisible. It serves as a clear demonstration that the political values and goals articulated in the North Atlantic Treaty's preamble remain as valid for allied governments today as they were in 1949.

The continuing rationale for a collective defense mission is therefore closely related to the ability of the alliance to serve as an instrument for conflict management and defense cooperation. Conceptually, the conventional wisdom among NATO governments appears logical and relevant to the likely challenges of the coming years. Some critics in the United States and Europe will continue to question the legitimacy of this conventional wisdom. However, the main weakness of the approach may be in its execution, not its conceptualization. Will sufficient resources be made available by allied governments to implement a multiple-mission approach? Will the emerging gap in deployed military technologies between the United States and Europe increasingly impede coalition operations, creating a dual or three-tier alliance? Part of the answer to these questions may lie in whether the European allies will be able to turn their aspirations for a true Common European Security and Defense Policy into effective military capabilities.

NOTES

1. Elizabeth Pond, *The Rebirth of Europe* (Washington, D.C.: Brookings Institution Press, 1999), 56, 57.

2. Speech by Guyla Horn, Hungarian foreign minister, at the meeting of the Hungarian Society of Political Sciences, Budapest, February 20, 1990.

3. For a variety of perspectives on the process by which Germany's was reunified, particularly the role of the United States, see Stephen F. Szabo, *The Diplomacy of German Unification* (New York: St. Martin's, 1992); Philip Zelikow and Condoleezza Rice, *Germany Unified and Europe Transformed: A Study in Statecraft* (Cambridge, Mass.: Harvard University Press, 1995); James A. Baker, *The Politics of Diplomacy: Revolution, War and Peace, 1989–1992* (New York: G. P. Putnam's, 1995); George Bush and Brent Scowcroft, *A World Transformed* (New York: Knopf, 1998); Hans-Dietrich Genscher, *Rebuilding a House Divided* (New York: Broadway Books, 1998); and Alexander Moens, "American Diplomacy and German Unification," *Survival* 33 (November–December 1991): 531–45.

4. Woerner, a German Christian Democrat and former West German defense minister, played an important creative role in the process of adapting NATO to the new international circumstances.

5. North Atlantic Council, London Declaration on a Transformed North Atlantic Alliance, July 6, 1990.

6. For an excellent, thoroughly documented account of NATO's transformation in the 1990s, see David S. Yost, *NATO Transformed: The Alliance's New Roles in International Security* (Washington, D.C.: United States Institute of Peace Press, 1998).

7. North Atlantic Council, Strategic Concept, November 8, 1991.

8. North Atlantic Council declaration, January 11, 1994.

9. The origins and purposes of the Partnership for Peace as a key element of NATO's post–Cold War outreach program is discussed in more detail in chapter 8.

10. Susan Woodward, *Balkan Tragedy, Chaos and Dissolution after the Cold War* (Washington, D.C.: Brookings Institution Press, 1995).

11. "The Situation in Yugoslavia" (statement issued by the heads of state and government participating in the meeting of the North Atlantic Council in Rome, November 7–8, 1991), paras. 1, 4.

12. Stanley R. Sloan, "NATO beyond Bosnia" (CRS Report for Congress 94-977 S, December 7, 1994), 3.

13. As cited by James Gow, *Triumph of the Lack of Will: International Diplomacy and the Yugoslav War* (New York: Columbia University Press, 1997), 48, 50.

14. For in insider's perspective on the role of the Western European Union, see the account by the Union's secretary-general of the time, Willem van Eeckelen, *Debating European Security, 1948–1998* (The Hague: Sdu Publishers, 1998), 140–83.

15. For an excellent, concise account of Clinton administration decision making concerning "the problem from hell," see Ivo H. Daalder, *Getting to Dayton: The Making of America's Bosnia Policy* (Washington, D.C.: Brookings Institution Press, 2000).

16. Daalder, *Getting to Dayton*, 16.

17. For a discussion of the UN–NATO relationship during the early stages of the Balkan conflicts, see Dick A. Leurdijk, *The United Nations and NATO in Former Yugoslavia, Partners in International Cooperation* (The Hague: Netherlands Atlantic Commission, 1994).

18. Daalder, *Getting to Dayton*, 68.

19. For Holbrooke's perspective on the Bosnia peace process and his role in it, see Richard Holbrooke, *To End a War* (New York: Random House, 1998).

20. For an excellent insider's perspective on the political and bureaucratic struggles within NATO during the adaptation process through 1996, see Rob de Wijk, *NATO on the Brink of the New Millennium: The Battle for Consensus* (London: Brassey's, 1997).

21. Subsequent discussions with US and French officials.

22. North Atlantic Council, Berlin Accord, June 3, 1996.

23. For background on the development of NATO's missions in addition to Article 5 contingencies, see Stanley R. Sloan, *NATO's Future: Beyond Collective Defense* (Washington, D.C.: National Defense University Press McNair Papers, 1996). This study was originally issued as a Congressional Research Service Report for Congress in 1995, advancing the idea of strengthening the Deputy SACEUR's role, a concept that became one of the key reforms in the June 1996 Berlin Accord.

24. For discussion of the development of Europe's defense profile, see chapter 9.

25. From the author's discussions with participants in the US decision-making process for the Berlin meeting.

26. The Contact Group had been formed in April 1994 among the United States, Russia, Great Britain, France, and Germany as a way of coordinating Bosnia policy in a small group of major powers. Italy was very unhappy about its original exclusion from the group, engineered by its European partners, not the United States. Italy joined the group in 1996 during its six-month term as president of the European Union's Council of Ministers and remained in the group thereafter. The tradition of smaller groups of allies forming a special committee is well established in the alliance, even if not always appreciated by allies excluded from the group. For example, during the Cold War, the Berlin Group, consisting of the United States, France, the United Kingdom, and Germany, used to meet prior to NATO ministerial meetings to discuss issues related to Berlin and Germany.

27. For a dispassionate assessment of NATO's operations in the Kosovo conflict, see John E. Peters, Stuart Johnson, Nora Bensahel, Timothy Liston, and Traci Williams, *European Contributions to Operation Allied Force: Implications for Transatlantic Cooperation* (Washington, D.C.: Rand, 2001).

28. Wesley K. Clark, *Waging Modern War: Bosnia, Kosovo, and the Future of Combat* (New York: Public Affairs, 2001).

29. US General Accounting Office, "Kosovo Air Operations: Need to Maintain Alliance Cohesion Led to Doctrinal Departures" (GAO-01-784), Washington, D.C., July 27, 2001, 2.

30. For a US perspective on the Kosovo campaign, see Ivo H. Daalder and Michael E. O'Hanlon, *Winning Ugly: NATO's War to Save Kosovo* (Washington, D.C.: Brookings Institution Press, 2000).

31. This claim was made in off-the-record administration briefings to the Senate NATO Observer Group, in which the author participated.

32. North Atlantic Council, Washington Summit Communiqué, April 24, 1999, para. 7.

33. North Atlantic Council, Defense Capabilities Initiative, April 25, 1999.

34. NATO Parliamentary Assembly, Defense and Security Subcommittee on Future Security and Defense Capabilities, "Interim Report on NATO's Role in Defence Reform" (Brussels: NATO Parliamentary Assembly, October 2001), para. 90.

35. North Atlantic Council, The Alliance's Strategic Concept, April 24, 1999.

36. The author originally developed this concept in *NATO in the 21st Century*, a special publication of the North Atlantic Assembly (now the NATO Parliamentary Assembly), for which he was rapporteur. See Senator William V. Roth Jr., president, North Atlantic Assembly, *NATO in the 21st Century* (Brussels: North Atlantic Assembly, September 1998).

NATO Nuclear Strategy and Missile Defense

THE POST–COLD WAR CONTEXT

From the very beginning, nuclear weapons questions played a central role in the transatlantic bargain. Ensuring that Germany would not become a nuclear weapons power was part and parcel of the transatlantic bargain. In the early 1950s, domestic financial considerations led the Eisenhower administration to make NATO's strategy heavily reliant on the threat of massive retaliation against the Soviet Union should it attack Western Europe. After Soviet advances in long-range missilery and nuclear weapons undermined massive retaliation, the allies shifted to a flexible response strategy based on deploying a spectrum of nuclear and nonnuclear forces to deter a Soviet-led Warsaw Pact attack. Soviet deployment of SS-20 missiles that could target all of NATO European territory provided the rationale for NATO's decision to deploy ground-launched cruise and Pershing II missiles that could hit Russian targets from bases in Western Europe.

When the Cold War ended, the allies faced many decisions concerning whether NATO strategy still required a nuclear component and what should be done about new threats from terrorists and rogue states for which traditional deterrence might not work. Beginning in 1989, the allies focused particularly on countering nuclear proliferation. They reaffirmed that nuclear weapons remained central to NATO's deterrence strategy. In the early glow of the post–Cold War era, the allies called them weapons of last resort, although they subsequently backed away from this description and put more emphasis on the constructive uncertainty that NATO's nuclear capabilities would raise in any potential adversary's mind.

Throughout the 1990s, the allies dramatically reduced NATO nuclear weapons beyond the cuts called for in arms control agreements with the Soviet Union. However, in terms of the transatlantic bargain, nuclear weapons policy was "the dog that didn't bark." The allies chose to move carefully and quietly on nuclear weapons policy, perhaps reflecting the concern that dramatic changes could begin to unravel the transatlantic bargain in which nuclear weapons had played such an important role.[1] At the dawn of the new century, however, the missile defense plans of the US administration under President George W. Bush brought a challenging philosophy to US nuclear strategy with potentially profound implications for NATO and transatlantic relations.

CHANGES TO NATO NUCLEAR STRATEGY AND FORCES

NATO's nuclear strategy and forces were key to the alliance's ability to deter Soviet aggression during the Cold War. In the new political and strategic environment of the 1990s, NATO had to take a long, hard look at the nuclear component of its strategy. Considering that nuclear weapons and strategy had been a prominent and controversial aspect of the transatlantic bargain from the beginning, nuclear issues assumed a relatively low-key role in the 1990s. However, without formal negotiations and with no treaty to bind the two sides, the United States took the initiative to reduce short-range nuclear weapons in its arsenal, many of which were deployed in Europe, and the Soviet Union responded in kind.

On May 3, 1990, President George Bush told a Washington press conference that the United States would not modernize the obsolescent LANCE tactical nuclear missile system or US nuclear artillery shells deployed in Europe. The president's move came in response to the dramatic changes in Europe and resulting opposition in the US Congress to costly programs that made little sense in terms of the new political and military situation there. He called for a NATO summit conference to agree, among other things, on "broad objectives for future negotiations between the United States and the Soviet Union on the current short-range nuclear missile forces in Europe, which should begin shortly after a CFE [Conventional Forces in Europe] treaty has been signed."

The London Declaration, issued by NATO leaders at their summit meeting in London on July 5–6, 1990, concluded that with eventual withdrawal of Soviet forces from their deployments in Eastern Europe and implementation of an agreement reducing conventional armed forces in Europe, the alliance would be able "to adopt a new NATO strategy making nuclear forces truly weapons of last resort."[2] This shift in approach would alter NATO's long-standing flexible response doctrine in which the use of nuclear weapons could conceivably have been authorized early in a military conflict. The summit declaration did not, however, forgo the allied option of using nuclear weapons first in a conflict if necessary, and it left open the possibility that nuclear forces will be "kept up to date where necessary." The leaders nonetheless decided that NATO no longer would require all of its existing inventory of short-range nuclear weapons consisting largely of nuclear artillery shells, bombs on dual-capable attack aircraft, and the obsolescent LANCE missile system.

On September 27, 1991, following the failed attempt of hard-line communists to seize control in Moscow, President Bush announced a set of wide-ranging changes in US nuclear policy and deployments. He decided to remove and destroy all US land-based nuclear missiles from Europe and withdraw all US sea-based tactical nuclear weapons while inviting the Soviet Union to take reciprocal actions. The president said that the United States should keep a nuclear capability for NATO, but at the same time he discontinued the program to develop the SRAM-II missile, intended for deployment on strategic bombers. A tactical version of this system, the SRAM-T, intended for deployment in Europe, also was discontinued. This left the US nuclear deployment in Europe limited to free-fall nuclear bombs on dual-capable ground attack aircraft.

The president's decisions were positively received throughout Europe and in the Soviet Union. On October 5, 1991, then–Soviet President Mikhail Gorbachev announced his reciprocal intent to eliminate short-range ground-launched nuclear weapons and proposed US–Soviet limitations on air-delivered tactical nuclear weapons as well. On October 17, 1991, the process of reducing such weapons was taken a step further when NATO ministers of defense, meeting as the Nuclear Planning Group, announced a 50 percent reduction in the inventory of some 1,400 free-fall nuclear bombs deployed primarily by the United States (the United Kingdom also deploys some free-fall nuclear bombs) in Europe.

FROM THE 1991 NEW STRATEGIC CONCEPT TO THE 1999 ALLIANCE STRATEGIC CONCEPT

The new NATO strategic concept approved by NATO leaders on November 7, 1991, in Rome declared that "the fundamental purpose of the nuclear forces of the allies is political: to preserve peace and prevent coercion and any kind of war." The allies, at US urging, rejected a no-first-use posture. Some allied governments would have favored a pledge not to be the first to use nuclear weapons. But the United States and some other allies believed that future aggression might be deterred by a potential aggressor's lingering concern that it might face a nuclear counterattack.

The new concept placed principal reliance on the strategic nuclear capabilities of the United States, France, and the United Kingdom. But it also asserted that peacetime basing of nuclear forces on European territory (meaning the residual US free-fall bombs) "provide an essential political and military link between the European and the North American members of the Alliance."[3] Even as the leaders met to approve the new concept, however, the Soviet Union itself was breaking apart, raising new issues that allied officials had not been able to take into account in drafting the new approach.

A main focus of NATO and US concern from 1992 forward was to ensure that the tactical and strategic nuclear forces of the former Soviet Union remained under reliable control. The United States and its allies sought to diminish the chances that the dissolution of the Soviet Union would result in nuclear proliferation, either from a number of former republics retaining nuclear weapons or from the transfer of nuclear weapons–making technology and know-how to other nations. By June 1992, all tactical nuclear weapons of the former Soviet Union had been consolidated within Russia, where many of the warheads were scheduled for elimination.[4] By June 1996, Ukraine and Kazakhstan had returned all their strategic warheads to Russia. Belarus did so by the end of 1996.

Early in 1992, with regard to another issue (one much less serious than issues raised by the breakup of the Soviet Union), various French officials suggested that French nuclear forces might some day be placed in the service of a unified European political and defense entity. French President François Mitterrand raised the issue by asking, "Is it possible to develop a European doctrine? That question will rapidly become one of the major considerations in the building of a common European defense."[5] French officials and politicians subsequently answered Mitterrand's rhetorical question in a variety of ways, many of them supporting the idea of eventually dedicating French nuclear capabilities to the European Union. But France's European partners were skeptical about French willingness to make any real sacrifice of national sovereignty on behalf of European integration, and French nuclear strategy remained based on French national deterrence requirements.

In other respects, NATO nuclear issues stayed largely out of sight during 1993 and 1994. In 1995, they began to resurface in the context of the debate on NATO enlargement and as a consequence of French President Jacques Chirac's renewed offer of French nuclear capabilities on behalf of the European Union's defense.[6]

When the NATO defense ministers met in Brussels on June 13, 1996, they reiterated the fundamental purposes of NATO nuclear policy outlined in the new strategic concept. The communiqué also observed that NATO's nuclear forces had been "substantially reduced," and in a direct message to Moscow, the ministers declared that NATO's nuclear forces "are no longer targeted against anyone." The ministers appeared to reinforce the point by noting that the readiness of NATO's dual-capable aircraft "has been recently adapted," presumably to a lower level of readiness for nuclear missions.[7]

The ministers concluded the very brief statement on nuclear policy by expressing satisfaction that NATO's nuclear posture would "for the foreseeable future, continue to meet the requirements of the Alliance." They then reaffirmed the strategic concept's conclusion that "nuclear forces continue to fulfill an indispensable and unique role in Alliance strategy" and emphasized that the remaining US free-fall nuclear bombs for delivery by dual-capable aircraft were still essential to link the interests of the European and North American members of NATO.

In the 1999 strategic concept, the allies essentially reiterated their view that "the fundamental purpose of the nuclear forces of the allies is political: to preserve peace and prevent coercion and any kind of war." They maintained that deploying nuclear weapons on the soil of several allied nations was an important demonstration of alliance solidarity. Finally, following another line taken consistently since the 1991 concept, the 1999 concept declared that substrategic forces based in Europe "provide an essential link with strategic nuclear forces, reinforcing the transatlantic link."[8] Since 1999, NATO has made no significant changes in its nuclear strategy. No link has been made between allied nuclear weapons capabilities and deterrence of threats of potential weapons of mass destruction from terrorist groups or rogue states.

DEPLOYMENTS OF US NUCLEAR WEAPONS IN EUROPE

Reductions in the early 1990s brought US nuclear deployments in Europe to very low levels. By the mid-1990s, all US nuclear weapons had been removed from Europe except for several hundred (fewer than 700) free-fall bombs.[9] In 1995, according to one unclassified source,[10] US deployments were limited to some B61 nuclear free-fall bombs at thirteen different sites in seven allied nations.[11] The deployments reportedly included weapons at four sites in Germany, one site in the United Kingdom, three sites in Turkey, two sites in Italy, and at one site each in Greece, Belgium, and the Netherlands. A portion of the US submarine-launched intercontinental ballistic missile force remained committed to NATO.

POLICY CHALLENGES

Notwithstanding consistent allied declarations concerning NATO strategy and the continued importance of US substrategic weapons deployed in Europe, a number of questions were left unanswered as NATO entered the twenty-first century. The most basic questions were whether a US nuclear guarantee for European security remained essential and, if so, why and how to implement that guarantee.[12]

It is possible to argue that for the foreseeable future Russia will deploy strategic nuclear forces far superior to the French and British nuclear capabilities. Given continued uncertainties about the future of democracy in Russia, it is only prudent, according to this perspective, to sustain a US nuclear guarantee for Europe and to deploy the nuclear and conventional forces that will make that guarantee credible. Others have argued that, in addition to uncertainties about Russia, potential security threats from North Africa and the Middle East warrant a continued US nuclear contribution to NATO.[13]

On the other hand, it can be argued that even an implicit US nuclear threat against Russia is inconsistent with US and Western attempts to support Russian reform and democracy or that the French and British nuclear systems should be sufficient to deter any credible threats from a weakened Russia or from others. In addition, even if it is deemed in the US interest to extend deterrence to Europe against potential non-Russian military threats, there are questions about whether the United States needs to deploy nuclear weapons in Europe itself to do so. And it remains unclear whether nuclear weapons have a significant deterrent effect on the behavior of nonnuclear rogue states or terrorist groups in any case.

Even though the Soviet threat vanished in the early 1990s, some Europeans still worry about residual Russian nuclear forces and the potential for Germany at some point to become a nuclear power. The US nuclear presence in Germany and the nuclear umbrella for the Germans have been seen as eliminating the motivation for Germany to become a nuclear power. This raises several questions. Do other European allies still value the US nuclear commitment for this purpose? Do the Germans still want some form of US nuclear guarantee? Will France offer nuclear guarantees to its European partners, including Germany, as part of its commitment to the goal of European political union on terms that would be acceptable and as a new alternative to a German nuclear option? If so, would the Germans see a French guarantee as preferable to the US commitment?

What Role for Residual US Nuclear Weapons in Europe?

As noted previously, there remain questions about whether a US nuclear guarantee for Europe is warranted by prevailing political and military conditions in Europe. The NATO countries continue to emphasize that collective defense, in which nuclear strategy played a key role, remains the core function of the alliance. But the activities of US forces stationed in Europe and of NATO forces more generally are concentrated on NATO's new "crisis management" missions. NATO is still in the process of "adaptation," reorganizing itself to accommodate new missions and challenges, and the role of nuclear weapons and NATO nuclear planning could logically be seen as part of that reassessment.

Before the Warsaw Pact was disbanded and the Soviet Union dissolved, it was argued that the mere presence of some US nuclear weapons in Europe played a role in deterring threats to the security of European NATO members. Now, however, NATO cannot say specifically who or what is being deterred. The rest of NATO strategy has been reoriented largely toward non–Article 5 challenges, but NATO's nuclear posture and strategy have become strategic orphans. Even when there was a Soviet threat, many analysts believed that the US commitment to extend nuclear deterrence to its European allies was made credible simply by the presence of US military forces in Europe, now dramatically reduced, much more than by the deployment of US nuclear weapons there. Other analysts for many years have questioned whether the United States would be willing to use nuclear weapons to defend its European allies if it meant risking nuclear strikes on the American homeland. This logic, of course, provided ammunition for the George W. Bush administration's argument that the ability of the United States to defend itself against missile attacks makes its extension of deterrence to its allies more credible.

Another question still unanswered at the opening of the twenty-first century was the military role that free-fall bombs deployed in Europe should play in NATO or US strategy. NATO projects no imminent military threat against the territorial integrity or security of its members within the unrefueled range of the fighter bombers that would carry the free-fall bombs. Even in the extreme case of a newly antagonistic

Russia, the free-fall bombs would likely be the least credible component of any Western response to a Russian military threat. The fighter bombers currently available in Europe to deliver the bombs cannot reach targets in Russia and return without air refueling arrangements, and other nuclear systems (such as US submarine-launched ballistic missiles, some of which are still dedicated to NATO) have longer range and are more likely to survive defenses and arrive on target.

The apparent conclusion is that, from a purely military perspective, the bombs are intended largely as placeholders, designed to keep open the option of developing a new air-delivered standoff system or deploying some existing air-launched cruise missiles from the US strategic nuclear triad in support of NATO strategy. This rationale presumably is based on the assumption that withdrawal of the bombs could foreclose, or at least make politically more difficult, future US deployment of any nuclear weapons in Europe. In addition, the presence of US nuclear weapons on European soil both ensures continued nuclear risk sharing and affords European governments a consultative relationship with the United States concerning nuclear weapons strategy and doctrines.

Perhaps the most important rationale for a continuing US nuclear presence in Europe is that virtually all European governments apparently still believe that the American military presence in Europe makes a significant contribution to European stability and peace. NATO's 1999 strategic concept asserted that the basing of US nuclear weapons in Europe provided "an essential political and military link between the European and the North American members of the Alliance." But unless there is some credible military or deterrence role for these weapons, their "linking" power may be quite limited.

On the other hand, there has been no significant government or public opposition to this residual nuclear presence, and it is possible that withdrawal would, over time, invite fundamental questions about the US commitment. A survey by the Atlantic Council of the United States in the mid-1990s observed that "the overwhelming consensus among political leaders and strategic thinkers in Europe is that it is premature to address major changes in future nuclear force postures." The survey noted that "Europe has long depended on the American nuclear umbrella, and few European leaders want that to change."[14] Nevertheless, the question of whether the deployment of free-fall nuclear bombs on European soil is essential to sustain extended deterrence remains open.

Nuclear Weapons and NATO Enlargement

The question of the US nuclear commitment became part of the debate on NATO enlargement in the mid-1990s and probably will have to be addressed with each new enlargement step in the coming years. The NATO allies have told prospective candidates that the commitments they will receive as NATO members must be matched by their willingness to assume full responsibilities of membership. According to the NATO enlargement study released in September 1995, "New members will be full members of the Alliance, enjoying all the rights and assuming all the obligations under the Washington [North Atlantic] Treaty. There must be no 'second tier' security guarantees for members within the Alliance."[15] It could, of course, be argued that they already have second-tier status because the NATO allies have told Russia that they see no need to deploy nuclear weapons on the territory of new member states. In response, it could be argued that many current allies do not have nuclear weapons deployed on their territory (and there is no plan to deploy them there, either), yet they are not regarded as second tier. In terms of the responsibility of new members, the study noted that they "will be expected to support the concept of deterrence and the essential role nuclear weapons play in the Alliance's strategy of war prevention as set forth in the Strategic Concept."[16]

In practice, and as declared in the NATO enlargement study, NATO has no intention of deploying nuclear weapons on the territory of any new member state. In fact, any plan to station NATO nuclear weapons forward in central Europe would destroy NATO's attempt to demonstrate to Russia that enlargement is not contrary to Russian interests. The study specifically notes that "there is no *a priori* requirement for the stationing of nuclear weapons on the territory of new members." This is so because, according to the allies, "in light of both the current international environment and the potential threats facing the Alliance, NATO's current nuclear posture will, for the foreseeable future, continue to meet the requirements of an enlarged Alliance."[17]

In the debate on the first round of enlargement, when the Czech Republic, Hungary, and Poland joined the alliance, opponents raised an old question in a new format: they asked whether the United States would be willing to put Chicago at risk for the sake of Warsaw. This formulation echoed similar Cold War questioning of whether the United States would ultimately be willing to risk nuclear strikes on American cities in the cause of defending German cities from Soviet attack. To some extent, this argument reflects a residual Cold War threat assessment rather than current circumstances. Russia's present leaders and even their main political opponents appear to have no desire to return to military confrontation with the West, and even if they did, they would find it difficult or impossible to do so with available military and financial resources. This, of course, could change in the long run, forcing NATO and the United States to reexamine their strategy, forces, and nuclear commitments.

The contemporary reality, however, is that NATO strategy and force deployments in response to the new threat environment have fundamentally altered the circumstances under which the United States would be making decisions on the use of nuclear weapons. As noted earlier, during the Cold War, the strategy of flexible response, combined with the forward deployment in Germany of US nuclear weapons, suggested that the United States would have to make nuclear use decisions early in any conflict. The nuclear umbrella therefore appeared likely to be forced open in the case of a Warsaw Pact attack (even though the process would have required requests for nuclear use through the NATO command structure and political decisions by the president of the United States to employ the weapons).

Today, the nuclear umbrella is much less "automatic."[18] NATO strategy now suggests that "the circumstances in which any use of nuclear weapons might have to be contemplated by them are . . . extremely remote." This is not quite the same as calling them "weapons of last resort," as NATO had in 1991. But it surely means that the alliance does not now contemplate circumstances in which the use of nuclear weapons would come early in a conflict. Second, the fact that the United States has withdrawn all its militarily significant nuclear weapons from their forward deployments in Europe means that, in a crisis, the old "use 'em or lose 'em" formula would no longer apply.

Although nuclear weapons remain a central part of NATO's deterrence strategy, they no longer are on the front lines in that strategy. In fact, they currently play no direct role in the main threat to the interests of NATO country: terrorism. One might speculate, however, that if NATO countries continue to reduce their nonnuclear forces, defense of an enlarged NATO against some future threat could actually become more dependent on nuclear deterrence than it was in the past. This could particularly be true if terrorist groups or rogue states develop weapons of mass destruction and sophisticated ways of delivering them on US or European targets.

Reassuring Russia

One of the most difficult policy issues confronting the process of enlarging NATO, particularly to the Baltic states of Latvia, Lithuania, and Estonia, is the question of how to reassure Russia that a growing NATO does not diminish Russian security. The allies are faced with the challenging task of keeping their commitment to enlarge while avoiding a new confrontational relationship with Moscow. The issue is a very broad one that includes important political, psychological, security, and economic dimensions. But one key element relates to nuclear weapons.

Russian officials have expressed particular concern that NATO enlargement could lead to the deployment of nuclear weapons on Russia's borders. This complaint could be dismissed as, at best, a bargaining strategy to the extent that Russian defense officials and experts know that NATO has no nuclear-armed missiles or other nuclear weapons systems that it would want to deploy forward on European territory. As noted previously, there are even questions about the continued need for the United States to deploy the several hundred free-fall bombs on West European territory. However, this information may be well understood only among Russian defense specialists and not by average citizens or even many political leaders.

The Russian concern is one that the NATO countries continue to take seriously. The nuclear issue did not become a major question with Russia during the enlargement process that resulted in the Czech Republic, Hungary, and Poland joining NATO. However, it could become more prominent when NATO decides to invite one or more of the Baltic states to join the alliance. The fact is that deploying nuclear weapons on the territory of new member states would only create tension and instability in Europe and would not enhance the security of the host states. If admitted to NATO, their main defense against a future attack from Russia under current circumstances is the simple fact that they will be members of the European Union and allied to the United States in NATO, and Russia needs good relations with the United States and Europe to survive economically. This is a calculated risk but one that, on balance, seems sensible.

In 2002, Russian President Vladimir Putin appeared ready to accept, if not fully approve of, Baltic state membership in NATO. If this comes to pass with Putin's tacit acceptance, however, the Russians will expect some serious concessions in return. At a minimum, Putin will expect NATO to recognize Russia's importance and international standing in Moscow's new working relationship with NATO. Further, Putin undoubtedly hopes for economic concessions by the United States and the European Union as partial compensation. In addition, the allies will have to repeat emphatically their pledge to the Russians that, under current circumstances, the alliance has no intention of deploying nuclear weapons on the soil of any new member states. Beyond this, development of more intense cooperation with Russia on a wide range of issues would likely alleviate some of Moscow's concern. In addition to making the NATO–Russia dialogue more formal and meaningful, the allies might consider inviting Russia to participate in special sessions of the Nuclear Planning Group aimed at discussing nuclear nonproliferation, strategic stability, and related issues. In general, any measures to make the military aspects of the enlargement process more transparent could help mitigate legitimate Russian concerns.

It could be argued that such "concessions" to Moscow would create problems for Latvia, Lithuania, and Estonia, which want to enter NATO as full and equal partners with something more than a "paper promise" from the other allies concerning their future security. However, these three countries are likely to be more than satisfied simply to be members of NATO. In fact, their comfort level will likely increase to the extent that Russia's new relationship with the alliance ties Moscow even more intimately into a cooperative European security system.

The Role of British and French Nuclear Forces

Another important NATO nuclear issue is the role to be played by British and French nuclear forces. If Europe were sufficiently united to have common foreign and security policies, the French and British nuclear forces presumably would become instruments of those policies. In December 1991, the members of the European Community pledged at Maastricht, the Netherlands, to take additional steps toward foreign policy and defense cooperation The French and German governments formed the Eurocorps (along with Belgium, Spain, and Luxembourg) as the possible foundation for a future European military force. And at the end of the decade, the members of the European Union (EU) began establishing a Common

European Security and Defense Policy with decision-making institutions and deployable forces.

Despite the impressive scope of such commitments, however, the process of developing such cooperation may stretch out over many years, perhaps decades. The agreement among all the EU members to create a rapid intervention force of 60,000 troops, 400 aircraft, and 100 ships within the framework of a Common European Security and Defense Policy does not encompass nuclear weapons. Even though France has become more willing to identify its nuclear deterrent forces as a contribution to European rather than just French defense, Paris has yet to make specific commitments to its nonnuclear European partners. French President Chirac did renew the French offer to extend nuclear deterrence to its EU partners after the French government decided to resume nuclear testing in 1995.[19] Because the offer was made as part of the reaction to widespread European opposition to the French testing program, it was regarded cynically by most observers. Most of France's European partners saw the offer as designed simply to wrap the French testing decision in the protective garb of European unity. In any case, the strong outpouring of opposition to the French nuclear testing program clearly revealed profound differences among European nations about the role of nuclear weapons in the post–Cold War world.

A number of factors therefore suggest that there are sufficiently substantial differences between the nuclear and nonnuclear EU member states as to make extensive European-level nuclear cooperation unlikely in the near future. In fact, until the European allies develop much closer foreign and defense cooperation, and perhaps even after they do so, some sort of US nuclear link may still appear desirable for many European nations as a hedge against an uncertain future. The link to the United States might seem even more critical to those allies who are not members of the European Union.

Until recently, the very different British and French positions in NATO appeared to constrain development of Franco-British nuclear cooperation. Great Britain still sees its force within the framework of the alliance and participates fully in NATO's Nuclear Planning Group. French capabilities remain completely outside NATO. As France moves toward a more regularized relationship with NATO in other areas, NATO's adaptation process might lead to a closer French nuclear relationship with the alliance. A revision of the role and functioning of the Nuclear Planning Group as part of a more general reform of NATO to adjust to new political and military realities could open the way for France to join with other allies in Nuclear Planning Group consultations.

Germany's Nonnuclear Status

One of the major factors affecting attitudes toward NATO's nuclear strategy is the position of Germany. No government in Europe wants Germany to become a nuclear weapons power. For the past four decades, the US nuclear guarantee for Europe has served in lieu of a national German nuclear role. Germany apparently remains comfortable with the US guarantee and has not sought a "European" replacement for it despite past French suggestions that its nuclear force could serve as a nuclear umbrella for Germany. There is no indication that a united Germany has any desire to become a nuclear power, and it has reasserted the pledge made earlier by the Federal Republic of Germany to abstain from production or possession of atomic, biological, or chemical weapons.[20] The absence of a direct military threat to Europe suggests that there is even less reason today for a united Germany to aspire to nuclear power status than there was for the Federal Republic of Germany, which consistently denied any nuclear aspirations throughout the Cold War. Yet there are residual concerns among Germany's European neighbors that, without the US nuclear guarantee, Germany could aspire to nuclear status in the future.

Many European governments still see a continuing US military presence and role in Europe as additional reassurance that Germany will remain a nonnuclear power. European governments do not articulate this concern openly because they do not want to be seen as distrustful of Germany, which has made significant constructive contributions to the Atlantic alliance, as a leader for the process of European integration, and in relations with the East. This understood, it is not clear that the United States needs to keep nuclear weapons in Europe to reassure both Germany and its neighbors.

The Nuclear Commitment as a Source of US Influence

One reason the United States may continue to offer extended deterrence to its NATO allies and keep some nuclear weapons in Europe is to maximize the influence and ability of the United States to advance its interests in relations with European nations. There is no way of proving that the United States derives influence as a result of its military commitment in Europe. It seems logical, however, to suggest that as long as European nations want the United States to make a contribution to military security in Europe, they will take US interests and perspectives into account in their policy decisions. Whether or not the United States will derive influence based on the nuclear guarantee and a nuclear presence in Europe will therefore depend largely on how much European nations value this US contribution to their security.

In the past, some US critics of extended deterrence have argued that the United States risks much with the policy without receiving meaningful benefits in return. Now, as long as US relations with Russia continue to develop essentially along cooperative lines, the risks inherent in a US nuclear guarantee for NATO will be substantially lower than in the past. However, as noted previously, the greatly reduced military threat to Europe also diminishes the necessity for and value of a US nuclear commitment, and therefore presumably a nuclear commitment will yield less influence for the United States in the future than in the past.

ISSUES FOR THE FUTURE

If allied governments could avoid dealing with NATO nuclear strategy, they probably would do so, given all the sensitive political issues raised in such an undertaking. But they may not be able to pursue an avoidance strategy indefinitely.

It could be argued that the core of a new strategy already has been tentatively presented by NATO's suggestion in the early 1990s that nuclear weapons are weapons of last resort. Such a strategy would have much popular appeal to the extent that it suggested a much reduced reliance on nuclear weapons. But it might also have some unattractive aspects. For example, a last-resort strategy could suggest to a potential aggressor that it had much leeway to make military advances with nonnuclear weapons before NATO would call on its nuclear weapons in response. In addition, it can be argued that nuclear weapons might be helpful in deterring rogue state employment of chemical or biological weapons.

The allies therefore appear to face a basic question: Should they replace flexible response with a strategy that limits the role of nuclear weapons to a last resort, or should they develop a new approach that makes use of the potential deterrent value of nuclear weapons for threats short of a last-resort scenario? Such a strategy would leave open the possibility that the allies would respond to threats with defenses and weapons that are required to deter attacks at any level and defend against them if necessary. The main difference from flexible response would be that nuclear weapons would not be woven into the fabric of conventional defense forces, and there would be a much wider gap between nonnuclear military options and nuclear options.

Developing any new strategy would require a serious and focused discussion among the allies, particularly among those who are nuclear weapons states. Therefore, one task for the allies is to find a way to expand nuclear consultations to include France in a way that would enhance the potential for the United States, Britain, and France to work in concert when facing a military threat that might invoke the threat or use of nuclear forces.

This analysis gives rise to some central questions that might be asked relating to future US defense strategy, nuclear policy, and NATO enlargement:

1. What are the costs and benefits of maintaining a US extended nuclear guarantee for its European allies?
2. Is it necessary for the United States to deploy nuclear free-fall bombs, which are of questionable military utility, on European soil in order to maintain the credibility of the extended nuclear guarantee? Is such deployment useful to promote sharing of nuclear risks with allies?
3. Does the continued enlargement of NATO entail acceptable nuclear risks for the United States under current and foreseeable threat circumstances?

4. What can or should the United States and the NATO allies do to try to reassure Russia that further NATO enlargement will not increase nuclear risks to Moscow?
5. What are the costs and benefits of potential French participation in NATO nuclear consultations? Is there potential for a European nuclear deterrent within NATO that might obviate the need for the United States to station nuclear weapons in Europe?
6. What changes in the structure and procedures of the Nuclear Planning Group might be required to involve France routinely in the work of the group? Include Russia in periodic consultations with the group?

NATO nuclear strategy per se is not generally seen to be an urgent issue for NATO or for the United States. But these questions suggest that some difficult issues of nuclear strategy and consultations may have to be addressed in the context of the dual processes of enlargement and adaptation of NATO that will continue well into this decade.

MISSILE DEFENSE

Perhaps the most difficult "nuclear" question the allies will face in the years immediately ahead will be how to adapt to the reality that the United States, having abandoned the Anti-Ballistic Missile (ABM) Treaty with Russia, is creating a new strategic environment by embarking on an ambitious program to develop and deploy antiballistic missile systems. The Bush administration has said that it does not aim to develop a "star wars" system capable of defending all US territory against an all-out nuclear attack. In fact, it says that it is not intent on deploying a "national missile defense" but rather a missile defense system capable of protecting US territory, deployed forces, and both allies and friends against limited ballistic missile attacks mounted by rogue states or terrorist organizations. The administration added protection of allies and friends to the equation to respond to European concerns that a US missile defense system would create unequal zones of security and effectively divide the alliance into a vulnerable Europe and a protected United States.

Despite the reassurances by the Bush administration, many questions remain open. Divergent US and European positions regarding the 1972 ABM Treaty have complicated the transatlantic dialogue on the issue. The Bush administration has argued, with good reason, that continuing to base relations with a post–Cold War Russia on premises and agreements that governed relations with a Cold War Soviet Union will not lead to new, constructive ties. They saw the ABM Treaty as a relic of the Cold War. Moreover, the treaty blocked the testing the United States deemed necessary to develop critical missile defense capabilities.

Europeans accept that relations with Russia need to be set on new ground but generally believe that treaties such as the ABM accord still help shape a framework of stability that should not be thrown away lightly. The US announcement in December 2001 that it would withdraw from the ABM Treaty forced the issue with both Russia and the European allies. On May 24, 2002, Presidents Bush and Putin signed a new strategic nuclear arms reduction treaty confirming the large reductions they had agreed to when they met in November 2001. The two leaders also signed a declaration on US–Russian cooperation, including collaboration on the missile defense issue. The treaty and declaration mitigated European fears that voiding the ABM Treaty would undercut friendly relations with Russia. Nonetheless, most Europeans—as well as many Americans—remained seriously concerned about the strategic implications, feasibility, and costs of Bush's missile defense plans.

The sharing of burdens in the alliance has never been as successful as the original bargain intended, and the missile defense issue illustrates that there is no perfect formula for the sharing of vulnerability to threats. However, both burdens and vulnerabilities will have to remain in tolerable balance between the United States and Europe, or the partners to the transatlantic bargain will drift toward separation and possibly divorce. Therefore, the manner in which the missile defense issue is managed could have profound implications for the future of the transatlantic bargain.

NOTES

1. This discussion is based on my chapter in *Controlling Non-Strategic Nuclear Weapons: Obstacles and Opportunities,* ed. Jeffrey A. Larsen and Kurt J. Klingenberger (Colorado Springs, Colo.: USAF Institute for National Security Studies, 2001).

2. North Atlantic Treaty Organization, "London Declaration on a Transformed North Atlantic Alliance, Issued by the Heads of State and Government Participating in the Meeting of the North Atlantic Council in London on 5–6 July 1990" (printed in *NATO Review* 38, no. 4 [August 1990]: 32–33).

3. North Atlantic Treaty Organization, "The Alliance's New Strategic Concept, Agreed by the Heads of State and Government Participating in the Meeting of the North Atlantic Council in Rome on 7–8 November 1991" (printed in *NATO Review* 39, no. 6 [December 1991]: 25–32).

4. For recent status, see "NRDC Nuclear Notebook, 2002," *Bulletin of Atomic Scientists,* July/August 2002, 71–73.

5. Mitterrand was speaking at a meeting in Paris on January 10, 1992, as reported by *Atlantic News,* no. 2387, January 14, 1992, 4.

6. Many Europeans looked skeptically on the French offer as an effort to deflect criticism of France's nuclear testing program.

7. M-DPC/NPG 1(96)88, Meeting of the Defense Planning Committee in Ministerial Session, Brussels, June 13, 1996.

8. "The Alliance's Strategic Concept, Approved by the Heads of State and Government Participating in the Meeting of the North Atlantic Council in Washington D.C. on 23rd and 24th April 1999" (NATO press release NAC-S[99]65).

9. See the description of these withdrawals in William M. Arkin, Robert S. Norris, and Joshua Handler, *Taking Stock: Worldwide Nuclear Deployments 1998* (Washington, D.C.: Natural Resources Defense Council, March 1998), 8–9; for a summary of current US deployments, see *Taking Stock,* 24.

10. "US Nuclear Weapon Locations, 1995" (citing the "Nuclear Notebook" prepared by Robert S. Norris and William M. Arkin for the Natural Resources Defense Council in *The Bulletin of the Atomic Scientists,* November/December 1995, 74).

11. For an assessment of the military and political utility of these deployments, see the section "What Role for Residual US Nuclear Weapons in Europe?" later in this chapter.

12. For an analysis of the role of nuclear weapons in US military strategy and foreign policy in the post–Cold War era, see Jan Lodal, *The Price of Dominance: The New Weapons of Mass Destruction and Their Challenge to American Leadership* (New York: Council on Foreign Relations Press, 2001), and the review of Lodal's book by Robert Jervis, "Weapons without Purpose? Nuclear Strategy in the Post–Cold War Era," *Foreign Affairs,* July/August 2001, 143–48.

13. The argument has been made, for example, by Thomas-Durell Young, who proposes that the United States, France, and the United Kingdom cooperate to develop a tactical air-to-surface missile (a "tripartite TASM") to provide a "state-of-the-art" air-delivered nuclear capability for NATO countries. Thomas-Durell Young, "NATO's Substrategic Nuclear Forces and Strategy: Where Do We Go from Here?" Strategic Studies Institute, US Army War College, Carlisle Barracks, Pennsylvania, January 13, 1992.

14. "Nuclear Weapons and European Security" (policy paper, Atlantic Council of the United States, April 1996), 3.

15. North Atlantic Treaty Organization, "Study on Enlargement," September 1995, chap. 5, para. 68.

16. North Atlantic Treaty Organization, "Study on Enlargement," para. 45, d.

17. North Atlantic Treaty Organization, "Study on Enlargement," chap. 4, B, iv, para. 58.

18. Larry Chalmer, director of the NATO Staff Officer Orientation course at the US National Defense University, has drawn the image out a little further, arguing that the nuclear umbrella, which was virtually automatic during the Cold War, has become more of a manual opening umbrella in post–Cold War circumstances.

19. President Chirac announced on June 13, 1995, that France would conduct eight underground nuclear tests between September 1995 and May 1996 to ensure the security and reliability of its nuclear weapons and programs.

20. The Treaty on the Final Settlement with Respect to Germany, known as the "2+4 Treaty," reaffirmed Germany's renunciation of the manufacture and possession of nuclear, biological, and chemical weapons as well as Germany's commitment to the Treaty on the Non-Proliferation of Nuclear Weapons. Germany agreed not to deploy nuclear weapons or foreign forces on that part of united Germany that used to be the German Democratic Republic.

NATO Outreach and Enlargement: The Legacy of Harmel

Particularly after NATO adopted the Harmel Report in 1967, NATO actively sought to promote dialogue and cooperation with the Soviet Union and its Warsaw Pact allies. The goal was to try to overcome the East–West division in Europe and prevent the war for which NATO nonetheless continued to prepare. This commitment to détente (discussed in chapter 4) led the allies to join with the Warsaw Pact and other European countries in 1972 to begin preparations for the Conference on Security and Cooperation in Europe (CSCE) and to open East–West talks on Mutual and Balanced Force Reductions (MBFR) in 1973. It provided the underlying political rationale for negotiations with Moscow on Intermediate Range Nuclear Forces (INF), which opened in 1985.

The CSCE, originally proposed by the Soviet Union to win recognition of the European status quo, was used by the West to promote human rights and other fundamental principles that should govern the behavior of states—in relations with their own peoples as well as with other states. The Helsinki Process, as the CSCE forum was called, was widely credited with legitimizing human rights groups in Eastern Europe and weakening the hold of communist regimes on those countries. The CSCE process also included negotiations on confidence-building and stabilizing measures. In 1986, these talks resulted in an agreement signed in Stockholm, Sweden, on Confidence and Security Building Measures and Disarmament. The MBFR talks, after many years of stalemate, were converted into negotiations on Conventional Forces in Europe, which yielded an agreement limiting conventional armaments and forces in Europe just as the Cold War was ending in 1990. The INF negotiations resulted in an agreement to eliminate Intermediate Range Nuclear Forces from Europe in 1987.

NATO's active pursuit of détente through arms control negotiations and security cooperation initiatives in the 1970s and 1980s demonstrated that the allies were prepared to take diplomatic steps to reduce the chance of war even if Warsaw

Pact military strength required NATO to maintain a credible defense and deterrence posture. Some political conservatives in the United States doubted the relevance or utility of NATO's détente role, seeing it as useful mainly as a palliative for the left in Europe. Meanwhile, some on the left in Europe saw NATO's détente role as a political sham, designed for show but not likely to help overcome Europe's division. Seen at some distance more than a decade after the end of the Cold War, it appears that a combination of allied détente, deterrence, and defense policies contributed to the events that culminated in the end of the Cold War, the dissolution of the Warsaw Pact, and the disintegration of the Soviet Union. Meanwhile, the Harmel formula provided a sufficiently broad rationale for NATO to sustain the alliance before public opinion in Europe and in the United States, even if the formula was not highly valued by those on the political extremes on either side of the Atlantic.

It therefore was not a desperate or illogical step for the NATO allies in the first years of the post–Cold War period to adopt a new version of the Harmel concept to adapt to the radically new circumstances that had emerged in just a matter of months. In so doing, the NATO allies began the process of engineering another fundamental adjustment to the transatlantic bargain, extending the bargain's reach to include potentially all of democratic Europe.

FROM THE CSCE TO THE OSCE

One of the first necessities was to adapt the CSCE, shaped as it was by Cold War conditions, to the new circumstances in Europe. The CSCE had played an important role in the Cold War, helping regulate relations among European states and also keeping up a human rights critique of Soviet and East European communist regimes. The Helsinki Final Act, signed by all these states in 1975, was not legally binding on the participants. But the Final Act provided the "rules of the road" for interstate relations in Europe and constructive guidelines for the development of democracy in all European countries.

At their meeting in London in July 1990, NATO leaders had agreed that one of their goals was to strengthen the CSCE as one of the critical supports for European peace and stability. NATO reasserted this approach at its summit in Rome in November 1991. As an important token of NATO's intentions, a NATO summit meeting in Oslo, Norway, in June 1992 agreed that, on a case-by-case basis, NATO would support peacekeeping operations initiated by the CSCE. Subsequently, NATO called for strengthening the CSCE's ability to prevent conflicts, manage crises, and settle disputes peacefully.

The key to the CSCE's ability to take on an expanded operational mandate was resources. As a "process," the CSCE had only an ad hoc structure that was not capable of supporting a more ambitious role. In December 1994, a CSCE summit meeting agreed to turn the process into an organization—hence the name change to the Organization for Security and Cooperation in Europe (OSCE) and the decision to provide staff and financial resources so that the OSCE could send missions into European nations to mediate disputes, monitor elections, and conduct other activities designed to prevent conflict.

By the end of the 1990s, NATO and the OSCE were working hand in hand to deal with potential threats to peace. In Bosnia, the OSCE played a critical role in helping to establish a process of free elections and respect for human rights. NATO provided the military presence to give such efforts a chance to succeed. OSCE monitors and mediators played important roles in helping to resolve conflicts and build democracy from Abkhazia and Tajikistan to South Ossetia and Ukraine. The relationship between NATO and the OSCE became one of the key ingredients in an evolving cooperative European security system.

WRAPPING UP COLD WAR CONVENTIONAL ARMS NEGOTIATIONS

In 1990, negotiations aimed at cutting nonnuclear forces in Europe, which had begun in 1973 as MBFR talks, concluded with the Treaty on Conventional Armed Forces in Europe (CFE). This landmark agreement produced reductions and controls on nonnuclear military forces from the Atlantic Ocean in the west to the Ural Mountains in the Soviet Union.

The CFE Treaty of November 19, 1990, is the most comprehensive, legally binding agreement on conventional arms control ever produced. Its goal, now largely accomplished, was to reduce imbalances in the numbers of major conventional weapon systems in Europe to eliminate the potential for surprise attack or large-scale offensive operations. Since the treaty entered into force on November 9, 1992, some 60,000 battle tanks, armored combat vehicles, artillery pieces, attack helicopters, and combat aircraft have been removed from the area and destroyed.

Perhaps the CFE Treaty's biggest accomplishment has been its contribution to transparency—making all military establishments and forces more visible to all other states. The treaty's required declarations of information and inspection procedures help reduce concern about intentions and capabilities of neighboring states. It would be very difficult to hide any significant military capabilities in today's system of military relations in Europe, in part because of the provisions of the treaty.

Throughout the 1990s, the countries that signed the CFE Treaty worked to adapt the treaty to the new security conditions in Europe. This was a difficult process, as the treaty was originally developed in a framework provided by two opposing alliance systems and subsequently had to reflect the reality of an evolving system of cooperative security in Europe. At the same time, the adaptation had to take into account special concerns of states located on the southern and northern flanks of Europe. An adapted version of the treaty was negotiated in 1999 but has not been ratified because Russia remains outside the limits on forces that it can maintain on its flanks. The overage is relatively small and apparently is related to Russia's perceived need for continued military action against rebel activity in Chechnya. According to one source,

> Within its borders, Russia is abiding by its overall CFE Treaty limits but it continues to deploy tanks and ACVs [armored combat vehicles] above sub-limits that cap its weapons deployments in its northern and southern regions, according to data from a recent treaty information exchange. The Kremlin claims its non-compliance is necessary to combat "terrorism" in Chechnya.[1]

Despite Russia's failure to come fully into compliance with the treaty, it remains a keystone of the European security system. Its provisions run in close parallel with cooperation in the OSCE, being intended also to promote transparency and stability through annual exchanges of information on military forces, random verification inspections, and the presence of observers at military exercises. It can be hoped that, over the long run, the process of military cooperation that cuts across all former Cold War lines will make arms control arrangements among European states unnecessary. Until that comes to pass, the adapted CFE Treaty is likely to remain an essential part of the foundation on which the future European security system is being built.

DIALOGUE AND COOPERATION AS A NEW MISSION

As democratic governments emerged from the shadow of communism in Eastern and central Europe at the end of the Cold War, many of the new democracies sought membership in NATO as one of their main national goals. The NATO countries approached these desires carefully, offering the new democracies friendship and cooperation but not initially membership.

In July 1991, the Warsaw Pact was dissolved, leaving NATO standing but still in need of greater clarity concerning its future relationship with former members of the Pact. NATO took the first formal step in the November 1991 Rome Declaration, inviting former Warsaw Pact members to join in a more structured relationship of "consultation and cooperation on political and security issues." They created the North Atlantic Cooperation Council (NACC) and invited the foreign ministers of the former Pact countries to the first meeting of the new council in December 1991. When the Soviet Union was dissolved in the same month, the NATO countries immediately invited Russia to join the NACC, and Russia became one of the founding members. The main goal of the NACC was to serve as a forum for dialogue between NATO members and nonmember states on a wide range of security topics.[2] Sixteen NATO members and twenty-two former Warsaw Pact members and former Soviet republics participated in the new body.

The NACC represented a major statement of intent by the allies. They said, in effect, that NATO was not going to remain an exclusive club. Although the allies at that point were reluctant to envision offering NATO membership to former

Warsaw Pact members, the creation of the NACC opened the door to the future. The East European leaders who wanted their countries to join NATO saw the NACC as totally inadequate for their needs, but they accepted the first move and immediately began working for more.[3]

The NACC was essentially the brainchild of President George Bush's administration in the United States. President Bush and his foreign policy team had played a major role in the process of negotiating German reunification and ensuring that a united Germany would remain a member of NATO. German reunification in effect represented the first expansion of NATO in the post–Cold War era and the first since Spain had been admitted in 1982.

In addition, President Bush made a major contribution to the process of winding down the Cold War by declaring substantial unilateral US reductions in its short-range nuclear forces (discussed in chapter 7). At the same time, Bush developed and maintained a sympathetic working relationship with Soviet President Mikhail Gorbachev, helping support the transition to a postcommunist political system in Russia after the Soviet Union was dissolved.

In 1990, neither the Bush administration nor any of the European allies were prepared to signal public acceptance of the possibility that countries that had just left the Warsaw Pact might in the near future become members of NATO. After all, in 1990 the question was whether NATO remained necessary, not whether its membership should be expanded. Moreover, most European governments, as well as President Bush, were focused primarily on how to ensure that the transition in the Soviet Union and then in Russia would confirm the end of the Cold War and not lead to a new one.

Nevertheless, toward the end of the Bush presidency, senior administration officials began acknowledging that the desires of East European governments to join NATO were indeed legitimate. Late in 1992, after Bill Clinton had beaten George Bush in the presidential elections, both Secretary of Defense Richard Cheney and Secretary of State Lawrence Eagleburger suggested that the process of opening up NATO that had begun with the NACC could lead toward NATO membership for some NACC partners.[4]

The advent of the Clinton administration was to bring new and dramatic developments to the process of NATO outreach. The Bush administration had put the process on track but had not had time to move beyond the relatively limited and "easy" NACC initiative.

FROM PARTNERSHIP TO MEMBERSHIP

When President Bill Clinton came to office in January 1993, the administration took over without a clear line on the issue of NATO enlargement. Its top priority was the economy, following the political rhetoric ("it's the economy stupid") that had helped pave Clinton's way to the presidency. In the administration's first year,

Europe was seen mainly as a problem: the source of economic competition for the United States and the locale for a bloody conflict in Bosnia that would not go away.

However, one of the important rituals for any new US president is the first NATO summit. Officials in charge of preparations for President Clinton's inaugural NATO summit, scheduled for January 1994, were not of one mind on NATO's future in general and on enlargement in particular. One high-level National Security Council staffer, Jenonne Walker, had written in 1990 that the United States should pull all its troops out of Europe as an incentive for the Soviet Union to withdraw from Eastern Europe.[5] This official was skeptical that the Clinton administration should promote NATO enlargement and had the task of chairing the initial interdepartmental review of the issue. Strobe Talbot, a close personal friend of the president and leading Russian expert at the Department of State, was concerned that moving too quickly on enlargement would sour prospects for reform in Russia. At the Pentagon, Secretary of Defense Les Aspin and his top officials, including Deputy Assistant Secretary of Defense Joseph Kruzel, were skeptical that the United States and NATO should take on the potential burdens of preparing countries for NATO membership that were so far from meeting NATO military standards.

However, as James M. Goldgeier has documented, two key officials leaned in favor of enlargement: National Security Adviser Tony Lake and President Clinton himself.[6] Clinton had not spent much time or energy on foreign policy issues in the campaign, but one of his campaign themes had emphasized that US foreign policy should be focused on "enlarging" the democratic and free-market area in the post–Cold War world. Both he and Lake apparently came to believe that NATO enlargement would directly serve this end. This approach made Clinton ripe for the message from the new democracies in central Europe, a message that he heard loud and clear when he met with several central European leaders, including Poland's Lech Walesa and the Czech Republic's Vaclav Havel, at the opening of the US Holocaust Memorial Museum in Washington, D.C., on April 21, 1993. Clinton subsequently reflected on the meeting, saying, "When they came here a few weeks ago for the Holocaust dedication, every one of those presidents said that their number one priority was to get into NATO. They know it will provide a security umbrella for the people who are members."

From the Holocaust meetings on, Clinton had an emotional as well as philosophical predisposition toward enlarging NATO.[7] And even if other administration officials favoring enlargement had geostrategic rationales for the move, such as hedging against future Russian power and ensuring continued US prominence in European security affairs, it was the value-based rationale that would tip the balance in convincing the public and members of the US Congress that NATO enlargement was in the US interest.

Even as official policy largely favored deferring a decision on enlargement at the January 1994 summit, some administration officials and others outside the

administration were putting together a case for moving ahead. In an assessment for Congress at the end of 1992, I noted the logic of the case for enlargement, writing,

> How can the existing members of Western institutions, who have throughout the
> Cold War touted the western system, now deny participation in the system to coun-
> tries that choose democracy, to convert to free market economic systems, respect
> human rights, and pursue peaceful relations with their neighbors? This suggests the
> need for creative and flexible attitudes toward countries making credible efforts to
> meet the criteria for membership.[8]

And in a statement to a special committee of the North Atlantic Assembly in January 1993, he added that "Poland, Hungary and the Czech Republic deserve
serious consideration for NATO membership in the near future."[9]

In Europe, German Minister of Defense Volker Rühe became the most out-
spoken official European proponent of enlargement.[10] Early in 1993, he organized
a small conference of US and European experts designed to provide ammunition
for his position on Europe's future (at the time, Rühe was considered not only a
leading official expert on defense but also a potential candidate for the chancel-
lorship). The conference outside Bonn, Germany, provided some of the initial
foundations for Rühe's enlargement position.[11] To augment his resources, Rühe
contracted the services of a team from the well-respected US think tank Rand.
The Rand analysts—Ronald Asmus, F. Stephen Larrabee, and Richard Kugler—
had been developing an advocacy of enlargement based on work they were doing
under a contract with the US Army and Air Force. In June 1993, Rühe and the
Rand analysts were joined by Republican Senator Richard Lugar (R-Ind.), who became the most forceful of US official proponents of enlargement, arguing for early
consideration of the membership desires of Poland, Hungary, and the Czech Republic. The Rand team published a major statement of the case for enlargement
in the fall of 1993, providing a key reference point for the coming enlargement debate.[12] Senator Lugar remained a strong supporter of NATO and of enlargement,
even though his cool relationship with Senate Foreign Relations Committee
Chairman Jesse Helms prevented Lugar from playing a formal role in the process.

These proponents of enlargement were in a minority in Europe as well as in the
United States, but they were not alone. While most of the US foreign policy bureaucracy was working on finessing the enlargement issue at the January 1994
summit, others, including Lynn Davis, undersecretary for arms control and international security affairs, and two key staffers on the Department of State policy
planning staff—Stephen Flanagan and Hans Binnendijk—were developing the
case for moving enlargement ahead. Both Flanagan and Binnendijk had leaned
forward on enlargement in the early 1990s; Davis had close ties to the work of the
Rand team.

However, the ship of state changes directions slowly, and the weight of thinking in the bureaucracy and even among the majority of policy-level officials was to continue to develop ties to the new democracies but to defer the more difficult and demanding enlargement issue. As the administration prepared for President Clinton's first NATO summit meeting, the more cautious approach dominated. Secretary of State Warren Christopher observed that NATO enlargement, while possible down the road, was currently "not on the agenda." Deputy Secretary of State Strobe Talbot, with his focus on facilitating Russia's transition to democracy and free markets, reinforced the secretary's cautious inclination.

Meanwhile, US civilian and military officials were searching for a concept to serve as the centerpiece for NATO outreach activities. The concept that developed in collaboration between General John Shalikashvili (the Supreme Allied Commander, Europe), his staff, and senior Pentagon officials, particularly Deputy Secretary of Defense Joseph Kruzel,[13] was premised on the need for aspiring members to meet certain political and military criteria before being considered for membership. The second assumption was that NATO should help such countries become producers, not just consumers, of security. The end result of this thinking was the proposal for the Partnership for Peace (PFP).

The PFP concept was a policymaker's dream. It signaled to those who aspired to NATO membership that they had been heard. Yet it made no commitment concerning the future. Perhaps most crucial, it bought time. It avoided destabilizing relations with Russia at a perilous moment in that country's post-Soviet development. It (temporarily) bridged differences between those in the US administration who favored enlargement and those who were skeptical.

The PFP initiative also served some practical needs. Countries that wanted to join NATO could not expect to do so until they had begun to adapt old Warsaw Pact military systems and habits to those of NATO. Partnership would provide a channel for US and other NATO assistance to aspiring members. And the PFP would serve as a vehicle for aspirants to make contributions to NATO's new role as a regional peacekeeping instrument, potentially spreading burdens among NATO and non-NATO countries.

On the negative side, PFP clearly would not be the end of the story. The central European democracies recognized that, although active engagement in PFP was essential to their longer-term goal of NATO membership, it could also serve as a long-term excuse for NATO to postpone serious consideration of their membership objective (hence the occasionally heard derogatory references to PFP as a "Policy for Postponement"). In addition, as experience would come to show, under PFP scrutiny of their defense reform and modernization, shortcomings could not be as easily hidden from their publics or from NATO members.

The Cooperation Track

In any case, at the NATO summit meeting in Brussels in January 1994, allied leaders endorsed the PFP program to give countries that wished to develop a detailed cooperative relationship with NATO the opportunity to do so. The program would provide the possibility for nonmember military leaders and forces to interact with and learn from NATO militaries. This created a formal framework for the development of NATO military outreach activities and, incidentally, began to shape a new mission for NATO military forces. The PFP was destined to become a successful program in its own right, helping reform regimes in central and Eastern Europe accelerate the process of democratization as well as to become NATO compatible.

Because these countries were at a variety of stages of political, economic, and military evolution, US and allied officials knew that a program of association with NATO would have to be sufficiently flexible to accommodate such diversity. The NACC already had provided a forum in which such countries could discuss military security issues with NATO allies. The PFP added a way for individual countries to tailor their relationship with NATO to meet their national needs and circumstances.

The PFP sought initially to promote greater transparency in national defense planning and budgeting as a way of building confidence in the peaceful intentions of all participants. It also aimed to encourage effective democratic control of defense forces; to help develop each partner as a potential contributor to NATO-led peacekeeping, search-and-rescue, or humanitarian missions; and to enhance the ability of partners' military forces to operate with NATO units. Each partner was invited to identify the extent and intensity of cooperation it wished to develop within the broad agenda of the program.

Since 1994, some twenty-nine countries have become PFP partners—three graduated to the status of NATO membership in 1999, and more will do so in the future. Some partners see their participation as a road to NATO membership. The Czech Republic, Hungary, and Poland all used their PFP involvement constructively as a way to strengthen their bid for membership. Other partners simply see participation in PFP as a unique and important way of contributing to peace and security in Europe.

In mid-1997, the allies decided to add some new and important elements to the PFP agenda to "enhance" the program. When the Clinton administration proposed the PFP, it could not decide what to do with the NACC, even though it could logically have served as a communal consultative forum to complement the more individualized partnership program. (NATO officials observed that the Clinton administration, perhaps in a "not invented here" mode, wanted to ensure that the focus was on the PFP, not on the NACC, which Clinton officials saw as a Bush administration initiative.[14]) The PFP and the NACC existed in parallel but mostly-separate worlds until the Clinton administration proposed replacing NACC with the Euro-Atlantic Partnership Council (EAPC). The EAPC was formally established by the foreign ministers of NATO and partner nations when they met in Sintra, Portugal, in May 1997.

Also at Sintra, the allies gave partners a much stronger role in developing and deciding on PFP programs. They created the concept of partnership "cells," or units made up of partner military and civilian officials working hand in hand with NATO international and member-state officials. A special Partnership Coordination Cell was established in Mons, Belgium, where NATO's top European command is located, to coordinate activities directly with the Supreme Allied Commander, Europe, and his staff. Through the new Planning and Review Process, partner countries that were making contributions to NATO operations, such as those in Kosovo and Bosnia-Herzegovina, could participate more actively in planning and overseeing conduct of such operations. As a result of these changes, the PFP became an important part of the evolving cooperative European security system, even if it was seen as a transitional device by many of its participants.

The EAPC continued as a forum that brought together all NATO allies with all partner countries. The EAPC had forty-five members in 2002. The purpose of the EAPC was to serve as the overarching framework for political and security-related consultations and enhanced cooperation under the PFP program. This framework was designed to provide partners the opportunity to develop a direct political relationship with the alliance. It also gave partner governments the chance to participate in decisions related to activities involving NATO and partner nations.

The EAPC meets twice a year at both foreign and defense minister levels and on a more routine basis at the ambassadorial level monthly in Brussels. The EAPC originally adopted the NACC Work Plan for Dialogue, Partnership and Cooperation, which included regular consultations on political and security-related matters, and then enlarged and adapted that agenda. Consultations came to include a wide range of topics, such as crisis management issues; regional matters; arms control issues; nuclear, biological, and chemical weapons proliferation; international terrorism; defense planning and budgets; defense policy and strategy; and security implications of economic developments. In addition, the agenda covered consultations and cooperation on emergency and disaster preparedness, armaments cooperation, nuclear safety, defense-related environmental issues, civil–military coordination of air traffic management and control, scientific cooperation, and issues related to peace support operations.

In recent years, the EAPC has been used as a forum for discussions among the allies and partner countries about the situation in the former Yugoslavia, including developments in Bosnia and Herzegovina and the crises in Kosovo and Macedonia. Under the auspices of the EAPC, a Euro-Atlantic Disaster Response Coordination Center was created in the spring of 1998.

Both allies and partners alike regard the EAPC as an important token of NATO's commitment to openness, cooperation, and extending the benefits of peace and stability to all European nations. However, given the large EAPC membership, formal meetings have consisted largely of set-piece statements by participating governments. This has provided an opportunity for participants to put their national positions on the record but hardly a chance for discussion and dialogue. As with many other international organizations, those opportunities come as part of the "corridor" conversations and informal meetings on the margins of the routine EAPC sessions. The EAPC as an institution, therefore, has played an important informal role but has not become an important factor in NATO's decision-making process.

In recognition of their special significance and special circumstances, two countries—Russia and Ukraine—were given additional opportunities for partnership and dialogue with NATO. As noted earlier, when the Soviet Union was dissolved in December 1991, the NATO countries set the goal of developing a partnership with Russia, the primary successor state to the former Soviet Union. Russia became a founding member of the NACC, and the partnership became more formal when Russia and NATO agreed in June 1994 to develop a "broad, enhanced dialogue and cooperation."

The NATO–Russia relationship was further strengthened in January 1996 when Russian forces joined NATO troops in the Implementation Force, organized to implement the military aspects of the Peace Agreement in Bosnia-Herzegovina. They remain in Bosnia today as part of NATO's Stabilization Force, and Russia contributes forces to the NATO presence in Kosovo.

Despite the generally positive development of cooperation, the issue of NATO enlargement troubled the relationship. In response to the strong desires of new democracies in central and Eastern Europe to join NATO, the allies agreed in December 1994 to study the "why and how" of NATO enlargement. Most Russians viewed this and subsequent steps toward enlargement as a threat to Russian prestige or at least as NATO rubbing salt in Russia's open wounds.

Russia's negative attitude toward NATO enlargement reflected feelings about the alliance that had been reinforced by four decades of Soviet propaganda. Even sophisticated Russians found it difficult to understand the fundamental differences between NATO, a voluntary alliance among independent countries, and the Warsaw Pact, where membership was imposed by the Soviet Union. Expansion of NATO's role and membership meant that US power and influence would stretch ever closer to Russia's borders, displacing what had been Soviet/Russian zones of influence in central and Eastern Europe. Some Russian officials believed that when Moscow agreed to facilitate German reunification, the Soviet Union had been promised that NATO would not expand up to its borders—a claim rejected by Bush administration officials who represented the United States in the negotiations.[15] The Russian perception may help explain Moscow's strong reaction to NATO's enlargement plans. The bottom line, of course, was that even if the negotiations led the Russians to such a conclusion, no such commitment was ever made formal.

The NATO allies decided that it was important to respond to the enthusiastic desire of the new democracies to join NATO while at the same time trying to overcome Russian opposition with a cooperative embrace. NATO's attempt to reassure the Russians took several forms. The NATO allies pledged that they had "no intention, no plan, and no reason" to deploy nuclear weapons on the territory of new members. They also said that they planned no permanent, substantial deployments of NATO soldiers in any new member states. Perhaps most important, the allies authorized NATO Secretary-General Javier Solana, acting on behalf of the member states, to negotiate a more permanent cooperative relationship with Russia. Those negotiations, guided by Strobe Talbott and other US officials, resulted in the Founding Act on Mutual Relations, Cooperation and Security between NATO and the Russia Federation, signed in Paris in May 1997 just before NATO announced its decision to invite three former Warsaw Pact nations to join NATO.

The Founding Act set a large agenda of topics on which NATO and Russia would attempt to collaborate. It created a Permanent Joint Council (NATO nations plus Russia) as a framework for continuing consultations. Creating this channel for communications was an important step, but there were limits on its effectiveness. From the beginning, there was a tension between the Russian desire to use the forum to "participate in" NATO decision making while the NATO allies sought to ensure that the Permanent Joint Council remained a place for consultations and not co–decision making. In 2001, following the terrorist attacks on the United States and Russian support for the war on terrorism, NATO and Russia moved toward a new relationship that would give Russia a "vote" on some issues that NATO decided to handle jointly with Moscow (see chapter 10 for further discussion of this issue).

NATO's relationship with the next most significant independent country formed by a former Soviet republic, Ukraine, has been of an entirely different character than that with Russia. Ukraine gave up the nuclear weapons deployed on its territory by the Soviet Union in return for Western financial assistance and the tacit promise of acceptance into the Western community of nations. By the mid-1990s, many in the Ukraine elite quietly aspired to eventual membership in both NATO and the European Union (EU). However, political divisions in the country called for a cautious approach. Ukraine did not ask to be considered for NATO membership but strongly supported the process of NATO enlargement. The NATO allies responded to Ukraine's aspirations at their summit meeting in Madrid in July 1997, agreeing with Ukraine on a Ukraine–NATO Charter on Distinctive Partnership, establishing an intensified consultative and cooperative relationship between NATO and Ukraine.[16] In subsequent years, Russia worked hard to ensure its future political and economic influence in Ukraine, leaving Ukraine's future orientation and role in Europe open to question.

The Enlargement Track

NATO has expended considerable time and energy developing or supporting a variety of cooperative security arrangements in its relations with nonmembers. But the membership track of NATO's outreach program generated the greatest controversy. Although the January 1994 Brussels summit deferred decisions on enlargement and put the PFP forward as the most recent outreach vehicle, the allies did agree to keep the membership door open.

The drafters of the North Atlantic Treaty in 1949 anticipated that other European states might subsequently wish to join the alliance. The Treaty's Article 10 said that the allies may, "by unanimous agreement, invite any other European state in a position to further the principles of this Treaty and to contribute to the security of the North Atlantic area to accede to this Treaty." The twelve original members were, over the years, joined by Greece and Turkey, Germany, and then Spain.

At the NATO summit meeting in Brussels in January 1994, allied leaders said that the commitment in Article 10 would be honored and that NATO's door would be opened to qualified candidates. The allies began a study in December 1994 of the "why and how" of NATO enlargement.

More important, President Clinton left the Brussels summit apparently ready to move on to the next step, even as those who favored a go-slow approach were reassured that the PFP would buy time and defer tough decisions on enlargement. On a visit to Warsaw in July 1994, in an interview with Polish television, Clinton pushed the issue further down the road, saying,

> I want to make it clear that, in my view, NATO will be expanded, that it should be expanded, and that it should be expanded as a way of strengthening security and not conditioned on events in any other country or some new threat arising to NATO. . . . I think that a timetable should be developed, but I can't do that alone.[17]

Clinton's comments affirmed that NATO should be enlarged because it was the right thing to do. The Warsaw remarks were taken by proenlargement officials in Washington as a green light to move ahead.

According to Goldgeier, a number of factors combined to get enlargement on track inside the US administration. These included the appointment as assistant secretary of state for European and Canadian affairs of Richard Holbrooke, who had become an enlargement believer during his time as US ambassador to Germany; the shift of Strobe Talbot from enlargement skeptic to enlargement supporter; and the appointment of several enlargement enthusiasts to key positions on the National Security Council staff, including Alexander (Sandy) Vershbow to direct European affairs and Daniel Fried covering central and Eastern European policy. While the Pentagon remained largely skeptical, administration policy began moving slowly but surely toward an activist enlargement approach.[18]

Meanwhile, the opposition Republicans took control of the US House of Representatives in the fall 1994 midterm elections. The new leaders of the House brought with them a "Contract with America," listing their policy priorities. Perhaps the only priority on which Clinton and the Republicans could agree was the Contract's advocacy of NATO enlargement. The Contract's enlargement position suggested that despite disparate motivations, NATO enlargement might enjoy a fairly wide bipartisan base of support in Congress.

In Brussels, necessary NATO work on enlargement moved ahead. In September 1995, the allies released the "Study on NATO Enlargement," which explained why enlargement was warranted.[19] It also drew out a road map for countries seeking membership to follow on their way to the open door. The report said that enlargement would support NATO's broader goal of enhancing security and extending stability throughout the Euro-Atlantic area. It would support the process of democratization and the establishment of market economic systems in candidate countries. They said that enlargement would threaten no one because NATO would remain a defensive alliance whose fundamental purpose is to preserve peace and provide security to its members.

With regard to the "how" of enlargement, the allies established a framework of principles to follow, including that new members should assume all the rights and responsibilities of current members and accept the policies and procedures in effect at the time of their entry; no country should enter with the goal of closing the door behind it, using its vote as a member to block other candidates; countries should resolve ethnic disputes or external territorial disputes before joining NATO; candidates should be able to contribute to the missions of the alliance; and no country outside the alliance (e.g., Russia) would have the right to interfere with the process. In this area, the report drew on a set of principles, articulated earlier in 1995 by Secretary of Defense William Perry, which had become known as the "Perry Principles," and on further enlargement analyses by the Asmus, Kugler, and Larrabee Rand team under their contract with the German Ministry of Defense.[20]

The NATO allies made clear that one of the key factors influencing readiness for membership would be the applicant country's ability to work within NATO's Integrated Command Structure. NATO military leaders were expected to help applicant countries help themselves prepare for becoming effective military contributors to the alliance, adding another important task to NATO's military mission profile.

During 1996–97, NATO officials conducted intensified dialogues with twelve countries that had expressed an active interest in NATO membership. The candidacies of all countries were thoroughly examined from a wide range of perspectives. It was clear, however, that the United States would play the decisive role in the question of whom to invite for the first round of enlargement.

Bringing new members into the alliance constitutes an "amendment" to the North Atlantic Treaty and, as such, has to be ratified by all NATO members. On balance, NATO enlargement had not been a hot issue in Congress, but to the extent that there was interest, there was sustained bipartisan support for NATO and for bringing in new members.[21] This support included passage of the NATO Participation Act of 1994 (Title II of P.L. 103-447), which backed NATO enlargement as a way of encouraging development of democratic institutions and free-market structures in the new democracies. The low-intensity but fairly consistent support was a good foundation for the collaboration between the White House and the

Senate that would be critical to eventual ratification of any enlargement decision. Meanwhile, the private, nonprofit Committee to Expand NATO was established in 1996 to support the enlargement cause. This group, which involved an impressive collection of corporate leaders, former civilian officials, and retired senior military officers, largely from the ranks of the Republican Party, actively courted congressional support for enlargement and played a major role in the lobbying effort on behalf of the initiative over the next two years.

The United States entered a presidential election year in 1996. Once again, foreign policy was not a big issue in the campaign. On the issue of NATO enlargement, President Clinton and his Republican opponent, Senator Robert Dole, competed mainly to see who could get closer to the enlargement flagpole. Dole criticized the president for being too attentive to Russia's views—Clinton had worked hard to reassure Russian President Boris Yeltsin that legitimate Russian interests would not be threatened while keeping enlargement moving ahead. But Dole's criticism had virtually no political impact, and most observers saw very little difference between the Republican and Democratic positions on the issue. It was yet another sign of the bipartisan nature of support for bringing new members into NATO, although it certainly did not guarantee that the approach to be taken by the president and the alliance would win the necessary two-thirds majority in the Senate.

The election campaign provided the opportunity for the administration to move ahead decisively. President Yeltsin had survived his reelection campaign in July 1996 and was no longer in imminent danger of being undercut by the US position on enlargement. In September 1996, Clinton called for a NATO summit in 1997 to name the first post–Cold War candidates for NATO membership. In October 1996, Clinton told an audience in Detroit that "by 1999, NATO's 50th anniversary and 10 years after the fall of the Berlin Wall, the first group of countries we invite to join should be full-fledged members of NATO."[22]

The prominent use of the enlargement issue during Clinton's campaign visits to the Midwest—home to many central European immigrant communities—was subsequently cited by opponents of enlargement in the United States and by skeptics in Europe as evidence that the US position was driven primarily by domestic politics. The history of administration policy, as documented by Goldgeier and observed personally by me, suggests a different conclusion. The president's commitment to enlargement grew much more fundamentally out of his acceptance of and belief in fairly basic Wilsonian principles of international relations, promoting peace and stability through inclusive and cooperative relations among democratic states. Ethnic communities in the United States provided important support for both the president and the issue. But had enlargement not made sense in terms of basic US values and interests, it would have withered on the vine despite the enthusiasm of Polish and other central European lobby groups.

By the end of 1996 and Clinton's successful reelection effort, collaboration between the White House and Congress was becoming more serious. The White
House was fully aware that if the Senate felt it had not participated directly in the
enlargement process, the issue could fail to gain the required two-thirds majority
even if two-thirds of the Senate leaned toward enlargement, as appeared to be the
case. The administration was sensitive to the fact that President Woodrow Wilson
had failed to win US involvement in the League of Nations because he had not made
the effort to get the Senate on board. It therefore followed President Harry Truman's
strategy for Senate consideration of the North Atlantic Treaty in 1948–49, a strategy
that brought key senators into the process early enough to win their commitment
but not too early to complicate the policymaking process prematurely.

As the White House began developing working relationships with critical Capitol Hill staff, a related but more immediate question was which countries should
be invited when the NATO "enlargement" summit convened in Madrid, Spain, in
July 1997. There was virtually unanimous agreement in the administration and
among the European allies that the Czech Republic, Hungary, and Poland were a
lock. Only Poland would add significantly to the military strength of the alliance.
But these three probably could be sold to the Senate as strategically important and
politically acceptable. From Germany's point of view, these three satisfied its desire
to move off the "front lines" in central Europe. Being surrounded by NATO members would give Germany a political and military buffer between it and Russia. The
United Kingdom preferred to keep the package as small as possible, not being a big
fan of the process of enlargement in any case, concerned that too rapid or large an
increase in membership would weaken the alliance. However, France, Italy, and
some other allies wanted to give enlargement a southern focus as well and favored
including Slovenia and Romania in the first tranche. Several members of the Senate, led by Senator Joseph Biden (D-Del.), ranking minority member of the Senate
Foreign Relations Committee, and Senator William V. Roth Jr. (R-Del.) favored the
inclusion of Slovenia—a small former Yugoslav republic that would add a land
bridge between existing NATO territory and Hungary.

The Clinton administration decided, despite the senatorial sentiments for Slovenia, that the core package of three candidates would be a sufficient challenge for the
process of ratification in the United States as well as for absorption by the alliance.
Romania, with an important geostrategic position in southeastern Europe and with
substantial military forces, lagged far behind the three core candidates in political and
economic development. Slovenia could be kept as a given for the next round. The administration came to an internal consensus on putting just three candidates forward.

Even though intensive discussion had been held at NATO and among NATO
allies in preparation for the Madrid meeting, the US choice of three and only three
was publicly revealed in a Pentagon press briefing by Secretary of Defense William
Cohen in mid-June. Cohen's suggestion that, as far as the US government was
concerned, the case was closed by the White House, which claimed that a NATO

decision had been made before NATO consultations had in fact been completed. The way the United States appeared to close the door to further discussion stunned the allies and was instantly interpreted by the French and others as just one more sign of hegemonistic US behavior. The United States had always been "first among equals" in NATO, where decisions are taken by consensus but where US preferences almost always carried the day. Nonetheless, the allies resented the cavalier US approach to the consultation process.

The challenge for the Clinton administration and for administrations before and after was to be a hegemon without acting like one. The administration had made the mistake of acting like one. The Madrid meeting endorsed the US preference, but not without significant grumbling by French President Jacques Chirac and others. The allies found much to complain about, including the fact that the United States wanted seats in the session for US senators who had been brought along to help ensure a favorable ratification process.

At Madrid, to help smooth the many feathers ruffled by US actions, other candidate states were encouraged to continue to work toward eventual membership by following the guidelines laid out in the "Study on NATO Enlargement" and developing bilateral cooperation with NATO through the PFP program. The allies reaffirmed their commitment to the open-door policy in which all European countries meeting the conditions of Article 10 and the guidelines of the study could be considered for eventual membership.

The next task for NATO was to negotiate the terms of entry with the candidate states. The Clinton administration, however, had its own challenging task: to convince at least two-thirds of the members of the Senate that NATO enlargement was in the US interest. The administration had already begun preparing the ground. A respected former Clinton White House aide and expert on congressional–executive relations, Jeremy Rosner, was brought back to serve as coordinator of the ratification process with both a State Department position and staff and the status of special adviser to the president. The administration had been wise to include senators in the Madrid delegation, but now the serious lobbying work would begin.

In the Senate, the Committee on Foreign Relations, chaired by arch-conservative Jesse Helms, would have primary jurisdiction over the legislation, with the Senate Committee on Armed Services also playing an important advisory role. Senate Majority Leader Trent Lott (R-Miss.) had already created the Senate NATO Observer Group, chaired by Senators Biden and Roth, designed to help manage the process in support of the Senate's advise and consent role.

In the summer of 1997, even though it appeared that Rosner and his administration team were starting with a good core of support in the Senate, they would need a strong lobbying effort to ensure final victory. In the course of a luncheon meeting in August hosted by a Scandinavian embassy officer, Rosner and I had a few moments to discuss his challenge. I said that I presumed that President Clinton would be personally involved in the lobbying effort. Rosner assured me that, in the coming months, the president would invite senators to the White House for dinners and private meetings focused on lining up the required votes. However, despite the fact that Clinton had played an important part in getting NATO enlargement on the US and NATO agenda, the fall of 1997 and spring of 1998 found him increasingly captured by impeachment proceedings against him in Congress. He never conducted the lobbying dinners and meetings Rosner had expected. At the numerous official events marking various stages of the ratification process, the president was present and involved, but one had to wonder whether his mind was not on other problems.[23]

Opponents of enlargement in the United States, right up until the Senate vote on April 30, 1998, complained that the issue had not been given the kind of serious attention that was warranted by such an important national commitment. It is true that the issue did not set the public on fire. Public opinion polls showed broad but somewhat shallow support for enlargement. The positive numbers seemed to reflect the public's positive image of NATO and of the idea that the US approach to international cooperation should be inclusive. However, a large percentage of those queried in polls showed a lack of basic knowledge about what was going on. For example, a large number of respondents in some polls believed that Russia was already a NATO member.[24]

The debate that did rage on editorial and op-ed pages of major American newspapers was largely among the academic and policy elite and was not of great interest to the American public. On the other hand, most foreign policy issues, such as NATO enlargement, are debated and decided largely by the elite public. The public at large is moved to action and involvement only by more headline-making events, particularly those with imminent life-or-death consequences.

In the deliberative body that had to debate and decide the issue, however, there was a thorough and serious process of consideration[25] in keeping with the Senate's role as a "partner" to the transatlantic bargain. Despite the president's "absence" from the process,[26] the work of the NATO Observer Group moved into high gear in close collaboration with the administration. The process relied heavily on teamwork between Rosner and key Senate staffers, particularly Senate Foreign Relations Committee staffer Steve Biegen, Ian Brzezinski, who worked for Senator Roth, and Michael Haltzel, who worked for Senator Biden. Other staffers, including Ken Myers of Senator Lugar's staff and David Stevens, who worked for Senator Jon Kyl (R-Ariz.), played key roles in the period leading up to the Senate debate.

The Senate NATO Observer Group, almost completely out of public view, organized a steady stream of classified and unclassified briefings and meetings in the course of 1997–98. Some of these sessions were intended largely for administration officials to communicate information to Senate staff. Others provided the opportunity for members to meet with senior NATO-nation military officials.

One critical session of the NATO Observer Group brought senators together with the foreign ministers of the candidate countries. The meeting appeared to be a turning point for at least one senator who had been skeptical about enlargement. Senator Kay Bailey Hutchison (R-Tex.) had profound concerns about the plan and engaged deeply in the issue, asking her staff, with the help of the Congressional Research Service, to research a number of enlargement issues. At the session with the candidate country foreign ministers, however, it became clear to this observer that Senator Hutchison's feeling of respect and admiration for the accomplishments of the three new democracies would likely bring her into the "yea" column. It did.

The Senate Committee on Foreign Relations held a series of public hearings in October and November 1997 in which both supporters and opponents of enlargement were invited to address the committee.[27] Proponents and critics of enlargement in the Senate engaged their staffs in investigation of major issues, calling in a wide range of outside experts to brief senators and staff and engaging hundreds of hours of support from Congressional Research Service analysts.

One of the most sensitive challenges for Jeremy Rosner and other administration officials was to hold together a coalition of Senate supporters and potential supporters who were motivated by substantially different assumptions and objectives. Supporters ranged from conservative Republicans to liberal Democrats. Senator Helms and a few other conservative Republican senators saw NATO enlargement first and foremost as an insurance policy against a resurgent Russia laying claim once again to the sovereignty of central and East European states. Helms was particularly interested in how the administration saw the future of NATO–Russia relations. In the process of introducing Secretary of State Madeleine Albright at the committee's opening enlargement hearing, Helms cautioned, "NATO's relations with Russia must be restrained by the reality that Russia's future commitment to peace and democracy, as of this date, is far from certain. In fact, I confess a fear that the United States' overture toward Russia may have already gone a bit far."[28]

In addition, many senators had not signed off on the "new NATO" (in which members cooperated to deal with new security challenges, including peace operations in the Balkans) and still believed that the "old NATO" (focused primarily on Article 5, the commitment to assist a fellow member that has come under attack) was what was still needed. On the other hand, some senators found the old NATO to be of decreasing relevance and were more interested in the idea of expanding the number of democratic states that could help deal with new security challenges in and beyond Europe. Others (e.g., Senator Barbara Mikulski, D-Md.) were motivated most strongly by the fact that Poland, the Czech Republic, and Hungary had thrown off communism and committed themselves to a democratic path. How, such proponents asked, could they be denied membership in the Western system, of which NATO was a core part?

The Senate opponents of enlargement were also all over the map politically and philosophically. Senator John Warner (R-Va.) became one of the most severe critics of enlargement. He believed that too many members would make the alliance impossible to manage and would doom it to future irrelevance because it would be unable to make timely consensual decisions with nineteen-plus members. Senator Warner's attempt to impose a formal pause on the enlargement process was rejected, but a number of senators who voted for enlargement voted with Warner in favor of a pause. Some forty-one senators voted for the Warner amendment, enough to block a two-thirds majority of the Senate for the next candidate(s) if they were all to vote against.

The most strongly committed enlargement opponent, Senator John Ashcroft (R-Mo.), simply believed that the United States was already overburdened and that NATO enlargement would perpetuate a responsibility that had long ago outlived its utility. Among the opponents, Ashcroft's position came closest to representing a neoisolationist stance. His perspective related in part to concerns about the potential cost of NATO enlargement. The cost question promised at one point to be the most difficult of issues in the Senate debate. However, conflicting and confusing estimates of the cost blurred the issue and made it a virtual nonfactor in the final debate. Ashcroft's attempt to amend the resolution of ratification to mandate a narrow interpretation of NATO's future mission was defeated through deft parliamentary procedures on the Senate floor. Instead, the Senate passed an amendment offered by Senator Jon Kyl (R-Ariz.) that affirmed the continuing importance of NATO's collective defense role while allowing that NATO now had utility in non–Article 5 missions as well.

The other main school of thought motivating opponents of enlargement was concern about the impact on relations with Russia. George Kennan, the highly respected Russia expert who played a major role in developing the US containment strategy toward the Soviet Union, had opined[29] that NATO enlargement would be a disaster for US–Russian relations, and some members, including Senators Paul Wellstone (D-Minn.) and Patrick Leahy (D-Vt.), cast their votes against enlargement largely on the basis of Kennan's warning.[30] Another opponent, Senator Daniel Patrick Moynihan (D-N.Y.), argued that the European Union, not NATO, should take the lead in including the new democracies in Western institutions.

After several abortive attempts to organize a debate and final vote in the Senate, Senator Lott devoted the entire day of April 30 to the enlargement issue. The opponents, led by Senators Warner, Robert Smith (R-N.H.), Moynihan, Ashcroft, and Wellstone, put on a strong show of their concerns. Because Senator Helms was not well, Senator Biden managed the bill for the Senate Foreign Relations Committee with single-minded energy and enthusiasm that left some of his democratic colleagues standing impatiently waiting to be given the floor. Several senators made impressive contributions to the advocate's side, including Mikulski, Joseph Lieberman (D-Conn.), and Gordon Smith (R-Ore.).

The decisive vote was taken late that evening. At the suggestion of Senator Robert Byrd (D-W.Va.) in his role as the unofficial guardian of the procedures and practices of the Senate, all senators took their seats and then rose when called to deliver their "yea" or "nay" vote. Byrd suggested that "the Senate would make a much better impression . . . [if senators would] learn to sit in their seats to answer the rollcall . . . [rather than] what we have been accustomed to seeing down here in the well, which looks like the floor of a stock market."[31] The Senate, seated with the decorum requested by Senator Byrd, voted 80 to 19 to give the Senate's advise and consent to ratification of the membership of Poland, the Czech Republic, and Hungary in NATO. The missing vote was that of Senator Kyl, an enlargement supporter who left Washington on an official overseas trip a few hours before the vote was taken, reassured that his side would win by a clear margin. After observing the daylong drama from the floor of the Senate, I walked out of the Capitol into a pleasant Washington night feeling that I had witnessed a historic event. That impression had been enhanced by the sight of the entire Senate seated in the chamber, thanks to Senator Byrd.

Although enlargement supporters managed to beat back all potential "killer" amendments, the number of votes garnished by Senator Warner's proposed "pause" in the enlargement process reflected an important sentiment. Few enlargement advocates were anxious to take on a new round in the near future. Even Jeremy Rosner, who had dedicated so much time and energy to NATO enlargement, judged that the system would not be able to support another round until the first candidates had demonstrated their successful entry into the NATO system.[32]

Some enlargement proponents, however, thought it was important to keep the process moving ahead. The first package had left aside Slovenia, a small but relatively attractive candidate. Senator William V. Roth Jr., one of the leading forces behind the enlargement process, argued that the process should "be carefully paced, not paused." In a special report for the North Atlantic Assembly (now the NATO Parliamentary Assembly) in September 1998, for which the author was rapporteur, Roth proposed that when the allies met in Washington in 1999 to celebrate NATO's fiftieth anniversary, "Slovenia should be invited to begin negotiations aimed at accession to the North Atlantic Treaty. In addition to reflecting Slovenia's preparedness for membership, the invitation would demonstrate that the enlargement door remains open without overloading the enlargement process."[33] Senator Roth's advocacy was considered by, and had some supporters in, the Clinton administration. But the administration ultimately decided that it was too early to move ahead with new candidates. That step was left for the next US administration to handle.

The European allies were relieved that the United States did not want to push ahead immediately with another round of enlargement. The strongest European proponent of enlargement, Germany, accomplished its main objectives with the accession of the first three candidates. It no longer stood on NATO's front lines looking east, and it no longer manifested such great enthusiasm for the enlargement process. Most of the other allies did not look forward to negotiating the next round, in which the potential candidates would likely include one or more of the three Baltic states—former Soviet republics whose NATO membership was strongly opposed by Moscow.

At the fiftieth-anniversary NATO summit in Washington on April 23–25, 1999, all aspiring candidates for NATO membership were given some cause for hope, even though Slovenia was left standing outside the door. The leaders pledged that "NATO will continue to welcome new members in a position to further the principles of the Treaty and contribute to peace and security in the Euro-Atlantic area." The allies created the Membership Action Plan (MAP), which promised cooperation beyond possibilities in the PFP and, perhaps more important, feedback from NATO concerning their progress toward membership. Nine aspirants—Albania, Bulgaria, Estonia, Latvia, Lithuania, Romania, Slovakia, Slovenia, and the former Yugoslav republic of Macedonia—initially signed up for the program. These nine were promised that NATO would formally review the enlargement process again no later than 2002.

According to NATO, "The MAP gives substance to NATO's commitment to keep its door open. However, participation in the MAP does not guarantee future membership, nor does the Plan consist simply of a checklist for aspiring countries to fulfil." What MAP did do, however, was to provide "concrete feedback and advice from NATO to aspiring countries on their own preparations directed at achieving future membership." The MAP did not substitute for full participation in NATO's PFP Planning and Review Process, which, in NATO's view, "is essential because it allows aspirant countries to develop interoperability with NATO forces and to prepare their force structures and capabilities for possible future membership."[34]

In 2000, with the United States preparing to elect its next president—the man who would make the next critical decisions on enlargement—the nine candidate states joined together in support of a "big bang" approach to enlargement. Meeting in Vilnius, Lithuania, the nine foreign ministers pledged that their countries would work for entry in NATO as a group rather than compete against each other for a favored position in 2002. Both major presidential candidates in the United States, Vice President Al Gore and Texas Governor George W. Bush, sent letters of support to the session.[35]

With his close victory in the November 2000 election, it was Bush who would take on the challenge of leading the alliance toward its enlargement decision, as promised, in Prague in November 2002. Table 8.1 outlines participation in the main Euro-Atlantic security institutions.

MOVING TOWARD THE NEXT ENLARGEMENT ROUND

The Bush administration and the NATO allies faced a number of issues as they confronted the next enlargement decision. They included several questions that played into the first enlargement debate and some others that were created by

Table 8.1 Participation in Euro-Atlantic Security Institutions, August 2002

	NATO	EAPC	PFP	EU	OSCE
Belgium	X	X	X	X	X
Canada	X	X	X		X
Czech Republic	X	X	X	2	X
Denmark	X	X	X	X	X
France	X	X	X	X	X
Germany	X	X	X	X	X
Greece	X	X	X	X	X
Hungary	X	X	X	2	X
Iceland	X	X	X		X
Italy	X	X	X	X	X
Luxembourg	X	X	X	X	X
Netherlands	X	X	X	X	X
Norway	X	X	X		X
Poland	X	X	X	2	X
Portugal	X	X	X	X	X
Spain	X	X	X	X	X
Turkey	X	X	X	3	X
United Kingdom	X	X	X	X	X
United States	X	X	X		X
Austria		X	X	X	X
Finland		X	X	X	X
Ireland		X	X	X	X
Sweden		X	X	X	X
Switzerland			X	X	X
Albania	1	X	X		X
Bulgaria	1	X	X	2	X
Estonia	1	X	X	2	X
Latvia	1	X	X	2	X
Lithuania	1	X	X	2	X
Fmr. Yugoslav Rep. of Macedonia	1	X	X	3	X
Romania	1	X	X	2	X
Slovakia	1	X	X	2	X
Slovenia	1	X	X	2	X
Armenia		X	X		X
Azerbaijan		X	X		X
Belarus		X	X		X
Georgia		X	X		X
Kazakhstan		X	X		X
Kyrgystan		X	X		X
Moldova		X	X		X
Russia		X	X		X
Tajikistan		X	X		X
Turkmenistan		X	X		X
Ukraine		X	X		X
Uzbekistan		X	X		X
Bosnia-Herzegovina		X	X		X
Croatia	1	X	X		X
Fmr. Rep. of Yugoslavia		X	X		X
Others (4)					X

1 Participates in NATO's Membership Action Plan; intends to join.
2 EU accession negotiations under way.
3 Applicants for EU membership in addition to twelve in previous category.
4 Andorra, Cyprus (2), the Holy See, Liechtenstein, Malta (2), Monaco, and San Marino.

specific circumstances surrounding the next batch of candidates. The issues, all of which will likely be considered during Senate debate on the next candidates for membership, include the following:

1. Had the first round of enlargement (with the Czech Republic, Hungary, and Poland) proceeded successfully enough to warrant a second round? Did shortcomings in military reform and defense improvements of the three new members suggest that leverage on candidate states disappears when they become members?
2. Did the increase to nineteen members have any discernible effect on NATO's decision-making ability? Is there a magic number beyond which NATO's consensus-based deliberative process will become unworkable?
3. If countries that do not fully meet the military guidelines for membership laid out in the NATO enlargement study[36] are nonetheless invited to join, does this imply that NATO is becoming "more political," making military capabilities of potential members less relevant?
4. What are the likely consequences for relations with Russia of various possible enlargement scenarios?
5. How will further enlargement interact with other policy initiatives, for example, the Bush administration's attempt to develop a collaborative approach with Moscow on nuclear missile reductions and ballistic missile defenses?
6. Can the financial costs of the next enlargement be kept reasonable and shared effectively?
7. Will senators be more wary of extending defense commitments to additional, less familiar countries than they were for the first three candidates?[37]
8. How should further NATO enlargement be linked to the process of EU enlargement, given that several leading candidates for NATO enlargement are headed for EU membership?[38]
9. Will enlargement be linked in any way to the process of further reforming NATO to make it more relevant to the war on terrorism?[39]
10. Will membership of the Baltic states in NATO and a closer NATO–Russia relationship lead Finland and Sweden to seek membership? If they do, will Austria and Ireland, the other two of four formerly neutral EU members, follow suit?

In the United States, the Bush administration will have to be even more assiduous than was the Clinton administration in developing congressional support for any membership approach. In a speech in Warsaw on June 15, 2001, President Bush outlined his vision of a Europe "whole, free, and at peace" and said that all new European democracies, "from the Baltic to the Black Sea and all that lie between," should be able to join European institutions, especially NATO. To pursue this goal, the administration's strategy requires bipartisan support, particularly if the Democrats continue to control the Senate. President Bush would have to engage Democratic and

Republican senators early and consistently to ensure that two-thirds of the Senate would be willing to give favorable advice and consent for ratification.

The process of opening NATO to new members and to working partnerships with all European states has already changed the transatlantic bargain in fundamental ways and is likely to produce more change in the future. NATO already is less exclusive, is more cumbersome, and has a more complex mission than during the Cold War. The transition from a club whose geostrategic environment made it quite exclusive to one whose circumstances require it to be more open has so far been difficult but, on balance, successful.

It seems highly unlikely that the United States and its NATO allies can now turn their backs on the hopes and hard work of new democracies that have demonstrated their fitness for NATO membership. The only question is how the allies will manage the process and whether they can minimize the negative consequences and maximize the potential gains.

NOTES

1. Wade Boese, "Russia Has Mixed Success with CFE Implementation," *Arms Control Today,* September 2001, 30–31.

2. David Yost has documented the fact that France was the only NATO ally to have serious reservations about the NACC. According to Yost, "The French had two preoccupations in this regard: resisting the tendency to give more substantial content to NACC activities, which might increasingly compete with those of the CSCE and maintaining coherence with the Alliance participation policy they had pursued since 1966." It is also evident that France's Socialist President François Mitterrand did not want to strengthen NATO's position in post–Cold War Europe at a time when other options might better suit French preferences. See David S. Yost, *NATO Transformed: The Alliance's New Roles in International Security* (Washington, D.C.: United States Institute of Peace Press, 1998), 95–96.

3. In the fall of 1990, on one my lectures at the NATO College in Rome, I served on a panel with a West European security expert and a Polish professor to discuss the future of NATO. The Polish panelist urged that the NATO countries take Polish pleas seriously, while the West European judged that the question of membership in NATO was many years away from serious consideration. Sympathetic to the Polish case, the best I could do was to suggest that Poland be patient and that the logic of their case would bring them through.

4. James M. Goldgeier, *Not Whether but When: The U.S. Decision to Enlarge NATO* (Washington, D.C.: Brookings Institution Press, 1999), 18. Goldgeier's account of the enlargement decision-making process in the Clinton administration is an insightful look at the US decision-making process that led to the entry of the Czech Republic, Hungary, and Poland into the alliance.

5. Jenonne Walker, "U.S., Soviet Troops: Pull Them All Out," *New York Times,* March 18, 1990, E19.

6. Goldgeier, *Not Whether but When,* 23–24. Goldgeier reports that at the first meeting of the interagency working group formed to prepare for Clinton's first NATO summit in January 1994, "Walker announced that there were two people in the White House who thought NATO expansion was a good idea—Bill Clinton and Tony Lake."

7. Goldgeier, *Not Whether but When,* 20.

8. Late in 1992, within constraints imposed by the Congressional Research Service mandate to produce "objective and non-partisan" analyses, I anticipated the issue facing the new administration:

> The goals of supporting democracy, the development of free market economics, and the observance of human rights probably will be served best by an inclusive rather than an exclusive approach to participation in components of a new European security system. In spite of the complications involved, inclusion may have to be the rule; exclusion the exception. How can the existing members of Western institutions, who have throughout the Cold War touted the western system, now deny participation in the system to countries that choose democracy, attempt to convert to free market economic systems, respect human rights, and pursue peaceful relations with their neighbors? This suggests the need for creative and flexible attitudes toward countries making credible efforts to meet the criteria for membership.

Stanley R. Sloan, "The Future of U.S.–European Security Cooperation" (Congressional Research Service Report for Congress 92-907, Washington, D.C., December 4, 1992), 2–3.

9. In a statement to the North Atlantic Assembly Presidential Task Force on America and Europe, on January 21, 1993, I carried the point to its logical conclusion, arguing at that early date for an approach that eventually became US policy:

> Full membership in specific institutions, such as NATO, should be based on the desire and demonstrated ability of countries to adopt the norms and obligations of membership. Not all former members of the Warsaw Pact may be able to meet such standards in the near future. But can the allies in good conscience deny participation in their security system to countries that have overthrown communist dictatorships and committed themselves to a democratic future?
>
> This suggests, in practical terms, that Poland, Hungary, and the Czech Republic deserve serious consideration for NATO membership in the near future. Clearly, taking such a step would require that the NATO countries reassure Russia and other non-NATO European states that growing membership in the alliance will help create conditions of stability and peace that will support their own attempts to become constructive participants in the international community.

Stanley R. Sloan, "Trends and Transitions in U.S.–European Security Cooperation" (statement before the North Atlantic Assembly Presidential Task Force on America and Europe, Washington, D.C., January 21, 1993).

10. Gebhard Schweigler, "A Wider Atlantic?" *Foreign Policy,* September/October 2001, 88.

11. The invitation to me and others suggested that the session was designed as an off-the-record opportunity to think and talk prospectively about transatlantic security issues.

12. Ronald D. Asmus, Richard L. Kugler, and F. Stephen Larrabee, "Building a New NATO," *Foreign Affairs* 72 (September–October 1993): 28–40.

13. Kruzel, a central and creative participant in NATO policy formulation in the early Clinton years; Col. Nelson Drew, the main architect of the Combined Joint Task Force concept; and respected career diplomat Robert Frasure, who played a key role in the process leading to the peace accord in Bosnia, all lost their lives when the vehicle in which they were riding plunged off a dirt road outside Sarajevo. Just days before the tragic accident, my wife and I were guests along with Kruzel and his wife at an informal dinner in Washington hosted by then–Danish Minister of Defense Hans Haekerrup. In the course of our conversation over dinner, I asked Joe if he did not sometimes regret the price he had to pay in lost time with his family given his demanding job. He acknowledged that this cost was the most difficult part of the job. In the end, he and his family paid a much larger price than either of us could have contemplated that enjoyable evening.

14. Off-the-record interviews with the author.

15. Yost, *NATO Transformed*, 133–34.

16. For an excellent collection of analyses of Ukraine's role in European security, see David E. Albright and Semyen J. Appatov, *Ukraine and European Security* (New York: St. Martin's, 1999).

17. Goldgeier, *Not Whether but When*, 68.

18. Goldgeier, *Not Whether but When*, 69–70.

19. NATO, "Study on NATO Enlargement" (Brussels: NATO, September 1995).

20. Goldgeier, *Not Whether but When*, 94–95.

21. At the time, I was the lead Congressional Research Service NATO expert and a source for Congress of objective and nonpartisan analysis on NATO issues. When the NATO Observer Group was established in the Senate to manage the process of NATO enlargement, I was asked to serve as adviser to the group and as the Congressional Research Service liaison with both the Senate Observer Group and the Senate Foreign Relations Committee on NATO enlargement issues.

22. White House, "Remarks by the President to the People of Detroit," October 22, 1996.

23. As a participant in several such ceremonies, I was impressed by the distant look in the president's eyes, suggesting, even as he artfully presented prepared remarks, that his thoughts and priorities were elsewhere.

24. See, for example, results of polls conducted by the Pew Research Center for the People and the Press, Washington, D.C., in *America's Place in the World, Part II.* The data, released on October 7, 1997, found that support for enlargement ran more than three to one in favor (63 percent for, 18 percent opposed); however, only 10 percent of the public could identify even one of the potential new members.

25. A partial record of Senate activities related to NATO enlargement, along with the Foreign Relations Committee's Resolution of Ratification and separate views of the Senate Committee on Armed Services and the Senate Select Committee on Intelligence can be found in US Senate Committee on Foreign Relations, *Protocols to the North*

Atlantic Treaty of 1949 on Accession of Poland, Hungary and the Czech Republic, 105th Cong., 2d sess., Exec. Rept. 105-14, March 6, 1998.

26. This aspect of the ratification process went completely unnoted in Goldgeier's otherwise excellent account of NATO enlargement decision making.

27. US Senate Committee on Foreign Relations, *The Debate on NATO Enlargement,* 105th Cong., 1st sess., October 7, 9, 22, 28, and 30 and November 5, 1997, S. Hrg. 105-285.

28. US Senate Committee on Foreign Relations, *The Debate on NATO Enlargement,* 2.

29. George F. Kennan, "A Fateful Error," *New York Times,* February 5, 1997, A23.

30. Following one Senate NATO Observer Group session in the weeks before the Senate vote, Wellstone engaged me in a discussion of the Russia issue. I attempted to provide a balanced perspective but suggested that Kennan's prediction was probably exaggerated. It was clear from that discussion, however, that Wellstone's vote probably would be with the enlargement opponents.

31. Even though the Standing Order of the Senate says that "votes shall be cast from assigned desk," roll-call votes are routinely taken with senators walking into the chamber and milling about the clerk's desk until their names are called. Byrd's comments can be found in *Congressional Record,* 105th Cong., 2d sess., April 30, 1998: S3906.

32. Discussion with author in 1998.

33. William V. Roth Jr., *NATO in the 21st Century* (Brussels: North Atlantic Assembly, September 1998), 53.

34. NATO, "NATO's Membership Action Plan," NATO on-line-library fact sheet (Brussels: NATO, April 20, 2000).

35. William Drozdiak, "9 NATO Candidates Pledge to Join in a 'Big Bang' Bid," *International Herald Tribune,* May 20–21, 2000, 1.

36. In 2001, a Rand Corporation study evaluated the qualifications of potential candidates and produced the following conclusions:

> Of the MAP states, Slovenia and Slovakia largely meet the criteria outlined by NATO [in the 1995 "Study on NATO Enlargement"] and their accession poses no major strategic problems for NATO. Estonia, Lithuania, and Latvia are advanced in terms of meeting NATO's preconditions, but the strategic ramifications of their accession [vis-à-vis Russia] loom large. Bulgaria and Romania have the opposite problem of being unable to meet NATO's preconditions, even though the strategic implications of their accession are not problematic. Macedonia and Albania are least advanced in meeting NATO's preconditions and their prospects for membership are distinctly long term. Of the European Union members currently not in NATO, Austria is in a good position to join if it chooses to do so. To a lesser extent, so is Sweden. Finnish membership, however, would entail some difficulties because of the strategic cost it would impose on NATO [also with regard to relations with Russia].

Thomas S. Szayna, "NATO Enlargement 2000–2015: Implications for Defense Planning," Rand Research Brief 62 (Santa Monica, Calif.: Rand Corporation, 2001). The brief summarizes the analysis completed by Szayna in *NATO Enlargement 2000–2015: Determinants and Implications for Defense Planning and Shaping* (MR-1243-AF) (Santa Monica, Calif.: Rand Corporation, 2001). See also Jeffrey Simon, *Roadmap to NATO Accession: Preparing for Membership*, (Washington, D.C.: Institute for National Strategic Studies, National Defense University, October 2001).

37. For a discussion of this issue by Professor Lawrence S. Kaplan, a distinguished NATO historian and enlargement skeptic, see Lawrence S. Kaplan, "NATO Enlargement: The Article 5 Angle," *Bulletin of the Atlantic Council of the United States* 12, no. 2 (February 2001), entire issue.

38. The European Union is conducting accession negotiations with twelve applicant states: Bulgaria, Cyprus, the Czech Republic, Estonia, Hungary, Latvia, Lithuania, Malta, Poland, Romania, Slovakia, and Slovenia. Three of the candidates—the Czech Republic, Hungary, and Poland—are now NATO members; six more—Estonia, Latvia, Lithuania, Romania, Slovakia, and Slovenia—are MAP participants. Turkey, a NATO member, is a candidate for EU membership but is not expected to be able to join the European Union in the foreseeable future.

39. Sean Kay, "Use NATO to Fight Terror," *Wall Street Journal Europe*, November 16, 2001.

9

A New Transatlantic Bargain Taking Shape: ESDI and CESDP

Post–Cold War adaptations in NATO's military missions, nuclear deployments, and outreach initiatives responded to the new international realities that emerged in the early 1990s, importantly reshaping the ways and means of the transatlantic alliance. None of those changes, however, altered the basic relationship between the United States and Europe in the alliance. The transatlantic bargain that emerged in the mid-1950s following the failure of the European Defense Community remained fundamentally in place.

Transatlantic discomfort with that bargain was on display as the end of the Cold War neared, with members of the US Congress complaining loudly about inadequate defense burden sharing and European officials grumbling about excessive European reliance on US leadership. As Michael Brenner has reflected on the transatlantic relations in the 1980s, "Strategic dependency did not cause European governments to suspend their critical judgment in assessing the wisdom of U.S. policy."[1]

Questions about the sustainability of a relationship that depended so heavily on the United States had been around for a long time. In the mid-1980s, I observed, "The only way to maximize the benefits of alliance will be to encourage a process of gradual evolutionary change in US–European relations toward a new transatlantic bargain." That bargain "must bring greater European responsibility and leadership to the deal; it must ensure continued American involvement in European defense while at the same time constructing a new European 'pillar' inside, not outside, the broad framework of the Western alliance." I then raised questions that are still open in the early years of a new millennium: "Will the European allies find the vision and courage to take on added responsibilities? Will the United States be wise enough to accept a more independent European partner?"[2]

In the 1990s, with the main threat to European security gone, that evolutionary process of change accelerated, perhaps destined to lead to the new bargain that I wrote about in 1985. That process of change, however, has unfolded in fits and starts—not a surprise, given the magnitude of the task. And just as the potential for a new bargain holds potential benefits for both US and European interests, it also contains risks that have weighed heavily on US officials over the last decade. However, success in this endeavor remains critical to the future of transatlantic relations. As Sean Kay has put it, "Balancing the transatlantic relationship is critical to keeping the US–European security partnership vibrant in the future. Indeed, it is a founding task of NATO that remains unfulfilled."[3]

As with the rest of the story of the alliance, the emergence of a more coherent Europe in the area of foreign policy and defense is part of a continuum. In chapter 4, I discussed the development of European-level foreign and defense policy coordination as one of the significant elements of change in the transatlantic bargain. In this chapter, I look at how this process developed in the 1990s, first as an attempt to build a European Security and Defense Identity in NATO and then as a major new initiative to develop an autonomous Common European Security and Defense Policy within the framework of the European Union (EU).

THE EUROPEAN SECURITY AND DEFENSE IDENTITY

The first response of European governments to the end of the Cold War was to begin cutting defense expenditures to realize a "peace dividend." The United States also hoped for a peace dividend. But the higher priority for President Bush and his top officials was ensuring continuity in US international leadership, including leadership of NATO. At a time when some were questioning whether NATO had any future, administration officials were suspicious of the moves within the European Union to give the Union a defense dimension.

American public opinion remained very favorable toward Europe and, in particular, toward EU members, reflecting deep European roots in American society, perceptions of shared values, and alliance relationships, among other factors. But the United States had always been schizophrenic about Europe's role in the world. Throughout the Cold War period, the United States supported the goal of enhanced European economic, political, and defense cooperation. However, the United States had not been forced to confront directly the prospect of European defense cooperation that could actually substitute for what in the past had been done in or through NATO and that could supplant traditional US–European roles in the alliance. Even though the United States has always welcomed the potential of a stronger "European pillar" in the transatlantic alliance, it has been wary of approaches that would divide the alliance politically, take resources away from NATO military cooperation, and not yield additional military capabilities to produce more equitable burden sharing. The US approach could accurately be called a "yes, but" policy, supporting the European effort but warning of the potential negative consequences.

In the early 1990s, traditional support for European integration still dominated the rhetoric of US policy, but the tendency to look somewhat skeptically at US support for European integration became more influential in the absence of the strong geostrategic requirement to support European union during the Cold War. In a "yes, but" policy environment, the "but" therefore received more emphasis.

National Security Adviser Brent Scowcroft was known to be skeptical about French motivations, and his relationship with officials in Paris was strained. In addition, there may have been a concern that bringing defense issues within the purview of the European Commission would open the way for anti-American sentiment present in the Commission to influence the evolution of transatlantic defense ties. The administration was also concerned that too much European rhetoric and declarations about taking on responsibility for defense would provide ammunition for traditional US critics of the US commitment to NATO.[4]

As the United States perceived the increased momentum toward European agreement on a defense identity early in 1991, a number of alarm bells were rung by US officials. The US ambassador to NATO, William Taft IV, in speeches delivered in February and March, supported a stronger European pillar in the alliance based on a revival of the Western European Union but cautioned that the European pillar should not relax the central transatlantic bond, should not duplicate current cooperation in NATO, and should not leave out countries that are not members of the European Community. (These themes returned prominently in the Clinton administration's 1998 warning that the European Union should avoid the dreaded "three Ds": duplication, decoupling, and discrimination.)

The message was put more bluntly in a closely held memorandum sent to European governments by Undersecretary of State for International Security Affairs Reginald Bartholomew in February. According to published reports, the memorandum expressed concern that the United States might be "marginalized" if greater European cohesion in defense led to the creation of an internal caucus within NATO.[5]

Following further warnings issued by Deputy Assistant Secretary of State James Dobbins on visits to European capitals and expressions of concern by Secretary of Defense Dick Cheney, the US approach to European defense integration appeared to have settled on five main points: the United States supported the development of common European foreign, security, and defense policies; NATO must remain the essential forum for consultations and venue for agreement on all policies bearing on the security and defense commitments of its members under the North Atlantic Treaty; NATO should retain its integrated military structure; the United States supports the European right to take common military action outside Europe to preserve its interests or ensure the respect of international law; and European members of NATO that do not belong to the European Union should not be excluded from European defense policy deliberations.[6]

Toward the end of 1991, the United States backed away from overt protests about a European defense identity, even though substantial ambiguity remained regarding what the United States really wanted from Europe. Tactically, US policymakers concentrated on diplomatic efforts to ensure that the definition of that identity that emerged from the NATO summit in Rome and the EU summit in Maastricht, the Netherlands, was consistent with US interests in NATO as the primary European security institution.

As discussed in chapter 6, NATO's 1991 new strategic concept established three areas of particular emphasis for future NATO policies. First, the allies said that, as part of a "broader" approach to security, they would actively seek cooperation and dialogue among all European states and particularly with the former Warsaw Pact adversaries (discussed in chapter 8). Second, they declared that NATO's nuclear and nonnuclear military forces would be reduced and that remaining forces would be restructured to take into account the need for militaries that could handle crisis management tasks (such as the one that later developed in Bosnia) as well as collective defense. Third, the allies agreed that the European members of NATO would assume greater responsibility for their own security. Specifically, the NATO leaders judged that "the development of a European security identity and defense role, reflected in the further strengthening of the European pillar within the alliance, will reinforce the integrity and effectiveness of the Atlantic Alliance." At that time, there was absolutely no concept of how this would come about, particularly when the allies were almost universally focused on how to cut defense expenditures in light of the reduced threats to produce a peace dividend for domestic spending programs. And in an important footnote to the support for a stronger European pillar, the leaders reiterated that NATO is "the essential forum for consultation among its members and the venue for agreement on policies bearing on the security and defense commitments of Allies under the Washington [North Atlantic] Treaty."[7]

In December 1991, in the wake of NATO's new strategic concept, the members of the European Community signed the Maastricht Treaty, transforming the European Community into the European Union and setting the goal of establishing a monetary union and a common currency, the Euro. The treaty importantly included, as part of that Union, a commitment to "define and implement a common foreign and security policy" that would eventually include "framing of a common defence policy, which might in time lead to a common defence." The key articles that follow set the path for enhancement of the role that defense and security would play in the future development of European unification:

Article J.1

The Member States shall support the Union's external and security policy actively and unreservedly in a spirit of loyalty and mutual solidarity. They shall refrain from any action which is contrary to the interests of the Union or likely to impair its effectiveness as a cohesive force in international relations. The Council shall ensure that these principles are complied with.

Article J.2

1. Member States shall inform and consult one another within the Council on any matter of foreign and security policy of general interest in order to ensure that

their combined influence is exerted as effectively as possible by means of concerted and convergent action.

2. Whenever it deems it necessary, the Council shall define a common position. Member States shall ensure that their national policies conform to the common positions.

3. Member States shall co-ordinate their actions in international organizations and at international conferences. They shall uphold the common positions in such fora. In international organizations and at international conferences where not all the Member States participate, those which do take part shall uphold the common positions.[8]

The treaty designated the Western European Union (WEU) as the organization responsible for implementing defense aspects of the European Union's decisions on foreign and security policy. The WEU members subsequently agreed (at Petersberg, Germany, in 1992) that they would use WEU military forces for joint operations in humanitarian and rescue missions, peacekeeping, crisis management, and peace enforcement—the so-called Petersberg tasks.

Although the outcomes in Rome and Maastricht appeared to resolve the conceptual differences between the United States and France about the relationship between a European defense identity and the transatlantic alliance, it may have just papered them over. This became patently clear in the first half of 1992, when the United States issued strong warnings to the German and French governments concerning their plans to create a Franco-German military corps of some 35,000 troops. American officials reportedly expressed reservations about the degree to which the corps would displace NATO as the focus of European defense efforts and undermine domestic support in the United States for a continuing US presence in Europe. National Security Adviser Brent Scowcroft was said to have sent a "strongly worded" letter to the German government suggesting that the Germans were not taking a strong enough position against what Scowcroft interpreted as French efforts to undermine cooperation in NATO.[9] The controversy reflected continuing differences between the US and French governments about the requirements for future European security organization.

The US policy toward European defense has always been set within a broader US concept of its role in the world and the way in which allies relate to that world. During the Bush administration, internal administration studies that suggested that the United States should establish and sustain unquestioned superpower status raised questions in Europe as well as in the United States. Concern arose when a draft of the US Department of Defense "defense guidance" memorandum was leaked to the press early in 1992.[10] The document's vision of far-flung US military requirements in the post–Cold War era, apparently designed to ensure that the United States remained the only global superpower, provoked an outcry from a wide variety of observers who saw the draft plan as seriously out of touch with current political and economic realities.

The reaction among the European allies was that the Pentagon approach seemed to view Europe as a potential adversary rather than an ally. The implication was that the United States should undermine efforts at closer European unity to ensure that no European rival emerged to "balance" the US role in the world. White House and State Department officials characterized the draft as "a 'dumb report' that in no way or shape represents US policy,"[11] suggesting that, even within the Bush administration, there was no consensus on the US role in the world to serve as *political* guidance for the Department of Defense's strategy.

Following the strong reactions to the leaked draft, a new version was produced that reportedly eliminated most of what the European allies and other observers found objectionable.[12] Nonetheless, the controversial draft, by framing one clear perspective on the future US role in the world, may have made an important, albeit worrisome, contribution to the ongoing discussion.

Because the American people clearly wanted the United States to focus its energies on economic and social problems at home, the 1992 election campaign produced very little heat or light on the definition of the future US role in the world. President Bill Clinton's administration came to office against the backdrop of an election in which those voting sent a clear message calling for more attention to domestic issues, including the still-mounting federal deficit.

The Clinton administration hoped to dispel any residual impression that the United States did not want the Europeans to take on more burdens and responsibilities in the alliance. As noted in chapter 8, at least one of Clinton's foreign policy advisers had even argued that withdrawal of US forces from Europe would signal US willingness to envision a "Europeanization" of NATO. Less radical approaches prevailed, however, and in January 1994, at Clinton's first opportunity for major initiatives on NATO issues, the NATO Brussels summit acknowledged the important role that a European Security and Defense Identity (ESDI) could play in the evolving European security system.

The January 1994 NATO summit meeting in Brussels approved the idea, initially proposed by the United States, of creating Combined Joint Task Force (CJTF) headquarters as part of NATO's integrated command structure. As discussed in chapter 6, the CJTF initiative was designed to give NATO's command structure additional flexibility to accomplish a variety of objectives, including to facilitate the dual use of NATO forces and command structures for alliance and/or operations run by the Western European Union. The purpose was to encourage European nations to undertake missions with forces that are "separable but not separate" from NATO in the context of an emerging ESDI.

The Brussels summit yielded multiple references in the allied declaration to the importance of European-level cooperation and the constructive role played by the Western European Union. (The declaration included no fewer than eight references to the Western European Union, seven references each to the ESDI and European Union, and two each to the Maastricht Treaty on European Union and the Union's Common Foreign and Security Policy goal.)

NATO's work to implement the January 1994 agreements in principle moved ahead slowly but remained hampered by different US and French visions of the future. Many French analysts and officials had interpreted the summit outcome as a US vote for Europeanization of the alliance. In fact, the administration had not intended to go so far and wanted only to open the way toward a stronger European role in the alliance. The perceptual split was suggested by the way each looked at CJTF. The French and many other Europeans saw CJTF mainly as a way for the European allies to engage in more autonomous military actions. The United States saw this as one of the functions of CJTF but regarded the concept's first role as making it possible for NATO itself to operate in more flexible formations and combinations.

In the second half of 1995, the British government began actively searching for ways to create an ESDI within the framework of the alliance and in a fashion that would facilitate France's return to full military integration. Early in 1996, the French and British governments proposed what became known as the "Deputies proposal."[13] NATO forces in Europe have always been commanded by an American officer who occupies the position of Supreme Allied Commander, Europe (SACEUR). The British and French suggested that the Deputy SACEUR, traditionally a senior European officer, and other European officers in the NATO command structure wear WEU command hats as well as their NATO and national command hats. This multiple-hatting procedure would, without duplication of resources and personnel, permit the WEU countries to use the NATO command structure to organize and command a military operation under largely European auspices.

The Deputies proposal reportedly raised serious issues for the US Joint Chiefs of Staff and SACEUR General George Joulwan. Senior US military commanders were concerned that the WEU command arrangements might weaken the European commitment to the NATO structure as well as lessen the American commitment to NATO. However, other US officials, including senior officials at the White House, believed that a continued active US role in the alliance depended on being able to demonstrate to Congress and the American public that the European allies were willing and able to take on greater responsibility for military missions both inside Europe and beyond.[14] The reinvolvement of France in the alliance, with its willingness and ability to participate in military interventions beyond national borders, was seen as the key to the construction of a meaningful and coordinated European contribution to post–Cold War security concerns.

The spring 1996 session of NATO ministers, scheduled to be held in Berlin, Germany, emerged as the opportunity to tie the loose ends together. In a discussion that spring with a key administration diplomat responsible for NATO policy, I asked whether he would support the Deputies proposal. His answer was, "I'll support it as soon as General Joulwan does," suggesting the depth of resistance from the SACEUR and the Joint Chiefs of Staff more generally. Just days prior to the Berlin meeting, US uniformed military leaders were still resisting the transformation of the Deputy SACEUR position. Senior advisers to the president realized that the time had come for a deal, and the White House overruled the Joint Chiefs—a step not easily taken by a president whose credentials with the military were so suspect.[15] As a consequence, the 1994 summit goals were transformed at Berlin into a plan to build a European defense pillar inside the NATO alliance despite objections from the Joint Chiefs.

In Berlin, NATO foreign ministers agreed to move ahead with implementation of the CJTF concept. In addition, they agreed that an ESDI would be created within the alliance by making NATO "assets and capabilities" available for future military operations commanded by the Western European Union. Such decisions would be made by consensus on a case-by-case basis. To facilitate such operations, European officers in the NATO structure would, when appropriate, shift from their NATO responsibilities to WEU command positions.

The allies determined that adaptation of the alliance should be guided by three fundamental objectives: to ensure the alliance's military effectiveness and ability to perform its traditional mission of collective defense while undertaking new military roles, to preserve the transatlantic link by strengthening NATO as a forum for political consultation and military cooperation, and to support development of an ESDI by creating the possibility for NATO-supported task forces to perform missions under the direction of the WEU nations.

The Berlin ministerial marked a watershed in the development of US and NATO policy toward creation of a more coherent European role in the alliance. The Clinton administration had clearly gone on the record as supporting a stronger European pillar, but when it came to making significant structural changes in NATO to help bring the concept to fruition, there was profound resistance in the US policy community.

Even after Berlin, the question was what military operations the European allies could actually take on within the framework of the new arrangements. During the intervening years, it was demonstrated that they did not have the combination of military resources and political will to take on operations such as the Implementation Force (IFOR) or Stabilization Force (SFOR) in Bosnia, and the United States provided most of the key resources for the air war against Serbia over Kosovo. In 1997, when impending chaos in Albania threatened to destabilize southeastern Europe, the Europeans were not even able to agree on organizing an intervention under the Western European Union but rather sent in an ad hoc coalition force under Italian command. All these experiences led observers to bemoan the fact that Europe did not have the military capacity required to maintain stability on the borders of EU–WEU member states, to say nothing of the capacity to project force beyond the Balkans. As Michael Brenner has written,

The cumulative record of EU failure and NATO's recovery (in the Balkans) sharpened the issue of whether an ESDI built within NATO on the CJTF principle was satisfactory. For the European allies, the record could be read two ways: as making a compelling case for them to take more drastic measures to augment their military resources and to cement their union, or as providing telling evidence that the quest for an autonomous ESDI was futile. Few drew the first conclusion.[16]

In June 1997, the members of the European Union, in the process of updating and strengthening the Maastricht Treaty, approved the Treaty of Amsterdam. In the area of common defense policy, the Treaty of Amsterdam included a reference to the Petersberg tasks and authorized the adoption of EU common strategies. It also created the position of high representative for common foreign and security policy, one that was not filled until September 1999, when former NATO Secretary-General Javier Solana took on the job. Solana had performed well as NATO secretary-general and had won admiration in Washington—no small accomplishment for a Spanish socialist who had opposed his country's membership in NATO in the early 1980s. Solana's selection clearly was intended to reassure the United States. In retrospect, the question may be whether Solana's new job was more important than the one he gave up. In fact, it probably was. It would be important for the European Union to move into NATO's exclusive reserve in a way that did not create too much choppy water across the Atlantic, and Solana had a reputation not only for hard work but also for his diplomatic skills—skills that he surely would need in his new job.

AN "AUTONOMOUS" COMMON EUROPEAN SECURITY AND DEFENSE POLICY

In the autumn of 1998, the shape of the discussion on European defense was changed profoundly by British Prime Minister Tony Blair's decision to make a major push for an EU role in defense. Blair first tried out his ideas at an EU summit in Pörtschach, Austria, in October 1998 and then reaffirmed his approach on November 3 in a major address to the North Atlantic Assembly's annual session[17] in Edinburgh, Scotland. Blair bemoaned the fact that Europe's ability for autonomous military action was so limited and called for major institutional and resource innovations to make Europe a more equal partner in the transatlantic alliance. Blair's initiative may also have betrayed some uncertainty concerning NATO's future.[18]

Traditionally, Great Britain had been the most reliable, predictable partner of the United States when it came to dealing with defense issues. The British had shared US skepticism regarding initiatives that might create splits between the United States and Europe in the alliance, particularly those with roots in French neo-Gaullist philosophy. The fact that Blair was moving out in front on this issue produced mixed reactions in the United States.

On the one hand, the United States believed that it still could trust Great Britain not to do anything that would hurt the alliance, and Blair claimed that his goal was to strengthen NATO by improving Europe's ability to share security burdens in the twenty-first century. On the other hand, Blair's initiative sounded "too French" to skeptics, and even those who were hopeful were concerned about the political setting for Blair's initiative. It was said that Blair wanted to demonstrate commitment to Europe at a time when the United Kingdom was not going to join in the inauguration of the Euro, the European Union's common currency. Questions about the seriousness of the initiative were also raised by the fact that the proposal seemed to come out of nowhere. In discussions with British foreign office officials minutes after the Edinburgh speech was delivered, the author was told that the initiative until then consisted of the two speeches and that on their return to London, they would begin putting meat on the bones of the approach.

At the Edinburgh meeting, Blair and British officials got a foretaste of one of the key aspects of American reactions to the initiative. A report released at the meeting by US Senator William V. Roth Jr. said,

> The United States should give every possible help and encouragement to the continuing consolidation of European defense efforts. But the United States must not be held accountable for the inability of European states to develop a more coherent European role in the Alliance. It is the responsibility of the European Allies to develop the European Security and Defense *Capabilities* to give real meaning to a European Security and Defense *Identity*.[19]

Any doubts about the serious nature of the Blair initiative were removed when Blair met with President Jacques Chirac at Saint-Malo early in December 1998. The declaration, named for this French resort town, envisioned the creation of a Common European Security and Defense Policy (CESDP) with the means and mechanisms to permit the EU nations to act "autonomously" should NATO not decide to act in some future scenario requiring military action. The French delegation reportedly had lined up support from German Chancellor Gerhard Schroeder prior to the meeting, giving the declaration even more weight. The statement included the following key elements:

1. The European Union needs to be in a position to play its full role on the international stage.
2. On the basis of intergovernmental decisions, the Union must have the capacity for autonomous action, backed up by credible military forces, the means to decide to use them and a readiness to do so, in order to respond to international crises.
3. The NATO and WEU collective defense commitments of the EU members must be maintained, obligations to NATO honored, and the various positions of European states in relation to NATO and otherwise must be respected.

4. The Union must be given appropriate structures and a capacity for analysis of situations, sources of intelligence and a capability for relevant strategic planning, without unnecessary duplication.
5. Europe needs strengthened armed forces that can react rapidly to the new risks, and which are supported by a strong and competitive European defense industry and technology.[20]

US administration officials said the Blair initiative was given the benefit of the doubt.[21] The administration thought that British motivations were solid, even if they remained concerned about those of the French. When the Saint-Malo statement emerged, however, administration officials felt that the British had not been 100 percent transparent about the likely outcome. The administration's formal reaction took the traditional form of the "yes, but" approach characterized earlier. Secretary of State Madeleine Albright, presenting themes originally developed as an op-ed piece for publication by National Security Adviser Sandy Berger, formally declared the administration's support *but* cautioned the Europeans against "the three Ds": duplication, decoupling, and discrimination. Secretary Albright emphasized these concerns at the December 1998 ministerial meetings in Brussels, just days after the Saint-Malo meeting.

According to Albright, the allies should not duplicate what already was being done effectively in NATO. This would be a waste of defense resources at a time when defense spending in most European nations was in decline. More fundamentally, the new European initiative should not in any way "decouple" or "delink" the United States from Europe in the alliance or the European defense efforts from those coordinated through NATO. This could result from a lack of candor and transparency that the United States feared might be an intended or unintended consequence of the new European approach. A tendency to "gang up" on the United States or even its perception on the US side of the Atlantic could surely spell the end of the alliance. Finally, Albright insisted there be no discrimination against NATO allies who were not members of the European Union. This point applied in particular to Turkey but also to European allies Norway, Iceland, the Czech Republic, Hungary, and Poland, as well as Canada and the United States on the North American side of the alliance.

The "three Ds" accurately summarized the administration's main concerns and hearkened back to the Bush administration's earlier warnings in reaction to the Franco-German development of the Eurocorps. Despite these footnotes to US support for the initiative, it moved ahead in parallel with NATO's conduct of the air campaign over Kosovo intended to wrest the province from Serbian control and allow Kosovo refugees to return to their homes in peace. The campaign, which threatened to cast a dark shadow over NATO's fiftieth-anniversary summit meeting in Washington, also added impetus to the Blair approach. When the numbers were toted up at the end of the air campaign, the United States had conducted nearly 80 percent of the sorties.

From the US perspective, the fact that the allies for the most part were not able to contribute to such a high-tech, low-casualty campaign suggested the wisdom of the Defense Capabilities Initiative (DCI). The DCI, adopted at the Washington summit, was designed to stimulate European defense efforts to help them catch up with the US Revolution in Military Affairs. From the European perspective, the Kosovo experience clearly demonstrated Europe's (undesirable and growing) military dependence on the United States and the need to get together to do something about it. Even if Washington saw a more assertive European role as a challenge to American leadership, more capable European military establishments could relieve the United States of some of its international security burdens, improving the burden-sharing equation and thereby strengthening, not weakening, transatlantic ties.

The Washington summit communiqué and the strategic concept for NATO agreed upon at the meeting reflected transatlantic agreement that European defense capabilities needed a serious shot in the arm and that it had to be done in ways consistent with the US "three Ds." However, although the Saint-Malo accord was endorsed by all EU members at meetings in Cologne (June 1999) and Helsinki (December 1999), over the course of the year there were growing rumbles and signs of dissatisfaction on the American side. According to one former administration official, as the initiative took shape, British officials came to Washington regularly prior to each major stage of negotiations with France and the other EU members to reassure US officials that they agreed completely with American perspectives. However, the Saint-Malo outcome and its subsequent implementation at Cologne and Helsinki gave much more emphasis to "autonomy" than the administration would have liked. This official noted that British reassurances throughout this period were often followed by outcomes that reflected compromises with French positions that were not entirely to the liking of administration officials, raising concerns about the eventual impact of a "European caucus" on transatlantic cooperation.

On the European side, NATO and government officials chafed under the impression left by the "three Ds" that the US superpower was putting too much emphasis on the negative. European experts and officials openly cautioned US State and Defense officials at transatlantic discussions of defense issues not to allow this negative approach to capture US policy. Former British Minister of Defense George Robertson, after succeeding Javier Solana as NATO secretary-general, offered a more positive approach. Addressing the forty-fifth annual session of the NATO Parliamentary Assembly, Robertson said, "For my part, I will ensure that ESDI is based on three key principles, the three I's: *improvement* in European defense capabilities; *inclusiveness* and transparency for all Allies, and the *indivisibility* of transatlantic security, based on shared values (emphasis added)." Moving from "Ds" to "Is," Robertson tried to put a positive spin on the American concerns that would make the same points but in a fashion less offensive to the Europeans.

By the end of 1999, the European Union had tied a major package together based on the guidelines of the Saint-Malo statement. The EU members agreed that Javier Solana, in addition to serving as the Union's high representative for common foreign and security policy, would become WEU secretary-general to help pave the way for implementation of the decision confirmed at Cologne to merge the Western European Union within the European Union.

In Helsinki, the EU members declared their determination "to develop an autonomous capacity to take decisions and, where NATO as a whole is not engaged, to launch and conduct EU-led military operations in response to international crises." They noted that the process "will avoid unnecessary duplication and does not imply the creation of a European army." The EU members continued to reiterate that collective defense remained a NATO responsibility and would not be challenged by the new EU arrangements. They agreed on a series of substantial steps, called the "Helsinki Headline Goals," required to implement their political commitment, including the following:

1. To establish by 2003 a corps-size intervention force of up to 60,000 persons from EU member-state armed forces capable of deploying within sixty days and being sustained for at least one year;
2. to create new political and military bodies to allow the European Council to provide political guidance and strategic direction to joint military operations;
3. to develop modalities for full consultation, cooperation, and transparency between the European Union and NATO, taking into account the "needs" of all EU member states (particularly the fact that four EU members—Austria, Ireland, Finland, and Sweden—are not NATO members);
4. to make "appropriate" arrangements to allow non-EU European NATO members and others to contribute to EU military crisis management;
5. to establish a nonmilitary crisis management mechanism to improve coordination of EU and member-state political, economic, and other nonmilitary instruments in ways that might mitigate the need to resort to the use of force or make military actions more effective when they become necessary.

The EU members moved quickly to implement the goals. By March 2000, the Political and Security Committee (PSC, also known by the French acronym COPS), the European Union Military Committee (EUMC), and the EU Military Staff (EUMS) started functioning as interim organizations. The PSC was to be the political decision-making body for CESDP, preparing decisions for EU Council consideration on foreign policy and crisis situations and implementing decisions of the EU members. The EUMC, like the NATO Military Committee, was designed to provide military advice and recommendations to the PSC and to implement the military aspects of EU decisions. The EUMS was to support the work of the Military Committee.

The most immediate task was to prepare a catalog of forces that would be made available to actions authorized under the CESDP. This work resulted in the European Union Capabilities Commitment Conference, which convened November 20–21, 2000. The conference produced an impressive inventory of resources, including about 100,000 soldiers, 400 combat aircraft, and 100 ships, including two aircraft carriers. In addition, non-EU NATO members and EU associate partners pledged capabilities that could join in future EU operations. One observer has emphasized that there were "certain realities" about the pledging operations that were missed by some observers. According to former high-level British defense official Michael Quinlan,

> First, there was no suggestion that the forces to be contributed by countries towards the Goals would be entirely new and additional ones created for that purpose; they would be existing ones though . . . much improvement or redesign might be required. Second, there was no suggestion that they would be separate from forces declared to NATO. European countries in the integrated military structure already customarily declared all that they could to NATO; there was no separate reservoir of similar forces available beyond those. Nothing in the CESDP concept rested on hypotheses of extensive autonomous EU action at a time when NATO itself needed to employ forces, and alternative earmarking did not therefore entail illegitimate or confusing double-count (any more than did the long-familiar fact that almost all Alliance members had sometimes used their NATO-declared forces for national or U.N. purposes). Third, the capability was not intended as a European Army—a description specifically rejected in EU utterances—or even a European Rapid Reaction force in the customary usage of that term in NATO.[22]

The main issue during 2000, however, was how these new EU institutions would relate to their NATO counterparts. The problem grew out of the strong desire of some in the European Union, particularly in French diplomatic and political circles, for an "autonomous" EU approach, less vulnerable to US influence, and the hope in NATO that the European Union's role in defense would be integrated as fully as possible within the overall transatlantic alliance.

The New NATO–EU Relationship

Until the opening of the new millennium, the relationship between NATO and the European Union had been informal and lacking much substance. Even though these two organizations constituted the core of intra-European and Euro-Atlantic relations, they largely existed as separate, disconnected organizations with bureaucracies and political cultures, particularly on the EU side, that were interested primarily in keeping a safe distance from one another. Because the United States had in so many ways been the dominant influence in NATO, EU national and international officials historically feared that too close a relationship with the alliance would bring too much US influence into European councils. In the 1990s, former US

Ambassador to NATO Robert Hunter frequently lamented the lack of any working communication and coordination channels between NATO and the European Union. During Hunter's years at NATO in the mid-1990s, NATO Secretary-General Javier Solana met informally with the president of the European Commission, the European Union's top official. And the NATO Berlin decisions of 1996, intended to give life to NATO's support for development of an ESDI, led to closer coordination between NATO officials and those from the Western European Union. But a huge gap remained between NATO and the European Union.

With the proclaimed EU goal of establishing an "autonomous" CESDP, a more formal NATO–EU relationship clearly was required. The process was slow in developing, partly because of the residual concern among a few EU governments, particularly the one in Paris, that the construction of CESDP not be overly influenced by the United States. For the first half of 2000, this view led the French government to argue that CESDP institutions should be developed prior to serious discussions of how the European Union's decision-making process would relate to NATO. However, according to NATO Secretary-General Lord Robertson, by September 2000 the process of linking NATO and EU institutions was well under way and moving in positive directions. Speaking to the SACLANT Symposium in Reykjavik, Iceland, on September 6, 2000, Robertson noted that

> already, NATO and the EU are working together closely—meeting together to decide on how to share classified information and drawing on NATO's experience to help the EU flesh out the requirements of its headline goal. . . . Put simply, NATO-friendly European defence is finally taking shape—and it is taking the right shape.[23]

In September 2000, NATO's North Atlantic Council (NAC) and the European Union's "Interim" Political and Security Committee (COPSI) began meeting to work out details of the arrangement and to establish a pattern and format for cooperation. The first joint NAC/COPSI meeting took place on September 19, 2000, followed by a second meeting on November 9, 2000. Meanwhile, four EU–NATO working groups began to work on their assigned issues: security of sensitive information, Berlin-plus (ESDI initiatives designed to facilitate more coherent European contributions within the NATO framework), military capabilities, and permanent EU–NATO institutional arrangements. In addition, Robertson and his predecessor, Javier Solana, actively collaborated to ensure that the NATO–EU liaison worked effectively.

In the Clinton administration's last major initiative regarding EU–NATO relations, Secretary of Defense William Cohen on October 10, 2000, delivered informal but important remarks to a meeting of NATO defense ministers in Birmingham, United Kingdom.[24] Cohen strongly endorsed the development of CESDP, saying that "we agree with this goal—not grudgingly, not with resignation, but with wholehearted conviction." At the same time, Cohen dismissed the logic sometimes used to provide a rationale for CESDP, saying, "The notion that Europe must begin to prepare for an eventual American withdrawal from Europe has no foundation in fact or in policy."

In addition, Secretary Cohen suggested that it was hard to imagine a future case in which the United States and the European Union would diverge dramatically on whether a crisis situation warranted a joint response. According to Secretary Cohen,

> It is overwhelmingly likely that in any situation where any ally's involvement on a significant scale is justified, and where there is a consensus in Europe to undertake a military operation, the United States would be part of the operation. In addition, it is difficult to imagine a situation in which the United States was prepared to participate, but our European Allies would prefer to act alone.

With regard to the question of whether the European Union should establish its own military planning capacity, Cohen argued for a NATO–EU approach that would be "unitary, coherent, and collaborative." He suggested that NATO and the European Union should create a "European Security and Defense Planning System" that would involve all twenty-three NATO and EU countries. In Cohen's judgment, "It would be highly ineffective, seriously wasteful of resources, and contradictory to the basic principles of close NATO–EU cooperation that we hope to establish if NATO and the EU were to proceed along the path of relying on autonomous force planning structures."

Cohen concluded,

> The NATO–EU relationship, Ministerial Guidance, and implementation of DCI [an initiative agreed to at the NATO Washington summit in 1999 designed to improve allied defense capabilities] are not separate, parallel processes that we can allow to proceed in isolation from one another. Rather, they are all vital strands in the powerful and enduring fabric of Euro-Atlantic security.

Secretary Cohen's remarks made it clear how important it would be to ensure that NATO and EU military planning move forward hand in hand in whatever institutional construct proved acceptable to all parties. In the best case, NATO and EU military planners would in fact be largely the same people working toward the same ends, whether they wore NATO or EU hats. It was also hoped that the dynamics created by the European Union's defense objectives might help reinvigorate and give new sense of direction to the NATO planning process.

The fact that the Cohen proposal for resolution of the planning issue was not received enthusiastically by the European Union (particularly by the French) led the secretary of defense, at his last NATO meeting in December 2000, to put more emphasis on the "but" side of the "yes, but" equation. Cohen warned that CESDP could, if handled incorrectly, turn NATO into a "relic of the past."[25]

At the end of the year, the NATO–EU negotiations came close to agreement on how to work together in the future. During the December 14–15 meeting of the NAC, the NATO allies were able to note that progress had been made in the four working groups. They welcomed the European Union's agreement at its summit in Nice, France, earlier in December that there should be a "regular pattern" of meetings at all levels between the European Union and NATO. According to the NAC communiqué, "Meetings between the North Atlantic Council and the Political and Security Committee outside times of crisis should be held not less than three times, Ministerial meeting once, per EU Presidency (in other words, every six months); either organization may request additional meetings as necessary."[26] The communiqué also noted favorably the European Union's agreement that consultation would be intensified in times of crisis. In addition, the allies welcomed the Nice provisions for inviting the NATO secretary-general, the chairman of the Military Committee, and the Deputy SACEUR to EU meetings. NATO reciprocated by agreeing to invite the EU presidency and secretary-general/high representative to NATO meetings and providing that the chairman of the EUMC or his representative would be invited to meetings of the NATO military committee.

The allies also stated their intention to make arrangements for

> assured EU access to NATO planning capabilities able to contribute to military planning for EU-led operations; the presumption of availability to the EU of pre-identified NATO capabilities and common assets for use in EU-led operations; the identification of a range of European command options for EU-led operations, further developing the role of DSACEUR in order for him to assume fully and effectively his European responsibilities; and the further adaptation of the Alliance's defence planning system, taking account of relevant activities in and proposals from the European Union. Allies will be consulted on the EU's proposed use of assets and capabilities, prior to the decision to release these assets and capabilities, and kept informed during the operation.[27]

However, at the end of the day, the government of Turkey blocked consensus to permit the European Union "assured access" to NATO planning and therefore prevented final agreement on the whole NATO–EU package. Ankara had wanted the European Union to grant the Turkish government veto power over the Union's deployment of a military force under circumstances that could affect Turkey's security. That, of course, was a nonstarter with the European Union.

When the George W. Bush administration came to office in the United States, most details of the NATO–EU arrangement had been agreed to, but it was left to the new administration in Washington to help find a way around the EU–Turkish impasse and perhaps also to review aspects of the NATO–EU agreement that it found of concern. Well into 2002, however, the European Union had not been able to resolve the issue with Turkey, largely because of Greek reluctance to go along with a proposed compromise, and so formal consummation of the EU–NATO relationship remained in abeyance.

The Bush administration was alert to any signs that CESDP might be undermining NATO. British Prime Minister Blair hurried to Washington to reassure President Bush. In his meetings with Blair in February 2001, President Bush accepted on good faith that CESDP would not hurt NATO. Following Camp David discussions with Blair, the president said,

> He [Blair] assured me that NATO is going to be the primary way to keep the peace in Europe. And I assured him that the United States will be actively engaged in NATO, remain engaged in Europe with our allies. But he also assured me that the European defense would no way undermine NATO. He also assured me that there would be a joint command, that the planning would take place within NATO, and that should all NATO not wish to go on a mission, that would then serve as a catalyst for the defense forces moving on their own. And finally, I was very hopeful, when we discussed the prime minister's vision, that such a vision would encourage our NATO allies and friends to bolster their defense budgets, perhaps. And so, I support what the prime minister has laid out. I think it makes a lot of sense for our country.[28]

Some observers speculated that Bush had endorsed CESDP in return for Blair's support for the new administration's missile defense goals, but it seems more likely that the two issues were considered on their own merits by both sides.

The reaffirmation of US support for the CESDP initiative was necessary because the incoming administration was known to have concerns similar to those expressed earlier by the Clinton administration and by private experts outside the administration—some of whom were appointed to positions of influence inside the new administration.[29]

Even among Euro-enthusiasts, there was lingering concern that CESDP would produce rhetoric, promises, and institutions but no additional capabilities. The EU pledge to create a 60,000-troop intervention force with 400 aircraft and 100 ships was impressive. But still in 2002, there was little evidence that European governments were increasing defense spending to buy the strategic lift and other assets required to make the force credible. On balance, the Europeans still lagged well behind the United States in deployed military capabilities for force projection, intervention, and high-tech warfare.

Making a point heard at many other transatlantic meetings in recent years, Senator John McCain, speaking at the Thirty-Seventh Conference on Security Policy in Munich, Germany, on February 3, 2001, observed that

> the European members of NATO should have the means—and, as importantly, the will—to act in response to crises without the direct involvement of the United States. However, to date there is little reason for confidence that this will be the outcome. . . . What the transatlantic partnership requires is not new institutions, but improved capabilities.[30]

Following President Bush's meeting with Prime Minister Blair, the new administration appeared to settle into a relatively passive approach toward CESDP, perhaps in the belief that nothing dramatic affecting US interests was likely to happen in the near term. The more urgent priority was to develop US policy toward ballistic missile defense and sell it to the allies, Russia and China, as well as to reform and repair the US defense establishment. Another priority—the war against terrorism—displaced all others on September 11, 2001, when terrorists killed more than 3,000 Americans and citizens of more than eighty other countries by hijacking four civilian passenger aircraft and flying them into the World Trade Center in New York, the Pentagon outside Washington, D.C., and the Pennsylvania countryside (the implications for the alliance of the terrorist attacks and the war against terrorism are discussed in chapter 10).

As the United States, Europe, and the world turned their eyes toward the war against terrorism, important questions remained unanswered about the relationship between the United States and Europe in the alliance.

The Bush administration, despite the Blair reassurances, seemed wary of the potential for CESDP to create artificial distinctions among NATO allies, undermining NATO's political cohesion. The CESDP process and the demands of its institutional creations could encourage "we/they" distinctions between Europeans and the United States and even among European members of NATO. The Clinton administration was quite restrained in its response to French diplomatic initiatives in Eastern and central Europe that appeared designed to convince states that were candidates for EU membership that they should line up with EU positions in the ongoing negotiations with NATO concerning the EU–NATO relationship.[31]

Down the road, the tactics of European and US policymakers may occasionally lead to further bouts of NATO–EU competition, particularly as many central and Eastern European states try to adjust to the demands of membership in both organizations. The challenge will be to keep the competitive instincts of policymakers on both sides of the Atlantic under control in the interest of NATO–EU convergence.

A key question about CESDP and NATO remains that of what military responsibilities the European allies are capable of taking on in the near future. In recent years, it has been demonstrated that they do not yet have the combination of military resources and political will to take on large and complex peace operations. But there is good news as well. According to Michael Quinlan, one should be encouraged by the fact that "most European countries now accept that their forces should in the future be configured, equipped, trained, and available much more than before for expeditionary or similar use, in support of international order, rather than for direct homeland defense against massive aggression."[32]

The Bush administration largely followed a policy of benign neglect toward CESDP during its first eighteen months in office. However, many administration officials, particularly several high-level Department of Defense political appointees, are skeptical about European pledges and prefer the United States not rely too much on the prospect of significantly improved European military capabilities.[33] As the administration looks more systematically at CESDP, perhaps with more skepticism than hope, a number of issues may remain of concern, including the following:

1. Might CESDP come to be seen in the United States as designed to "balance US power," undermining the potential for transatlantic cooperation across the board?
2. Could CESDP strengthen European resistance to NATO actions that are not blessed by a UN mandate? (Into 2002, the European Union had not yet decided how to shape the relationship between CESDP and the United Nations.[34])
3. Will CESDP include a European "regional" perspective on security, spreading a minimalist security perspective from certain EU states to the entire membership?
4. Might CESDP lead resources and political energy to be spent on enhancing the credibility of the European Union's military efforts while allowing real security needs, such as those identified in NATO's DCI, to go uncovered?
5. Will internal EU differences, such as those that blocked progress at the European Union's summit in Laeken, Belgium, in December 2001 ensure that CESDP remains more talk than action?

Governments of the European Union have attempted to address many US concerns in the design of the CESDP initiative. Most of the US concerns, however, could not be put to rest in the near term. The way in which CESDP evolves will determine its impact on transatlantic relations. Management of the issue will therefore be a continuing challenge for US and European officials for years to come.

Thus, the foundation has been laid for a fundamental change in the transatlantic bargain. If all goes well, the change could carry the alliance back toward the original 1949 bargain, which anticipated an equitable sharing of burdens and responsibilities between the United States and Europe. A successful transition, however, will require a high level of statesmanship, hard work, and more than a little luck. There are obstacles down that path. Those obstacles and additional challenges are addressed in the next chapter.

NOTES

1. Michael Brenner, *Terms of Engagement: The United States and the European Security Identity,* The Washington Papers no. 176, Center for Strategic and International Studies (Westport, Conn.: Praeger, 1998), 23.

2. Stanley R. Sloan, *NATO's Future: Toward a New Transatlantic Bargain* (Washington, D.C.: National Defense University Press, 1985), 191.

3. Sean Kay, *NATO and the Future of European Security* (Lanham, Md.: Rowman & Littlefield, 1998), 149.

4. This discussion draws on the author's examination of US attitudes toward European defense published in Stanley R. Sloan, "The United States and European Defence," Chaillot Paper no. 36 (Paris: Western European Union Institute for Security Studies, April 2000).

5. Catherine Guicherd, "A European Defense Identity: Challenge and Opportunity for NATO," Congressional Research Service Report 91-478 (Washington, D.C.: Congressional Research Service, June 12, 1991). For the text of the "Bartholemew Telegram" of February 20, 1991, see Willem van Eekelen, *Debating European Security, 1948–1998* (The Hague: Sdu Publishers, 1998), 340–44.

6. Guicherd, 60–61.

7. Rome Declaration on Peace and Cooperation, Issued by the Heads of State and Government Participating in the Meeting of the North Atlantic Council in Rome on 7–8 November 1991.

8. Single European Act, Title V: Provisions on a Common Foreign and Security Policy, Articles J 1, 2.

9. Frederick Kempe, "US, Bonn Clash over Pact with France," *Wall Street Journal*, May 27, 1992, A9.

10. Patrick E. Tyler, "Senior US Officials Assail Lone-Superpower Policy," *New York Times*, March 11, 1992, A6.

11. Tyler, "Senior US Officials Assail Lone-Superpower Policy," 6.

12. Barton Gellman, "Pentagon Abandons Goal of Thwarting US Rivals," *Washington Post*, May 24, 1992, A1.

13. This concept was developed in a Congressional Research Service report originally prepared for Senator William V. Roth Jr. (R-Del.). See Stanley R. Sloan, "NATO's Future: Beyond Collective Defense," Congressional Research Service Report 95-979 S (Washington, D.C.: Congressional Research Service, September 15, 1995), 21–24, 30–32. French officials subsequently acknowledged that the report contributed to what eventually became a British–French initiative. British officials have suggested that London was beginning to think along similar lines when the report appeared.

14. Discussions with administration officials in 1996.

15. This point is based on interviews with US officials involved in the decision.

16. Brenner, *Terms of Engagement*, 35.

17. In the course of that session, the Assembly renamed itself the NATO Parliamentary Assembly to emphasize its role as the parliamentary component of the transatlantic alliance.

18. Jolyon Howorth, *European Integration and Defence: The Ultimate Challenge?* (Paris: Western European Union Institute for Security Studies, 2001), 108.

19. Willam V. Roth Jr., *NATO in the 21st Century* (Brussels: North Atlantic Assembly, September 1998), 57.

20. "Statement on European Defence" (text of a joint statement by the British and French governments, Franco-British summit, Saint-Malo, France, December 4, 1998).

21. Interviews conducted with Clinton administration officials.

22. Michael Quinlan, *European Defense Cooperation: Asset or Threat to NATO?* (Washington, D.C.: Woodrow Wilson Center Press, 2001), 38.

23. Lord Robertson, "NATO's New Agenda: More Progress Than Meets the Eye" (remarks at the SACLANT Symposium, Reykjavik, Iceland, September 6, 2000).

24. William Cohen, "Meeting the Challenges to Transatlantic Security in the 21st Century: A Way Ahead for NATO and the EU" (remarks at the Informal Defense Ministerial Meeting, Birmingham, United Kingdom, October 10, 2000).

25. Reuters News Service, "Cohen Warns Europe That NATO Could Become 'Relic,'" *International Herald Tribune,* December 6, 2000, 7.

26. Final Communiqué, Ministerial Meeting of the North Atlantic Council held at NATO Headquarters, Brussels, December 14–15, 2000, para. 31.

27. Final Communiqué, para. 33.

28. Transcript of President Bush and British Prime Minister Tony Blair's news conference following their first meeting at Camp David, February 23, 2001, www.whitehouse.gov/news/releases/2001/02/20010226-1.html [accessed August 5, 2002].

29. For example, Peter Rodman, who had written and commented widely on CESDP from his position at the Nixon Center, moved into a senior policy position at the Department of Defense; Robert Zoellick, a supporter of European defense cooperation, became the US trade representative; and John Bolton, a strong skeptic, moved to a position at the National Security Council.

30. Transcript of remarks of Senator John McCain to the 37th Munich Conference on Security Policy, February 3, 2001.

31. The perception among many Eastern and central European officials was that this was the intent of French diplomacy for a period early in 2000, even though it has been denied by French officials.

32. Quinlan, *European Defense Cooperation,* 54.

33. Based on personal contact with several of the officials over many years.

34. Martin Ortega, *Military Intervention and the European Union* (Paris: Western European Union Institute for Security Studies, March 2001), 108.

10

The Future of the Transatlantic Bargain: Crisis, Continuity, or Community?

We are All Americans

—Headline in *Le Monde* (Paris), September 12, 2001

THE CHALLENGES AHEAD

This reassuring but perhaps misleading headline in *Le Monde* after the terrorist attacks on the United States suggested the extent to which terrorism would affect the future of the transatlantic bargain.

On September 11, 2001, the challenges to transatlantic relations became much more complex and demanding. The terrorist attacks on the United States, organized by the al-Qaeda radical Islamic group led by Osama bin Laden, left more than 3,000 people dead. Bands of terrorists hijacked four civilian airliners, crashing them into both towers of the World Trade Center in New York and the Pentagon outside Washington, D.C. A fourth hijacked aircraft, perhaps headed for the White House or the US Capitol, crashed in a field in Pennsylvania after passengers learned of the other three hijackings and decided to try to wrest control of the aircraft from the terrorists.

President George W. Bush declared a war on terrorism in response to the attacks, and the United States prepared to mount a campaign against the Taliban leadership and forces in Afghanistan, which had hosted and supported the al-Qaeda organization and bin Laden and had refused to turn bin Laden and his associates over to the United States for prosecution.

Within twenty-four hours, the attack on the United States was addressed by the North Atlantic Council in Brussels, which decided to invoke Article 5 of the North Atlantic Treaty if it was determined that the attack was the responsibility of a foreign source and not domestic terrorism, from which many allies had suffered but which does not fall under the collective defense provisions of the Treaty. On September 12, the North Atlantic Council declared,

> The Council agreed that if it is determined that this attack was directed from abroad against the United States, it shall be regarded as an action covered by Article 5 of the Washington Treaty, which states that an armed attack against one or more of the allies in Europe or North America shall be considered an attack against them all.
>
> The commitment to collective self-defence embodied in the Washington Treaty was first entered into in circumstances very different from those that exist now, but it remains no less valid and no less essential today, in a world subject to the scourge of international terrorism. When the Heads of State and Government of NATO met in Washington in 1999, they paid tribute to the success of the alliance in ensuring the freedom of its members during the Cold War and in making possible a Europe that was whole and free. But they also recognised the existence of a wide variety of risks to security, some of them quite unlike those that had called NATO into existence. More specifically, they condemned terrorism as a serious threat to peace and stability and reaffirmed their determination to combat it in accordance with their commitments to one another, their international commitments and national legislation.
>
> Article 5 of the Washington Treaty stipulates that in the event of attacks falling within its purview, each ally will assist the Party that has been attacked by taking such action as it deems necessary. Accordingly, the United States' NATO allies stand ready to provide the assistance that may be required as a consequence of these acts of barbarism.[1]

On October 2, 2001, NATO Secretary-General Lord Robertson announced that the allies had concluded that the attacks had been directed from abroad and therefore would be regarded as covered by Article 5. The United States had made it clear that, even though it appreciated the alliance's declaration of an Article 5 response, it would conduct military operations itself, with ad hoc coalitions of willing countries. Initially, this included only the United Kingdom among NATO allies. The United States decided not to ask that military operations be conducted through the NATO integrated command structure. Such a request would have created serious political dilemmas for many allies. The discussion of NATO's area of operation had basically been put aside since the debates leading up to the 1999 strategic concept, and there was no enthusiasm for reopening these debates in the middle of this crisis. Furthermore, the United States obviously preferred to keep tight control of any military operations.

Nonetheless, NATO was asked to provide a number of services on behalf of the war against terrorism. On October 4, NATO allies agreed to

> enhance intelligence sharing and co-operation, both bilaterally and in the appropriate NATO bodies, relating to the threats posed by terrorism and the actions to be taken against it; provide, individually or collectively, as appropriate and according to

their capabilities, assistance to Allies and other states which are or may be subject to increased terrorist threats as a result of their support for the campaign against terrorism; take necessary measures to provide increased security for facilities of the United States and other Allies on their territory; backfill selected Allied assets in NATO's area of responsibility that are required to directly support operations against terrorism; provide blanket overflight clearances for the United States and other Allies' aircraft, in accordance with the necessary air traffic arrangements and national procedures, for military flights related to operations against terrorism; provide access for the United States and other Allies to ports and airfields on the territory of NATO nations for operations against terrorism, including for refueling, in accordance with national procedures.[2]

The North Atlantic Council also agreed that the alliance was prepared to deploy elements of its Standing Naval Forces to the eastern Mediterranean in order to provide a NATO presence and demonstrate resolve and that NATO was ready to deploy elements of its Airborne Early Warning force to support operations against terrorism. In fact, on October 8 it was announced that NATO AWACS aircraft would be deployed to the United States to help patrol US airspace. The move freed up US assets for use in the air war against Taliban forces in Afghanistan. Just as NATO had invoked Article 5 for the first time ever, the dispatch of NATO forces to protect US territory, according to General Joseph Ralston, NATO's Supreme Allied Commander, Europe, was "the first time NATO assets will have been used in direct support of the continental United States."[3]

NATO's reaction to the terrorist attacks was quick and unequivocal. The reaction was initially applauded by the Bush administration. Two months after the attacks, the US ambassador to NATO, R. Nicholas Burns, argued that NATO had responded strongly to the terrorist challenge and that the response demonstrated NATO's continuing relevance: "With the battle against terrorism now engaged, it is difficult to imagine a future without the alliance at the core of efforts to defend our civilization."[4]

The terrorist attack and the actions required to respond militarily demonstrated in many ways the wisdom of the allied approach to adaptation of the alliance that had been under way since the early 1990s. NATO never abandoned the critical Article 5 commitment, but it began preparing for the new kind of security challenges alliance members thought were likely in the twenty-first century. The implications for force structure, discussed in more detail in chapter 6, were clear: NATO needed more forces capable of being moved quickly to conflicts beyond national borders and prepared to fight as allies in a variety of topographic and climatic conditions in coalitions using a synergistic mix of conventional and "high tech" weaponry. Even though the September 11 attacks constituted a clear case for invocation of Article 5, the response required the kinds of forces and philosophies that the allies had been seeking to develop for so-called non–Article 5 contingencies.

Unfortunately, the directions suggested by NATO strategy documents and incorporated in the 1999 Defense Capabilities Initiative (DCI) had not been taken seriously by most European governments. NATO formally acknowledged this reality in December 2001, when allied defense ministers in a special statement observed that

> efforts to improve NATO's ability to respond to terrorism must be an integral, albeit urgent, part of the more general ongoing work to improve Alliance military capabilities. There has been some progress in this wider regard since our last meeting, but a great deal more needs to be done. We are especially concerned about persistent long-standing deficiencies in areas such as survivability; deployability; combat identification; and intelligence, surveillance, and target acquisition. The full implementation of DCI is essential if the Alliance is to be able to carry out its missions, taking into account the threat posed by terrorism.[5]

In 1999, the allies had finessed the issue of whether NATO could be used for military operations beyond Europe despite their commitment to combat terrorism. The United States had argued strongly that most likely applications of allied cooperation in the future would be well beyond allied borders, but most European allies had opposed any open-ended commitment to employ NATO on a more global basis. As the war in terrorism unfolded in Afghanistan, far from Europe, the alliance had no agreement in principle concerning where NATO could be used. Legally, they needed no such agreement once they had declared the attacks on the United States to fall under NATO's collective defense provisions. But the lack of any planning for operations far from NATO's borders—created by the 1999 finesse—meant that the alliance was not ready to be used for such operations.

Preparing for and conducting operations in Afghanistan, the US administration sought help from the allies mainly through bilateral channels, not through NATO. In the weeks following the attacks, some Pentagon officials privately dismissed NATO's formal invocation of the alliance's mutual defense provision and complained that the alliance was not relevant to the new challenges posed by the counterterror campaign. Meanwhile, some NATO allies were led to believe that the United States did not value or want contributions that they might make in the battle against terrorism. The Italians, for example, were embarrassed by their exclusion from British–French–German talks about counterterrorist operations held on the fringes of a European Union (EU) summit in Ghent, Belgium, combined with rumors, apparently from French sources, that the United States had rejected Italian offers of military assistance.[6]

By November, many allies, including Germany, had pledged forces to the counterterrorist campaign, and their offers had been explicitly welcomed by the administration. As the campaign stretched into 2002, more NATO country forces were brought to bear on the conflict. Many allies pledged forces for postconflict peacekeeping duties. Several Danish and German soldiers were killed trying to destroy Taliban munitions. Canadian forces saw combat against al-Qaeda and Taliban elements in the eastern Afghan mountains, and the British deployed a force of some 1,700 Royal Marines to join in the fight against residual al-Qaeda and Taliban forces. But these important national contributions did not produce any formal role for the alliance in the affair.

This experience therefore left many questions unanswered about the future of the allied response to the terrorist challenge and to the other issues that remained on the alliance platter. Would NATO countries follow up their Article 5 commitment with resources that would be helpful in the conduct of a far-reaching and long-running campaign against international terrorism? Would the NATO cooperative framework prove to be helpful, or would it be seen by the United States as inappropriate and unhelpful for the kinds of operations required by the war on terror? How would the new circumstances created by the terrorist attacks and their aftermath affect other key issues for the alliance, including NATO's future role in the Balkans; the coordination of US, allied, and NATO approaches to ballistic missile defense; relations with Russia; the continuation of the enlargement process; and the future development of the Common European Security and Defense Policy (CESDP) and the European Union's relationship to NATO?

DEALING WITH TERRORISM

Few would question how important it will be to ensure that the members of the Atlantic Community stay united and strong against the insidious threat of terrorism that struck at America's heart on September 11 and that will strike again if given the opportunity to do so. NATO's initial response to the attacks was impressive and appropriate but also reflects some limitations on the alliance that will influence its future role.

Most observers of transatlantic security issues remember the debates in the 1990s, particularly those leading up to NATO's 1999 strategic concept, in which the United States imagined a NATO mandate without artificial geographic limitations while many European countries wanted to prevent the appearance of an open-ended role for the alliance in dealing with future security challenges. The September 11 events demonstrated that the United States was right concerning the nature of future threats to transatlantic security—most of them have roots outside Europe and must be dealt with well beyond NATO's borders. However, the differing perspectives among NATO members concerning the best instruments to employ against disparate threats have not disappeared. They are based on fundamentally different historical experiences, political and military traditions, and available power and military capabilities. Britain and France have force projection philosophies and global strategic perspectives. But Germany's concepts and perspectives will continue to inhibit the Federal Republic's military role beyond its borders despite the dramatic progress Berlin has made in breaking out of outdated constraints on the use of its forces since the end of the Cold

War.[7] Such differing perceptions will, on occasion, make consensus and cooperation difficult to find. The passage of time and other developments will inevitably put some distance between the allies and the coalescing shock of the September 11 atrocities. The challenge will be to keep the alliance on track despite the inevitable disagreements on military tactics and political strategies.

In the aftermath of the terrorist attacks and the US reactions, one British expert judged that the US choice not to use NATO to run the military operations against terrorist targets in Afghanistan means that "it's unlikely the Americans will ever again wish to use NATO to manage a major shooting war."[8] This judgment may or may not be accurate. The Bush administration presumably did not ask that NATO run the military actions in Afghanistan because they did not want to repeat the Kosovo experience, where US management of the conflict was complicated by allied criticism of US targeting strategy. Specifically, the French government on several occasions vetoed targets that had been identified by US planners. Complaints by Bush administration Pentagon officials about NATO's limited utility apparently were registered without the administration even asking the allies to give the alliance a more substantial role.

With regard to the other US partner to the transatlantic bargain, the US Congress, the traditional burden-sharing debate took on a new and pointed direction. Leading members of the US Senate argued strongly that Europe's failure to take the war on terrorism seriously could undermine the US commitment to NATO and destroy the alliance altogether. At the Thirty-Eighth Annual Munich Conference on Security Policy, defense expert Senator John McCain (R-Ariz.) joined leading Bush administration officials, stressing "the need for the European allies to acquire better capabilities for their armed forces so that they can cope with sudden terrorist threats and possibly join U.S. troops in a campaign to overthrow Saddam Hussein in Iraq."[9] This argument came in the wake of President Bush's State of the Union Address in which he argued that Iraq, Iran, and North Korea constituted an "axis of evil" that could be the target of US preemptive strikes.[10]

Senator Richard G. Lugar (R-Ind.), longtime NATO supporter and leading commentator on the alliance, hit hard in a speech to the US–NATO Missions Annual Conference in Brussels on January 19, 2002, arguing that a division of labor in which the United States did the war fighting and Europe did the peacekeeping was unacceptable. Senator Lugar summed up his view, saying,

> America is at war and feels more vulnerable than at any time since the end of the Cold War and perhaps since World War II. The threat we face is global and existential. We need allies and alliances to confront it effectively. Those alliances can no longer be circumscribed by artificial geographic boundaries. All of America's alliances are going to be reviewed and recast in light of this new challenge, including NATO. If NATO is not up to the challenge of becoming effective in the new war against terrorism, then our political leaders may be inclined to search for something else that will answer this need.[11]

On the European side, allied officials complained that, after showing their support and willingness to contribute, the United States proceeded with a strategy focusing largely on dividing, not sharing, responsibilities. According to press reports, the situation

> irritated European leaders. Behind their unflagging public political support for Washington are private complaints about the constant risk of being caught flat-footed by the US refusal to limit its own options by revealing its plans. Accustomed to being consulted about or at least alerted to US moves, these leaders are now embarrassed.[12]

One French official reportedly observed that the message from the United States was, "We'll do the cooking and prepare what people are going to eat, then you will wash the dirty dishes."[13] It subsequently became popular to observe that the new formula for international security management was "the US fights, the UN feeds, and the EU finances and does peacekeeping."

To some extent, the situation can be attributed to factors for which the Europeans themselves are to blame. First, they did not, for the most part, have significant military assets to contribute to the first phase of the Afghan campaign, which relied heavily on air-delivered precision-guided munitions. Second, officials in the Bush administration were fully aware of past NATO nation resistance to involving the alliance in military operations beyond their borders, to say nothing of beyond Europe.

On the other hand, it appeared that the United States missed an opportunity to move the NATO consensus well beyond the 1999 strategic concept following the September 11 events. Given invocation of Article 5 and the explicit willingness of many NATO allies to contribute military capabilities to the war against terrorism, a political consensus existed that perhaps could have been used to expand NATO's horizons and establish a mechanism for NATO contributions in the future. For example, the allies could have taken NATO's involvement at least one step further by creating a NATO counterterrorism combined joint task force.[14] Creation of a special task force would have provided the organizational focus required for a serious NATO contribution to the counterterrorist campaign. It would have provided a reliable framework for allied involvement in the campaign—built on the foundation of NATO's integrated command structure—for as long as such support were required.

If, however, the war against international terrorism remains for some years the main focus of US security policy, NATO's ability to be part of the solution could exert a major influence on US perceptions of the alliance's utility. It seems likely that the United States, despite unilateralist tendencies in Washington, will want to ensure that the response to the terrorist attacks strengthens America's most important alliance instead of undermining it. Europeans, despite their skepticism about the US approach to the war on terrorism (particularly President

Bush's formula for dealing with Iran, Iraq, and North Korea as an axis of evil), will not want to risk diminished US support for the alliance specifically and transatlantic cooperation more generally.

Dealing with this challenge will require sophisticated political handling on both sides of the Atlantic. The United States will have to be careful to ask allies to do things that they are capable of doing. At the same time, the NATO allies must avoid at all cost the perception that they do not support the United States in responding to the terrorist threat. For NATO, not doing enough risks losing US interest in the alliance. On the other hand, trying to push the alliance beyond the political consensus concerning NATO's mission could create splits among the allies and even domestic unrest in some allied countries. In any case, the war against international terrorism could for many years remain the most important part of the political and strategic environment in which the NATO allies deal with every issue they face as allies.

NATO'S ROLE IN THE BALKANS

NATO's involvement in the Balkans developed with reluctance and considerable political difficulty during the 1990s but now can be seen as an example of NATO's continued relevance to twenty-first-century security requirements. Only NATO could have organized and conducted the peacekeeping mission in Bosnia-Herzegovina and the air war against Serbia over Kosovo. NATO's continuing involvement in Bosnia-Herzegovina, Kosovo, and Macedonia helps sustain a degree of security and stability that provide the opportunity for the development of liberal institutions in the states that are emerging from former Yugoslavia in a more peaceful regional environment.

NATO's experiences in the Balkans have made it clear that running a war with multiple centers of political direction can be a demanding, frustrating task. On the other hand, if NATO had not existed, it is unlikely that the many NATO and non-NATO military forces that have played important roles in the Balkan operations could have worked together as effectively as they have. The NATO focus on interoperability and on the development of habits of cooperation in both political and military relations makes operations among the forces of NATO members states possible. It also has created a framework that can accommodate contributions by other countries. It is no coincidence that the European Union is developing the forces for its CESDP under "NATO standards" and that all countries that want to become NATO members are working hard to bring their forces into line with those same standards. The bottom line is that the day-to-day collaboration that takes place under the NATO banner has positive practical consequences whose potential benefits stretch well beyond collective defense requirements and well beyond Europe's borders. Even when NATO's integrated command structure is not used to run military operations, the fact that participants in ad hoc coalitions led by the United States or EU members start out with a degree of interoperability will make such operations more effective.

In addition, the NATO role in Balkan operations has created a framework in which all the NATO allies share responsibility for the security challenges there, even as they divide up tasks required to fulfill the missions. In the early 1990s, some Europeans were tempted to see the Balkan challenge as one that could and should be handled by Europeans, not the Americans. Throughout the 1990s, many Americans felt that the United States should not be required to play such a major military role in the Balkans, given that the Europeans were closer to and had a greater stake in the region. For some, this had meant that the European Union should take over responsibility for Balkan security, allowing the United States to move on to other military tasks. The Bush administration came to office having made such an argument during the 2000 presidential election campaign. Once in office, however, wiser heads in the administration, notably Secretary of State Colin Powell, decided that a unilateral US withdrawal from the Balkans could undermine prospects for continued development of liberal institutions and regional stability. Moreover, a unilateral US withdrawal would begin the process of dividing security responsibilities between the United States and its European allies, making a trip down the slippery slopes of US unilateralism and European autonomy much more likely and the future of NATO much more questionable. Secretary of State Powell therefore pledged that the NATO allies had "come in together and would go out together," reestablishing, at least temporarily, continuity in US policy toward both Balkan security and NATO cooperation.

At the end of 2001, the bulk of the political, military, and financial burdens in the Balkans were being borne by the Europeans. Since 1991, the European Union has been the largest single provider of aid to the western Balkans, having given close to $6 billion through its various aid programs. The European Union also provided some 800 civilian police to help maintain civil order in Kosovo.[15] Meanwhile, in December 2001, US forces constituted under 20 percent of the total NATO and non-NATO forces committed to NATO Balkan operations in Bosnia-Herzegovina, Croatia, Macedonia, and Kosovo.[16] In other words, the European allies and partner countries, taken together, were carrying the bulk of peacekeeping tasks in the Balkans, albeit under a NATO flag. This demonstrated their willingness to take responsibility for important missions within the NATO framework at a time when the European Union did not have the requisite internal command arrangements to assume full responsibility.

Perhaps some day it will be appropriate to turn over remaining military tasks in this region to the European Union. For the time being, however, NATO's continued involvement signals US commitment to stability in the region. Even with less than 20 percent of the military forces now deployed under NATO command there, the US involvement carries political weight that is at least helpful, if not essential, to peace and the development of liberal democratic institutions in the region.

BALLISTIC MISSILE DEFENSES

One of the most difficult issues remaining on NATO's agenda after September 11, 2001, was the question of missile defense. Early in 2001, the new Bush administration's strong commitment to development of missile defenses appeared to pose one of the most fundamental challenges to NATO unity in the history of the alliance. Early that year, experts wrote about the dangers of "strategic disconnect" between a United States that, in the future, had insulated itself from missile threats that would then allow it to isolate itself from security problems around the world and to disengage from security in Europe. From this perspective, the United States would become a secure "island," and the rest of the alliance would remain in a vulnerable, separate strategic space. This would sever the sharing-of-risks principle underlying the transatlantic bargain. Missile defense proponents, on the other hand, argued that if the United States could protect itself from rogue state or terrorist-launched missile threats, it would be in a better position to come to the aid of its allies in Europe and elsewhere.

On the one hand, those who had been skeptical about Bush missile defense plans could interpret the September 11 attacks as demonstrating that building defenses against strategic missiles was pointless. Terrorists and rogue states clearly could find ways around US defenses to attack and destroy select US targets, create fear, and disrupt the US economy and way of life.

On the other hand, those who supported a robust missile defense program could see the September 11 events as fully justifying their position. The demonstrated willingness of the al-Qaeda network to attack US targets using hijacked aircraft made it even more likely that such groups or rogue states in the future might acquire ballistic missiles to deliver weapons of mass destruction on US or allied targets.

In the months following the attacks, it appeared that those in the second school of thought retained the upper hand regarding future US policy. The United States, on balance, while sensitized to the many ways that it could be attacked, nonetheless concluded that the September 11 events warranted the search for effective defenses against ballistic missiles as part of the overall threat posed by terrorists and rogue states. Public opinion, strongly supporting the war against terrorism and demonstrating the will to take casualties to achieve the war's objectives, also demonstrated increased support for developing missile defenses. For example, in the wake of the attacks, a poll by the Gallup organization found that some 70 percent of the adults questioned supported spending money to develop defenses against nuclear missiles. That was up from 53 percent in favor a year before.[17]

However, not all aspects of the post–September 11 situation necessarily support more rapid development of missile defenses. The economic consequences of the attacks, which helped push the United States into what had been an impending economic recession, reduced the resources available for government programs. The costs of the war in Afghanistan, of other aspects of the war against terrorism, and of enhanced homeland security will compete with missile defense funding. In addition, the fact that Russia's President Vladimir Putin has been helpful in the war against terrorism strengthened Putin's relationship with President Bush and increased the incentives for developing the US missile defense program in ways that are compatible with continued US–Russian cooperation on other issues. Moreover, in 2002, test programs for missile defense technologies had not yet demonstrated the level of success likely to be required to move systems toward development and deployment.

This combination of factors suggests that the United States will continue to pursue missile defenses against terrorist or rogue-state threats but in a fashion constrained by finances, relations with Russia, and the record of technological success. This means that the United States and its allies will remain challenged to find approaches to missile defenses that strengthen, not weaken, the alliance. On balance, the September 11 events probably enhanced prospects for the United States and the allies to find more common middle ground. The attacks demonstrated that the world remains a dangerous place and that terrorists are willing to commit acts that appear irrational by standards accepted in Western liberal democracies. In addition, the attacks did serious damage to the image of a United States becoming invulnerable and disengaged from Europe as the result of missile defenses. One post–September 11 transatlantic conference, sponsored by the Royal United Services Institute in London, reportedly concluded that "European views were becoming closer to US positions" and that "the Europeans now understand the United States will deploy defenses for itself and its allies and friends . . . [and] will accept American deployment and cooperate in missile defense development."[18]

Despite such tentative signs of converging US and European positions, however, ballistic missile defense remains a difficult issue for the alliance. Perhaps the best next step for the United States and all the NATO allies would be to conduct bottom-up reviews of homeland defense requirements, including defenses against ballistic missiles. Such an approach might shed light on areas of common interest and perceptions that were not evident before September 11.

RELATIONS WITH RUSSIA

The military and ideological threat posed by the Soviet Union, with Russia at its core, along with European concerns about a resurgent Germany, provided the original stimulus for the transatlantic bargain. These two factors also provided motivation for the steps taken in the 1940s and 1950s to initiate the process of European unification. The German "threat" was dissipated by decades of liberal German democracy, loyalty to the Western alliance, and the process of European integration. When the Soviet Union imploded at the end of the Cold War, the United States and its European allies discovered that even though this founding threat was also disappearing, the cooperation that had developed over the years not only was based on solid common values and interests but also had continuing utility in a post-Soviet world.

Nevertheless, Russia remained a major factor in allied calculations. Despite Russia's devastated economy and military forces so weakened as to be incapable of putting down rebellion in the former Soviet republic of Chechnya, Russia remained a world-class nuclear power and a huge variable in Europe's future. The development of a liberal democratic system in Russia would be a dramatic gain for international peace and stability. An autocratic, deprived, and dissatisfied Russia would constitute a major source of instability for the indefinite future. As a consequence, the transatlantic allies moved carefully throughout the 1990s trying to assess how steps that they were taking to adapt their alliance would affect and be affected by Russia.

As the European Union and NATO began their separate processes of outreach to the new democracies emerging in Eastern and central Europe and figuring how to respond to their long-repressed desires for membership in Western institutions, neither NATO nor the European Union thought that Russia would qualify for membership in either organization for as far out as the eye could see. It was clear, however, that Russia, even as weak as it was, remained a major player in European security.

NATO in particular reached out to Russia as it moved toward including the Soviet Union's former central and East European "allies" in the Western security system. Russia was offered participation in NATO's partnership program and then, in the context of the first round of NATO enlargement, was given a special relationship to the alliance with negotiation of the Founding Act on Mutual Relations, Cooperation and Security between NATO and the Russia Federation, establishing a Permanent Joint Council—NATO nations plus Russia—as a framework for continuing consultations.

Russia's acceptance of the Permanent Joint Council was always grudging. Russian leaders wanted something more—something that would more directly acknowledge Russia's importance in European security. The NATO countries, on the other hand, did not want to give Russia a direct say in NATO deliberations and certainly not a veto over NATO actions—a concern directly expressed by American conservatives during the debate on NATO enlargement.

However, under the leadership of Vladimir Putin, a democratically elected but autocratic leader with pragmatic foreign policy inclinations, Russia and NATO have moved toward a more meaningful relationship. The most important stimulus was provided by the September 11 terrorist attacks and Putin's offer of assistance in the US-declared war against terrorism. Putin's position clearly helped strengthen his relationship with President Bush and facilitated work toward agreements on dramatic cuts in strategic nuclear weapons arsenals and possible agreements on missile defenses. Putin also hinted at new Russian perspectives on its relationship to NATO and Russia's attitude toward NATO enlargement.

Once again, British Prime Minister Tony Blair, who had played such an important role in getting the European Union's CESDP on track, started the ball rolling for a new Russia–NATO initiative by proposing creation of a new forum for Russia–NATO cooperation. Blair, in a letter to NATO Secretary-General George Robertson, suggested the creation of a Russia/North Atlantic Council that would take decisions by consensus on certain issues affecting both NATO and Russia, for example, terrorism, arms proliferation, and peacekeeping. According to press reports, British officials suggested privately that post–September 11 events could lead to a new world order, ending old enmities and building new bridges. "The prime minister believes the fact that the world is such a different place since September 11 does give us opportunities as well as threats," one official said.[19]

Apparently with the blessing of the Bush administration, Secretary-General Robertson put the idea forward during an official visit to Moscow. Headlines blared, "Russia Could Get Veto Power in New NATO."[20] Russian conservatives worried that Putin was about to give away the store, while other Russian analysts speculated that the move would give Russia associate membership in the alliance. American conservatives were concerned what the move might do in NATO. Polish observers fretted that this might be the first step toward Russian membership in NATO. French observers wondered whether events were moving too fast for rational consideration of their consequences.[21]

Two former officials responsible for President Clinton's NATO enlargement policy, Jeremy D. Rosner and Ronald D. Asmus, argued for simply revitalizing current NATO–Russia relations:

> Mr. Putin has complained that the existing NATO–Russia relationship is moribund. He is right. But the reason why it is moribund is that Russia walked away from the table in protest over NATO's air campaign in Kosovo and has since pursued an obstructionist policy. That fact alone should give us pause. There is nothing wrong with the NATO–Russia Permanent Joint Council that a dose of good will and hard work could not fix.[22]

On December 6, 2001, despite such arguments, the allies agreed to establish a new NATO–Russia council to identify and pursue opportunities for joint action between Russia and the NATO allies. The ministers made it clear that the new council would not give Russia a veto over NATO decisions.

The Permanent Joint Council would be replaced by a new NATO–Russia Council. The new council, formally agreed to by NATO and Russia on May 28, 2002, is intended to meet more regularly and to make decisions on some subjects. However, the regular agenda of the North Atlantic Council will not be shifted to the new framework. The North Atlantic Council will decide when issues should be submitted to decision by the Russia–North Atlantic Council and when they should be kept within usual NATO decision-making channels. Unlike the Permanent

Joint Council, however, the allies will not bring "pre-cooked" NATO positions to the table with Russia. If the Russia–North Atlantic Council becomes deadlocked on an issue because of Russian disagreement, this would not block the NATO members from acting in the North Atlantic Council without Russian agreement or participation. Russia will not have a "veto" over NATO decisions, even though it clearly will exercise more influence on those decisions than previously.

The way in which the new arrangement will work depends largely on political judgments made in Moscow and in NATO governments. Lord Robertson argues that the real differences between the former "19 + 1" arrangement and a new "20" forum is a matter of "chemistry rather than arithmetic, as even the best format and seating arrangements can be no substitute for genuine political will and open mind on both sides."[23] One of the early issues that will have to be tackled in the NATO–Russia relationship, bilaterally and perhaps in the new council, is how to deal with the Kaliningrad enclave, that is, Russian territory between Poland and Lithuania that would be surrounded by NATO (and EU) territory in the future.

The advent of a more meaningful, action-oriented NATO–Russia relationship could be a very positive development for European security. It will not block NATO decisions on enlargement of the alliance. In fact, just as creation of the Permanent Joint Council with Russia "accompanied" and facilitated the first round of NATO enlargement, development of the new NATO–Russia Council will parallel implementation of NATO's next enlargement round. The step will not presage imminent Russian membership in the alliance. Militarily, Russia obviously could make major military contributions to the alliance. However, Russia's size and importance suggest that geopolitical factors will play a large role in deciding when Russia might be acceptable as a member. Politically, Russia is a long way from meeting the guidelines for membership laid out in NATO's 1995 "Study on Enlargement." Russia falls far short particularly in terms of the internal development of liberal democratic institutions, including a free press, and a Western-style human rights regime. If Russia some day meets these guidelines, there truly will be a "new world order," and Russia should then be considered a legitimate candidate for membership. Until then, there should remain a clear distinction between what issues are decided with members of the alliance and which are decided with this very important Russian partner.

NATO ENLARGEMENT

Before the September 11 events, political interest in and support for NATO's second enlargement round could not be compared to that for the first round, which brought the Czech Republic, Hungary, and Poland into the alliance. President Bush said that his administration was a strong supporter of NATO enlargement. But the administration had no eager European partner on this issue. Germany, the key European architect of the first round, has less of a strategic stake in the next stages and, until late in 2001, had been reluctant to upset Moscow.

Launched in the early 1990s, NATO enlargement aims at stabilizing Europe and at furthering the spread of democracy in former Warsaw Pact countries. Together with the European Union's admission of new members, expansion of Euro-Atlantic institutions has been a key part of the strategy aimed at extending the benefits of democracy, economic prosperity, and international multilateral cooperation to a region cut off from such opportunities for more than fifty years. More than a decade after the fall of the iron curtain, the basic rationale for this strategy has not changed.

In the wake of the terrorist attacks on the United States, some observers questioned the wisdom of moving ahead with NATO enlargement. However, within a few months of the attacks, it appeared that a consensus was growing in favor of a major enlargement initiative when allied leaders meet in Prague, the Czech Republic, in November 2002.

According to a study by the Brookings Institution released late in 2001,

> The case for enlargement . . . is stronger than before. Enlargement will contribute to the process of integration that has helped stabilize Europe over the past fifty years and promote the development of strong new allies in the war on terrorism. . . . Far from backing away from NATO enlargement, the Bush administration should welcome all those European democracies whose political stability, military contributions, and commitment to NATO solidarity would be assets to the Alliance. Now more than ever, Alliance leaders can and should pursue a wider, integrated NATO and a strong and cooperative relationship with Russia at the same time.[24]

Ten countries were seeking membership in NATO prior to the Prague summit. Judged by the standards set in NATO's 1995 "Study on Enlargement," some of these countries were very close to qualifying for an invitation. They included Slovenia, the Slovak Republic (presuming that it stays on a democratic path), and the Baltic states: Estonia, Latvia, and Lithuania. Two candidates, Romania and Bulgaria, supported particularly by NATO states in southeastern Europe, could be strategic assets to the alliance and have made significant contributions to the war against terrorism, enhancing their chances of receiving an invitation in Prague. The other candidates—Albania, Macedonia, and Croatia—were less well prepared to begin formal negotiations. In the run-up to Prague, it looked increasingly as if all seven of the leading candidates might receive invitations.

One of the options available to the members was to invite all seven countries in Prague but to spread their accession out over several years. A 2001 report to the NATO Parliamentary Assembly, for example, suggested the enlargement process could be converted from one of "waves" to a "stream" of invitations—otherwise known as the "regatta" approach.[25]

Beyond the question of formal invitations and negotiation of membership terms lies another major challenge. The Bush administration will have to convince sixty-seven of the one hundred members of the Senate that further enlargement is in the interest of the United States. Ratification of enlargement will be an issue in all NATO and candidate countries, but the decision in the United States is the most critical. Senator John Warner (R-Va.), a leader of the opposition to enlargement the first time around, remains skeptical that enlargement is in the US interest. In February 2002, Senator Warner, speaking at a Senate Armed Services Committee hearing, asked,

> Are the people willing to risk US military troops and expend significant taxpayer dollars to defend the nine additional nations seeking NATO membership? If NATO expands beyond its current 19 members, some fear—and I share that fear—that the alliance will become increasingly inefficient, indecisive and just about a mini–United Nations for Europe.

Warner suggested it was time to "consider proudly retiring the colours of NATO and start over again."[26] His perspective may be shared by other conservative Republicans as well as some Democrats who will want to be reassured once again that enlargement will not come with a large price tag for the United States. In any case, the process of ratification of enlargement will demonstrate once again the important role of Congress and particularly the Senate in management of the transatlantic bargain.

Beyond the ratification question, it will be important that the integration of new members into the alliance be coordinated effectively with their role in the European Union's CESDP. Three current NATO members (Poland, the Czech Republic, and Hungary) and all seven leading candidates for NATO membership are engaged in accession negotiations with the European Union. Although there is no formal link between NATO and EU enlargement, the fact is that every EU member is effectively part of the Western security system that is organized around NATO. In some European capitals, this reasoning gave rise to the idea of delaying the Baltic states' accession to NATO in favor of a quick admission to the European Union coupled with an implicit defense guarantee. However, as the European Union is not yet able to issue convincing defense guarantees, this approach was not a compelling alternative to moving both enlargement processes ahead on their own merits. Working these two processes together successfully will be high on the security agendas of both NATO and the European Union in the years ahead.

US HEGEMONY, EU AUTONOMY, AND THE NATO–EU RELATIONSHIP

The most fundamental challenge to the Atlantic Community is to overcome natural but ominous tendencies on both sides of the Atlantic that could tear the alliance apart. The combination of a United States drifting toward unilateralism and European concentration on creating an "autonomous" defense policy could feed on each other, creating circumstances that could lead the transatlantic bargain from one crisis to another.

The Hegemony Challenge: How to Be a Hegemon without Acting Like One

The United States did not by itself create the circumstances that have left it as the world's only surviving superpower. But it does face the challenge of dealing with this new reality. Since the Cold War ended, there has been an ongoing elite debate about the role the United States should play in an international system that is no longer dominated by the bipolar confrontation of two alliance systems led by the United States and the Soviet Union.[27]

In recent years, the debate over US foreign policy among experts and editorialists has included those who argue for a more restricted US world role and those who call for the United States to take full advantage of its position as the sole surviving superpower. Public opinion polls suggest that the American people reject both options and in fact favor an engaged US world role based on sharing international burdens and responsibilities with other nations.[28]

At the end of the Cold War, President George Bush clearly believed that the United States was required to play a strong international leadership role. Some of his advisers apparently thought that the United States should use its position as the sole superpower to discourage challenges to that position, even among current allies. President Bush nonetheless accepted the importance of building consensus in the United Nations and constructing coalitions to deal with international challenges (both illustrated by his orchestration of the response to Iraq's invasion of Kuwait).

In the first year of his presidency, Bill Clinton and his foreign policy advisers experimented with a number of different approaches to US foreign policy. Clinton sought to convert his successful campaign slogan, "It's the economy, stupid," into a pillar of US foreign policy. In part as a consequence of this philosophy, some Clinton administration officials argued that Asia (rather than Europe) should be the central focus of US foreign policy because of the opportunities presented by growing Asian markets.

Early on, many friends and allies of the United States worried that the United States was turning inward or at least away from Europe. Those concerns were heightened by the Clinton administration's initial "tilt" toward Asia (1993), the US reaction to the peacekeeping disaster in Somalia (1993), US reluctance to become deeply involved in the conflict in the former Yugoslavia (1991–94), and an emerging tendency toward "self-deterrence" in which the United States appeared to be increasingly less inclined to risk the use of military force on behalf of international stability.[29]

For most of Clinton's first term, many observers saw the administration as vacillating between active internationalism and foreign policy reticence. As Clinton moved toward the end of his first term, however, he appeared to have decided that an assertive US international leadership role could be more of an advantage than a burden. In 1996, as he campaigned for a second term in office, Clinton argued that the United States was the world's "indispensable power," suggesting the international system required the active involvement of the United States to function effectively. Clinton maintained that such activism was in the US interest.

The Clinton administration mostly attempted to avoid policies that were or that could be perceived as isolationist or unilateralist. But, on occasion, it misjudged or chose to ignore how its actions would be seen by its friends and allies. The administration was also pushed by Congress in some directions that apparently would not have been its first choice, such as on the issues of extraterritorial sanctions and nonpayment of US arrears at the United Nations. Administration setbacks in Congress over payment of UN arrears and "fast track" authorization for international trade negotiations were perceived abroad as further evidence of unilateralist tendencies.

In addition, self-confident US behavior on occasion rubbed many Europeans the wrong way. When the Clinton administration revealed its choice of three candidates—Poland, the Czech Republic, and Hungary—to participate in the first wave of NATO enlargement, many allies privately applauded. But the fact that the United States appeared to have abandoned the process of NATO consultations to make its choice clear and then said that its decision was nonnegotiable troubled even America's closest allies. It strengthened the hand of those in Europe who claimed that the United States is acting like a "hegemonic" power, using its impressive position of strength to have its way with its weaker European allies. One official of a pro-American northern European country that supported the package of three commented, "We liked the present but were troubled by the way it was wrapped."[30]

American officials said that they wanted to keep the issue within alliance consultations but that their position was leaked to the press by other allies. They decided to put an end to "lobbying" for other outcomes. Their choice to go strong and to go public may have been understandable and even defensible. However, the acknowledged leader of a coalition of democratic states probably needs to set the very best example in the consultative process if it wants other sovereign states to follow its lead willingly. The case demonstrated that it is hard being number one, and US officials always note in such cases that the United States is "damned if it does, and damned if it does not" provide strong leadership.

Whatever the explanation, US–European relations would have been better served by a US approach that allowed the outcome to emerge more naturally from the consultative, behind-the-scenes consensus-forming process. In NATO councils, votes are weighed, not counted, and the US vote carries more weight than any other. The final result would have been the same, and the appearance of a US "diktat" to the allies would have been avoided.

By the end of the Clinton administration and with the advent of the George W. Bush administration, concerns had shifted strongly toward the expectation that the United States would pull its troops out of the Balkans (as candidate Bush had recommended) and behave increasingly like the international hegemon that it had become. The approach taken by the Bush administration during the early stages of the war against terrorism, beginning with the campaign in Afghanistan, produced mixed reactions. On the one hand, the administration's strategy was based on building a broad international coalition against terrorism. The rhetoric and formal approach of US policy remained true to this goal. On the other hand, the United States conducted the campaign with little reference to offers from the allies to help out and without making much institutional use of the NATO framework.

Part of the danger in this debate lies in the language that is used to discuss the issue. Not all foreign commentaries are benign, but many foreign observers do use "hegemony" as a descriptive, academic term intended to characterize the structure of current international power relationships. *Webster's New Collegiate Dictionary* defines "hegemony" as "preponderant influence or authority esp[ecially] of one nation over others." This presumably is a condition that can exist even if the country in question does not seek a hegemonic position.

The American people and their leaders, however, do not perceive the United States as a hegemonic power and do not aspire to hegemony. "Hegemony," to the American ear, is an offensive term; it is recognized as the word that was appropriately used to describe the policies and practices of the Soviet Union during the Cold War. How, most Americans might wonder, can our friends use terminology to describe us that was once appropriate for an expansionist, dictatorial communist regime?

Beyond the reaction to the term, there are immediate and practical implications. If the United States appears to be overbearing in its relations with other countries, it may find it difficult to build international consensus on behalf of its policies. There may be occasions on which the United States will choose to pursue a dominating line, even at the expense of dissonance with its allies, when it feels that important interests are at stake. But it is clear that there are costs associated with policies that build coalitions only by the use of overwhelming political force rather than by consultation, persuasion, and compromise.

The underlying reality—that the United States occupies a central and unmatched position in international politics—will not change in the foreseeable future. This, German commentator Joe Joffe has argued, cannot be seen simply in classic balance-of-power terms. He argues the United States is different from previous dominant powers: "It irks and domineers, but it does not conquer. It tries to call the shots and bend the rules, but it does not go to war for land and glory." Further, he argues, the dominating US position is based on "soft" as well as "hard" power: "This type of power—a culture that radiates outward and a market that draws inward—rests on pull, not on push; on acceptance, not on conquest."[31]

Under these circumstances, the United States faces the challenge of using its power in ways that reflect US values and draw on the American public's desire to cooperate with other countries while not inspiring opposition as a result of appearing too domineering. If US allies still believe that US leadership is essential on many international issues, as they apparently do, then their challenge is to express their criticism of US leadership style in terms that are appropriate for frank and honest discussions among friends.

If the United States and its allies do not deal effectively with this problem, it could intrude dramatically on a wide range of issues in which their common interests are likely served by pragmatic cooperation rather than conflict inspired by current international power realities. In particular, a healthy transatlantic relationship will require that the United States master the art of being a hegemon without acting like one.

The Autonomy Challenge: How to Pursue European Autonomy Inside an Atlantic Community

On the other side of this equation, there is the danger that the European Union's pursuit of ever-deeper integration and autonomy will divide the transatlantic partners. American interests would benefit from a European partner that could assume serious military burdens and play a more substantial role dealing with international security problems. However, the unintended consequences of international policies can be the most important—and threatening—in the long run.

Since the end of World War II, the United States has actively supported the process of European integration and a stronger European role in defense. For most of the Cold War period, the United States, particularly Congress, constantly berated the Europeans about their inadequate defense efforts. At the same time, however, the United States was growing accustomed to its role as the dominant alliance leader, and inadequate European defense efforts only enhanced US predominance. Therefore, when the European allies pledged to include military aspects of security in the process of European integration, the United States had mixed emotions. On the one hand, a more substantial European defense effort would help relieve the United States of European and perhaps even some global defense burdens. On the other hand, serious European efforts promised to disturb what had become the normal balance of power and influence in the alliance.

The United States made a serious effort in the mid-1990s to respond to the European desire to take on more responsibility for defense and to give the process of European integration a meaningful security component by creating room within which a European Security and Defense Identity could grow within NATO. The subsequent—and substitute—initiatives for an "autonomous" CESDP (discussed in chapter 9) therefore created immediate US suspicions that the new approach would bypass the mechanisms and principles established between NATO and the Western European Union in the mid-1990s and replace them with arrangements that are more likely to create separate and even competing EU and NATO decision-making processes and commitments.

American concerns were perhaps exaggerated but not entirely unwarranted. Despite the European Union's best intentions, there is the danger that CESDP could create artificial divisions and distinctions among NATO allies, undermining NATO's political cohesion. Perhaps even more important than duplicating US/NATO capabilities at a time when EU countries are not increasing spending on defense is the risk that CESDP and the demands of its institutional creations could encourage "we/they" distinctions between Europeans and the United States and even among European members of NATO. Despite all the declarations on behalf of transparency and cooperation, EU governments and officials may occasionally seek to promote the European Union's or their own standing by distinguishing European from American or "NATO" positions. The United States and the European allies share a wide range of common interests and values, but they are not always identical and are not always pursued identically. NATO's "golden rule of consultation" does not eliminate such differences but does provide a setting in which differing approaches can be compromised or at least accommodated. The dynamic of the new arrangements may impose subtle barriers to communication and compromise that did not exist before.

By way of example, US suspicions of EU motivations were heightened in 2000 by concern that reports that some EU officials and governments had pressured candidates for EU membership—the Czech Republic, Hungary, and Poland—to support an EU "line" in the EU–NATO relationship. Apparently, the tactic was suspended, but the incident illustrates the potential for the "autonomy" aspect of CESDP to divide the alliance into European and American components.[32]

There remains a potent residue of suspicion in Washington about France's intentions and likely behavior. Particularly with the United Kingdom as strongly committed to CESDP as it has become, some in the United States are concerned that it will become increasingly enmeshed in an anti-American device manipulated by French neo-Gaullists. In addition, successful French guidance of CESDP down an anti-American road could pull Germany in the same direction, undermining the close relationship that the United States and Germany developed during the Cold War and the post–Cold War transition period.

There is also the danger that CESDP could be used by some European countries to join forces with Russia and China in working against "US hegemony." Very little irritates US officials and experts more than European officials singing along with a chorus of Russian, Chinese, and Third World commentators against "US hegemony." Some past examples that raised hackles in Washington have included French President Jacques Chirac joining the Chinese in a communiqué at the end of his state visit to Beijing in May 1997 praising the virtues of a "multipolar world"—thin cover for criticism of US hegemony. In June 1997, on a state visit to Moscow, Chirac failed to dispute Russian President Boris Yeltsin's view of a Europe organized between Russia, France, and other members of the European Union. This recalled all too clearly old Soviet proposals for a "European house" that excluded the United States. If CESDP were to become a European platform for criticism of the US world role, it would probably spell the beginning of the end for the transatlantic alliance.

A CESDP that focuses too strongly on "autonomy" could convince US leaders and members of Congress that the United States is no longer needed or wanted as a security partner in Europe. During the Cold War, European allies occasionally expressed the concern that if they did too much for their own defense, the United States would decide it was no longer needed in Europe and pull out. For those who believe that the alliance is still vitally important for US interests, there is a concern that the appearance of greater European self-reliance (even before it becomes a fact) might lead US political leaders and members of Congress to conclude that NATO and US military involvement in Europe is no longer necessary. Representative Douglas Bereuter warns, "It needs to be clear to our European Allies that the creation of competing institutions in Europe that detract from NATO's capabilities and solidarity would endanger public and congressional support for its commitment to the North Atlantic alliance."[33]

Another challenge will be in the area of defense industrial relations. There is a danger that US unilateralism combined with the EU desire for "autonomy" will increase transatlantic trade and industrial tensions by supporting development of a "fortress Europe" mentality in defense procurement. This is an area where the United States can take much of the blame for the lack historically of a "two-way street" in transatlantic armaments trade and for failure to devise ways of sharing new technologies with the European allies to help them participate in the "revolution in military technology." The CESDP does not necessarily require that Europe increase protectionism or favoritism for its own defense industries. Lagging far behind American defense firms in adjusting to post–Cold War market conditions, the necessary mergers and consolidations are finally beginning to rationalize the European defense industrial base. The next logical step is for rationalization of the transatlantic industrial base through a variety of means. This next step would have to be facilitated by governments, and both the United States and the EU members would have to make alliance solidarity and cooperation a high priority to overcome existing barriers to transatlantic armaments cooperation. An EU that puts a higher priority on developing CESDP could easily put new obstacles in the way of alliance cooperation in armaments and particularly in the way of purchasing US systems.[34]

Future US policy toward CESDP will in any circumstances remain conflicted. Bush administration and congressional concerns about negative consequences of CESDP are likely to increase in direct proportion to the emphasis EU governments put on "autonomy" when describing what they hope to accomplish in CESDP.

A politically united Europe is not likely to emerge for many years, perhaps not for many decades. It is difficult to imagine the EU nations making commitments in the defense area that are more far reaching than those they have made to political union at any given point in time. It seems very unlikely, in other words, that defense union can proceed ahead of political union; rather, it must develop in parallel or lag somewhat behind the process of developing greater political cohesion among the member states. Unless and until the members of the European Union have achieved something approaching political union, a CESDP will remain an intergovernmental exercise, subject to variable perceptions of national interests among current and potential EU members.

Dealing with the process of transition from an alliance dominated by the United States to one that is at least somewhat more balanced between the United States and Europe will therefore be one of the major challenges for the transatlantic democracies in the years, probably decades, ahead. However, the degree to which the United States pursues unilateralist policies internationally is likely to intensify support in Europe for more cohesive European foreign policy and defense positions, even if on a purely intergovernmental level.

The Bottom Line

At the end of the day, neither the United States nor the European allies are likely to allow the unilateralism-versus-autonomy mix to destroy the transatlantic bargain. This is true in part because when the United States looks around the world and asks which countries can help it deal with future international security challenges, it is likely to find mainly European nations that have both the will and the capacity to be serious partners. And if Europeans look around for allies that broadly share European values and interests, most will conclude that the United States, with all its flaws, will remain the most important, reliable, and important world partner for a more united Europe. It is sometimes difficult to see this European reality through our allies' frequent complaints about their big-power partner. But particularly in the eyes of the new European democracies in central and Eastern Europe, the transatlantic tie remains essential to European and international security and well-being. In fact, the perception that some European countries were putting good relations with the United States at risk for the sake of European autonomy would divide the EU members and seriously disrupt the process of European integration.

The transatlantic allies need to breathe new life into the sense of common destiny among the Atlantic community of nations. This is a bigger task than simply reaffirming the goal of NATO unity or avoiding disastrous unilateralist policies. It requires policies that reflect and acknowledge the mutual dependence and shared values that still make the Euro-Atlantic community special. Without such a sense of community, the United States would be weaker and less predictable and Europe less confident and secure.

THE TRANSATLANTIC BARGAIN RECONSIDERED: ALTERNATIVE FUTURES

Against the backdrop of these challenges, it may be useful to consider some of the theoretical directions that an evolving European security system could take in the next decade or two. One way of looking ahead is to examine several different tendencies. One tendency could be toward continued domination by NATO and the United States. Another tendency could be toward a system increasingly dominated

by the European Union. A third tendency could be toward a loosely organized cooperative security system along the lines of the Organization for Security and Cooperation in Europe (OSCE). The system could tend toward disintegration and
disorganization. Or, in theory, it could become more thoroughly integrated.

NATO Dominant

This tendency would be characterized by a NATO that is successfully reinvigo-
rated with a new sense of purpose—provided in part by the war on terrorism—
as well as additional and enthusiastic members from Eastern and central Europe
and a stronger, more effective collaboration with Russia. Its most important char-
acteristic would be a continued strong leading role for the United States that ensures transatlantic management of European security affairs. In this direction, a
greater degree of defense cooperation among the members of the European
Union would be likely, but the CESDP would remain insufficiently developed and
equipped to "Europeanize" NATO or for the European Union to take over NATO's
responsibilities. A degree of European resentment for continued US hegemony in
Europe would be the source of continuing transatlantic frictions. The OSCE
would remain handicapped by its unwieldy membership, limited operational
mandate, and negligible resources. The United Nations would continue to lack the
full support of the United States that would be required to transform it into an effective manager of military operations that go beyond traditional peacekeeping
activities. NATO therefore would remain the only effective organizer of multilateral military forces and operations.

EU Dominant

The directions outlined in the Maastricht Treaty, reinforced by CESDP developments in the late 1990s and the emergence of the Euro as a major force in world
currency markets, would dominate in this tendency. As the members of the European Union progressively coordinated their foreign and defense policies and developed military assets and capabilities, the Union would take on principal responsibility for managing security in Europe. The European Union would also
develop the capacity and political will to intervene internationally on behalf of
European interests and policy goals. With the European Union emphasizing its
autonomy and independent world role and the United States acting in progressively more unilateralist directions, NATO would soldier on but would increasingly be relegated to a role of trying to sustain minimal transatlantic military cooperation. The United States would withdraw all substantial military units from
Europe. The OSCE and the United Nations would remain handicapped by the factors discussed previously in the NATO-dominant model. The new democracies
increasingly would see membership in the European Union as their major source
of security and well-being, and Russia would cut separate deals with the European
Union and with the United States to protect its future interests.

OSCE Influenced

In the OSCE-influenced direction, the United States and the European states would accede to long-standing Russian preferences for a European security system constructed on a pan-European foundation. NATO would remain a viable framework for coordinating military cooperation, and EU defense cooperation would continue to develop, but all with the understanding that ultimate political decision making on European security issues resides in the OSCE. The United States would become increasingly distanced from the system, remaining involved largely to balance Russian influence.

Fragmenting

In a fragmenting European security system, all the existing organizations would have failed to attract sufficient political support and cohesion to provide the operational center for the system. Competition among nations preferring different directions would have undermined the effectiveness of all the key institutions. NATO would have faded toward irrelevance, and the United States would have withdrawn most of its forces from Europe and dramatically lowered the level of day-to-day military cooperation with the European allies. Interoperability among Euro-Atlantic military forces would be steadily declining. The United States would be focused on dominating international arms sales, while the Europeans would be constructing a fortress Europe within which strong preference was given to European-developed and -produced arms. The European Union would have failed to develop sufficient consensus on foreign and defense policies to substitute for NATO even though cutbacks in defense spending throughout Europe had stimulated a variety of defense cooperation projects. Defense would not have been thoroughly "renationalized" only because no country would want to devote sufficient resources to become militarily self-sufficient. The OSCE would remain weak and racked by divisions among the members, and Russian influence would have increased in part because of the general incoherence in NATO and the European Union.

Integrating

In an integrating system, all the building blocks of a European security system would be in the process of linking to each other and to the UN system. In such an approach, each level of institutionalized cooperation would ideally be consistent with and supportive of the next level—a building-block, instead of a bloc-to-bloc, approach to European security. Nation-states would remain the basic building blocks for the system, but EU integration would have progressed, NATO would effectively have combined US leadership with a stronger European role in defense, and the OSCE would provide the "rules of the road" for relations among states in Europe and, operationally, would be playing an effective role in preconflict resolution and mediation efforts as well as postconflict settlement and democratization/liberalization of political systems. The institutions would be truly "interlocking" rather than "interblocking," to use terms that became popular in NATO circles in the late 1990s. A sense of community among Euro-Atlantic democracies would be enhanced and perhaps even captured in new "Atlantic Community" institutions. An increasingly democratic Russia would be playing a constructive role in a cooperative European security system with a more formal and meaningful relationship to NATO. Good working relations would have been established between the integrated European system and the global UN system. Military cooperation in NATO would make it possible for the transatlantic allies to make combined joint task forces available for OSCE- and UN-authorized missions, and NATO's autonomous ability to act would contribute to deterrence of aggressive international behavior.

Current Preferences and Tendencies

The fragmenting and integrating tendencies are clearly extreme outcomes. The vision of a fragmented European security system is the nightmare scenario for most governments and experts even if their actions and recommendations occasionally push developments in this direction. Such a system would be highly unstable, and the potential for discord among European states would be greater than any other direction suggested here. The integrated system suggests a kind of ideal direction (at least from my perspective) in which the competing interests of all the states and organizations involved are successfully resolved in a highly cooperative and stable set of relationships. Even though these two directions are extreme, they nonetheless may be helpful to policymakers. The fragmented scenario may provide some guidance concerning what to avoid; the integrated scenario may help define useful goals and desirable tendencies.

The NATO-dominant tendency remains the default position for the United States. As long as an integrated system remains a long-term vision but a complicating factor for the short term, the United States is likely to continue to prefer NATO's preeminent role in European security affairs as in its best interests. This does not preclude support for greater European cohesion on defense and security issues, and in fact it presupposes more substantial sharing of international security burdens by European allies. However, there is the danger, discussed previously, that unilateralist US behavior will undermine both the NATO-dominant approach and the integrating approach.

France still must be regarded as the most ardent advocate for the EU-dominant direction. France has accepted and even embraced a continuing role for the transatlantic relationship and NATO in the twenty-first-century world. But the strongest strain in French policy remains the promotion of autonomous policies and capabilities for the European Union. However, France has been mostly reluctant to sacrifice core elements of national sovereignty for the sake of the European integration process, therefore limiting the potential for a fully EU-dominant tendency.

The Europe that France seeks is in some respects different from that traditionally sought by some other European states. Germany, for example, is a strong proponent of a process of European integration that eventually erodes and overwhelms national sovereignties. A similar vision influences perspectives in the Netherlands, Belgium, and a few other countries. The United Kingdom, while increasingly enmeshed in the European integration process, remains reluctant to go as far as many continental EU members have by giving up their national currency for the new EU Euro. (On January 1, 2002, the Euro became the official legal tender of twelve of the fifteen EU countries, replacing their national currencies.[35]) In November 2001, British Prime Minister Tony Blair called his country's traditional ambivalence toward Europe a "tragedy" of lost opportunity and argued that "Britain's future is inextricably linked with Europe; that to get the most of it, we must make the most of our strength and influence within it; and that to do so, we must be wholehearted, not halfhearted, partners in Europe."[36] His argument demonstrated his personal commitment to a leading British role in Europe but also a pragmatic acceptance that substantial British resistance to joining the Euro still made a wholehearted partnership difficult.

Independent British views are mirrored to some extent in Sweden and Finland. These two nations, along with Austria and Ireland, have national histories of "neutrality" that, in varying ways, influence their attitudes toward the integration process. "Neutrality," of course, has very little meaning in the post–Cold War world, and participation in the process of European integration has already brought these countries into the Western community structure. But all four formerly neutral countries face domestic political obstacles to full acceptance of their new circumstances. The Danish public has so far refused to approve joining the Euro zone, and Norway has not joined the European Union. These and other factors reflect both the strength of the integrating tendencies (e.g., the advent of the Euro) and the persistence of national sovereignty and tradition as a brake on those tendencies.

The OSCE-dominant direction for European security was a popular vision for many Europeans in the early days of the post–Cold War era. That popularity faded quickly, however, partly because the first Bush administration in the early 1990s made it clear that the United States was not prepared to see the OSCE (then the Conference on Security and Cooperation in Europe [CSCE]) take the lead away from NATO and partly because the OSCE became seen increasingly as an unwieldy operational instrument for military cooperation. Since the early 1990s, only Russia has remained a strong proponent of the OSCE-dominant European security system, and that position has begun to shift with President Putin's move toward a closer relationship to NATO in 2001. Perhaps one question is whether Putin's shift is based on his judgment that NATO will continue as an influential player in European security or on the belief that NATO is of declining relevance militarily and no longer a threat to Russia.

One of the more thoughtful observers of European security developments, Michael Rühle, argues that speculating about the future of the European security system can be "hazardous" but has the virtue of forcing "thinking about a 'preferred future,' the means necessary to achieve this outcome, and the variables that could interfere."[37] Rühle has developed what he calls "a benevolent scenario 2011," in which he projects what a "good" set of developments for the European security system would produce in the coming decade. According to his projection, a "realistic" benevolent scenario would feature the following:

1. An alliance of twenty-five or more members that still is able to make decisions, led by an active US political and military role;
2. a stronger European military role in the Balkans and more coherent EU foreign policies but a Europe still lacking key capabilities for high-intensity warfare;
3. intense and regular NATO–EU cooperation with back-to-back ministerial meetings;
4. a reduced NATO military presence in the Balkans with Bosnia-Herzegovina and Yugoslavia joining the ranks of applicants for NATO membership;
5. US deployment of a limited strategic missile defense system and European deployments of tactical missile defenses with their forces, in company with a strategic convergence in the alliance on the role of missile defenses;
6. formal links between the Euro-Atlantic Partnership Council and the OSCE with both working on issues such as disaster relief and stability in the Caucasus and central Asia;
7. a continued and intensified role for the Partnership for Peace, even as the number of partners declines as countries join NATO;
8. quasi-associate status with NATO for Russia, with a political solution to Kaliningrad and many areas of cooperation, including tactical missile defenses;
9. a formal and effective NATO relationship with the United Nations;
10. a more global NATO outlook, featuring intensified cooperation with Mediterranean nations, modeled on the Partnership for Peace, and a formal Asia–NATO dialogue.

Rühle identifies a number of variables that could have a fundamental impact on this benign projection. Russia's evolution is a major unknown. How NATO and the European Union handle the enlargement process will be important. The development of CESDP and the US reaction to it are critical, as is the willingness of the United States to remain an active alliance leader. Should the gap in deployed military technology between the United States and the Europeans widen, the burden-sharing problem will be aggravated. If European countries do not devote additional resources to defense, the gap surely will widen. And the evolving threat picture, particularly with the unpredictable nature of international terrorism, could produce fundamental changes in transatlantic attitudes, perceptions, and commitments.

Rühle's analysis is a form of the integrating approach discussed previously. Because he is focused particularly on the military and security aspects of a future Euro-Atlantic system, he does not address directly the need for the transatlantic allies to deepen their cooperation in other aspects of the relationship to complement their military and security ties. One of the first lessons learned about NATO after the terrorist attacks of September 11, 2001, is that the alliance does not have all the instruments of cooperation at hand to be relevant to all aspects of a war on terrorism. Military operations in Afghanistan against Taliban forces that were harboring the al-Qaeda terrorist network and its leaders were the most dramatic and visible aspect of the response. But dealing with the threats posed by terrorism and managing most other aspects of transatlantic relations demand more effective transatlantic cooperation in political, economic, financial, and social as well as military aspects of the relationship. This suggests the need to consider a new framework for the transatlantic bargain, a challenge discussed in chapter 11.

NOTES

1. Statement by the North Atlantic Council (NATO press release [2001] 124), September 12, 2001.

2. George Robertson, NATO secretary-general (statement to the press on the North Atlantic Council Decision on implementation of Article 5 of the North Atlantic Treaty following the September 11 attacks against the United States), October 4, 2001.

3. "NATO Airborne Early Warning Aircraft Begin Deploying to the United States" (SHAPE news release), October 9, 2001.

4. R. Nicholas Burns, "NATO Is Vital for the Challenges of the New Century," *International Herald Tribune,* November 10–11, 2001, 8.

5. NATO North Atlantic Council in Defence Ministers Session, "Statement on Combating Terrorism: Adapting the Alliance's Defence Capabilities" (NATO press release [2001] 173), December 18, 2001.

6. Not-for-attribution discussion with Italian government officials in October 2001.

7. Mary Elise Sarotte, *German Military Reform and European Security,* Adelphi Paper 340, International Institute for Strategic Studies (Oxford: Oxford University Press, 2001), 9–12.

8. Charles Grant, "Does This War Show That NATO No Longer Has a Serious Military Role?" *The Independent,* October 16, 2001.

9. Joseph Fitchett, "Pentagon in a League of Its Own," *International Herald Tribune,* February 4, 2002, 3.

10. George W. Bush, State of the Union Address, January 29, 2002 (for the text, see the White House website at www.whitehouse.gov/news/releases/2002/01/20020129-11.html).

11. Richard G. Lugar, "NATO Must Join War on Terrorism" (speech to the US–NATO Missions Annual Conference, January 19, 2002; for the text, see Senator Lugar's website at www.senate.gov/~lugar/011702.html).

12. Joseph Fitchett, "US Allies Chafe at 'Cleanup' Role," *International Herald Tribune,* November 26, 2001, 1.

13. Fitchett, "US Allies Chafe at 'Cleanup' Role," 1.

14. As discussed in chapter 6, NATO in 1994 accepted the US idea of creating Combined Joint Task Force (CJTF) headquarters as a means of making the alliance's command structure more flexible to deal with new threats to security. A NATO Counterterrorism Task Force would not have been designed to run military operations against terrorist targets. However, such a task force could have been developed as a support mechanism for Afghanistan and future operations. In addition to military officers, the task force could have involved participation by representatives from the foreign and finance ministries of task force countries to bring to bear the wide range of resources needed to wage the campaign. One of the beneficial attributes of the CJTF structure is that non-NATO allies can be invited to participate. In addition, a Counterterrorism Task Force would have provided a framework for enhanced NATO–Russia cooperation. Russia could have been represented in the task force command and support counter terrorist operations even if it did not join openly in attacks on terrorist targets. The author recommended such an initiative following the September 11 attacks, first in an October 7, 2001, presentation to the Political Committee of the NATO Parliamentary Assembly during the Assembly's annual meeting in Ottawa, Canada (titled "A Perspective on the Future of the Transatlantic Bargain"), in a lecture at the NATO Defense College on October 22, 2001, and then in "Give NATO a Combined Task Force against Terrorism," *International Herald Tribune,* November 13, 2001, 8.

15. Information as of June 2001 provided by the European Commission at europa.eu.int/comm/external_relations/see/index.htm.

16. According to the International Institute for Strategic Studies, the United States deployed some 6,830 forces in support of operations in Bosnia-Herzegovina and Croatia out of a total of 21,150, some 5,400 forces in support of operations in Kosovo out of a total of 38,820, and 340 forces in support of operations in Macedonia out of a total of 5,000. *The Military Balance 2001–2002,* International Institute for Strategic Studies (London: Oxford University Press, 2001), 28, 30.

17. Gallup Poll results can be found summarized at www.gallup.com/index.html.

18. Robin Ranger, David Wiencek, and Jeremy Stocker, "New Start for European–U.S. Missile Defense," *Defense News,* November 26–December 2, 2001, 21.

19. Mike Peacock, "Blair Pushes for a New NATO/Russia Relationship," Reuters, November 16, 2001.

20. Michael Wines, "Russia Could Get Veto Power in New NATO," *International Herald Tribune,* November 23, 2001, 1.

21. For detailed coverage of these reactions and other issues related to NATO and NATO enlargement, a good source is the "NATO Enlargement Daily Brief (NEDB)," which can be found at groups.yahoo.com/group/NEDB.

22. Ronald D. Asmus and Jeremy D. Rosner, "Don't Give Russia a Veto," *Washington Times,* December 5, 2001, A19.

23. Lord Robertson, "NATO in the 21st Century" (speech at Charles University, Prague, March 21, 2002; for the full text, see NATO's website at www.nato.int).

24. Phillip H. Gordon and James B. Steinberg, "NATO Enlargement: Moving Forward" (policy brief, Brookings Institution, Washington, D.C., December 2001), 1.

25. AU 214 PC/CEE (01) 5 (Report of the Sub-Committee on Central and Eastern Europe on "NATO Enlargement"), Rapporteur: Bert Koenders (Netherlands; Pays-Bas). The report suggests that "at the Prague Summit NATO should extend invitations to join the alliance to all of the nine applicant countries. Moving from a process in 'waves' to a continuous 'stream' requiring applicant countries to continue their reforms has a number of advantages. It will enhance NATO's credibility, as well as strengthening the reform process in applicant countries that is under way. Moreover, by following the 'regatta approach,' though it might make relations more difficult in the short term, the Alliance will avoid enlargement being a continuing controversial issue that disturbs the NATO–Russia relationship. Lastly, applicant countries joining one by one as they meet the required criteria, not two or three at the same time, would make enlargement more manageable for the Alliance."

26. Richard Wolffe, "Republicans Hit Out at NATO Expansion," *Financial Times,* February 28, 2002. See March 1, 2002, entry at www.expandnato.org/nedbmar02 .html [accessed August 4, 2002].

27. For background on this debate, see Stanley R. Sloan, *The U.S. Role in the Twenty-First Century World* (New York: Foreign Policy Association Headline Series, 1997).

28. Chicago Council on Foreign Relations polls over the last decade, as well as those from other polling organizations, have consistently shown that the vast majority of those questioned support an active US role in the world sharing burdens with other countries through multilateral organizations such as the United Nations and NATO. For polling data, see reports located at www.ccfr.org/publications/opinion/opinion .html and www.gallup.com/poll/specialReports/pollSummaries/sr020215iv.asp.

29. These tendencies and the concept of "self-deterrence" were discussed in Stanley R. Sloan, "The United States and the Use of Force in the Post–Cold War World: Away from Self-Deterrence?" Congressional Research Service Report 97-78 F(Washington, D.C.: Congressional Research Service), January 6, 1997.

30. Conversation with the author.

31. Josef Joffe, "How America Does It," *Foreign Affairs,* September/October 1997, 16.

32. When I confronted a senior French diplomatic official on this issue at a meeting in Paris, he denied that EU diplomats had taken any such approach. Several central

European officials participating in the meeting, however, subsequently told me that their governments had been lobbied to line up with the European Union on certain issues regarding the EU–NATO relationship in support of their desire to become EU members.

33. William Drozdiak, "US Seems Increasingly Uncomfortable with EU Defense Plan," *International Herald Tribune,* March 6, 2000, 8.

34. For an excellent survey of transatlantic defense industrial issues, see Burkard Schmitt, ed., with Gordon Adams, Christophe Cornu, and Andrew D. James, "Between Cooperation and Competition: The Transatlantic Defence Market," Chaillot Paper no. 44 (Paris: Western European Union Institute for Security Studies, January 2001). For additional background, see Gordon Adams et al., *Europe's Defence Industry: A Transatlantic Future* (London: Centre for European Reform, 1999), and Robert P. Grant, "Transatlantic Armament Relations under Strain," *Survival* 39, no. 1 (spring 1997): 111–37.

35. On January 1, 1999, the Euro became the single currency for eleven EU member states: Austria, Belgium, Finland, France, Germany, Italy, Ireland, Luxembourg, the Netherlands, Spain, and Portugal. On January 1, 2001, Greece joined this group. Denmark, Sweden, and the United Kingdom remain outside the Euro zone.

36. Eric Pfanner, "U.K. Future Tied 'Inextricably' to Europe, Blair Says," *International Herald Tribune,* November 24–25, 2001, 1.

37. Michael Rühle, "Imagining NATO 2011," *NATO Review* 49, no. 3 (autumn 2001): 18–21. Rühle is head of policy planning and speech writing in NATO's Political Affairs Division.

11

Toward a New Atlantic Community

With NATO, we are all Europeanists; we are all Atlanticists.

—*Lawrence S. Kaplan*[1]

NATO: A NECESSARY BUT INSUFFICIENT FOUNDATION

It is increasingly clear that the challenges faced by the Euro-Atlantic allies cannot be managed effectively within NATO's narrow confines or even in a treaty between the United States and members of the European Union (EU), which would leave out Canada and important European allies, such as Norway and Turkey. Furthermore, the US–EU bilateral relationship has a distinctly functional nature—it is mostly about the important but mainly technical details of US–EU relations and has very little political prominence or association with broader goals and values.

The diverse nature of twenty-first-century issues affecting allied interests suggests the need for a new initiative designed to broaden the context of the transatlantic relationship. The point of doing so would be to give form and substance to the apparent belief of all allied governments that, even in the absence of a Soviet threat and in the face of new terrorist challenges, they continue to share—and need to defend—many values, goals, and interests. The goal remains moving toward the integrating model discussed in chapter 10. The means would be a reinforced Atlantic Community as the central organizing mechanism.

The notion that current transatlantic institutions are inadequate to the tasks ahead did not emerge with the September 11 events. It has been around for many years. At the February 1995 Wehrkunde Conference in Munich, Germany, foreign and defense ministers from Britain, France, and Germany put forward complementary proposals to replace the existing transatlantic bargain with a new "contract" or "covenant." The result would be a new "Atlantic Community."

The 1995 proposals were aimed at something more modest than a federal organization of transatlantic relations but more ambitious than proposals for a treaty between the United States and the European Union. No country would give up sovereignty in the arrangement, but all would pledge their individual and joint efforts to promote common interests. The ideas, as put forward, sought to capture all aspects of transatlantic relationships in a single cooperative framework.

The officials offered two main arguments for their suggestions. First, they said that they believed that the current institutions were inadequate to meet the needs of US–European cooperation in the post–Cold War world. The German Christian Democrat Volker Rühe, then serving as defense minister, put it simply: "The foundation for transatlantic relations has changed. NATO as the sole institutional basis is no longer sufficient."[2] British Minister of Defense Malcolm Rifkind agreed, saying, "Defense issues alone do not offer a broad enough foundation for the edifice we need."[3] Alain Juppé, then serving as French foreign minister, suggested a similar motivation when he argued that "the end of the cold war and the political assertion of Europe will force us to think through the terms of a renewed partnership if we want to prevent an insidious disintegration of the transatlantic link."[4]

Second, these officials were concerned that the United States was drifting away from its close Cold War ties to Western Europe—a worry expressed during the Clinton administration that was not in any way laid to rest in the first year of the Bush administration. Foreign Minister Juppé observed that the United States might increasingly act unilaterally rather than in concert with its allies, saying, "Across the Atlantic . . . there is a temptation . . . not to draw back, but rather to act unilaterally."[5] Rühe concluded that the Euro-Atlantic partnership "must be given fresh impetus so that states on both sides of the Atlantic are not tempted to go their own ways."[6]

These 1995 initiatives were not, of course, without historical precedent or foundation. Following World War II, the United States provided many of the ideas and critical resources to help reconstruct Europe (through the Marshall Plan), encourage the process of European integration (promoting the development of what now is the European Union), and deploy a defense system against Soviet power through NATO. The post–World War II phase of institution building created a web of European and transatlantic organizations that, taken together, constituted a loosely knit cooperation community among the United States, Canada, and the West European allies.

Some North American and European advocates in the 1950s and 1960s wanted to extend the process of cooperation to build a full-fledged transatlantic community that would bring together the many strands of common political, cultural, economic, and security interests between North American and Western Europe. From the late 1940s through the 1970s, a number of proponents urged creation of an "Atlantic Union," and the US Congress considered a variety of proposals aimed at stimulating this process. Representative Paul Findley, a liberal Republican from Illinois and a prominent Atlantic Union advocate, argued in 1973 that "all is not well with our present institutional methods for dealing with problems confronting the Atlantic community."[7] However, the idea of a transatlantic federation as proposed by Findley and others never received serious intergovernmental consideration. There was little official enthusiasm in Washington for such an initiative. And in Paris, a formalized "Atlantic Community," presumably dominated by the United States, was seen as a threat to the autonomous development of the European integration process.

The 1995 proposals met virtually the same reaction. One US official observed that "the vision is important" for the future,[8] but it was clear that the administration's plate was already full with NATO enlargement, relations with Russia, and Bosnia. In France, policy officials were focused primarily on how the European Union could develop an autonomous military and security role within the overall framework of the transatlantic alliance but not subordinate to it.

Discussions at the February 2001 Munich Conference on Security Policy (formerly known as the Wehrkunde Conference) once again demonstrated the continuing relevance of this issue. The conference focused on the transatlantic divisions threatened by the fact that Europeans wanted to form an "autonomous" defense capability and the new Bush administration in the United States wanted to accelerate US national missile defense programs despite European concerns. Following the meeting, some experts and officials were attracted to the idea of negotiating a "grand bargain" in which the United States would support the European Union's Common European Security and Defense Policy (CESDP) and the Europeans would accept the validity of the US approach to missile defenses. Despite the superficial attractions of this approach, it was recognized that consummating such a deal would have been a disservice to the transatlantic relationship, giving a green light to unilateralist tendencies on both sides of the Atlantic. The exchange on this issue demonstrated that, despite the close US–European relationship, serious mutual misperceptions and misunderstandings remain, distressingly so among high-level US and European officials. Perhaps most important, the discussions revealed the need to revitalize the foundations of the transatlantic relationship.

This need has in recent years been explicitly acknowledged by a number of scholars and former officials, including Henry Kissinger, who has written that "NATO will no longer prove adequate as the sole institutional framework for Atlantic cooperation."[9] Kissinger goes on to caution,

> It is not an exaggeration to say that the future of democratic government as we understand it depends on whether the democracies bordering the North Atlantic manage to revitalize their relations in a world without Cold War and whether they can live up to the challenges of a global world order. If the Atlantic relationship gradually degenerates into the sort of rivalry that, amidst all its great achievements, spelled the end of Europe's preeminence in world affairs, the resulting crisis would undermine those values the Western societies have cherished in common.[10]

In his provocative book *The Clash of Civilizations and the Remaking of World Order,* Samuel P. Huntington argues, "If North America and Europe renew their moral life, build on their cultural commonality, and develop close forms of economic and political integration to supplement their security collaboration in NATO, they could generate a third Euroamerican phase of Western economic affluence and political influence."[11] Huntington, like Kissinger, concludes with a warning: "The futures of both peace and Civilization depend upon understanding and cooperation among the political, spiritual, and intellectual leaders of the world's major civilizations. In the clash of civilizations, Europe and America will hang together or hang separately."[12]

Convincing Americans and Europeans to expand the Euro-Atlantic relationship beyond NATO and bilateral US–EU ties would not be an easy task. For most Americans, NATO *is* the transatlantic relationship. But that relationship is more than just NATO, even though NATO has effectively carried most of the burden of relations for more than fifty years. It is also more than is captured by the growing US relationship with the European Union, which increasingly represents not only united European economic but also political and now security views in dealings with the United States. But the European Union does not yet include all European democracies, and different views of Europe's future among its members suggest that it will be years, if not decades, before the European Union equals "Europe" in all its aspects.

The Atlantic Community of transatlantic democracies still represents a core of values and interests that is unique, even if imperfect. Some might question whether the community's value foundation remains as strong as it once was and argue that new and important perceptions of interests increasingly divide America from Europe. Nevertheless, the United States has more in common with its transatlantic allies—from historical roots to contemporary interests—than with any other single nation or group of countries in the world. No single country has as much in common with Europe or is more important to Europe than is the United States.

The United States and Europe will continue to fight over trade and economic issues. But despite predictions to the contrary, the end of the Cold War did not nullify their common interest in resolving such conflicts successfully. The Western economic system thrives on competition. It is constantly perturbed by the conflicts that arise out of such competition, but it survives because the shared interests of the participants requires a constant process of resolving, or at least managing, conflicts.

Over the decades, successive administrations in the United States and in Europe have been preoccupied, not unreasonably, largely with the short term. Creation of a new Atlantic Community would require leaders to gamble on a long-term vision of continued and strengthened transatlantic partnership with new institutions to supplement the old ones. Such an initiative would require vision and leadership that all too often is missing in US and European government policies. Nevertheless, the transatlantic idea is not likely to die. Even as the alliance tries to cope with the demands of the war on terrorism, approaches to the missile defense issue, relations with Russia, NATO enlargement, and the EU–NATO relationship, the United States and its allies should consider the need for a new Atlantic Community Treaty.

A NEW ATLANTIC COMMUNITY TREATY

A new Atlantic Community Treaty could draw on the expressions of common values and shared interests articulated in the 1949 North Atlantic Treaty that established NATO (full text in appendix 1). It could reflect a contemporary appreciation of those values and interests and should include all members of the European Union and NATO.

A draft of an Atlantic Community Treaty could be based on the existing North Atlantic Treaty. The preamble would be slightly modified to reflect the broader goals of the Community (new language italicized):

> The parties to this Treaty reaffirm their faith in the purposes and principles of the charter of the United Nations and their desire to live in peace with all peoples and all governments.
>
> They are determined to safeguard the freedom, common heritage and civilization of their peoples, founded on the principles of democracy, individual liberty and the rule of law.
>
> They seek to promote stability and well-being in the *Euro-Atlantic area as a foundation for conditions of peace, democracy, the rule of law, and international cooperation among all member nations of the international community.*
>
> They are resolved to unite their efforts for the preservation of peace and security. They therefore agree to this *Atlantic Community Treaty:*

Articles 1 and 2 could remain exactly as they are written in the Washington Treaty. Article 1 includes a pledge by the parties to settle international disputes by peaceful means and to refrain from the threat or use of force "in any manner inconsistent with the purposes of the United Nations." In Article 2, the so-called Canadian article, the parties pledge to strengthen their free institutions, promote international conditions of stability and well-being, and encourage economic cooperation among them—all objectives that remain relevant and important for a new Atlantic Community.

A new Article 3 in an Atlantic Community Treaty could spell out the main purpose of the new Atlantic Community and could read as follows:

> *The Parties will promote mutually beneficial political, economic, and security cooperation at all levels of intergovernmental and multinational interaction among them and will particularly ensure the effective collaboration between the North Atlantic Treaty Organization (NATO) and the European Union (EU) in areas of mutually reinforcing activity.*

In Article 3 of the North Atlantic Treaty, the parties pledge that they "will maintain and develop their individual and collective capacity to resist armed attack." This article, whose pledge is a useful reminder that Community members need to keep up adequate defense efforts, could become Article 4 in the Atlantic Community Treaty. The North Atlantic Treaty's Article 4, which says that "the Parties will consult together whenever, in the opinion of any of them, the territorial integrity, political independence or security of any of the Parties is threatened," could become Article 5 in the Atlantic Community Treaty. This would provide the mandate for members to initiate a broad range of cooperative measures (political, financial, economic, policy, and so on) in response to threats.

The North Atlantic Treaty's collective defense provision, which is activated by an actual attack against a member, would remain at the core of that Treaty but would not be included in the Atlantic Community Treaty. Article 6, which in the North Atlantic Treaty qualified application of Article 5, would be replaced by a commitment to work together using all instruments available to promote peaceful resolution of disputes and to restore and keep international peace when it has been broken by conflict. It could read as follows:

> The Parties, through processes of consultation, cooperation and action, will contribute to world peace, individually and collectively, by promoting peaceful resolution of disputes that affect peace and well-being in the Euro-Atlantic area, discouraging resort to force in international relations, and providing civilian and military resources to help restore and keep international peace when it has been broken by conflict.

The North Atlantic Treaty's Article 7 importantly reserves primary responsibility for the maintenance of international peace and security to the United Nations Security Council. This could be preserved in the Atlantic Community Treaty, and a sentence could be added to make it clear that the new Atlantic Community would be a cooperative structure, not one that gives orders to either the European Union or NATO.

In addition, Article 7 in the new treaty could give members of the European Union the option of being represented in Atlantic Community councils by the European Union when such representation was consistent with or required by their membership in the European Union. For example, in areas where EU policy is conducted by the EU Commission, a Commission representative could speak for the European Union. When matters relating to the European Union's CESDP were being discussed, the European Union's high representative for common foreign and security policy could represent the European Union along with an official representing the president of the EU Council of Ministers. The Atlantic Community members might also wish to agree that the secretary-general of NATO, the president of the EU Commission, and the European Union's high representative for common foreign and security policy would become permanent observers in Atlantic Community councils. The new Article 7 could read as follows:

This Treaty does not affect, and shall not be interpreted as affecting in any way the rights and obligations under the Charter of the Parties which are members of the United Nations, or the primary responsibility of the Security Council for the maintenance of international peace and security. *This treaty establishes no authority superior to the decision-making bodies of the North Atlantic Treaty Organization or the European Union. Parties that are members of the European Union may when appropriate choose to be represented in Atlantic Community bodies by relevant EU authorities.*

Articles 8 in the North Atlantic Treaty could transfer without change to the new Atlantic Community Treaty. In Article 8, parties declare that there is no conflict between their existing international commitments and the provisions of the Treaty.

Article 9 provides the mandate for establishing a "Council" as its decision-making forum. The language of the North Atlantic Treaty's Article 9 would provide a flexible starting point for governments to begin organizing the new Atlantic Community. However, the second clause of the last sentence calling for creation of a defense committee could be adapted to reflect the growing interaction between NATO and the European Union's CESDP. That clause could direct an Atlantic Community defense committee to facilitate coordination of working relations between NATO and the European Union's CESDP. The Atlantic Community Treaty Article 9 could read as follows:

The Parties hereby establish a Council, on which each of them shall be represented, to consider matters concerning the implementation of this Treaty. The Council shall be so organized as to be able to meet promptly at any time. The Council shall set up such subsidiary bodies as may be necessary; in particular it shall establish immediately a defense committee *composed of NATO and EU representatives to facilitate coordination of the defense responsibilities and activities of the two organizations.*

Article 10, concerning membership, would have to be redrawn. The new language would make members of the European Union and NATO eligible to join the Atlantic Community. Thus, the enlargement processes of the EU and NATO would serve as the entry points for joining the Atlantic Community. Article 10 could read as follows:

All State Parties to the North Atlantic Treaty and members of the European Union are eligible to become Parties to this Treaty. Any qualified State may accede to this Treaty by depositing its instrument of accession with the Government of [to be determined]. The Government of [to be determined] will inform each of the Parties of the deposit of each such instrument of accession.

Articles 11 to 14 could remain essentially as they appear in the North Atlantic Treaty, with the provision that, as in Article 10, the depository government (presumably the government of the member state in which the treaty was signed) would have to be specified appropriately. In addition, the reference in Article 12 to the "North Atlantic area" might appropriately be revised to read the "Euro-Atlantic area." Article 11 specifies arrangements for ratification and entry into force of the Treaty; Article 12 provides for a review of the Treaty, if necessary, after ten years; Article 13 specifies the right of any party to leave the Treaty after twenty years; and Article 14 notes that English and French texts of the Treaty are authentic and shall be deposited in the archives of the depository government and transmitted by that government to the others.

A NEW ATLANTIC COMMUNITY IN PRACTICE

Such a treaty text would not answer all the questions in detail about how the Atlantic Community would do its work. That task is better left to governments to resolve in practice, just as they did with NATO based on the North Atlantic Treaty. However, some basic propositions might be considered.

Operation of a new Atlantic Community could include the organization of twice-yearly summit meetings among all members of NATO and the European Union as well as observers from all countries recognized as candidates for membership in those two bodies. The meetings could be scheduled in conjunction with the regular NATO and EU summits and would supplant the current US–EU summit meetings. The summit framework could be supported by a permanent council to discuss issues as they develop between summit sessions and working groups that meet as needed. To give the Community a representative dimension, the NATO Parliamentary Assembly could be transformed into the Atlantic Community Assembly, including representatives from all member states in the Community, with the mandate to study and debate the entire range of issues in the transatlantic relationship.

To help reduce institutional overlap and heavy meeting schedules for transatlantic officials, all items currently on the US–EU agenda could be transferred to the new forum, covering virtually all aspects of transatlantic relations and including all countries with interests in the relationship, unlike the more narrow US–EU consultations. When specific US–EU issues arise, they could be handled in bilateral US–EU negotiations. Atlantic Community institutions could be established in or near Brussels, Belgium, to facilitate coordination with NATO and EU institutions.

It might be beneficial to address some other consolidation issues at the same time. The Euro-Atlantic Partnership Council (EAPC) in NATO has never established itself as a uniquely useful forum for dialogue and cooperation. At the same time, the Organization for Security and Cooperation in Europe (OSCE) could be strengthened as the body that would bring together the members of the new Atlantic Community and all the other states in Europe that do not qualify for or do not seek Atlantic Community membership, including, most important, Russia and Ukraine. Shifting all relevant EAPC functions to the OSCE framework would be a useful consolidation of European structures. The main responsibility of the OSCE would be to provide the "collective security" function for relations among states in Europe, helping build peace and cooperation across the Continent through confidence building and arms control measures, early warning, conflict prevention, crisis management, and postconflict rehabilitation activities.

Approaching problems and issues from the broad perspective offered by an Atlantic Community framework would open up possibilities for discussions of issues that are discussed unofficially among allied representatives at NATO but are not within NATO's formal mandate. In an Atlantic Community forum, there would be a better opportunity for a dynamic problem-solving synergy to develop when all aspects of issues can be put on the table.

The war against terrorism is a good example. If there had been an Atlantic Community Council on September 11, it could immediately have established working groups to address all aspects of the campaign against sources of international terror. The North Atlantic Council would not have been required to wait for the Atlantic Community Council to act and could have invoked Article 5 on September 12 just as it did. However, in the meantime, discussions in the Atlantic Community Council could have been coordinating the response of police authorities in Community countries, discussing actions to cut off sources of financial support to terrorists, developing public diplomacy themes to accompany military and diplomatic action, and beginning consideration of long-term strategies designed to undermine support for terrorist activities.

A new Atlantic Community would embrace, not replace, NATO in the overall framework of transatlantic relations.[13] Because it would be a consultative forum only, it would not threaten the "autonomy" of the European Union or undermine NATO's Article 5 collective defense commitment. In fact, it could help bridge the current artificial gap between NATO discussions of security policy and US–EU consultations on economic issues, which have important overlapping dimensions. Because an Atlantic Community would encourage members to address issues that NATO does not tackle, the new structure would provide added value beyond that offered by the traditional alliance. It might also provide some additional options for shaping coalitions willing to deal with new security challenges in cases where using the NATO framework might not be acceptable to all allies and where action could be blocked by a single dissenting member.

Such an initiative would admittedly face some tough questions. Some critics might ask what another "talk shop" among the Western democracies would accomplish. Would consultations in the Atlantic Community framework eventually take precedence over those in NATO's North Atlantic Council? Would such a forum have avoided Euro-Atlantic differences over Bosnia and Kosovo? Would discussions in such a forum contribute to the settlement of transatlantic economic issues? Would US participation in such a setting simply add to the expense of US international involvement at a time when some want to reduce the scope and cost of the US role in the world? Some might question whether the proposal is an attempt to substitute process (more consultations) for a diminishing substance (common interests) in the relationship. Others might charge that such a community would threaten the "autonomy" of the European Union, others that the United States would be sacrificing sovereignty. The answer to all these questions is that no one outcome is guaranteed, and all such questions will be answered by the choices made by participating governments.

Some in Europe and in the United States might prefer to move away from alliance and toward something more like a "handshake relationship" in which cooperation continues but in a more ad hoc, less institutionalized setting. This formula might yield greater freedom of maneuver for the United States and a uniting Europe but would also likely produce more tensions and frictions, given the lack of a solemn commitment to cooperation as a frame of reference.

These questions and issues should all be considered in a debate on the need for a new Atlantic Community. The point, however, is that such a debate is required. No consultative arrangement will guarantee that the United States and Europe will be able to solve all problems between them. But without a renewed commitment to community and without the necessary institutional settings for dialogue and cooperation, the foundations of the transatlantic relationship could be at risk.

Reconsidered, the transatlantic bargain remains a critical, valid framework for the United States, Canada, and the European democracies. The bargain survived the Cold War and after by adapting to changing circumstances. Now Euro-Atlantic leaders need to face up to the need to adapt their bargain to the demanding challenges of the twenty-first-century world.

Creation of a new Atlantic Community may remain beyond the political will and energy of the Euro-Atlantic democracies in the years immediately ahead. However, the story that began following World War II and that has led to an unprecedented level of cooperation in the Euro-Atlantic area is far from over. The continued relevance and vitality of the bargain will depend on whether it continues to grow and adapt its institutions and processes to changing international circumstances.

NOTES

1. Lawrence S. Kaplan, "Atlanticists vs. Europeanists in NATO," in *NATO and the European Union, Confronting the Challenges of European Security and Enlargement,* ed. S. Victor Papacosma and Pierre-Henri Laurent (Kent, Ohio: Lyman Lemnitzer Center for NATO and European Union Studies, 1999), 17.

2. Volker Rühe, "Europe and America—A New Partnership for the Future" (speech to the annual Wehrkunde Conference, Munich, Germany, February 1995).

3. Joseph Fitchett, "Western European Proposes New Trans-Atlantic Pact," *International Herald Tribune,* February 7, 1995, 1.

4. M. Alain Juppé (speech on the occasion of the twentieth anniversary of the Centre d'analyse et de prévision, Paris, January 30, 1995).

5. Juppé (speech).

6. Rühe, "Europe and America."

7. For further details, see US House Committee on Foreign Affairs, Subcommittee on International Organizations and Movements, *Hearing on H.J. Res. 205, 206, 213, 218, 387, H. Cong. Res. 39, 67,* 93rd Cong., 1st sess., March 26, 1973.

8. Fitchett, "Western European Proposes New Trans-Atlantic Pact," 1.

9. Henry Kissinger, *Does America Need a Foreign Policy? Toward a Diplomacy for the 21st Century* (New York: Simon & Schuster, 2001), 80.

10. Kissinger, *Does America Need a Foreign Policy?* 81–82.

11. Samuel P. Huntington, *The Clash of Civilizations: Remaking of World Order* (New York: Simon & Schuster, 1996), 308.

12. Huntington, *The Clash of Civilizations,* 321.

13. In the mid-1990s, an opponent of NATO enlargement, Charles A. Kupchan, argued that NATO and the Article 5 commitment were outliving their utility and recommended the creation of a broadly based "Atlantic Union" to replace NATO. See Charles A. Kupchan, "Reviving the West: For an Atlantic Union," *Foreign Affairs* 75, no. 3 (May/June 1996): 92–104. Needless to say, the underlying rationale and intended product of the proposal made here differ substantially from the Kupchan approach.

A

The North Atlantic Treaty, Washington, D.C., April 4, 1949

The Parties to this Treaty reaffirm their faith in the purposes and principles of the Charter of the United Nations and their desire to live in peace with all peoples and all governments. They are determined to safeguard the freedom, common heritage and civilization of their peoples, founded on the principles of democracy, individual liberty and the rule of law. They seek to promote stability and well-being in the North Atlantic area. They are resolved to unite their efforts for collective defense and for the preservation of peace and security. They therefore agree to this North Atlantic Treaty:

ARTICLE 1

The Parties undertake, as set forth in the Charter of the United Nations, to settle any international dispute in which they may be involved by peaceful means in such a manner that international peace and security and justice are not endangered, and to refrain in their international relations from the threat or use of force in any manner inconsistent with the purposes of the United Nations.

ARTICLE 2

The Parties will contribute toward the further development of peaceful and friendly international relations by strengthening their free institutions, by bringing about a better understanding of the principles upon which these institutions are founded, and by promoting conditions of stability and well-being. They will seek to eliminate conflict in their international economic policies and will encourage economic collaboration between any or all of them.

ARTICLE 3

In order more effectively to achieve the objectives of this Treaty, the Parties, separately and jointly, by means of continuous and effective self-help and mutual aid, will maintain and develop their individual and collective capacity to resist armed attack.

ARTICLE 4

The Parties will consult together whenever, in the opinion of any of them, the territorial integrity, political independence or security of any of the Parties is threatened.

ARTICLE 5

The Parties agree that an armed attack against one or more of them in Europe or North America shall be considered an attack against them all and consequently they agree that, if such an armed attack occurs, each of them, in exercise of the right of individual or collective self-defense recognized by Article 51 of the Charter of the United Nations, will assist the Party or Parties so attacked by taking forthwith, individually and in concert with the other Parties, such action as it deems necessary, including the use of armed force, to restore and maintain the security of the North Atlantic area.

Any such armed attack and all measures taken as a result thereof shall immediately be reported to the Security Council. Such measures shall be terminated when the Security Council has taken the measures necessary to restore and maintain international peace and security.[1]

ARTICLE 6

For the purpose of Article 5, an armed attack on one or more of the Parties is deemed to include an armed attack:

- on the territory of any of the Parties in Europe or North America, on the Algerian Departments of France,[2] on the territory of or on the Islands under the jurisdiction of any of the Parties in the North Atlantic area north of the Tropic of Cancer;
- on the forces, vessels, or aircraft of any of the Parties, when in or over these territories or any other area in Europe in which occupation forces of any of the Parties were stationed on the date when the Treaty entered into force or the Mediterranean Sea or the North Atlantic area north of the Tropic of Cancer.

ARTICLE 7

This Treaty does not affect, and shall not be interpreted as affecting in any way the rights and obligations under the Charter of the Parties which are members of the United Nations, or the primary responsibility of the Security Council for the maintenance of international peace and security.

ARTICLE 8

Each Party declares that none of the international engagements now in force between it and any other of the Parties or any third State is in conflict with the provisions of this Treaty, and undertakes not to enter into any international engagement in conflict with this Treaty.

ARTICLE 9

The Parties hereby establish a Council, on which each of them shall be represented, to consider matters concerning the implementation of this Treaty. The Council shall be so organized as to be able to meet promptly at any time. The Council shall set up such subsidiary bodies as may be necessary; in particular it shall establish immediately a defense committee which shall recommend measures for the implementation of Articles 3 and 5.

ARTICLE 10

The Parties may, by unanimous agreement, invite any other European State in a position to further the principles of this Treaty and to contribute to the security of the North Atlantic area to accede to this Treaty. Any State so invited may become a Party to the Treaty by depositing its instrument of accession with the Government of the United States of America. The Government of the United States of America will inform each of the Parties of the deposit of each such instrument of accession.

ARTICLE 11

This Treaty shall be ratified and its provisions carried out by the Parties in accordance with their respective constitutional processes. The instruments of ratification shall be deposited as soon as possible with the Government of the United States of America, which will notify all the other signatories of each deposit. The Treaty shall enter into force between the States which have ratified it as soon as the ratifications of the majority of the signatories, including the ratifications of Belgium, Canada, France, Luxembourg, the Netherlands, the United Kingdom and the United States, have been deposited and shall come into effect with respect to other States on the date of the deposit of their ratifications.

ARTICLE 12

After the Treaty has been in force for ten years, or at any time thereafter, the Parties shall, if any of them so requests, consult together for the purpose of reviewing the Treaty, having regard for the factors then affecting peace and security in the North Atlantic area, including the development of universal as well as regional arrangements under the Charter of the United Nations for the maintenance of international peace and security.

ARTICLE 13

After the Treaty has been in force for twenty years, any Party may cease to be a Party one year after its notice of denunciation has been given to the Government of the United States of America, which will inform the Governments of the other Parties of the deposit of each notice of denunciation.

ARTICLE 14

This Treaty, of which the English and French texts are equally authentic, shall be deposited in the archives of the Government of the United States of America. Duly certified copies will be transmitted by that Government to the Governments of other signatories.

NOTES

1. The definition of the territories to which Article 5 applies was revised by Article 2 of the Protocol to the North Atlantic Treaty on the accession of Greece and Turkey.

2. On January 16, 1963, the North Atlantic Council heard a declaration by the French representative who recalled that by the vote on self-determination on July 1, 1962, the Algerian people had pronounced itself in favor of the independence of Algeria in cooperation with France. In consequence, the president of the French Republic had, on July 3, 1962, formally recognized the independence of Algeria. The result was that the "Algerian departments of France" no longer existed as such and that at the same time the fact that they were mentioned in the North Atlantic Treaty had no longer any bearing. Following this statement, the Council noted that insofar as the former Algerian departments of France were concerned, the relevant clauses of this Treaty had become inapplicable as from July 3, 1962.

B

Atlantic Community Chronology: 1941–2001

Louis R. Golino

The following chronology records key events in the evolution of the Atlantic Community in reverse chronological order from the end of 2001 to 1941. It is not intended to be comprehensive and does not include coverage of World War II events other than signing of the Atlantic Charter. It focuses particularly on the development of NATO and the European Union. For an updated, more detailed version of this chronology, see the website of the Atlantic Community Initiative at www.AtlanticCommunity.org.

2001

December 18—NATO defense ministers discussed how the alliance needs to adapt to the requirements of the war on terrorism, in particular by acquiring more forces that can be deployed far from alliance territory. NATO Secretary-General Roberston and US Defense Secretary Donald Rumsfeld said this meant that NATO allies needed to devote more resources to defense. Rumsfeld also called for reducing the NATO peacekeeping presence in Bosnia "by at least 6,000" troops no later than next year, reducing the US presence in Bosnia from about 3,100 to about 2,100 troops.

December 14–15—At a summit in Laeken, Belgium, EU leaders appointed former French President Valery Giscard d'Estaing to head a Convention on the Future of Europe to review institutional changes needed in advance of the European Union's planned enlargement. The European Union expects to complete accession negotiations with ten candidate countries (Cyprus, Estonia, Hungary, Latvia, Lithuania, Malta, Poland, the Slovak Republic, the Czech Republic, and Slovenia) by the end of 2002. They said that the EU rapid reaction force "is now capable of conducting some crisis management operations." They were not able to reach final agreement on the EU–NATO relationship because of objections from Greece about a presummit deal between the European Union and Turkey that would give Turkey a consultative role in the EU force. EU leaders also reached agreement on a European arrest warrant and a common definition of terrorist offenses.

December 13—US President Bush gave Russia formal notice that the United States will withdraw from the 1972 ABM treaty in six months in order to pursue unrestricted testing of US missile defense systems. Russian President Vladimir Putin called the move a "mistake" but said it was not a threat to Russia's security interests.

December 6—NATO foreign ministers announced they had decided to create, with Russia, "a new NATO–Russia Council to identify and pursue opportunities for joint action at 20." They said that "new, effective mechanisms for consultation, cooperation, joint decision, and coordinated/joint action" should be in place by the time of their next meeting in Reykjavik, Iceland, in May 2002. The ministers made it clear that the new council would not give Russia a veto over NATO decisions.

November 25—US Marines moved into southern Afghanistan. As many as 2,000 US conventional ground troops may eventually be deployed. The US-led international coalition in Afghanistan includes troops from many nations including Australia, Canada, Japan, and Turkey as well as many European nations. The European countries participating in military action are the Czech Republic, France, Germany, Italy, the Netherlands, Poland, Spain, and the United Kingdom. Germany's deployment marked its first military action outside Europe since World War II.

November 22—NATO Secretary-General George Robertson proposed the creation of a Russia–North Atlantic Council in which Russia would have status equal to NATO's nineteen member states and would have veto power on certain subjects. British Prime Minister Tony Blair made a similar proposal the previous week.

November 19–20—EU foreign and defense ministers held a Capabilities Improvement Conference in Brussels to assess progress made since their meeting a year ago to acquire the capabilities their planned rapid reaction force would require. They said they had acquired two-thirds of the necessary capabilities.

October 8—French General Marcel Valentin became the first French military official to head the NATO-led KFOR peacekeeping force in Kosovo, which consists of 42,000 troops, most of which are European. NATO deployed its Standing Naval Force Mediterranean (STANAVFORMED) to the eastern part of the Mediterranean and announced it would deploy five AWACS (airborne warning and control system) reconnaissance and surveillance planes to the United States to assist with domestic counterterrorism operations, marking the first time NATO assets were used to protect the continental United States.

October 7—The United States and the United Kingdom launched the first wave of strikes against targets in Afghanistan associated with the al-Qaeda terrorist network and the Taliban regime. Australia, Canada, France, and Germany contributed to the US-led military effort.

October 4—Following a US request, NATO agreed to provide eight measures, individually and collectively, to support the US-led campaign against terrorism.

October 3—Following meetings in Brussels with EU officials and NATO Secretary-General Robertson, Russian President Putin pledged Russian cooperation in the struggle against terrorism. Putin said that the fight against terrorism was leading Russia to take "an entirely new look" at NATO's plans for enlargement.

October 2—NATO Secretary-General Robertson said that since it had been determined that the September 11 terrorist attacks were directed from abroad, they were considered an action covered by Article 5 of the North Atlantic Treaty. The North Atlantic Council agreed to issue the Execution Directive authorizing the SACEUR to issue the activation order for Operation Amber Fox. This new NATO mission, led by Germany, had a specific mandate to protect international monitors overseeing implementation of a peace plan in the former Yugoslav republic of Macedonia.

September 21—EU leaders held an emergency summit in Brussels to express their solidarity with the United States in the aftermath of the September 11 terrorist attacks and endorse a series of counterterrorism proposals.

September 20—In a historic address before a joint session of the US Congress, US President George W. Bush proclaimed the "Bush doctrine," saying, "From this day forward, any nation that continues to harbor or support terrorism will be regarded by the US as a hostile regime."

September 19—The United States launched the first phase of its response to the September 11 terrorist attacks on New York and outside Washington, D.C. More than 100 fighter planes, bombers, and other aircraft left the United States for bases in the Indian Ocean, the Persian Gulf, and the former Soviet republics of Tajikistan and Uzbekistan.

September 12—For the first time, NATO's North Atlantic Council provisionally invoked Article 5 of the North Atlantic Treaty (which states that an attack against one ally is considered an attack against all allies) pending evidence that the terrorist attacks carried out against the United States on September 11 were directed from abroad.

September 11—In the worst terrorist incident in US and world history, terrorists destroyed the twin towers of the World Trade Center in New York and a wing of the Pentagon outside Washington, D.C., killing just under 3,900 people and injuring thousands more.

August 22—The North Atlantic Council authorized NATO's SACEUR to issue the activation order for Operation Essential Harvest, a NATO mission to collect and destroy the weapons of ethnic Albanian insurgents in the former Yugoslav republic of Macedonia (FYROM).

June 15–16—All twelve EU candidate countries attended an EU summit in Gothenburg, Sweden, and EU leaders agreed to plan to complete entry negotiations with these countries by the end of 2002. Some of these countries are expected to accede to the European Union by 2004.

June 15—In a speech in Warsaw, US President Bush outlined his vision of a Europe "whole, free, and at peace" and said that all new European democracies, "from the Baltic to the Black Sea and all that lie between," should be able to join European institutions, especially NATO.

June 12—NATO's Military Committee met for the first time with the European Union's Military Committee at NATO headquarters in Brussels.

May 29–30—NATO foreign ministers met in Budapest, Hungary, where they held the first-ever high-level NATO meeting in a former Warsaw Pact country. On May 30, the first formal NATO–EU ministerial meeting was held.

March 26—During a visit to Skopje, NATO Secretary-General Robertson and EU High Representative Javier Solana urged ethnic Albanian insurgents and government forces in the former Yugoslav republic of Macedonia to show restraint. NATO and the European Union coordinated their efforts to resolve the conflict between these parties.

February 26—Following the December 2000 European Council meeting held in Nice, France, EU foreign ministers signed a new treaty amending the Treaty on European Union and the Treaties establishing the European Communities (the Treaty of Nice).

February 15–21—NATO conducted its annual crisis management exercise (CMX 2001) involving, for the first time, the participation of fourteen Partnership for Peace countries.

January 31—The North Atlantic Council and EU Political and Security Committee held their first-ever meeting at ambassadorial level.

2000

December 14—NATO foreign ministers met to discuss NATO–EU defense cooperation. They reached agreement on NATO's approach to permanent arrangements between the alliance and the European Union, but work remained in the area of modalities for EU access to NATO assets and planning. Ministers also welcomed proposals made by EU ministers at their Nice summit to work toward a NATO–EU strategic partnership in crisis management.

December 7–9—A European Council was held in Nice during which EU leaders welcomed progress of accession candidates in meeting the conditions for EU membership and, following protracted negotiations, reached political agreement on a Treaty of Nice.

November 23–24—The European Union held a Balkans summit in Zagreb, Croatia, bringing all the countries of the Balkans region together for the first time.

November 20-21—During the EU Capabilities Commitment Conference, EU member states pledged contributions to a planned corps-sized rapid reaction defense force. Candidate countries Norway and Iceland also agreed to contribute to the force.

October 9–10—In response to dramatic developments in Serbia, including the removal from office of Serb President Slobodan Milosevic, the European Union lifted sanctions on Serbia and proposed extending the Stabilization and Association Process for Southeastern Europe that was launched in 1999.

September 28—In a referendum, a majority of Danish citizens voted against their country participating in the European Monetary Unit (EMU).

September 19—The first-ever meeting of NATO and the European Union at the ambassadorial level was held at the EU Council of Ministers building.

July 24—The first meetings of the NATO–EU Ad Hoc Working Groups took place in Brussels as a consequence of decisions taken by both organizations to work together on the development of an EU military crisis response capability.

June 19–20—At a two-day summit in Feira, Portugal, EU leaders identified mechanisms to allow non-EU European allies to contribute to EU military crisis management and principles for consultation with NATO on military issues in four areas: security issues, capability goals, the modalities for EU access to NATO assets, and the definition of permanent consultation arrangements. In addition, Greece's entry in the EMU was approved.

April 18—The Eurocorps assumed command of KFOR. It replaced LANDCENT forces in this rotational function at KFOR headquarters and assumed command of all KFOR troops for the next six months.

February 23—The first-ever joint crisis management exercise between NATO and the Western European Union ended. The scenario of the exercise was based on a peace support mission in which the Western European Union led an operation using NATO assets and capabilities.

February 14—The EU Intergovernmental Conference on institutional reform opened in Brussels, Belgium.

January 31—EU member states downgraded their bilateral relations with Austria to protest the inclusion of the far-right and populist Freedom Party in the new Austrian coalition government. This action did not affect Austrian ties to the European Union itself.

January 24—EU foreign ministers agreed on limited sanctions against Russia because of its renewed campaign against separatists in Chechnya.

January 15—The opening session of the EU Intergovernmental Conferences for accession negotiations of Bulgaria, Latvia, Lithuania, Malta, Romania, and Slovakia to the European Union was held in Brussels, Belgium.

1999

December 10–11—At European Council held in Helsinki, Finland, EU leaders decided to open accession negotiations with Bulgaria, Malta, Latvia, Lithuania, Romania, and Slovakia and to recognize Turkey as an applicant country. They agreed to call an Intergovernmental Conference to revise the treaties establishing the European Communities in February 2000. Key decisions were taken toward the development of an EU rapid reaction defense force, specifically, a plan to create by 2003 a 60,000-person corps-sized force for humanitarian, peacekeeping, and crisis management missions as well as political and military institutions to provide political guidance and strategic direction for the force.

July 30—A stability pact for southeastern Europe was agreed upon at a meeting of the European Union Council of Ministers in Cologne, Germany.

June 21—At an EU–US summit in Bonn, Germany, the European Union and the United States issued a joint statement to strengthen their partnership under the New Transatlantic Agenda and, in particular, to work together to prevent and resolve international crises.

June 20—NATO announced that all Yugoslav military and police forces had left Kosovo.

June 11—Russian troops entered Pristina, Kosovo, in advance of KFOR troops. NATO's first KFOR troops arrived three hours later.

June 10—NATO announced the suspension of air operations following Yugoslav President Milosevic's agreement to withdraw his troops from Kosovo after seventy-eight days of air strikes. The UN Security Council authorized the deployment of an international peace enforcement force to Kosovo (KFOR) with NATO at its core.

June 3–4—At a European Council meeting in Cologne, Germany, EU leaders adopted a common EU strategy toward Russia and issued declarations on Kosovo and the strengthening of European Common Foreign and Security Policy (CFSP). They also designated former NATO Secretary-General Javier Solana high representative for the CFSP and secretary-general of the Council.

April 23–25—NATO heads of state and government held a fiftieth-anniversary summit in Washington. Alliance officials approved a new strategic concept to guide the alliance in the twenty-first century and a Defense Capabilities Initiative designed to address shortcomings in the military capabilities of NATO members.

April 12—The North Atlantic Council specified the five conditions the Serb leadership had to fulfill regarding Kosovo: an end to military action and repression of Kosovar Albanians, withdrawal of all Serb forces, acceptance of an international military presence, the return of refugees, and a willingness to enter into negotiations for a political settlement based on the Rambouillet formula.

March 24—NATO Secretary-General Solana announced NATO's intention to take military action against the Federal Republic of Yugoslavia. He said the objectives of NATO actions were to prevent further human suffering and violence and the spread of instability in the region and were directed against the repressive policies of the Serb leadership toward Kosovo. NATO initiated air operations against military targets.

March 19—The Paris negotiations on an Interim Peace Agreement for Kosovo were suspended when the Federal Republic of Yugoslavia announced that it would not sign the agreement.

March 12—The Czech, Hungarian, and Polish foreign ministers deposited their instruments of accession to the North Atlantic Treaty at the Truman Library in Independence, Missouri, in accordance with Article 14 of the Treaty. With this action, the Czech Republic, Hungary, and Poland officially became members of NATO.

February 9—The Hungarian parliament voted overwhelmingly in favor of NATO membership.

February 7—Kosovo peace talks began between Serb and Kosovo Albanian representatives in Rambouillet, France.

January 30—NATO announced that it was prepared to support the Contact Group's Kosovo peace efforts with military force, if necessary, including the use of air strikes against targets in the Federal Republic of Yugoslavia should both parties refuse to comply with the conditions set out by the international community.

January 28—NATO Secretary-General Solana issued a statement in support of the six-nation Contact Group's proposals to mediate the conclusion of an interim political settlement in Kosovo within a specified time frame. NATO decided to increase its military preparedness to ensure that the demands of the international community were met. (The Contact Group included France, Germany, Italy, Russia, the United States, and the United Kingdom.)

January 1—The Euro was officially launched. Austria, Belgium, Finland, France, Germany, Ireland, Italy, Luxembourg, the Netherlands, Portugal, and Spain adopted the Euro as their official currency for banking and financial transactions. On the first day of trading, the Euro's value climbed to $1.19 (the value fell below $1.00 on December 3, 1999).

1998

December 31—The European Council adopted fixed and irrevocable conversion rates between the national currencies of the eleven participating member states and the Euro.

December 4—Meeting in the French resort town of Saint-Malo, British Prime Minister Blair, French President Jacques Chirac, and French Prime Minister Lionel Jospin issued a joint statement calling for the European Union to develop an autonomous military capability. The Saint-Malo declaration said that the European Union should have "the capacity for autonomous action, backed up by credible military forces, the means to decide to use them, and a readiness to do so, in order to respond to international crises."

December 2—The former Yugoslav republic of Macedonia agreed to allow a NATO force to be stationed on its territory. The NATO force was designed to evacuate Organization for Security and Cooperation in Europe (OSCE) verification personnel from Kosovo.

October 13—In light of the noncompliance of the Federal Republic of Yugoslavia with UN resolutions, the North Atlantic Council issued activation orders for limited air strikes and a phased air campaign in Yugoslavia.

October 9—NATO and Russia expressed full support for diplomatic efforts aimed at securing a political solution to the crisis in Kosovo and stressed the need for compliance with relevant UN Security Council resolutions.

July 15—The Commission to Assess the Ballistic Missile Threat to the United States issued a report that said "rogue states" would be able to launch ballistic missile attacks on the US homeland within five years.

May 3—At a special European Council, EU leaders decided that eleven member states satisfied the conditions for adoption of the single currency on January 1, 1999.

April 30—In an 80–19 vote approving the Resolution of Ratification, the US Senate gave its advice and consent to NATO enlargement.

April 29—The Kyoto Protocol on climate change was signed in New York.

March 30—An EU ministerial meeting launched the accession process for the ten central and Eastern European applicant countries and Cyprus.

March 25—The European Commission adopted the monetary convergence report and recommended that eleven member states adopt the Euro on January 1, 1999. Denmark, Great Britain, and Sweden decided not to adopt the Euro, and Greece did not yet meet the convergence criteria necessary to adopt it.

March 16—The drachma entered the European Monetary System exchange rate mechanism.

1997

December 16–17—Meeting in Brussels, NATO foreign ministers signed Protocols of Accession for the Czech Republic, Hungary, and Poland in the presence of their respective foreign ministers.

December 12–13—The European Council met in Luxembourg and launched the EU enlargement process by endorsing the European Commission's recommendation to begin accession negotiations in March 1998 with Cyprus, the Czech Republic, Estonia, Hungary, Poland, and Slovenia.

September 26—NATO and Russian foreign ministers met for the first time as the NATO–Russia Permanent Joint Council.

July 8—At a North Atlantic Council meeting in Madrid, NATO heads of state and government agreed to invite the Czech Republic, Hungary, and Poland to begin accession talks with NATO with a view to becoming members of the alliance after completion of the ratification process.

June 16–17—The European Council met in Amsterdam and reached consensus on a draft Amsterdam Treaty to revise the Maastricht Treaty on European Union.

May 30—The final meeting of the North Atlantic Cooperation Council (NACC) and the inaugural meeting of the Euro-Atlantic Partnership Council were held in Sintra, Portugal.

May 29—On the margins of a meeting of NATO foreign ministers in Sintra, Portugal, NATO Secretary-General Solana and Ukrainian Foreign Minister Udovenko initialed a "Charter for a Distinctive Partnership Between NATO and Ukraine."

May 27—A NATO–Russia summit was held in Paris during which leaders signed the Founding Act on Mutual Relations, Cooperation and Security between NATO and the Russian Federation, establishing the NATO–Russia Permanent Joint Council.

April 15—The first of 6,000 Italian-led multinational security landing forces arrived at the Tirana airport in Albania. Operation Alba was designed to protect humanitarian aid deliveries to Albania.

1996

December 20—The Bosnia Stabilization Force (SFOR), with an eighteen-month mandate, took over from the Implementation Force (IFOR) in Bosnia-Herzegovina as the NATO-led peace enforcement force.

December 10—At a meeting in Brussels, NATO foreign ministers agreed to convene a NATO summit in July 1997 to invite "one or more" candidate countries to join NATO.

December 4–5—At a European Council in Dublin, EU leaders agreed on various elements necessary for introduction of the single European currency and approved the Irish government's draft treaty for the Intergovernmental Conference to revise the Maastricht Treaty.

November 14—The Spanish Parliament endorsed the decision of the Spanish government to take the steps necessary to integrate Spain into NATO's military structure.

June 3—NATO foreign ministers, meeting in Berlin, agreed that a European Security and Defense Identity would be built within NATO, allowing European officers in the NATO structure to occupy command positions in a parallel WEU structure. They agreed that NATO structures and assets could be made available for future WEU-led military missions. In addition, they agreed to implement the Combined Joint Task Force concept.

May 2—NATO Secretary-General Solana and WEU Secretary-General Jose Cutileiro signed a security agreement that established procedures for protecting and safeguarding classified information provided by either organization.

March 29—The European Union's Intergovernmental Conference to revise the Maastricht Treaty opened in Turin, Italy.

1995

December 18—The first US troops arrived in Bosnia-Herzegovina, and command of the peacekeeping mission in Bosnia-Herzegovina was transferred from the UN Protection Force (UNPROFOR) to the NATO-led IFOR.

December 14—President Alva Izetbegovic of Bosnia-Herzegovina, President Franjo Tudjman of Croatia, and President Milosevic of Serbia signed the Bosnian Peace Agreement in Paris.

December 5—At a meeting in Brussels, NATO foreign and defense ministers approved the SACEUR's operation plan "Joint Endeavor" for the implementation of the Dayton peace agreement, including the deployment of 60,000 troops in Bosnia-Herzegovina. France returned to the participation in nonintegrated military bodies of NATO for the first time since 1966. French leaders said that they would take part regularly in NATO's Military Committee and Defense Planning Committee and in other NATO bodies except for the Nuclear Planning Group.

December 3—US President Bill Clinton, European Commission President Jacques Santer, and European Council President Felipe Gonzalez signed the New Transatlantic Agenda in Madrid, Spain.

November 14—At a meeting in Madrid, Spain, WEU foreign and defense ministers affirmed the objective of developing the Western European Union as a means to strengthen the European pillar of NATO.

September 21—NATO's North Atlantic Council approved a "Study on NATO Enlargement" outlining the membership requirements for countries wanting to join NATO.

August 1—The US House of Representatives voted to end the Bosnian arms embargo. NATO launched Operation Deliberate Force, during which they attacked Bosnian Serb positions with aircraft and artillery in response to the shelling of Sarajevo.

July 26—EU member states signed the Europol Convention on police cooperation.

July 2—Srebrenica came under the heaviest shelling it received since being declared a UN safe area. The UN War Crimes Tribunal formally indicted Bosnian Serbs Radovan Karadzic and General Ratko Mladic with charges of genocide and crimes against humanity.

May 30–31—Russia formally accepted the Russian Individual Partnership Program under the Partnership for Peace.

March 26—The Schengen agreement on removing border and passport controls between Belgium, France, Germany, Luxembourg, the Netherlands, Portugal, and Spain entered into force.

March 20–21—The Stability Pact for Central and Eastern Europe was signed and adopted in Paris.

January 1—Austria, Finland, and Sweden joined the European Union.

1994

December 5–6—CSCE participating states renamed the Conference on Security and Cooperation in Europe as the Organization for Security and Cooperation in Europe (OSCE) at a summit in Budapest, Hungary. This change took effect January 1, 1995.

November 11—The US government announced that it would stop enforcing the arms embargo on the Bosnian government and Bosnian/Croat Federation.

September 12–16—Thirteen NATO and partner nations participated in the first joint Partnership for Peace training exercise, which was held in Poland.

September 8—France, the United States, and the United Kingdom removed their remaining troops from Berlin.

September 2–10—The first joint US–Russian peacekeeping exercises were held on Russian territory.

September 1—The last Russian troops left Berlin, completing Russian withdrawal from Germany.

August 31—The last Russian troops left Estonia, completing Russian withdrawal from the three Baltic states.

July 12—The German Federal Constitutional Court ruled that German participation in UN, NATO, or WEU peacekeeping missions would not violate the German constitution.

May 26–27—An inaugural conference for a Stability Pact for Central and Eastern Europe was held in Paris. The Stability Pact was designed to help avert conflicts over borders and minority rights and strengthen regional cooperation and democratic institutions in central and Eastern Europe.

April 26—The first meeting of the Contact Group was held in London. This group consisted of representatives from France, Germany, Russia, the United States, and the United Kingdom who attempted to craft a political settlement in the former Yugoslavia.

April 19—The Council of the EU decided to take joint action under the CFSP in support of the Middle East peace process.

February 6—UN Secretary-General Boutros Boutros-Ghali asked NATO to prepare for possible air strikes against artillery positions in and around Sarajevo in the aftermath of a deadly February 5 Bosnian Serb mortar attack on a crowded market in the city.

January 10–11—A Brussels NATO meeting launched the Partnership for Peace and invited all NACC partner countries and CSCE states capable and willing to participate to join the Partnership for Peace. The leaders also endorsed the concept of Combined Joint Task Forces to give NATO greater flexibility in future deployments of allied forces and stated their support for the development of a European Security and Defense Identity in NATO.

1993

November 1—The Treaty on European Union entered into force, and the European Union came into being.

October 4—Troops loyal to Russian President Yeltsin stormed the headquarters of the Russian Parliament with tanks and machine guns. This ended the occupation of the headquarters that Russian parliamentarians who opposed Yeltsin's reform program had begun on September 21.

August 9—The North Atlantic Council approved operational plans for air strikes in Bosnia-Herzegovina to be implemented under the authority of UN Secretary-General Boutros-Ghali.

June 18—The UN Security Council approved deployment of 300 US troops to the former Yugoslav republic of Macedonia to join the 700 UN troops already there to help prevent the Bosnian conflict from spreading.

June 8—NATO and the WEU ministers approved a single command and control arrangement for the combined NATO–WEU naval operation in the Adriatic to enforce the UN embargoes against Serbia and Montenegro.

May 25—The International Criminal Tribunal for the former Yugoslavia was created under UN Security Council Resolution 836. The tribunal was tasked to prosecute people accused of serious criminal violations of international and humanitarian law.

January 21—The French and German Chiefs of Defense and NATO's SACEUR signed an agreement that defined the relationship between NATO and the Eurocorps.

January 14—NATO allies agreed on plans for enforcement of a no-fly zone over Bosnia-Herzegovina, if requested to do so by the United Nations.

1992

October 2—NATO inaugurated its Allied Command Europe Rapid Reaction Corps.

October 1—The US Senate gave its advice and consent to ratification of the START Treaty, which, if implemented, would cut US and Russian nuclear forces by one-third.

September 20—In a referendum, 51.05 percent of French citizens voted in favor of ratification of the Treaty on European Union.

September 16—During what came to be called "Black Wednesday," the United Kingdom suspended its participation in the exchange-rate mechanism of the European Monetary System because of one of the worst-ever runs on the British pound. Italy withdrew its participation in the ERM the same day. These moves led to a major European currency crisis.

September 2—The North Atlantic Council agreed on measures to enable NATO resources to be made available to support EC, CSCE, and UN efforts to establish peace in the former Yugoslavia, including provisions for the protection of humanitarian relief and support for UN monitoring of heavy weapons.

June 19—WEU foreign and defense ministers meeting in Petersberg, Germany, issued a declaration setting out guidelines for the Western European Union's future development. The declaration defined what came to be known as the Petersberg tasks, which include "humanitarian and rescue tasks; peacekeeping tasks; tasks of combat forces in crisis management, including peacemaking."

June 2—In a referendum, 50.7 percent of Danish citizens voted against ratification of the Treaty on European Union.

May 21—French President François Mitterrand and German Chancellor Helmut Kohl formally founded the Eurocorps, an autonomous European rapid reaction force that includes 50,000 troops from Belgium, France, Germany, Luxembourg, and Spain.

May 21—The first formal meeting was held between NATO's North Atlantic Council and the Council of the Western European Union at NATO headquarters in Brussels.

April 10—The first meeting of the NATO Military Committee in Cooperation Session was held with Chiefs of Defense and Chiefs of General Staffs of central and Eastern European states.

April 7—The European Community officially recognized Bosnia-Herzegovina as independent.

March 3—President Izetbegovic proclaimed Bosnia-Herzegovina's independence from Yugoslavia.

February 21—The UN Security Council established UNPROFOR to help end the conflict in the former Yugoslavia.

January 9—Bosnian Serbs declared establishment of their own republic.

1991

December 20—The inaugural meeting of the North Atlantic Cooperation Council was attended by foreign ministers and representatives of sixteen NATO countries and nine central and Eastern European countries. The Soviet Union effectively ceased to exist. The German government recognized the independence of Croatia and Slovenia. However, formal recognition was given only on January 15, 1992, in a collective EC decision.

December 9–11—At a historic European Council in Maastricht, the Netherlands, EC leaders reached agreement on a Treaty on European Union (TEU—often referred to as the Maastricht Treaty), amending the Treaties of Rome. EC foreign ministers signed the treaty on February 7, 1992, and it entered into force on November 1, 1993. The TEU included agreements on endorsing Economic and Monetary Union and creating European Political Union and a Common Foreign and Security Policy. The TEU created a new organization, the European Union, which subsumed the European Communities. WEU member states held a meeting during which they invited members of the newly created European Union to accede to the Western European Union or become observers and other European members of NATO (that are not in the European Union) to become associate members.

December 8—Representatives of the three former Soviet republics of Belarus, Russia, and Ukraine met in Minsk, Belarus, and agreed to establish a Commonwealth of Independent States to replace the Soviet Union.

November 7–8—NATO leaders held a summit in Rome during which they issued a new strategic concept for the post–Cold War era and the Rome Declaration on Peace and Cooperation.

October 14—German Chancellor Kohl and French President Mitterrand proposed that the existing Franco-German brigade be expanded into a European army corps that would include troops from other nations and be answerable to the Western European Union and the European Community rather than NATO.

August 19—Soviet President Mikhail Gorbachev was removed from office in a coup and replaced by an "emergency committee."

July 4—Germany for the first time suggested to its EC partners that they collectively recognize the independence of Croatia and Slovenia in order to facilitate international intervention to end the conflict in the former Yugoslavia. On June 28, Jacques Poos, foreign minister of Luxembourg, who was speaking for the Luxembourg EC presidency, had said, "If one problem can be solved by the Europeans, it's the Yugoslav problem. This is a European country and it's not up to the Americans and not up to anybody else."

June 25—The Croatian and Slovenian Parliaments proclaimed independence from Yugoslavia. Conflict resulted when the Yugoslav federal army attempted to reestablish control over the breakaway republics.

June 23—EC member states decided not to recognize any eventual unilateral declaration of independence by Croatia and Slovenia.

May 21—The US House of Representatives called for a reduction of US troop strength in Europe from 250,000 to 100,000 by 1995.

April 16—US Secretary of State James Baker sent a letter to EC leaders that articulated US opposition to making the Western European Union the European Community's defense arm.

February 28—Coalition forces liberated Kuwait. Iraq accepted unconditionally all twelve UN Security Council resolutions regarding the withdrawal of its forces from Kuwait, and US President George Bush suspended allied combat operations.

February 25—Representatives of the six Warsaw Pact countries, meeting in Budapest, Hungary, announced dissolution of the pact.

February 20—US Undersecretary of State for International Security Affairs Reginald Bartholomew sent a telegram to US diplomatic missions in Europe voicing strong opposition to any efforts to establish a European caucus within NATO or to create an autonomous European defense force under the European Community.

January 17—Following Iraq's refusal to withdraw from Kuwait in accordance with UN Security Council resolutions, US-led international coalition forces initiated air attacks against Iraq, marking the start of the Persian Gulf War.

1990

December 14–15—The European Council, meeting in Rome, launched Intergovernmental Conferences on European Political Union and Economic and Monetary Union.

November 22—US and EC officials signed the Declaration on US–EC Relations, in which they developed an institutional framework for regular consultations, including US–EC summits to be held once every six months.

November 19–21—At the end of a three-day CSCE summit held in Paris, the thirty-four participating states (the United States, the Soviet Union, Canada, and thirty-one European countries) signed the Charter of Paris for a New Europe. In addition, during the CSCE summit, twenty-two NATO and Warsaw Pact countries signed the Treaty on Conventional Armed Forces in Europe and Joint Declaration on Non-Aggression.

November 17—CSCE participants adopted the Vienna Document on Confidence and Security Building Measures.

October 3—The Federal Republic of Germany absorbed the German Democratic Republic in accordance with Article 23 of the Basic Law, creating a unified Germany.

September 4—The nine members of the Western European Union agreed on guidelines for the coordination of their naval operations in the Persian Gulf region to reinforce the international embargo against Iraq.

August 22—The legislature of the German Democratic Republic voted in favor of the unification of the Republic and the Federal Republic of Germany on October 3, 1990, and agreed to hold elections in the unified country on December 2, 1990.

August 2—Iraqi troops invaded Kuwait following a dispute between the two countries on exploration of oil rights in the Persian Gulf.

July 17—The "Two Plus Four" conference on the unification of Germany concluded in Paris.

July 6—During a meeting in London, NATO heads of state and government issued the London Declaration on a Transformed North Atlantic Alliance, which was their first major assessment of the impact on NATO of the changing situation in Europe.

June 25–26—At a European Council in Dublin, EC leaders agreed on convening a second Intergovernmental Conference on European Political Union in addition to the planned IGC on EMU.

February 27—The US and EC decided to establish a formal relationship with each other by holding regular meetings between their respective presidents.

1989

December 8–9—At a European Council in Strasbourg, France, EC leaders decided to convene an Intergovernmental Conference before 1990 to amend the Treaties of Rome for the final stages of EMU.

December 6—At a meeting in Kiev, Ukraine, Soviet leader Gorbachev and French President Mitterrand explored ways to slow down German unification. The two leaders issued a declaration that said it would be premature and destabilizing to change Europe's borders. British Prime Minister Margaret Thatcher shared Mitterrand's concerns about German unification.

November 28—In an address before the Bundestag, West German Chancellor Kohl proposed a ten-point plan for the peaceful reunification of Germany on the basis of free elections in the German Democratic Republic and the merging of the economies of East and West Germany. Kohl said that the reunified Germany would be fully integrated into the Western community and NATO.

November 9–10—East and West Berliners tore down the Berlin Wall, which was erected in 1961 to prevent East Germans from fleeing to West Germany, and celebrated the beginning of the reunification of Germany.

October 2—French General Jean-Pierre Sengeisen assumed command of the first French and German units of the Franco-German brigade, which consisted of about 4,200 troops.

July 10—In remarks at a state dinner in Warsaw, Poland, US President George Bush for the first time discussed his goal of a "Europe whole and free."

July 6—Soviet leader Gorbachev outlined his vision of Europe, a "common European home," which would include East and West Europe and the Soviet Union, in a speech before the Council of Europe's Parliamentary Assembly.

June 26–27—At a European Council in Madrid, European Community leaders adopted the Delors Committee's plan on Economic and Monetary Union.

April 5—Polish government and opposition negotiators signed agreements on political reforms in Poland, including free elections and registration of the banned trade union movement Solidarity.

1988

September 20—British Prime Minister Thatcher gave a speech in Bruges, Belgium, that strongly criticized the drive for a federal Europe and plans for Economic and Monetary Union.

January 22—On the twenty-fifth anniversary of the signing of the 1963 Elysee Treaty on Franco-German cooperation, France and Germany established a Defense and Security Council and an Economic and Financial Council. The French and German governments also signed an agreement on the formation of a joint Franco-German army brigade, proposed by Chancellor Kohl on June 19, 1987.

1987

December 8–10—US President Ronald Reagan and Soviet leader Gorbachev signed the Washington Treaty on Intermediate-Range Nuclear Forces and other agreements.

November 13—During the fiftieth Franco-German summit, West German Chancellor Kohl and French President Mitterrand proposed the creation of a Franco-German brigade of French and German forces.

October 27—WEU foreign and defense ministers adopted the Hague platform on European Security Interests in which WEU member states underlined their commitment to the defense of the West under the modified Brussels Treaty and their desire to strengthen the European pillar of NATO.

July 23—Soviet negotiators in Geneva proposed to their US counterparts a "double-zero option" to eliminate Soviet and US land-based intermediate-range nuclear weapons on a global basis.

February 17—Talks between NATO and Warsaw Treaty countries on a mandate for negotiations on conventional forces in Europe from the Atlantic to the Urals opened in Vienna.

1986

October 11–12—At a summit in Reykjavik, Iceland, US President Reagan proposed to Soviet leader Gorbachev the elimination of all offensive ballistic missiles within ten years, and Gorbachev countered with an offer to eliminate all strategic weapons. An agreement was not reached because it would have required President Reagan to renounce his strategic defense program, which he was unwilling to do.

September 22—The Stockholm Conference on Confidence and Security Building Measures and Disarmament in Europe ended with the signing of a document that set forth measures for notification, observation, and on-site inspection of signatories' military maneuvers.

February 17 and 28—The twelve EC member-state governments signed the Single European Act, which entered into force July 1, 1987. This amendment to the founding treaty of the European Community was necessary for passage of legislation to create a single European market.

1985

June 14—The Schengen agreement on the elimination of border controls was signed in Schengen, Luxembourg by Belgium, France, Germany, Luxembourg, and the Netherlands.

June 12—Spain and Portugal signed treaties of accession to the European Community. They formally acceded on January 1, 1986.

March 11—Mikhail Gorbachev became general secretary of the Communist Party of the Soviet Union following the death of Konstantin Chernenko.

January 1—The first European passports were issued in most EC member states.

1984

June 12—Foreign ministers of the Western European Union meeting in Paris decided to reactivate the Union.

1983

November 23—NATO's INF deployments began with deliveries of ground-launched cruise missile components to the United Kingdom. The Soviet Union decided to discontinue INF negotiations in Geneva.

June 17–19—At a European Council in Stuttgart, Germany, EC leaders issued a Solemn Declaration on European Union. (This document, which helped lead to the creation of the European Union, confirmed the 1966 Luxembourg compromise. The latter shifted the balance of power within the European Economic Community (EEC) from the supranational European Commission to the intergovernmental European Council.)

March 23—US President Reagan announced his Strategic Defense Initiative, a comprehensive research program aimed at eliminating the threat of strategic nuclear missiles.

January 19—In a historic speech before the West German Bundestag (or lower house of parliament), French President Mitterrand strongly supported the US and NATO plan to deploy Pershing II and cruise missiles in response to Soviet SS-20 deployments.

1982

June 4–6—During a Western economic summit in Versailles, US and EC leaders were unable to reach agreement on East–West trade and credit issues. EC leaders were opposed to sanctions put in place in December 1981 by the Reagan administration in the aftermath of the imposition of martial law in Poland.

May 30—Spain became the sixteenth member of NATO.

1981

December 13—Martial law was imposed in Poland.

November 30—The United States and Soviet Union opened negotiations on INF in Geneva.

January 6 and 20—Italian Foreign Minister Emilio Colombo and German Foreign Minister Hans Dietrich Genscher proposed strengthening European Political Cooperation.

January 1—Greece became the tenth member of the European Community.

1980

October 20—Greek forces were reintegrated into NATO's military command system.

August 31—The Gdansk agreements were signed in Poland, leading to the creation and official recognition of the independent Polish trade union Solidarity.

1979

December 12—A special meeting of NATO foreign and defense ministers was held in Brussels that resulted in the "double-track" decision. This was a plan to modernize theater nuclear forces in Europe by deploying US ground-launched cruise and Pershing II missiles and a parallel arms control effort to obviate the need for such deployments.

June 7–10—The first elections of the European Parliament by direct universal suffrage were held.

March 16—French statesman Jean Monnet, the "father of Europe," died.

1978

December 4–5—At a European Council in Brussels, EC leaders agreed to set up the European Monetary System based on a European Currency Unit and an Exchange Rate Mechanism, which entered into force on March 13, 1979. Britain opted out of the mechanism.

1977

May 7–8—For the first time, the EC countries participated as a unit in discussions at an economic summit of Western industrialized countries.

1976

December 9–10—The North Atlantic Council rejected proposals by the Warsaw Treaty countries to renounce first use of nuclear weapons.

February 2—The European members of NATO established the Independent European Program Group to provide cooperation on the research, development, and production of military equipment.

1975

December 1–2—At a European Council in Rome, EC leaders took decisions on election of the European Parliament by universal suffrage, a passport union, and a single EC representative for the North–South dialogue.

August 1—The Final Act of the Conference on Security and Cooperation in Europe was signed in Helsinki by representatives of thirty-five countries.

June 5—Following renegotiation of the United Kingdom's EC membership terms, a referendum found 67.2 percent of British voters to be in favor of continued UK membership in the European Community.

1974

December 9–10—At a summit in Paris, EC leaders formally launched the European Council, agreed to have direct elections to the European Parliament and a European Regional Development Fund (for poorer regions within the European Community), and resolved to establish an economic and monetary union. The European Council brings together heads of state and government of the European Community and the president of the European Commission.

August 14—Greek forces withdrew from NATO's integrated military command.

July 31—The Euro-Arab Dialogue, a diplomatic initiative that involved EC member states, the European Commission, and the Arab League, opened in Paris.

April 1—The new Labour government in the United Kingdom requested a renegotiation of the terms of British EC membership.

1973

October 30—NATO–Warsaw Pact negotiations on Mutual and Balanced Force Reductions formally opened in Vienna, Austria.

October 6–24—Egypt and Syria launched a two-pronged attack on Israel during the Jewish holiday of Yom Kippur. Other Arab states assisted Egypt and Syria, leading to the fourth Arab–Israeli war since 1948.

July 3–7—The CSCE opened in Helsinki, Finland.

January 1—Denmark, Ireland, and the United Kingdom acceded to the European Communities.

1972

September 25—Norway held a referendum on joining the European Community; a majority did not favor accession. Following the defeat of the referendum, the Norwegian government said that it wanted to negotiate a free-trade agreement with the European Community rather than accede to it.

May 26—The United States and Soviet Union signed an interim agreement on strategic arms limitations (SALT) and antiballistic missile systems (ABM) in Moscow.

January 22—The governments of Denmark, Ireland, Norway, and the United Kingdom signed treaties of accession to the European Communities.

1971

March 22—The Council adopted the Werner Plan on coordinating EC member states' economic policies. The report (which was issued in 1970) said that member states needed to harmonize their budget policies and reduce the fluctuation between their currencies.

1970

November 19—EC foreign ministers met for the first time to discuss how to advance European political cooperation, a task that their leaders delegated to them at the Hague summit in 1969. The ministers issued a report that recommended focusing on foreign policy cooperation, in particular, information exchanges, consultations, and efforts to coordinate member states' foreign policies.

October 27—EC member states approved the Davignon report on political cooperation. The report said that the European Community should seek to speak with a single voice internationally.

January 1—Responsibility for developing and implementing external trade policy passed from EC member states to the European Commission.

1969

December 1–2—EC leaders held a summit in The Hague, Netherlands, where they reaffirmed their plan to gradually build an economic and monetary union, harmonize member-states social policies, and enlarge the Community with new members. They also instructed their foreign ministers to report to them on "the best way of achieving progress in the matter of political unification" and working toward "a united Europe capable of assuming its responsibilities in the world."

April 28—French President Charles de Gaulle resigned from office following defeat of a referendum he had called.

1968

August 20–21—Soviet, Polish, East German, Bulgarian, and Hungarian troops invaded Czechoslovakia.

July 1—The EC customs union was completed eighteen months ahead of the schedule contained in the Treaty of Rome. Member states no longer imposed custom duties on products traded with each other, while the common custom tariff replaced national custom duties for trade with non-EC members. The Nuclear Non-Proliferation Treaty was signed by the United States, the Soviet Union, the United Kingdom and fifty-nine other countries. The treaty entered into force on March 5, 1970.

1967

December 13–14—The North Atlantic Council approved the Harmel Report on the Future Tasks of the Alliance. This document made the case that NATO's military posture should couple defense and deterrence with détente. The Defense Planning Committee adopted NATO's new strategic concept of flexible response, under which the use of nuclear weapons would be gradual and adapted to prevailing circumstances rather than automatic as called for by the doctrine of massive retaliation.

November 27—French President de Gaulle vetoed the United Kingdom's application to join the European Communities.

October 16—The new NATO headquarters in Brussels opened.

July 6—The new Commission of the European Communities took office, and Jean Rey of Belgium was elected its first president.

June 30—The Commission of the European Communities signed the final act of the Kennedy Round of the General Agreement on Tariffs and Trade.

March 31—Supreme Headquarters Allied Powers, Europe (SHAPE), officially opened in Casteau, near Mons, Belgium.

1966

March 10—French President de Gaulle formally announced France's intention of withdrawing from NATO's integrated military command.

1965

December 14–16—At a ministerial meeting in Paris, the North Atlantic Council adopted new procedures to improve the annual process of reviewing the defense efforts of member countries and agreeing on their military contribution to the alliance.

September 9—French President de Gaulle announced at a press conference that French military integration within NATO would end by 1969.

July 1—France broke off negotiations with its EEC partners on financing the Common Agricultural Policy, and the French government recalled its permanent representative to the European Economic Community. This was the beginning of the Empty Chair crisis. The crisis ended when the Council accepted the Luxembourg Compromise on January 28–29, 1966, under which France resumed its place in the Council (which used majority voting) in return for retaining unanimous EEC decision making when major national interests are affected.

April 8—The treaty merging the executives of the three European communities (EEC, ECSC, and Euratom) was signed in Brussels and entered into force on July 1, 1967. This treaty established a Council of the European Communities and a Commission of the European Communities.

1964

October 14—Soviet leader Nikita Khrushchev was removed from office and replaced by Leonid Brezhnev as general secretary of the Communist Party of the Soviet Union and Alexei Kosygin as prime minister.

1963

November 22—US President John F. Kennedy was assassinated in Dallas, Texas.

July 15–25—The United States, the United Kingdom, and the Soviet Union initialed an agreement banning nuclear tests in the atmosphere, outer space, and underwater. The Moscow Treaty on a partial nuclear test ban was signed on August 5 and entered into force October 10.

January 22—French President de Gaulle and West German Prime Minister Konrad Adenauer signed the landmark Treaty of Friendship and Reconciliation in Paris (the Elysee Treaty), which established a complex framework of institutional contacts between France and Germany.

January 14—French President de Gaulle effectively vetoed British membership in the European Economic Community by stating that he doubted the United Kingdom's political will to join the Community.

1962

December 18–20—US President Kennedy and UK Prime Minister Harold Macmillan met in Nassau, Bahamas, and agreed to dedicate part of their strategic nuclear forces to NATO.

October 22 to November 20—The United States partially blockaded Cuba following revelation that the Soviet Union had constructed missile bases on the island. The blockade was lifted after the Soviets agreed to dismantle the bases.

July 4—In an address at Independence Hall in Philadelphia, US President Kennedy said that the United States does not view "a strong and united Europe as a rival but as a partner." President Kennedy proposed "a concrete Atlantic partnership" between the United States and Europe "on a basis of full equality in all the great and burdensome tasks of building and defending a community of free nations."

May 6—At US insistence, NATO foreign and defense ministers agreed to review the circumstances under which the alliance might be compelled to use nuclear weapons.

January 10—The EEC Commission (today the European Commission, the European Union's executive body) took office with Walter Hallstein as president. Hallstein was a close foreign policy adviser to West German Chancellor Adenauer.

1961

December 13–15—A NATO North Atlantic Council ministerial in Paris reaffirmed the alliance's position on Berlin (which was that it should remain united), strongly condemned the building of the Berlin Wall, and approved the renewal of diplomatic contacts with the Soviet Union to determine whether there was a basis for negotiation with it (the Declaration of Paris).

August 13—Construction of the Berlin Wall was begun by the Communist government of East Germany to divide East and West Berlin.

1960

December 14—Eighteen European countries, the United States, and Canada signed the convention establishing the Organization for Economic Cooperation and Development (OECD), an international organization that promotes economic progress and world trade. The convention went into effect September 30, 1961. (The OECD superceded the Organization for European Economic Cooperation, created in 1948 to coordinate the Marshall Plan.)

January 4—The governments of Austria, Denmark, Norway, Portugal, Sweden, Switzerland, and the United Kingdom signed the Stockholm Convention establishing the European Free Trade Association (EFTA). The convention went into effect on May 3, 1960. The EFTA, which was comprised of European countries that were not in the European Economic Community, was formed to reduce barriers to trade among its members.

1959

December 15–22—New NATO headquarters opened at the Port Dauphine in Paris.

1958

November 10—Soviet leader Nikita Khrushchev announced that the Soviet Union wished to terminate the Four-Power agreement on the status of Berlin. Khrushchev gave the Western powers six months to agree to withdraw from Berlin and make it a demilitarized city.

March 19—The members of the European Economic Community held a meeting in Strasbourg, France, to set up the European Parliamentary Assembly. French statesman Robert Schuman was elected president of this group, which replaced the ECSC Common Assembly.

1957

October 4—The Soviet Union launched the first *Sputnik,* an unmanned satellite orbiting the earth, opening the space age and raising US concerns about Soviet military and technological advances.

March 25—The Rome Treaties were signed by the governments of Belgium, France, Germany, Italy, Luxembourg, and the Netherlands in Rome. These treaties established the European Economic Community and Euratom and entered into force January 1, 1958.

1956

December 13—NATO's North Atlantic Council approved recommendations in the Report of the Committee of Three on Non-Military Cooperation calling for more extensive consultations among NATO members.

November 5–6—British and French forces began occupying the Suez Canal area, but their action was stopped by growing opposition at home and in the United Nations, the threat of Soviet intervention, and US pressure on the United Kingdom.

November 4—The Soviet Union suppressed the Hungarian people's rebellion.

October 30—The British and French governments issued ultimatums to Israel and Egypt to withdraw ten miles on either side of the Suez Canal to allow Anglo-French occupation after Israeli brigades had invaded Egypt and advanced toward the canal.

July 26—The Egyptian government of Gamal Abdel Nasser declared martial law in the Suez Canal area and nationalized the Suez Canal, which had been owned by British and French companies.

February 24—At the Soviet Communist Party's Twentieth Congress, Khrushchev denounced Soviet leader Stalin in a secret speech.

1955

May 14—The Warsaw Treaty Organization, known as the Warsaw Pact, was established between the Soviet Union and Albania, Bulgaria, Czechoslovakia, the German Democratic Republic, Hungary, Poland, and Romania.

May 6—The Brussels Treaty Powers (the Benelux countries, France, and the United Kingdom), the Federal Republic of Germany, and Italy signed the modified Western European Union treaty, transforming the Western Union into the Western European Union.

May 5—The Federal Republic of Germany acceded to the North Atlantic Treaty, becoming the fifteenth member of NATO. The protocol was signed October 23, 1954, and entered into force May 5, 1955.

April 1—In a 76–2 vote, the US Senate gave its advice and consent to US ratification of a protocol to admit Germany into NATO.

January 12—The foreign ministers of Belgium, France, Germany, Italy, Luxembourg, and the Netherlands met in Messina, Italy, and agreed to work toward the economic integration of their countries.

1954

November 22—NATO's Military Committee approved MC 48, a report on the role of nuclear weapons in NATO military doctrine, and transmitted it to the North Atlantic Council.

November 10—Jean Monnet, president of the European Coal and Steel Community High Authority, resigned his position following the failure of the European Defense Community.

October 23—The Brussels Treaty Powers signed agreements on a modified Brussels Treaty to replace the Western Union with the Western European Union. The Federal Republic of Germany was invited to join NATO, and the Federal Republic of Germany and Italy acceded to the Western Union under agreements signed in Paris.

October 20–22—The Four-Power Conference (which consisted of France, the Federal Republic of Germany, the United Kingdom, and the United States) met in Paris. This group adopted a protocol that terminated the occupation regime in the Federal Republic of Germany.

September 28 to October 3—The Conference of Nine (which consisted of Belgium, Canada, France, the Federal Republic of Germany, Italy, Luxembourg, the Netherlands, the United Kingdom, and the United States) met in London. The purpose of this meeting was to seek an alternative to the European Defense Community in light of its rejection by France.

August 29—The French National Assembly voted 319 to 264 against ratifying the treaty to establish the European Defense Community. French Communists, Gaullists, and various right-wing parties were particularly opposed to the European Defense Community.

August 26—The US Mutual Security Act of 1954 was enacted into law. It contained a provision preventing future deliveries of military equipment to France and Italy, which had not signed the EDC (European Defense Community) treaty.

August 19–22—The Brussels Treaty Powers met in Brussels to consider modifications to the EDC treaty. French Prime Minister Pierre Mendès-France proposed a less supranational defense organization, but France's partners did not agree to it.

May 7—The United States and the United Kingdom rejected the Soviet Union's bid to join NATO.

1953

August 12—The Soviet Union tested its first hydrogen bomb.

July 23—The Korean armistice was signed in Panmunjon, Korea.

March 5—Soviet leader Joseph Stalin died.

1952

July 1—The US Senate gave its advice and consent to US ratification of a NATO protocol with the Federal Republic of Germany that extended NATO security guarantees to the Federal Republic of Germany.

May 27—The governments of Belgium, France, Italy, Luxembourg, the Netherlands, and the Federal Republic of Germany signed a treaty in Paris intended to create the European Defense Community.

March 12—Lord Ismay of the United Kingdom was appointed the first secretary-general of NATO and vice chairman of the North Atlantic Council. (All subsequent secretaries-general have also been European.)

February 20–25—NATO foreign, defense, and finance ministers met in Lisbon, Portugal, and established NATO as a permanent organization with a headquarters in Paris. They also reorganized the structure of NATO by establishing the North Atlantic Council as a permanent body of diplomatic representatives of member governments. In addition, they decided the proposed European Defense Community would be part of NATO's integrated military command.

February 7—The US Senate, in a 73–2 vote, gave its advice and consent to US ratification of a protocol inviting Greece and Turkey to join NATO. The two acceded to the treaty on February 18.

1951

April 18—The leaders of Belgium, France, Germany, Italy, Luxembourg, and the Netherlands signed a treaty creating the European Coal and Steel Community, a common market for the production and trade of coal, steel, and other materials. The treaty entered into force on July 23, 1952.

April 4—The US Senate approved deployment of four US Army divisions to Europe. It also requested the president consult with Congress before sending any additional troops and that the Joint Chiefs of Staff certify that Western Europe was making "appropriate efforts in collective defense" before the troops left home.

April 2—Allied Command Europe became operational with SHAPE in Rocquencourt, France, near Paris.

February 15—The French government convened a conference in Paris on creating a European army.

1950

December 20—The Brussels Treaty Powers decided to merge the military component of the Western Union into NATO.

December 19—NATO members appointed US General Dwight D. Eisenhower as the first Supreme Allied Commander, Europe (SACEUR). Eisenhower was tasked with creating a force capable of repulsing a Soviet attack against Western Europe.

His tenure as SACEUR began on April 2, 1951. (All subsequent SACEURs have also been US generals.)

October 24—French Prime Minister René Pleven outlined a plan for a unified European army within NATO that would eventually include West German regiments. European, especially French, concerns about West German rearmament would be addressed through controls on West German participation in this integrated force.

June 25—North Korean forces attacked the Republic of South Korea.

June 3—Belgium, France, Germany, Italy, Luxembourg, and the Netherlands signed the Schuman declaration. On May 9, French Foreign Minister Schuman had proposed that France and Germany and any other country wishing to join them pool their coal and steel resources (the Schuman declaration). Schuman believed that his plan would make war between France and Germany "not merely unthinkable but materially impossible."

1949

October 6—US President Harry Truman signed the Mutual Defense Assistance Act of 1949, which authorized the distribution of almost $1.3 billion in military aid, most of which was for Western Europe.

October 5—The Defense Committee of NATO's North Atlantic Council met for the first time and established a Military Committee headed by US General Omar N. Bradley.

August 29—The Soviet Union detonated an atomic bomb for the first time.

July 25—US President Truman announced the ratification of the North Atlantic Treaty. He also sent a message to Congress recommending it authorize $1.4 billion in military aid in 1950, the majority of which would go to Western Europe.

July 21—The US Senate gave its advice and consent to US ratification of the North Atlantic Treaty by a vote of 82 to 13.

June 25—The Council for Mutual Economic Assistance (Comecon) was created to facilitate and coordinate the economic development of Soviet bloc countries.

May 12—The Soviet Union lifted the blockade of Berlin. The US–UK airlift continued until September 30.

May 5—The statute creating the Council of Europe was signed in London. (The Council of Europe is an international organization that promotes democracy and human rights and seeks to foster unity and cooperation among European states on legal, cultural, and social issues. It is based in Strasbourg, France, and in 2001 had forty member states.)

April 4—The governments of the United States, Belgium, Canada, Denmark, France, Iceland, Italy, Luxembourg, the Netherlands, Norway, Portugal, and the United Kingdom signed the North Atlantic Treaty in Washington. The Treaty established a common security system based on a partnership among these twelve countries.

1948

June 26—In response to the Soviet blockade of Berlin, the United States and the United Kingdom launched a massive airlift to supply the city.

June 24—The Soviet Union announced that the Four-Power administration of Berlin had ceased and that the allies no longer had any rights over Berlin. Since March, Soviet occupation forces in East Germany had blocked ground access to Berlin.

June 11—The US Senate adopted the Vandenberg Resolution by a vote of 64 to 4.

April 16—The Organization for European Economic Cooperation was created to coordinate the Marshall Plan, or European Recovery Program, and promote European economic cooperation. The Marshall Plan provided funds for economic reconstruction to war-ravaged nations in Western and southern European nations as proposed in a June 5, 1947, speech by US Secretary of State George Marshall.

March 17—The governments of Belgium, France, Luxembourg, the Netherlands, and the United Kingdom signed the Brussels Treaty of Economic, Social and Cultural Collaboration and Collective Self-Defense, in which they pledged to come to each other's assistance if attacked and maintain cooperative political and economic relations with each other.

February 22–25—The Communist Party of Czechoslovakia gained control of the government in Prague through a coup d'état.

January 22—British Foreign Secretary Ernest Bevin, in a speech before the House of Commons, proposed a Western Union comprised of the United Kingdom, France, and the Benelux countries.

1947

September 22–27—Cominform, an organization that promoted the ideological unity of the Soviet bloc, was established following rejection of Marshall aid by the Soviet Union and its allies.

March 12—US President Truman promulgated the Truman Doctrine when he urged the United States "to support free peoples who are resisting attempted subjugation by armed minorities or by outside pressure."

March 4—The United Kingdom and France signed the Treaty of Dunkirk, agreeing to give mutual support to each other in the event of renewed German aggression. The treaty was the precursor of the 1948 Brussels Treaty.

1946

September 19—Former British Prime Minister Sir Winston Churchill called for "a United States of Europe" in a speech in Zurich, Switzerland.

March 5—In a speech in Fulton, Missouri, former UK Prime Minister Churchill warned of the expansionist tendencies of the Soviet Union and famously said, "From Stettin in the Baltic to Trieste in the Adriatic an iron curtain has descended across the Continent."

1945

June 26—The UN Charter, which created the United Nations, was signed in San Francisco.

1941

August 14—US President Roosevelt and UK Prime Minister Churchill signed the Atlantic Charter at sea. This document was a declaration of principles common to the people of both nations.

Selected Bibliography

Two key reference works for the study of the Atlantic Community are *The NATO Handbook* (Brussels: NATO Office of Information and Press, 2001) and *The History of the European Union: A Chronology from 1946 to 2001* (Brussels: European Union). Updated NATO information is at www.nato.int; EU information is on the Europa website at europa.eu.int. Other websites of interest include that of the EU Institute for Security Studies, at www.iss-eu.org, where the Chaillot Papers are located; the Atlantic Council of the United States, at www.acus.org; and the Atlantic Community Initiative, at www.AtlanticCommunity.org, where a "living history" of the Atlantic Community and related information can be found.

Acheson, Dean. *Present at the Creation: My Years in the State Department.* New York: W. W. Norton, 1969.

Arkin, William M., Robert S. Norris, and Joshua Handler. *Taking Stock: Worldwide Nuclear Deployments 1998.* Washington, D.C.: Natural Resources Defense Council, March 1998.

Asmus, Ronald D., Richard L. Kugler, and F. Stephen Larrabee. "Building a New NATO." *Foreign Affairs,* September–October 1993, 28–40.

Baker, James A. *The Politics of Diplomacy: Revolution, War and Peace, 1989–1992.* New York: G. P. Putnam's Sons, 1995.

Bannerman, Edward, Steven Everts, Heather Grabbe, Charles Grant, and Alasdair Murray. *Europe after September 11th.* London: Centre for European Reform, 2001.

Barzini, Luigi. *The Europeans.* New York: Simon & Schuster, 1983.

Boniface, Pascale. "The Specter of Unilateralism." *Washington Quarterly,* summer 2001, 155–62.

Brenner, Michael. *Terms of Engagement: The United States and the European Security Identity.* The Washington Papers no. 176. Center for Strategic and International Studies. Westport, Conn.: Praeger, 1998.

Buchan, Alistair. *NATO in the 1960s: The Implications of Interdependence.* New York: Praeger, 1963.

Bush, George, and Brent Scowcroft. *A World Transformed.* New York: Knopf, 1998.

Clark, Wesley K. *Waging Modern War: Bosnia, Kosovo, and the Future of Combat.* New York: Public Affairs, 2001.

Cleveland, Harlan. *NATO: The Transatlantic Bargain.* New York: Harper & Row, 1970.

Cole, Alistair. *François Mitterrand: A Study in Political Leadership.* New York: Routledge, 1994.

Congressional Research Service Reports for Congress: Stetzer, Suzanne, "NATO: A Brief History of Expansion," July 24, 1998; Golino, Louis R., "NATO's Evolution since July 1997: A Selected Chronology," December 24, 1997, and "NATO Internal Adaptation: The New Command Structure and the Future of the European Pillar," December 24, 1997 (also published in A. M. Babkina, *NATO's Role, Missions, and Future* [Commack, N.Y.: Nova Science Publishers, 1999], 83–88); Sloan, Stanley R., and J. Michelle Forrest, "NATO's Evolution: A Selected Chronology from the Fall of the Berlin Wall to the Madrid Summit 1989–1997," July 22, 1997.

Cook, Don. *Forging the Alliance.* New York: Arbor House, 1989.

Daalder, Ivo H. *Getting to Dayton: The Making of America's Bosnia Policy.* Washington, D.C.: Brookings Institution Press, 2000.

Daalder, Ivo H., and Michael E. O'Hanlon. *Winning Ugly: NATO's War to Save Kosovo.* Washington, D.C.: Brookings Institution Press, 2000.

de Wijk, Rob. *NATO on the Brink of the New Millennium: The Battle for Consensus.* London: Brassey's, 1997.

Dean, Jonathan. *Watershed in Europe: Dismantling the East-West Military Confrontation.* Lexington, Mass.: Lexington Books, 1987.

Dinan, Desmond, ed. *Encyclopedia of the European Union.* Boulder, Colo.: Lynne Rienner, 1998.

Drew, Nelson S. *NATO from Berlin to Bosnia: Trans-Atlantic Security in Transition.* Washington, D.C.: National Defense University Press, 1987.

Friend, Julius. *The Long Presidency: France in the Mitterrand Years, 1981–1995.* Boulder, Colo.: Westview, 1998.

Genscher, Hans Dietrich. *Rebuilding a House Divided.* New York: Broadway Books, 1998.

Goldgeier, James M. *Not Whether but When: The U.S. Decision to Enlarge NATO.* Washington, D.C.: Brookings Institution Press, 1999.

Golino, Louis R. "Europe, the War on Terrorism, and the EU's International Role." *Brown Journal of World Affairs* (winter 2002): 61–72.

Goodman, Elliot R. *The Fate of the Atlantic Community.* New York: Praeger, 1975.

Gordon, Phillip H., and James B. Steinberg. *NATO Enlargement: Moving Forward.* Washington, D.C.: Brookings Institution Press, 2001.

Gow, James. *Triumph of the Lack of Will: International Diplomacy and the Yugoslav War.* New York: Columbia University Press, 1997.

Halle, Louis J. *The Cold War as History.* New York: Harper & Row, 1967.

Harrison, Michael M. *The Reluctant Ally: France and Atlantic Security.* Baltimore: The Johns Hopkins University Press, 1981.

Heisbourg, François, Nicole Gnesotto, Charles Grant, Karl Kaiser, Andrez Karkoszka, Tomas Ries, Maartje Rutten, Stafano Silvestri, Alvaro Vasconcelos, and Rob de Wijk. *European Defence: Making It Work.* Chaillot Paper no. 42. Paris: Western European Union Institute for Security Studies, 2000.

Hill, Roger. *Political Consultation in NATO.* Toronto: Canadian Institute of International Affairs, 1978.

Hoffman, Stanley. "The Crisis in the West." *New York Review of Books,* July 17, 1980.

Holbrooke, Richard. *To End a War.* New York: Random House, 1998.

Howorth, Jolyon. *European Integration and Defence: The Ultimate Challenge?* Paris: Western European Union Institute for Security Studies, 2001.

International Institute for Strategic Studies. *The Military Balance 2001–2002.* London: Oxford University Press, 2001.

Ireland, Timothy P. *Creating the Entangling Alliance: The Origins of the North Atlantic Treaty Organization.* Westport, Conn.: Greenwood, 1981.

Joffe, Josef. "How America Does It." *Foreign Affairs* (September–October 1997): 13–27.

———. *The Limited Partnership: Europe, the United States and the Burdens of Alliance.* Cambridge, Mass.: Ballinger, 1987.

Kaplan, Lawrence S., ed. *American Historians and the Atlantic Alliance.* Kent, Ohio: Kent State University Press, 1991.

———. "Atlanticists vs. Europeanists in NATO." In *NATO and the European Union: Confronting the Challenges of European Security and Enlargement.* Edited by S. Victor Papacosma and Pierre-Henri Laurent. Kent, Ohio: Lyman Lemnitzer Center for NATO and European Union Studies, 1999.

———. *The Long Entanglement: NATO's First Fifty Years.* Westport, Conn.: Praeger, 1999.

———. *NATO and the United States: The Enduring Alliance.* New York: Twayne, 1994.

———. "NATO Enlargement: The Article 5 Angle." *Bulletin of the Atlantic Council of the United States* (February 2001): entire issue.

———. *The United States and NATO: The Formative Years.* Lexington: University Press of Kentucky, 1984.

Kaplan, Lawrence S., and Robert W. Clawson, eds. *NATO after Thirty Years.* Wilmington, Del.: Scholarly Resources, 1981.

Kay, Sean. *NATO and the Future of European Security.* Lanham, Md.: Rowman & Littlefield, 1998.

Kelleher, Catherine. *The Future of European Security.* Washington, D.C.: Brookings Institution Press, 1995.

Larson, Jeffrey A., and Kurt J. Klingenberger, eds. *Controlling Non-Strategic Nuclear Weapons: Obstacles and Opportunities.* Colorado Springs, Colo.: USAF Institute for National Security Studies, 2001.

Leurdijk, Dick A. *The United Nations and NATO in Former Yugoslavia: Partners in International Cooperation.* The Hague: Netherlands Atlantic Commission, 1994.

Lodal, Jan. *The Price of Dominance: The New Weapons of Mass Destruction and Their Challenge to American Leadership.* New York: Council on Foreign Relations Press, 2001.

Lunn, Simon. *Burdensharing in NATO.* London: Royal Institute of International Affairs, 1983.

———. *The Modernization of NATO's Long-Range Theater Nuclear Forces.* Report prepared for the US House Committee on Foreign Affairs. Washington, D.C.: Congressional Research Service, Library of Congress, 1981.

Moens, Alexander. "American Diplomacy and German Unification." *Survival* (November–December 1991): 531–45.

Myers, Kenneth A., ed. *NATO—The Next Thirty Years: The Changing Political, Economic, and Military Setting.* Boulder, Colo.: Westview, 1980.

Ortega, Martin. *Military Intervention and the European Union.* Paris: Western European Union Institute for Security Studies, 2001.

Osgood, Robert. *NATO: The Entangling Alliance.* Chicago: University of Chicago Press, 1962.

Papacosma, S. Victor, Sean Kay, and Mark R. Rubin, eds. *NATO after Fifty Years.* Wilmington, Del.: Scholarly Resources, 2001.

Peters, John E., Stuart Johnson, Nora Bensahel, Timothy Liston, and Traci Williams. *European Contributions to Operation Allied Force: Implications for Transatlantic Cooperation.* Washington, D.C.: Rand, 2001.

Pond, Elizabeth. *The Rebirth of Europe.* Washington, D.C.: Brookings Institution Press, 1999.

Quinlan, Michael. *European Defense Cooperation: Asset or Threat to NATO?* Washington, D.C.: Woodrow Wilson Center Press, 2001.

Raj, Christopher S. *American Military in Europe.* New Delhi: ABC Publishing House, 1983.

Roth, William V. Jr. *NATO in the 21st Century.* Brussels: North Atlantic Assembly, September 1998.

Rühle, Michael. "Imagining NATO 2011." *NATO Review* (autumn 2001): 18–21.

Rutten, Maartje, ed. *From St. Malo to Nice, European Defence: Core Documents.* Chaillot Paper no. 47. Paris: Western European Union Institute for Security Studies, 2001.

Sarotte, Mary Elise. *German Military Reform and European Security.* Oxford: Oxford University Press, 2001.

Schmitt, Burkard, ed., with Gordon Adams, Christophe Cornu, and Andrew D. James. *Between Cooperation and Competition: The Transatlantic Defence Market.* Paris: Western European Union Institute for Security Studies, January 2001.

Schweigler, Gebhard. *West German Foreign Policy: The Domestic Setting.* Washington Papers no. 106. New York: Praeger, 1984.

———. "A Wider Atlantic?" *Foreign Policy* (September–October 2001): 87–88.

Serfaty, Simon. *Stay the Course: European Unity and Atlantic Solidarity.* Washington, D.C.: Center for Strategic and International Studies, 1997.

Simon, Jeffrey. *Central European Civil–Military Relations and NATO Expansion.* Washington, D.C.: National Defense University Press, 1996.

———. *Roadmap to NATO Accession: Preparing for Membership.* Washington, D.C.: Institute for National Strategic Studies, National Defense University, October 2001.

Sloan, Stanley R., ed. *NATO in the 1990s.* Washington, D.C.: Pergamon-Brassey's, 1989.

———. *NATO's Future: Beyond Collective Defense.* Washington, D.C.: National Defense University Press, 1996.

———. *NATO's Future: Toward a New Transatlantic Bargain.* Washington, D.C.: National Defense University Press, 1985.

———. *The United States and European Defence.* Chaillot Paper no. 36. Paris: Western European Union Institute for Security Studies, 2000.

Stuart, Douglas, and William Tow. *The Limits of Alliance: NATO Out-of-Area Problems since 1949.* Baltimore: The Johns Hopkins University Press, 1990.

Szabo, Stephen F. *The Diplomacy of German Unification.* New York: St. Martin's, 1992.

Szayna, Thomas S. *NATO Enlargement 2000–2015: Determinants and Implications for Defense Planning and Shaping.* Santa Monica, Calif.: Rand, 2001.

Treverton, Gregory R., ed. *The Shape of the New Europe.* New York: Council on Foreign Relations, 1992.

US Government. Department of State. *Foreign Relations of the United States* (series).

US Senate Committee on Foreign Relations. Subcommittee on European Affairs. *NATO at 40.* Report prepared by the Congressional Research Service, Library of Congress, May 1989 (includes extensive annotated bibliography).

Van Eeckelen, Willem. *Debating European Security, 1948–1998.* The Hague: Sdu Publishers, 1998.

Van Heuven, Marten, and Gregory F. Treverton. *Europe and America: How Will the United States Adjust to the New Partnership?* Santa Monica, Calif.: Rand, 1998.

Williams, Phil. *The Senate and U.S. Troops in Europe.* London: Macmillan, 1985.

Yost, David S. *NATO Transformed, The Alliance's New Roles in International Security.* Washington, D.C.: United States Institute of Peace Press, 1998.

Young, Thomas-Durell. *NATO's Substrategic Nuclear Forces and Strategy: Where Do We Go From Here?* Carlisle Barracks, Penn.: Strategic Studies Institute, US Army War College, January 13, 1992.

Zelikow, Philip, and Condoleezza Rice. *Germany Unified and Europe Transformed: A Study in Statecraft.* Cambridge, Mass.: Harvard University Press, 1995.

Zoellick, Robert B. "The Lessons of German Unification." *The National Interest* (fall 2000): 17–28.

Index

debate in US Senate, 146–54; Madrid
(Spain) summit and, 148–49; nuclear
weapons and, 123–26, 129, 143;
Prague (Czech Republic) summit
and, 154, 199; "regatta" approach,
199; Study on, 123–24, 145–46, 149,
156, 198–99
NATO Parliamentary Assembly (NPA),
106, 139, 153, 171–72, 174, 199, 224
NATO Participation Act of 1994, 146
NATO. *See* North Atlantic Treaty
Organization
NATO-Russia Council, 197–98
Naumann, Klaus, 113
Netherlands, 14, 25, 33, 37, 61, 66, 121,
211; Balkans and, 96
"new world disorder," vi
Nine-Power Conference, 36
Nixon, Richard M., 50, 57;
administration of, 65, 83–84; Nixon
Doctrine, 84
North Atlantic Assembly (NAA). *See*
NATO Parliamentary Assembly
North Atlantic Assembly Presidential
Task Force on America and Europe,
139n9
North Atlantic Cooperation Council
(NACC), 136–37, 141–43; Work Plan
for Dialogue, Partnership and
Cooperation, 142
North Atlantic Treaty, 9, 14–16, 23, 25,
47, 80, 102, 124, 148, 221–224; Article
1, 221; Article 2, 74, 221; Article 3, 5,
24, 221–22; Article 4, 6, 109, 222;
Article 5, v, 5, 10, 97, 107–14, 151,
185–86, 222, 225; Article 6, 222;
Article 7, 222; Article 8, 223; Article
9, 223; Article 10, 8, 145, 149, 223;

Article 11, 223; Article 12, 223–24;
Article 13, 224; Article 14, 224;
community of values and, v, 3–4, 88,
221; mandate, 4–5, 90, 189; preamble,
73–4, 114, 221
North Atlantic Treaty Organization
(NATO), v, 3–4, 208–13, 217–26;
1991 strategic concept, 6, 89–93, 111,
119–20, 166; 1999 strategic concept,
105, 107–10, 120–21, 123, 189;
adaptation of, 89, 98–100, 110–14,
122, 133–37; Afghanistan and,
185–92; arms control and, 59–60,
130–31; authoritarian regimes in, 4,
74; Balkans and, 93–98, 111–12,
192–93; burden-sharing and, 7;
collective defense and, 5, 90–92,
110–14, 122, 185–86; counter
terrorism combined joint task force,
191, 214n14; crisis management and,
6, 110–14, 122; Defense Capabilities
Initiative (DCI), 106, 109–14, 178,
188; defense cooperation and, 5, 6,
10; détente and, 4–5, 47–52, 133–34;
Eastern and Central Europe and,
136–57; European Union, relations
with, 165–66, 169, 176–82, 189,
204–7, 208–13, 217–26;
Europeanization of, 99, 168; former
Soviet Republics and, 5, 136–37;
Greece-Turkey issue and, 9; "habit of
consultation," 48; habits of
cooperation, 7, 98; Integrated
Command Structure, 4, 5, 6, 26, 41,
92–93, 98, 146, 168; international
staff, 49; members, *155;* membership
candidates, 2, *155;* Middle East and,
121; Military Committee, 6, 113, 175,

About the Author

Stanley R. Sloan is director of the Atlantic Community Initiative (www. AtlanticCommunity.org), president of VIC-Vermont, a visiting scholar at Middlebury College, and an associate of the European consulting firm Strategy Consulting Partners and Associates (www.scpa.ch). Before retiring from thirty-two years of government service, he was the senior specialist in international security policy at the Congressional Research Service (CRS) of the Library of Congress, where he previously served as head of the Office of Senior Specialists, division specialist in US alliance relations, and head of the Europe/Middle East/Africa section, among other positions. Prior to joining CRS, he was a commissioned officer in the US Air Force and held a number of analytical positions at the Central Intelligence Agency, including Deputy National Intelligence Officer for Western Europe.

He has published a large number of CRS Reports for Congress, as well as journal articles, book chapters, and opinion editorials in major US and European publications on international security topics, US foreign policy, and European security. His books include *NATO's Future: Toward a New Transatlantic Bargain* (1985), *NATO in the 1990s* (1989), *NATO's Future: Beyond Collective Defense* (1995), and *The U.S. Role in the Twenty-first Century World: Toward a New Consensus?* (1997). He was rapporteur and study director for the North Atlantic Assembly's report on "NATO in the 1990s" (1988) and "NATO in the 21st Century" (1998). He lectures widely on international security topics in the United States and Europe.

Sloan received his B.A. from the University of Maine and his masters in international affairs from the Columbia University School of International Affairs; completed all but his dissertation for a Ph.D. at the School of International Service, American University; and is a distinguished graduate of the USAF Officers Training School.